Economic Miracles in the European Economies

Magdalena Osińska
Editor

Economic Miracles in the European Economies

Springer

Editor
Magdalena Osińska
Department of Econometrics and Statistics
The Faculty of Economic Sciences
and Management
Nicolaus Copernicus University
Toruń, Poland

ISBN 978-3-030-05605-6 ISBN 978-3-030-05606-3 (eBook)
https://doi.org/10.1007/978-3-030-05606-3

Library of Congress Control Number: 2019930842

This Springer imprint is published by the registered company Springer Nature Switzerland AG
The registered company address is: Gewerbestrasse 11, 6330 Cham, Switzerland

Preface

The theory of economic growth has been attracting attention of scholars since the very beginning of formulating economics as a branch of scientific interest, but it was fully developed in the second half of the twentieth century. At the beginning, the emphasis was put on direct factors of growth such as capital and labour. Gradually, these obvious resources were completed by various elements that could mark out the economy—technological progress, human capital development, energy consumption, institutional factors, etc. At present, due to strong globalization tendencies, increased capital, and labour mobility, it appears that many production and service processes can be located almost everywhere in the globe. However, these facts do not necessarily mean that each country is able to accelerate its aggregate growth rate easily and reach a higher level of its economic development. In such an environment, it is interesting how economies induce growth, the processes of which are responsible for intensive growth, and how countries manage to maintain the positive results of economic growth.

Not each economic growth rate is the subject of special interest. We focus on an economic miracle—a term coined by Seliger who in 2010 (*Theories of economic miracles*) described several miraculous stylized facts experienced by Germany, Japan, and East Asia, concluding that although there exists a certain applicability of the lessons of the countries that experienced miracles for economic policymaking, its imitability is limited to similar circumstances like the cultural embeddedness, international context, and pre-existing institutional system.

In this book, intense economic growth rates experienced by several European market-type economies in different periods after World War II, mainly in the 1970s and the 1980s, their determinants and consequences, are considered. Processes that occurred during the periods of miracles in the states selected for detailed investigation of country-specific path of growth, i.e. Ireland, the Netherlands, Spain, and Turkey, are considered based on growth and development processes observed in all European market-type economies at the turn of the twentieth and twenty-first centuries. All of the analysed examples of economic miracles are fairly different taking into account such features as the magnitude and the level of development of the economies and their position in the world economic system and the institutional system. The book is projected to fill a gap in identification and explanation of the causes, mechanisms, conditions, processes, and effects reported in social and economic practice of the intense economic growth.

The main research objectives can be summarized as follows:

1. Identification of the economic and institutional factors underlying periods of intense economic growth and their interpretation in the context of mainstream economics theories and the imperfect knowledge economics (IKE)
2. Econometric modelling and testing of selected economies during the periods of accelerated growth and neighbouring periods as well as the detailed analysis of results
3. Examination and measurement of the structural changes in the periods of economic growth as well as the periods of recession

It has been assumed that changes observed in resources, institutions, and economic policy in the periods of increasing growth rate generate changes concerning expectations of the state of the economy in the future. The characteristics of the changes in the periods of increasing growth rate depend on the initial level of economic development and institutional order as well as on the resources possessed.

The discussion on measurement of economic growth is quite wide in the economic literature. It has been widely accepted that Gross Domestic Product (GDP) is the right measure of the state of the country's economy and consequently its growth rate is a comparable indicator of economic growth among the countries. However, the aggregate measure and its dynamics are not sufficient to determine whether inhabitants of a given territory gain advantages from the processes of growth. That is why the GDP *per capita* determines not only economic growth but also the well-being of the population. Assuming relative stability of the country population in the short run, it is possible to calculate a relative increase in the share in GDP for each individual. These two measures are typically strongly correlated, which allows using one of them in practical applications. It should be emphasized that over the years the real GDP has increased both in the entire world and in each country. Does it mean that inhabitants have improved their standards of living? Or, has the difference between standards of living in different countries decreased substantially? These and similar questions are the subject matter of the convergence theory.

From the perspective of the problems considered in this book, the two measures, i.e. GDP and GDP *per capita*, constitute a basis for right interpretation of economic growth. However, the focus is placed on inducing and accelerating growth processes to the highest possible level and maintaining them at that level as long as possible by putting into motion such forces that allow the economy to be moved from the periphery to the centre. These forces activate and intensify growth *via* innovations, institutions, and reforms at each tier of the economy (i.e. micro-, medium, and macroscales) and result in the aggregate measure. As a consequence, it is visible also in *per capita* measure which indicates improvement in the standard of living and motivates people for further increases in productivity as well as innovation creation. It should be noticed, however, that the process of globalization erases differences between the countries when production and service processes are compared. Thus, it is important to indicate such specific advantages of the economies that allow moving them up to a higher level of development which, as is tacitly assumed, will improve the standard of living for each inhabitant. In some cases yet another measure of growth is used. Gross National Product (GNP) or Gross National Income (GNI) has been designed to exclude globalization effects that are disproportionately impacting the measurement of the size of such economies that intensively participate in the global production and service system.

The results of the research should be considered according to the following three dimensions: theoretical, applicative, and interpretational. The first one reflects establishing the criteria for the classification of the intense economic growth, selection of examples to be analysed in detail, and determining the entire necessary background for the analysis. It covers growth theory, new economic history, new economic geography, and economic policy. The second one is related to econometric modelling of intense economic growth and neighbouring periods in selected countries based on TECM models, as well as determining the impact of induced changes on the stability of structural parameters of the long- and short-term models. The idea of identification was essentially based on the Enders and Siklos approach, but it was significantly modified and broadened within the research. The modification consists in the fact that the identification of the regimes is allowed in the long and short run, thus letting individual variables to be possible threshold variables. The extension of the procedure is made by application of such tests for regimes changing as the Tsay test and the Hansen and Seo test. The empirical TECM models estimated for selected economies show differences between parameter estimates in different regimes and sets of variables being significant in different regimes and in different countries. They allow determining the time period(s) when a given regime was identified. It is worth noting that for comparison of the results—whenever possible—the same set of endogenous and exogenous variables was considered. The sample size covered the same time period, i.e. the years 1980–2016. The issue of interpretation of the results is proposed in the context of imperfect knowledge economics (IKE) in comparison with the current Neo-classical, Keynesian, and institutional paradigms. It is clear that the periods of accelerated growth, where the growth rate is higher than expected, may be an essential driver of economic development of specific countries, as well as the cause and the driving wheel of changes in the balance of power in the world. In some cases, on the contrary, periods of miracles may be followed by periods of economic regress, especially when the resulted level of resources or institutions was insufficient to sustain the effect of a miracle. This raises the question about the ways in which miracles are induced and the effects they generate in the long and short run. Using for this purpose the ideological and methodological concept of imperfect knowledge economics to study the impact of changes in resources and institutions on the historical process of economic growth in the selected examples of the intense economic growth allows an innovative contribution to the study of the historical process of economic change, conducted in contemporary econometrics framework, and the theory of economic development, political economy of growth, and new institutional economics.

This book is essentially the result of the research project no. 2015/17/B/HS4/01000 supported by the National Science Centre in Poland. In this project, we decided to concentrate on the accelerated economic growth that was observed in European countries in the second part of the twentieth and in the early twenty-first centuries. For the purpose of a detailed economic and econometric analysis, the following examples were selected: Ireland, the Netherlands, Spain, and Turkey. We worked on the project as a team of four persons representing Nicolaus Copernicus University in Toruń, Poland, and we also invited a few specialists to publish their research on the specified economies from the insider viewpoint that enabled us to deepen the interpretation of our findings and gave them an appropriate perspective for generalization.

The chapters of the book contain complete research topics, which can be considered separately, but the entire book should be considered as wholeness on economic miracles, since the content is revealed from general to specific. The content is divided into two parts. The first part entitled *Economic Miracles in Growth Theory and in Real Economy: An Overview* introduces and defines what is understood as an economic miracle, gives some theoretical perspective, as well as presents stylized facts about selected economies. Since the economies can be divided into three groups, i.e. well-developed economies, economies in transition, and underdeveloped economies, this idea was employed in both descriptive and empirical chapters. In the first part of the book, four economies are described: Ireland, Israel, Spain, and Turkey.

The second part *Statistical Identification and Econometric Modelling of Economic Miracles in Selected Economies* encompasses statistical and econometric methodology as well as empirical results for selected economies with a short description and interpretation. In the empirical research, three of the economies considered in the first part (i.e. Ireland, Spain, and Turkey) are investigated using econometric methods and models, but instead of modelling the Israeli economy, the Dutch economy was subjected to broad research. This selection is based on the fact that the European economies are of particular interest in this book. Thus, the Netherlands belongs to the well-developed economies group, and the country is considered as a benchmark for other European economies, mainly when economic convergence is taken into account. It is interesting to follow the Dutch path to economic growth and its place among developed economies. Ireland and Spain are typically categorized as the transition economies; however, there are symptoms that these economies, particularly the Irish economy, are fairly close to the Core. Turkey places itself among underdeveloped economies with a great potential for growth. It belongs to both European and Asian continents; thus, its presence here should not be questioned. The Israeli economy discussed in Chap. 6 is interesting for two reasons. Firstly, it is one of the most innovative, knowledge, and human-capital-based economies, and secondly, it is fully organized according to the Western standards, despite the fact that it is situated in Asia. The reader is then provided with a wide spectrum of economies that either experience intense economic growth periods or make efforts to accelerate their growth to induce progress towards developed economies group. Such considerations have yet another consequence. They attract one's attention to the results of intense economic growth and effectiveness of making growth policy; they also allow answering the question whether the effects are worth the costs that were endured.

A general overview of the issues considered in the sequent chapters is as follows. In the first chapter, definitions of economic miracles expressing the essence, features, and basis for further typology of intense economic growth are introduced. In the second chapter, Jerzy Boehlke discusses the concept of economic miracle based on the theory of economic growth and new economic history. The third one, authored by Ali T. Akarca, uncovers the cyclical pattern of Turkey's economy from the election cycle point of view. This approach is supported by empirical analysis and differs from the historical perspective presented in Chaps. 4–6. In Chap. 4, Rafael Myro considers and analyses the factors of growth in the Spanish economy after 1980 on the background of economic history. In Chap. 5, Małgorzata Szczepaniak discusses the factors of growth in Ireland from the pre- and postcrisis perspectives. An interesting example of the Israeli economy is the focus of Chap. 6, authored by Yochanan Shachmurove. This example gives a new insight in the factors of economic growth acceleration, but it is not analysed further using econometric methodology. The next four chapters result from the performed econometric analysis of intense economic growth in selected European economies. The first attempt at data analysis is testing for stationarity and for structural breaks. Marcin Fałdziński presents the methodology of the structural break analysis and the results of testing for stationarity and breaks in macroeconomic time series representing GDP as well as factors of its growth in four economies under study in Chap. 7. In Chap. 8, authored by Maciej Gałecki and Magdalena Osińska, the econometric threshold error correction model construction and testing as well as our modification are presented. Moreover, the specific tests for thresholds are discussed. They are used for validation of the empirical results presented in the next chapter. Chapter 9, authored by four authors from the aforementioned team, is the most crucial with regard to the focus of the research project. In this part, the econometric models for long-run growth paths as well as fluctuations around them in Ireland, Spain, Turkey, and the Netherlands are estimated and tested. The results are validated for the case of possible departures from the initial output. One can easily notice that the econometric analysis allows deepening our recognition of the mechanism of intense economic growth as well as identifying the impact of most important factors on growth rate in diverse economic realities. It should be mentioned that empirical results, presented in this part, remain in line with economic knowledge, historical perspective, and stylized facts. Finally, in Chap. 10, Maciej Gałecki and Jerzy Boehlke attempt to recapitulate the empirical findings in the framework of the imperfect knowledge economics relatively to the mainstream economic ideas.

Toruń, Poland Magdalena Osińska
September 25, 2018

Acknowledgements

I am extremely grateful to all of the authors who contributed to this book. First of all, I express my sincere thanks to Rafael Myro from Universidad Complutense de Madrid for his significant contribution to main characteristics of economic processes observed in Spain since 1980. Ali T. Akarca from the University of Illinois in Chicago supported us by preparing his chapter about the cyclical growth pattern in Turkey. I am also indebted greatly to him for all the fruitful discussions that helped to improve empirical results concerning the Turkish economy. I would also like to thank Małgorzata Szczepaniak from Nicolaus Copernicus University in Toruń for preparing a chapter on the evolution of the Irish economy before and after the recession of 2008–2009. I send many thanks to Yochanan Shachmurove from the University of New York, who cooperates with Nicolaus Copernicus University in Toruń, for his passion in describing the economy of Israel. Finally, let me express many thanks to all of the members of the research team from Nicolaus Copernicus University of Toruń—Jerzy Boehlke, Marcin Fałdziński, and Maciej Gałecki—that I have had a unique occasion to lead for almost 3 years working out the concept of the book and the methodological procedures and results that are presented in the book.

I am particularly grateful to Krzysztof Malaga from the University of Economics in Poznań, firstly for preparing the review of this book, and secondly for his valuable remarks and comments on the structure of the entire book and contents of particular chapters.

I gratefully thank Adam Czajkowski and his team for professional support in the text proofreading and Patrycja Rataj for her editorial assistance.

Contents

Contributors

Ali T. Akarca Department of Economics, University of Illinois at Chicago, Chicago, IL, USA

Jerzy Boehlke Department of Economics, The Faculty of Economic Sciences and Management, Nicolaus Copernicus University, Toruń, Poland

Marcin Fałdziński Department of Econometrics and Statistics, The Faculty of Economic Sciences and Management, Nicolaus Copernicus University, Toruń, Poland

Maciej Gałecki Department of Econometrics and Statistics, The Faculty of Economic Sciences and Management, Nicolaus Copernicus University, Toruń, Poland

Rafael Myro Departamento de Economía Aplicada, Estructura Económica e Historia, Facultad de Economicas de la UCM, Madrid, Spain

Magdalena Osińska Department of Econometrics and Statistics, The Faculty of Economic Sciences and Management, Nicolaus Copernicus University, Toruń, Poland

Yochanan Shachmurove Department of Economics, The Faculty of Economic Sciences and Management, Nicolaus Copernicus University, Toruń, Poland

The City College and the Graduate Center, The City University of New York, New York, USA

Małgorzata Szczepaniak Department of Economics, The Faculty of Economic Sciences and Management, Nicolaus Copernicus University, Toruń, Poland

Part I
Economic Miracles in Growth Theory and in the Real Economy: An Overview

Chapter 1
Economic Miracles: An Introduction

Jerzy Boehlke and Magdalena Osińska

Abstract This chapter presents definitions of economic miracles expressing the essence, features, and basis for further typology of intense economic growth. The main goal of this chapter is to introduce the reader into the subject matter as well as to lay foundations for further theoretical developments and real-life examples of economies that experienced the economic miracle. Furthermore, this chapter is a link between the other chapters presented in this book.

1.1 Introduction

The problem of economic miracles has attracted the attention of many politicians and economists for many years. A postulate to attempt to develop a theory of economic miracles has even appeared in recent years (Selinger 2010). Most often, the starting point for research in this area is the historically identified examples of economic miracles in some countries. The purpose of this chapter is to present different concepts and interpretations of the economic miracle phenomenon that can be found in the literature. It is organized as follows. In the next part, a discussion about definitions and examples of intense economic growth, called "an economic miracle" was provided. In the third part, a more precise definition of an economic

Financial support from research project no. 2015/17/B/HS4/01000 supported by the National Science Centre in Poland is gratefully acknowledged.

J. Boehlke
Department of Economics, The Faculty of Economic Sciences and Management, Nicolaus Copernicus University, Toruń, Poland
e-mail: jurekbo@umk.pl

M. Osińska (✉)
Department of Econometrics and Statistics, The Faculty of Economic Sciences and Management, Nicolaus Copernicus University, Toruń, Poland
e-mail: emo@umk.pl

M. Osińska (ed.), *Economic Miracles in the European Economies*,
https://doi.org/10.1007/978-3-030-05606-3_1

miracle coming from the institutional perspective and its consequences are discussed. In the last part, some conclusions are summarized.

1.2 Economic Miracle in the Interpretive and Growth Perspectives

The modern theory of scientific knowledge refers both to the interpretive epistemologies whose emergence is a consequence of, among others, the so-called "linguistic turn" in the philosophy of science, as well as of contemporary versions of empiricism and rationalism. A review of the literature allows indicating numerous examples and interpretations of the concept of the economic miracle phenomenon. The most frequent ones include the following:

1. A transition from pre-modernity to modernity (e.g., the European miracle with the history of the emergence and dominance of Western European capitalism) (Apter 1959; Albert 1999; Eisenstadt 1987; Kennedy 1987; Polanyi 2001)
2. A transition from feudalism to highly developed capitalism (e.g., Japan and South Korea) (Forsberg 2000; Berger 2002; Valdés 2003)
3. Periods of rapid growth in the economies of the countries of the so-called core, thus highly developed countries (e.g., Germany after the Second World War, Ireland) (Zweig 1980; Bradley and Birnie 2001; Eucken 2004; Kelly and Everett 2004; Reichel 2002; Spicka 2007)
4. A high rate of economic growth in the countries of the economic periphery (Chile) (Ząbkowicz 2001; Klein 2009)
5. A period of dynamic growth in the global history of the world defined by Iggers (1997) (e.g., China, India) (Qizheng and Yudong 2008)
6. Characteristics of a specific path of transformation from socialism to capitalism (China) (Fenby 2008)
7. The economic expansion of countries in a specific geographic region (e.g., Japan and the so-called Asian tigers) (Tsuru 1976; Krugman 1994; Lall 1994; Vietor 2007)
8. The creation of conditions for the so-called low wages and high growth economies (Malaysia) (Krugman 1994; Jomo 2001; Stiglitz and Yusuf 2001).

In the aforementioned context, one can easily add other examples of economies that can be referred to as economic miracles. One of popular examples is related to the so-called BRIC (Brazil, Russia, India, and China) group of countries (O'Neill 2011). On the one hand, each of them has formidable potential, on the other hand, however, spectacular achievements in economic transformation and growth are expected in different time periods in the future and conditionally in the speed in introducing reforms. Yet, the interpretative approach is relatively unattractive, since it does not use a precise definition of the notion of the economic miracle which very often can be used for political reasons.

The definition of the notion of the economic miracle typically involves the theory of economic growth, contemporary institutionalism, and political theory. According to one definition of the economic miracle, proposed on the basis of the theory of economic growth, it is a period of faster-than-expected economic growth (Sharma 2012). At the same time, it is commonly acknowledged that these expectations are a consequence of the achieved level of the aggregate GDP and the GDP per capita, and the place of a studied country in the world economic system. It follows from the above that in order to define the concept of the economic miracle the following factors are essential: expectations regarding the growth of the economy, the actual growth rate, the level of economic development measured by GDP per capita, and time. Taking into account the history of the period after World War II, it should also be added that miracles occur in market economies (probably the only arguable case is the "Chinese miracle"), and with different levels of economic development. It is worth mentioning the works analyzing this phenomenon in the context of the processes of economic convergence and divergence (Barro and Sala-i-Martin 1995), endogenous growth associated with investment in human capital and learning processes (Lucas 1993), and industrial policy (Lall 1994). The issue of economic miracles is also of interest of the new economic geography in relation to the regional development and demography (Bloom and Williamson 1998).

1.3 Economic Miracles in the Light of Institutional Economics

The most important works were edited by researchers associated with contemporary institutionalism and, in particular, with the new institutional economics (Fishlow et al. 1996; Dahlman and Sananikone 1997; Katz 1998). Most frequently, changes that have occurred in the countries of South-East Asia (Lucas 1993; Krugman 1994; Lall 1994; Stiglitz and Yusuf 2001; Jomo 2001), Japan (Tsuru 1976; Katz 1998; Valdés 2003), China (Fenby 2008), and Germany after the Second World War (Zweig 1980; Reichel 2002) form the empirical basis for theoretical considerations. Examples of economic miracles in other countries, such as Chile (the 1970s), Ireland (the 1980s and the 1990s), and Turkey (in the twenty-first century), have also been described extensively, and fairly accurately (see: Ząbkowicz 2001; Kelly and Everett 2004; Yeldan and Unuvar 2015, respectively).

Interesting deliberations on understanding the notion of the economic miracle and the characteristics of this phenomenon are included in a work edited by Balcerowicz and Rzońca (2014). Economic miracles are here a consequence of internal economic shocks caused by national economic policy, at the root of which lie institutional determinants of changes in the economic system that could be barriers to, or drivers of development. The authors of the aforementioned work distinguish between the two types of growth mechanisms, the first of which, based on innovations, is potentially sustainable and universal, whereas the "second type comprises specific growth mechanisms contained only in some situations formed by certain types of institutional systems, and/or deforming the economic policy, and they may be activated by respective reforms and, after some, sometimes a long, time, they die out" (Balcerowicz and Rzońca 2014, p. 44). Dividing further institutional systems into those blocking economic growth, and those conducive to the economic growth driven by innovations, either owing to strong restrictions or incentives for investment, or to the creation of direct barriers to innovations, the authors distinguish between periods covering the entire path of growth of a given country, and periods in which fast and institutionally determined growth concerns only a part of this path. "Periods of rapid growth in the first category occurred in countries which, since the beginning, had maintained an institutional system with strong property rights (of proper construction), along with the competition associated with them, and adequate protection of those rights" (Balcerowicz and Rzońca 2014, p. 77), thus a liberal system, guaranteeing a wide range of economic freedom. The second category of periods concerns the countries in which institutional changes were made in order to unblock innovation and introduce solutions closer to liberal systems.

According to Balcerowicz and Rzońca, sustained acceleration of economic growth is a result of the successful introduction of a package of reforms, which must have an appropriate direction (liberal), temporal scope and structure, and be irreversible. The liberal direction of reforms assumes "changes in the structure of property rights by lifting the ban on private property, by privatization, deregulation, lowering taxes, and weakening the fiscal position of the state, or strengthening the protection of these rights, if they have an appropriate structure" (Balcerowicz and Rzońca 2014, p. 80). The requirement of the liberal direction of reforms results from the fact that it is impossible to identify a single example of successful reforms that would have the opposite direction. Admittedly, these authors notice the opinions formulated in the literature regarding possible applications of the so-called unconventional, and thus alternative to liberal, packages of reforms (e.g., Rodrik 2008), but they express their doubts as to their effectiveness. On the other hand, the scope of reforms necessary for sustained acceleration in the economic growth depends mainly on institutional barriers at the initial condition (Balcerowicz and Rzońca 2014, p. 97). The occurrence of numerous barriers in the initial state is an argument for a broad package of reforms implemented in a short period, rather than for a gradualist approach. According to Balcerowicz and Rzońca, "a successful package of reforms can be defined as one that removes all barriers to growth occurring in the inherited institutional system. In contrast, an unsuccessful package allows some of the barriers to remain; as a result, economic growth is still slow, despite some reforms" (Balcerowicz and Rzońca 2014, p. 84). Moreover, the implemented reform packages should be the most productive in terms of the rate of economic growth. It is quite obvious that institutional systems of individual countries differ in the number and types of barriers to economic growth. Finally, in the deliberations of the abovementioned authors, economic miracles are the transition of the economy from very slow to very rapid, long-term growth, as a result of internal economic shocks caused by a package of reforms of liberal direction leading to the removal of at least one of the existing barriers to growth in the inherited institutional system. Thus defined, the concept of the economic miracle is a phenomenon associated with the shape and effects of a broader policy that is driven by the activity of the state and agencies representing it. Thus, at the current state of knowledge, the identification of periods of economic growth as a miracle always occurs *ex post*. According to Balcerowicz and Rzońca, historical experience suggests that in this case a reform package must significantly and permanently increase the pace of technology transfer from abroad, which requires a radical opening of the economy to the rest of the world, deregulation, fiscal reforms raising the rate of savings and investment, and strengthening the protection of private property rights, etc. At the same time, they note that in the literature there is no consensus as to the initial conditions under which an appropriate package of implemented reforms may result in an economic miracle.

Their proposal of a definition is not fully satisfactory, but from the point of view of empirical knowledge it allows a relatively detailed description and understanding of this phenomenon. This definition is also more precise than Sharma's. On the one hand, it requires such a miracle to be a result of a planned and implemented liberal reform package aimed at eliminating barriers limiting long-term economic growth based on innovations, in its scope depending on the initial conditions (mainly the inherited institutional system) which should be the most productive in terms of the growth rate, whereas, on the other hand, it links such miracles primarily to market economies, which Sharma does not do, relying probably on Rodrik's arguments that in studies of this phenomenon it is not the nominal, but the functional aspect of the institutions that must be considered. This means that in the light of Sharma's definition, in contrast to that of Balcerowicz and Rzońca, we can talk about the Chinese miracle. According to Balcerowicz and Rzońca, the acceptance of such a view requires the system of nominal institutions operating in China, or in any other non-market or quasi-market economies, to be treated, from the functional side, as liberal institutions characterizing systems of liberal market economies. This would mean that different institutional solutions can lead to similar economic results, which, according to these authors, raises serious doubts that are mainly empirical in nature.

An argument in favor of Balcerowicz and Rzońca's methodological proposals with regard to the research into economic development, in particular the phenomenon of miracles, could also be the studies by Acemoglu and Robinson (Acemoglu and Robinson 2013). Similarly to Balcerowicz and Rzońca, they recognize the decisive effect of the institutional structure of the economy on its level of development and growth rate. The so-called *inclusive* institutions, which guarantee freedom to the largest possible number of individuals and provide strong incentives for both cost and socially effective actions, are conducive to rapid growth, whereas barriers to it are the consequence of the dominance of the so-called *extractive* institutions restricting the freedom of the individual and broad access to resources. If the definition of the economic miracle proposed by Balcerowicz and Rzońca is to be accepted, one must remember that in the context of the cited views of these authors, the theoretical and empirical research of this phenomenon at the present state of knowledge requires combining both an interpretive and empirical approaches to epistemology.

Contrary to the description of the cases of particular economies in different periods, definitions of economic miracle phenomena are not very frequent in the literature. So the recent concept presented by Best (2018) is worth emphasizing.

Best's definition concentrates on economic framework and focuses on production, business organization, and skills. Best called it "the capability triad." He argues that government should create the institutional infrastructures that help this triad to link in order to make economic growth because "policies that address production capability, enterprise growth and skill formations separately and in isolation will not be successful" (Best 2018, p. 4). The novelty of the referred approach lies in the linkages between all of the elements of the triad and their creation, coordination as well as elimination. This is the area of economic governance where the role of policymakers is particularly important. Although Best's concept of economic miracle creation is fairly new (it comes originally from 2000, comp. Best 2018, p. 3), it can be included into the institutional framework discussed broadly in this section. However, it should be noted that in some cases it gives more precise economic indications than those offered by Balcerowicz and Rzońca; nevertheless, it can be considered as nested within their general concept.

1.4 An Economic Miracle: Metaphysical or Rational?

It is worth mentioning that the concept of economic miracles represented in this book is often considered as too metaphysical. As a matter of fact, this term is considered very seriously, and furthermore, it is based on a fully rational background. One can see this rationality in Chap. 2 of the book where factors of economic growth are considered from the historical, economic, and political viewpoints. Some stylized facts coming from the description of economic growth in Spain, Ireland, and Israel, presented in sequent chapters confirm that the intense economic growth results from different kinds of reforms and institutions. The case of Turkey seems to be different due to a great impact of political processes on economic performance.

Valuable conclusions about economic miracles can be formulated on the basis of econometric analysis presented in the second part of this book. The econometric methodology consists of structural breaks tests and threshold error correction models and tests. The structural breaks analysis discussed in Chap. 7 is strongly related with nonlinearities described by the threshold-type models (Chap. 8). It allows finding possible discontinuities in time series data, which result from a positive or negative structural change. A structural change, which is positive, can indicate a beginning of what is called "an economic miracle." On the other hand, threshold models allow evaluating whether the period of an economic miracle took place in a given economy and how much it differed from the neighboring periods. Due to the cointegration and division of the data into sub-periods, according to a threshold variable, the mechanism of a long-term growth path and fluctuations around is possible to be identified. The empirical results presented in Chap. 9 remain in line with the stylized facts discussed in Chaps. 3–6. A careful reader will certainly notice that there are many explanations of the obtained results. A framework for a possible wide and theory-consistent interpretation comes from Imperfect Knowledge Economics discussed in Chap. 10.

1.5 Summary

In this chapter, the existing definitions and interpretations of the concept of the economic miracle have been presented. However, this selection seems to be representative, yet not exhaustive. The broad study of the literature brings us to the conclusion that new definitions as well as new examples of what we call the economic miracle appear in the newest publications. The broad definition, coming from the analyses made by Acemoglu and Robinson, Balcerowicz and Rzońca as well as by Best, indicates the need of reforms and governance of mutual relationships between resources, output as well as legal, social, economic, and financial institutions. The definition formulated by Sharma, however, can be perceived as fairly general, since it concentrates on the features of growth and does not indicate the sources of growth.

Two conclusions can be derived on the basis of the analysis given in this chapter. The first one can help in the identification of miracles. If the reforms are planned and intentionally introduced with the support from appropriate legal, social, and economic institutions, they can bring better results in different indicators, among which the GDP and GDP p.c. are only two possible measures. Thus, making a miracle involves a sustained process of both development and convergence to the core economies. Yet this kind of both theoretical and empirical considerations is not based on any causal relationship, which results in different interpretations, in a different perspective and, finally, in different results, particularly predictions about the future.

The second conclusion is that many authors describe the examples of economic growth as miracles or potential miracles. The analyses are made on three tiers: deep quantitative analysis, descriptive analysis of the basis of economic theory as well as popular reading. All three perspectives, referring to a historical perspective, are very valuable and should be taken into account when economic comparisons or projections are made.

References

Acemoglu D, Robinson J (2013) Why nations fail: the origins of power, prosperity and poverty. Crown Business, New York

Albert H (1999) Between social science, religion and politics: essays in critical rationalism. Krit Rat

Apter DE (1959) Nationalism, government, and economic growth. Econ Dev Cult Chang 7 (2):117–136

Balcerowicz L, Rzońca A (2014) Puzzles of economic growth. The World Bank

Barro RJ, Sala-i-Martin X (1995) Economic growth. McGraw-Hill, New York

Berger PL (2002) The capitalist revolution. Fifty propositions about prosperity, equality and liberty. Published by Arrangement with Basic Books, a Division of Harper Collins Publisher, New York

Best MH (2018) How growth really happens? The making of economic miracles through production, governance, and skills. Princeton University Press, Princeton

Bloom DE, Williamson JG (1998) Demographic transitions and economic miracles in emerging Asia. World Bank Econ Rev 12(3):419–455

Bradley J, Birnie E (2001) Can the Celtic Tiger cross the Irish border? Cork University Press, Cork
Dahlman CJ, Sananikone O (1997) Taiwan, China: policies and institutions for rapid growth. Lessons from East Asia 7(7.1):83
Eisenstadt SN (1987) Patterns of modernity. Pinter, London
Eucken W (2004) Podstawy polityki gospodarczej. Poznańska Biblioteka Niemiecka, Poznań
Fenby J (2008) The penguin history of modern China: the fall and rise of a great power, 1850 to the present. The Penguin, Westminster
Fishlow A, Gwin C, Haggard S, Rodrik D, Wade R (1996) Miracle or design? Lessons from East Asian experience. Overseas Development Council, Washington, DC
Iggers GG (1997) Historiography in the twentieth century. From scientific objectivity to the postmodern challenge. Wesleyan University Press, Hanover
Jomo KS (2001) Growth after the Asian crisis: what remains of the east Asian model? G-24 Discussion Paper Series N° 10
Katz R (1998) Japan. The system that sourced. The rise and fall of Japanese miracle. Routledge, New York
Kelly J, Everett M (2004) Financial liberalisation and economic growth in Ireland. Central Bank and Financial Services Authority of Ireland. Quarterly Bulletin Article: 91–112
Kennedy P (1987) The rise and fall of the great powers. Random House, New York
Klein N (2009) The shock doctrine: the rise of disaster capitalism. Metropolitan Books, New York
Krugman P (1994) The myth of Asia's miracle. Foreign Aff 73(6):62–77
Lall S (1994) Industrial policy: a theoretical and empirical exposition. Queen Elizabeth House
Lucas R (1993) Making a miracle. Econometrica 61:251–272
O'Neill J (2011) The growth map. Penguin Books, London
Polanyi K (2001) The great transformation: the political and economic origins of our time. Beacon Press, Boston, MA
Qizheng Z, Yudong S (2008) Shanghai pudong miracle. China Intercontinental Press, Shanghai
Reichel R (2002) Germany's postwar growth: economic miracle or reconstruction boom? Cato J 21 (3):427–442
Rodrik D (2008) One economics, many recipes: globalization, institutions, and economic growth. Princeton University Press, Princeton
Selinger B (2010) Theories of economic miracles. OPO, Ordnungspolitische Discurse. Discurses in social market economy, Discurs 2010-01
Sharma R (2012) Breakout nations: in pursuit of the next economic miracles. W. W. Norton & Company, New York
Spicka ME (2007) Selling the economic miracle: economic reconstruction and politics in West Germany, 1949–1957. Berghahn, Oxford
Stiglitz JE, Yusuf S (eds) (2001) Rethinking the East Asia miracle. Oxford University Press, Oxford
Tsuru T (1976) Towards a new political economy. Kōdansha, Tokyo
Valdés B (2003) An application of convergence theory to Japan's post-WWII economic "miracle". J Econ Educ 34(1):61–81
Vietor RH (2007) How countries compete: strategy, structure, and government in the global economy. Harvard Business School, Boston
Yeldan E, Unuvar B (2015) An assessment of the Turkish Economy in the AKP Era. Research and Policy on Turkey. Routledge
Ząbkowicz A (2001) Instytucje i wzrost gospodarki w Chile. Neoliberalizm i sztuka kompromisu. Wydawnictwo Naukowe PWN, Warszawa
Zweig K (1980) The origins of the German social market economy: the leading ideas and their intellectual roots. Adam Smith Institute, London

Chapter 2
Intense Economic Growth in Economic History and Economic Theory

Jerzy Boehlke

Abstract The purpose of this chapter is to present basic ideas, views, and interpretations of intensive modern economic growth in economic history and economics theory. Periods of accelerated economic growth in the contemporary dual system of the world economy are primarily associated with the processes of industrialization and development of the capitalist market economy in peripheral countries and the fast-paced innovativeness of industrial and post-industrial economies of developed countries. A review of the literature shows a large diversity of views of economic theoreticians on the possibilities, mechanisms, and effects of accelerating economic growth. Phenomena associated with spectacular high rate of economic growth are defined as economic miracles. The industrial revolution, technological progress, specialization, and concentration of manufacturing processes as well as the rapid accumulation of capital caused an increase in the productivity of production factors not seen earlier in the history. Industrialization was, therefore, a necessary condition for the occurrence of economic miracles on the path of the historical development of capitalism. A result of the literature investigation is a proposal of an economic miracles classification which could be used for the description and interpretation of each identified case.

2.1 Introduction

The issue of economic growth in time and space and the characteristics of its types, conditions, effects, as well as the shape and experience of implementing different growth strategies, especially in the era of globalization, is the subject of intensive

Financial support from research project no. 2015/17/B/HS4/01000 supported by the National Science Centre in Poland is gratefully acknowledged.

J. Boehlke (✉)
Department of Economics, The Faculty of Economic Sciences and Management, Nicolaus Copernicus University, Toruń, Poland
e-mail: jurekbo@umk.pl

M. Osińska (ed.), *Economic Miracles in the European Economies*,
https://doi.org/10.1007/978-3-030-05606-3_2

research carried out by economists, economic historians, sociologists, and specialists in politics and international relations. Research in this area was significantly intensified in the twentieth century. Compared to previous historical periods, this was the time characterized by a high rate of economic growth and a high standard of living. An example is Japan, where the economic growth increased by as many as eight times since the 1950s (Dornbusch 2000, p. 11). The reasons for interest in economic growth are obvious and these were adequately formulated by Rodrik (2007, p. 15). He argued that economic growth, although not universal, was still the most important and the most effective instrument of fighting poverty. The question of how to lift out of poverty has always been troubling people. The areas of poverty currently occurring in the world are in places where from the beginning of modern economic growth, i.e. from the mid-eighteenth century, its rate has been the lowest. Rodrik (2007), Acemoglu and Robinson (2013), Dornbusch (2000), as well as Gomułka (2016) all agree that the analyses of the historical process of economic growth point out to the emergence of capitalism, industrial revolution, and the development of international exchange as the reason for the entry of Europe and consequently other parts of the world on the path of sustainable economic growth. Thus, modernization that took place in Western Europe became an impulse for accelerating economic growth. This modernization enabled Europe not only to overcome poverty and enter the path of long-term and rapid economic growth but also to achieve an unprecedented level of social welfare in history. The analysis of economic growth processes is very strongly related to economic development although it is assumed that one can think of growth without development and vice versa. According to Acocella, who made references to the work of Desai (1991) and reports of the United Nations from 1990 (Acocella 2002, p. 97), development occurs when prosperity increases. Measuring it requires the application of many indicators, the most commonly used being the human development index that covers three main elements, i.e. life expectancy, the level of human capital, and the standard of living. However, an increase in welfare does not require a positive rate of economic growth, as evidenced by an attempt to formulate a development concept with zero growth rate. This controversial economic concept appeared for the first time in debates in the Club of Rome that aimed at overcoming the problems resulting from global development. The postulate to freeze economic growth on the achieved level was formulated in the report entitled "Limits to Growth" (Meadows et al. 1972). The purpose was to stop the increase of the rate of exploitation of real-world resources and, as a result, stabilize the global economy system at the level of regenerative potential of the natural environment. The publication of the first report of the Club of Rome made the debate on the issue of sustainable development more dynamic (Mishan 1977). Descriptions and attempts by economists to explain and interpret on historical and theoretical grounds economic growth processes, especially accelerated growth that occurred in the twentieth and twenty-first century, usually refer to economic history, development economics, and theories of economic growth.

2.2 Economic History

Analysing from the perspective of research achievements of economic historians, the processes of the development of economic growth, especially the periods of accelerated economic growth, it should be noted at the outset that conducted studies are only an essential supplement to considerations in the field of economics, in particular the theory of economic growth development as well as evolutionary and institutional economics. By extending the analysed time range and describing the historical context of the observed periods of accelerated economic growth, these periods enable the study of the so-called historical path of dependences and the evolutionary nature or surging nature of these processes. Considerations of this kind usually confirm the views accepted by economists in this regard. They, however, show a much greater complexity of conditions, causes, mechanisms, and effects of accelerated growth. It means that from a methodological point of view, the views that exist in the theory of economics should be considered as formulated at such a high level of abstraction that they do not allow for the explanation, understanding, and interpretation of the course of growth processes in individual countries in different periods of their history. For this reason, the postulate to enrich the economic analysis of the process of economic growth, in particular the periods of accelerated growth, is indisputable and strengthens the empirical foundations of economic research. Analyses of processes of modern economic growth in the historical perspective usually include the problems of modernization, especially determinants and consequences of industrialization both in developed and backward economies, and its effects. The latter manifest themselves in the emergence of capitalism in Europe and its expansion to other geographical areas. The scope of this analysis might be perceived as not very precise due to the existing disputes regarding the understanding of the terms "modern age", "modernity", or "contemporary times" as pointed out, for example, by Golka (2012, ch. III). However, regardless of the above-mentioned semantic problems, the starting point for economic historians is always the question of the causes and effects of backwardness and ways of getting it out. An example confirming the correctness of the above statement is the historical analysis of economic backwardness put forward by Alexander Gerschenkron (Gerschenkron 1962). He presented the concept of the dependence of institutional forms and types of ideology on the degree of backwardness perceived by the author as a relative phenomenon, not an absolute one. This way of thinking led Gerschenkron to formulate both the conditions for entering the path of permanent and relatively fast economic growth as well as the regularity of processes of industrialization (Gerschenkron 1962). Considering the institutional forms of industrialization which includes solutions that are appropriate for economic liberalism on one pole, and on the other—top-down controls and the scale of social ideologies associated with industrialization which, in turn, at one end contains the laissez-faire ideology and, on the other, Marxism, Gerschenkron formulated the thesis according to which the further a given country is on the scale of backwardness, the more intensively it must utilize institutional solutions and types of ideologies that are more distant from the initial forms to implement industrialization. According to Gerschenkron (1962, p. 353), the differences in industrialization processes result from the degree of backwardness of the economies of individual countries. Consequently, the more backward economy:

- the more the industrialization process was characterized by a sharp surge with a high rate of industrial production growth
- the larger size and scale of enterprises and industrial facilities
- the stronger the preferences to produce capital goods and not consumer goods
- the greater the restrictions on society's consumption
- the greater the role of unique institutional forms that enable the growth of capital supply necessary for building industry and frequently the compulsory their nature
- the smaller the role of the agricultural sector as a distribution channel of investment goods regardless of increasing work efficiency in this sector

Finally, Gerschenkron formulates the thesis on developmental pluralism according to which it is necessary to allow for the diversification of industrialization processes in individual countries, and the development of a backward country may significantly differ from the development of a developed country. In the literature on economic history, the interpretation of the idea of developmental pluralism, however, is not unambiguous. For example, while Gerschenkron believes that in the context of historical experiences of the West the issue of the extent to which industrialization processes in European countries may be seen as a series of repetitions of England's industrial history or deviations from the English path, Kula suggests the departure from perceiving the paths of economic growth of individual European countries as repetitions or deviations from the English scheme (Kula 1967, pp. 67–70). He also draws attention to the fact that the consistent adoption of the thesis on developmental pluralism in relation to the processes of modern economic growth under capitalism requires the acceptance of pluralism in feudal relations in Europe. In other words, the legitimacy of analysing the so-called historical path of dependence should be recognized. Otherwise, despite the intentions of Gerschenkron, one must accept a version of the interpretation of a one-way vision of development. In practice, this means discussing the prerequisites of industrialization during the period of modernization (*prerequisites of modern industrialization*). The considerations on the issue of the primary accumulation of capital is an example in the context of economic history. According to Gerschenkron, primary accumulation may be a factor enabling industrialization, but it may also be the result of the country's entrance on the path of industrialization. Thus, while some factors in developed countries can be evaluated as prerequisites of industrialization, in the backward countries they will be perceived as its results (Gerschenkron 1962, p. 113). Berger's remarks also refer to this issue (1986, p. 203). Commenting on the concept of the Rostow growth stages well-known in the literature (Rostow 1960), according to which the development of individual countries can be placed on the path corresponding to modern British history, Berger states that accepting the idea of economic development as a process of going through specific stages does not mean having to mechanically go through other stages. Marks (1951) and Hobsbawm (1964) assumed the same line of argumentation. Development can be treated as a process of progressive economic growth leading to an increase in social welfare. It consists of many stages, the sequence of which may be modified due to the impact of cultural conditions, the international situation, the state economic policy, and other circumstances. This position is also expressed in the idea of surge development where the surge is not only omitting full stages or phases of development but also a rapid transition from traditional to modern branches of economy or modern production techniques and technologies (Kleer et al. 1989). The effect of the surge development is to be the acceleration of the development and growth processes. Acceleration evoked by a surge does not have to be associated with periods of economic miracles. The Rostov concept is known to have been subjected to harsh criticism not only as Eurocentric, but also as overly optimistic. The reality is that we are dealing with the coexistence of capitalist wealth and poverty, which, since Prebish's (1963) theory of "centre" and "periphery" developed, for example, in the well-known concept of the world economy of Wallerstein (1976, 1979) and the theory of dependent development (Frank 1969; Palma 1978; Furtado 1964), and in recent years as part of the research trend called colonial studies (Loomba 2005; Gandhi 1998; Said 2003), are perceived as mutually conditioned and functional. There is no doubt, therefore, that the processes of economic growth in capitalist economies, especially the conditions and effects of accelerated growth, must be analysed separately for developed and backward countries. History also does not confirm the continuity and durability of the processes of accelerated growth. This opinion is also consistent with the results of analyses carried out under other theories of long-term economic growth, such as the Rosenstein-Rodan theory of "big push" that is well-known in the history of economic thought (1959), the theory of the "vicious circle of poverty" by Nurkse (1962), Schumpeter's theory of economic development (Schumpeter 2017), Perroux's growth poles theory (Perroux 1950) and Chenery's theory of structural changes (Chenery 1979). The review and characteristics of these theories are included in the work of Fiedor and Kociszewski (2010). They all focus on the attempt to separate development and economic growth and present a specific point of view on the issues of conditions, objectives, strategies, and development policy, as well as on the general regularity of these processes. The theories recognize the fact that in less-developed countries the acceleration of development and growth, and especially periods of potential economic miracles, create opportunities to faster overcome the barriers of underdevelopment, to transform from the periphery to the centre, or strengthen the position in the centre. Regardless of the level of development achieved, industrialization and a marked acceleration of economic growth usually require a well-organized and effective state (Polanyi 1947), although according to Gerschenkron, the case of England proves that development could have occurred autogenously and was strengthened by the laissez-faire ideology. There is no doubt, therefore, that the methodological proposal regarding the need to accept the thesis on developmental pluralism is fully justified even though its interpretation may raise some controversy. For example, this thesis is maintained by Landes (2000) who is, however, of the opinion that the historical approach when trying to answer the question as to the reasons for wealth or poverty does not guarantee an answer. As for the wealth and dominance of the West, there are generally two ways of explaining it. The first approach maintains that it is the result of better organization, intelligence, hard work, and all kinds of innovation, whereas the second one points to the aggressiveness, greed, ruthlessness, and lack of scruples of the Europeans. In the light of the considerations under study, the statements of Eisenstadt (1966) and Levy Jr. (1968) in the point about the faster growth rate of capitalism in the form of a modernization process rather than in the form of changes in production methods and social structures are undoubtedly of interest. Development and backwardness are the results of the accelerated accumulation of capital that took place in Europe at the turn of the eighteenth and nineteenth centuries. However, to understand the durable character of backwardness, Eisenstadt and Levy Jr. regard it to refer to the mechanism of functioning of the world economy system in the understanding represented by Prebish and Wallerstein which is seen as the effect of the emergence of industrial capitalism. The institutional factors influencing modernization in individual countries have a dominant importance in describing, explaining, and interpreting the results of research on accelerated economic growth.

The difficulties in finding the causes of the economic growth of the West are also indicated by Rosenberg and Birdzell (1986). In their opinion, the richness of the West should be perceived as a historical phenomenon that occurred under certain historical conditions and which can be treated as the so-called European miracle. Such a thesis quite often formulated in the literature on the subject. As it is known, the so-called European miracle resulted in the economic, military, technological, and political supremacy of Europe in the world after 1500, i.e. in the period of modernization and the emergence of capitalism. It resulted in the formation of a bipolar model of the world in which the "centre" dominated the "periphery" (Hobson 2004; Jones 1981). According to Kennedy (1988, Chapter 1), the European miracle was a dynamic process driven primarily by technical and economic progress under specific geographic and social conditions, which was also decided by chance. Its understanding requires the analysis mainly of material and long-term factors. Because the European miracle was absolutely unique in history, it should be assumed that only the identification and reconstruction of all of its constituent elements could cause its repetition in other societies. According to Kennedy, the European miracle was a consequence of the combination of economic laissez-faire, political and military pluralism, and intellectual freedom. As it can be easily noticed, the acceptance of the thesis about the European miracle significantly limits both historical generalizations and the theoretical explanation of this phenomenon, because its logical consequence is the recognition of the European miracle as a unique, unplanned phenomenon, which was identified and described ex post. The idea of the European miracle is of course much more capacious than the cases of "economic miracles" described in the economic history and associated mainly with periods of accelerated economic growth in some countries. However, it is impossible to resist the impression that such an understanding of the "European miracle" and the characteristics attributed to this phenomenon is the basis for case studies used by economists of the so-called economic miracles that have occurred in some countries since the second half of the twentieth century. It should, therefore, be assumed that in the light of historical research, considerations on the concept and characteristics of the phenomenon of an economic miracle associated with periods of accelerated economic growth will require many interpretations depending on an individual case in question. In the context of research on the historical process of growth, and especially the periods of its acceleration, an interesting concept is presented by Gelei (1974). Recognizing that the research approach adopted by Clark (2008), Chenery (1979), Kuznetz (1971), and Perroux (1950) was the right approach to studying the process of economic growth, Gelei introduced the division of all processes into those differentiating, substituting, and shaping absolute growth. The phenomenon of differentiation as a complex multi-layer phenomenon includes:

- changes in the use of production factors affecting the development of the division of labour
- increase in labour productivity and capital
- inequality of development
- specialization, integration, and concentration processes

Substitution processes are, in turn, associated with changes in the systems of relations between the old and new areas of activity and combinations of production factors, as well as transformations of their structure. The concept of absolute growths, however, expresses the essence of the process of economic growth. These may, for example, include an increase in the resources of production factors, raising the level of absolute business activity, and increasing the number of goods and services produced. Differentiation, substitution, and absolute growth make an indivisible unity. According to Gelei, economic growth processes take place due to the creation of absolute growths through differentiation, which is the result of substitution. In her opinion, the process of long-term economic growth includes two periods, i.e. a period of stagnation and a period of accelerated growth. In the period of accelerated growth, the economy ceases to be a single-sector economy, namely a clear division into the agricultural and non-agricultural sector occurs. Within stagnation, industry develops. Differentiation phenomena are associated with a new division of production factors, the division of labour deepens, specialization progresses, and the "roundabout production methods" are extended. Integration processes of production factors accelerate both in space and in individual spheres of economic activity. Substitutions of live labour by objectified labour are observed, capital-intensive production techniques are increasingly used, and there take place changes in the structure of the economy consisting in limiting agricultural activity in favour of industry and services. There appears a phenomenon of increasing surplus of goods and services over the subsistence minimum in the area of growths. This surplus is of a permanent, systematic nature and allows accumulation to increase. The final effect of these developments is the change in the relationship between the natural and money-goods sectors of economy manifested in the much faster rate of development of the latter. Larger business units are created in individual sectors of the economy. A global market is also emerging. Its existence increases the economic interdependence of individual countries.

The typology of processes proposed by Gelei that are elements of economic growth is obviously one of many classifications. It shows a certain structure of this process and the regularity of its changes despite the necessity to include in its analysis the peculiarities of the economies of individual countries, regions, sectors, states, and forms as well as the scale of economic activity. Certainly, the author's way of explaining the economic growth process in capitalist economies differs from the theories based on the concepts that refer to the idea of the industrial revolution and industrialization. In Gelei's opinion, the formation and popularization of money-goods relations is of fundamental importance. The stages of growth specified by Gelei form an organic whole and show the interdependence, that got shaped in the processes of differentiation and substitution, of all entities operating in the economy. This constant adaptation to changing structures makes it possible to use production growths and thus cause an increase in its scale. As Gelei points out, she is not interested in the stages involving the initial growth prerequisites, which were mentioned by M. Kula, but subsequent stages related to the occurrence of the phenomenon of systematic economic growth. The research she conducted shows that the beginning of the first phase of systematic growth can be observed in the last 30 years of the nineteenth century, while the end of this period falls on the period of the First World War. The new change of development directions should by no means be attributed to cyclical influences but to the consequences of development and stabilization of new material relations defining new production techniques and technologies, new energy sources, products, and areas of economic activity, as well as internal and foreign markets. These new factors create an impulse for the growth of the differentiation process in subsequent stages, then for the continuation of the substitution process and further absolute growths expressed in the volume and rate of growth of the national income. Finally, Gelei formulates the thesis that accelerated economic growth cannot be expected without the tight and organic interdependence of material processes (Gelei 1974, p. 253). The prerequisite stage, however, is recognized by the author as the borderline period in which the capitalist economy was created. At the same time, there is a significant relationship between the volume of growths, the created production surplus that makes the basis for capital formation, the cumulative increase in national income and economic development. However, one cannot perceive economic growth in a relevant period as a simple continuation of the process that took place in the previous period, since differentiation, in terms of specific indexes of growth rate, is shaped in a different way. The high average rate of economic growth results from the levelling of the range of growth rate characteristic of particular sectors and areas of the economy. However, the condition for rapid growth requires the reference of range to the highest possible value indicators. Thus, the overall growth process should be the result of partial processes with a high acceleration coefficient. In general, accelerating the process of economic growth undoubtedly depends on the structure of the economy and the directions and rate of its changes.

Undoubtedly, a well-known work by Naisbitt (1984) entitled *Megatrends. Ten New Directions Transforming Our Lives* is, to some extent, the continuation of the proposal and method of studying the processes of growth and economic development advocated by Gelei. It is true that it refers to American experiences, but it is an attempt to identify phenomena and processes of a universal nature that define the future and the development rate of the economies of the modern globalized world.

The conclusion that comes from Naisbitt's publication is obvious. Faster and sustainable economic development can be expected when the identified megatrends of development are taken into account, the socio-economic policy is adjusted to those tendencies, and consequently, necessary institutional and technological changes are introduced.

From the point of view of considerations under study in this work, attention should be given to the discussion, that is both important and theoretically and empirically interesting, on the validity of recognizing the logistic curve as properly describing the historical course of the process of economic growth. This curve is even referred to as the growth curve and it can be used to illustrate many social phenomena. Cameron (1993, Chapter 1) indicates the possibility of using a logistic curve. The curve is divided into two phases, i.e. the phase of accelerated and delayed growth due to the reversibility of the economic growth process. According to Cameron, however, the question of the reversibility of development is debatable because the social structure, political, and economic organizations rarely have the same forms in individual phases. In turn, Kurowski (1963) states, when describing the mechanism of growth according to the logistic curve, that the growth takes place as a result of the opposing forces, and therefore has a dialectic character. At the same time, he accepts the thesis about the logistic nature of growth, which can be deduced in a deductive way from the law of geometric progress and from the statement on the finiteness of the material world. The truth of this claim is evidenced by the results of empirical research carried out by Kurowski on the historical process of economic growth based on the indicator analysis, which in this case was the production of iron and steel. It should be emphasized that the logistics curve does not imply the existence of any growth limit. Accepting the claim about the logistical nature of the growth process makes it possible to analyse both the processes of diversifying levels of economic development as well as the tendencies to accelerate their equalization. The phenomena of spatial reallocation of industrial potentials were the effects of successive periods of the tendency to differentiate and to equalize. The phenomenon of concentration of industrial potential in one or more countries was usually observed during periods of differentiation, while the tendency to shift it to many countries prevailed in the equalization periods. It is not indifferent whether the periods of changes in these levels occur in the accelerated growth phase or in the phase of delayed growth. Kurowski's research also showed an interesting fact that the later a given stage of the growth process took place, i.e. the later a certain level of metallurgical production per capita was reached, the faster the process occurred. It was the consequence of technological acceleration, which is always the largest in the range of the lowest production and the smallest in the highest range. This acceleration is, of course, a function of time (Kurowski 1963, pp. 333–334). Periods with exceptionally high growth rates are perceived as economic miracles. However, they differ in their conditioning, course, and effects in time and space. Therefore, it is worth examining separately cases of, for example, the Japanese and the Irish miracles in the twentieth century. The analysis of long-term growth trends leads to the adoption of the theory of the wave nature of secular growth. Its correctness is confirmed by the results of many empirical studies. Nevertheless, one should remember the differences characterizing the results of secular and medium- and short-term research. This means that the former cannot be the basis for reflections on an economic growth policy conducted by an individual country. They only extend the scope and number of possible interpretations of the conditions and effects of measures adopted, referred to by Kurowski (1963) as the logistic law of growth. Hence, it is not surprising that the concept of developmental waves in the economy emerged as part of economic history and the theory of economic development (Freeman 1984). The starting point is very often the Kondratiev cycle concept. As was already pointed out, the phenomenon of economic miracles is associated with periods of accelerated growth. An interesting interpretation of the occurrence of economic miracles was presented by Best (2018). In his opinion, the study of the historical process of the capitalist economy growth requires the characteristics of the so-called triad, that included the business model, production capacity, and knowledge and skills. Best recognized that the traditional analysis of the production function is far from sufficient to learn the real characteristics and mechanisms of functioning of the market economy since it interprets only those characteristics and mechanisms of the functioning of the market economy that are assumed in theory a priori. Not only are the resources of production factors and their structure important for the processes of economic growth, but also the interactions that take place between the elements of the triad. Rapid economic growth requires the coordination of organizational changes in each of the three above-mentioned elements of the triad and in their mutual relations. Best mentions on this occasion various mechanisms of this coordination, which may include, for example, competition, regulation, industrial policy, macroeconomic, or financial policy. They are all compatible with the system of the market economy. The adoption of the triad concept enables the study of both micro- and macroeconomic conditions of mechanisms and effects of economic growth. Best refers explicitly in his deliberations to the research achievements of the representatives of the new institutional economics, such as Williamson (1985) or Ostrom (1990), for whom the problems of coordination of measures were of the primary nature. The policy of the state, treating the elements of the triad separately, will not effectively create the process of economic growth, especially growth that is based on innovation. Finally, Best states that the processes of economic growth require a certain volume and structure of resources of production factors, efficient institutions for the coordination of measures adopted in the area of economy and a policy based on experience and knowledge. An effective policy means primarily an institutional policy that supports the elements of the triad and their coordination.

To sum up the above considerations on selected problems of accelerated economic growth and economic development in the historical perspective, it is first of all necessary to notice their methodological significance consisting in highlighting historical changes as mainly evolutionary, but also as a process of overcoming backwardness diversified both in time and in space. The process, nevertheless, is subject to certain regularities that can be deduced inductively on the basis of empirical studies or deductively from the adopted indicators regarding the nature of these changes and the ontological status of the material world. They also show that the phenomenon of accelerated economic growth is, as mentioned above, related to the history of the emergence of capitalism and the industrial economy. It resulted in institutional changes corresponding to the challenges of a market economy operating in structures with diversified levels of development. As North (2005, Chapter 10) notes, periods of growth occurred in history when the economy generated incentives to increase productivity. One can recognize the mutual relations between the economic and political organization of society in the context of changing beliefs guiding human actions when research focuses on the institutional and organizational structure. Therefore, when one looks for the roots of economic miracles in individual countries in the twentieth and twenty-first centuries, one should remember that from the point of view of historical experiences economic miracles may occur (though perhaps not only) in market economies that have successfully passed through the period of modernization. The history of the birth of capitalism in Western Europe is a spectacular example mentioned here many times before. The key to success was, in this case, a large variety of opportunities used and an increased probability of entering the path of economic growth due to the formation of a competitive economic and political order favouring the widening of the scope of human freedom (North 2005). From the point of view of economics, these are important conclusions. There is no doubt that the analysis and understanding of the process of long-term economic change is possible under the concept of path dependence (North 1990, p. 112) with the application of various research instruments, such as evolutionary game theory, simulation theory, or experimental economics (Elsner 2012, pp. 1–43). However, it should be remembered that understanding the processes of long-term growth and development does not mean they are explained.

2.3 Theory of Economic Growth

The methods of explaining and interpreting the phenomenon of fast economic growth as well as its diversification in time and space in the second half of the twentieth century that exist in the contemporary theory of economic growth usually refer to the savings rate that defines the rate of capital accumulation and broadly understood technological progress. Theories of economic growth developed in economics enable the description and explanation of the growth mechanism, its social, demographic, institutional, technological, and resource conditions, causes and effects, relations between various economic variables affecting its course, nature, and rate. The theories grew on the tradition of both neoclassical and Keynesian economics. However, it should be emphasized that Keynesian-type growth models play a secondary role (Malaga 2011) in research practice. The subject of the growth theory is the analysis of the economy in the long run, i.e. in the period in which changes in the capital stock affect the course of production processes. The subject literature in this field is abundant. An overview of various models of economic growth can be found, for example, in the works by Barro and Sala-I-Martin (1995), Jones (1981), Romer (1996), and Tokarski (2009). As noted by Dornbusch (2000), the high growth rate in the second half of the twentieth century revived the discussion on its causes, mechanisms, and effects as well as the assessment of the state of theory in this area. Regardless of the above-mentioned lack of agreement as to the methodological and ideological basis of various trends in the theory of economic growth and models that exist within the framework of these trends, the issue of accelerated economic growth plays an important role. The dependence that is universal for all economic systems at all times is the starting point for reflections on the subject. Clark (2008, Chapter 10) refers to it as the fundamental equation of growth and the model is widely known:

$$y = ak + bz + w$$

where y is production growth rate per capita, k represents capital growth rate per capita, w indicates labour productivity growth rate, while a and b indicate shares in the product represented by capital and land owners. Thus, economic growth rate depends on the changes in the volume of resources of production factors and technological progress. Since the publication of a well-known work by Dennison (1967), it has been recognized that technological progress is the main source of growth. To determine its effect on the growth rate, Solow (1956) introduced the concept of total productivity of production factors (the so-called Solow residual). This made it possible to specify the part of the growth that should be attributed to the accumulation of capital and the part to be attributed to the residual factors, mainly non-material technological progress, i.e. the progress which does not stem directly from the greater involvement of traditional factors in the fundamental equation of growth. The intensification of economic growth is, therefore, associated with the increase in innovation. It is now thought that the differentiation of growth rates results mainly from the total productivity of production factors. The productivity is a consequence of the creation and development of the IT sector and the absorption rate of information technologies by other industries. As noticed by Gomułka (2016), contemporary discussions on the mechanisms and sources of growth must necessarily include at least the following two stylized facts. The first one includes the reasons for growth acceleration in recent decades and the circumstances for its possible reduction, while the second one is the phenomenon of the duality of the world economy (the emergence of the centre and the periphery) characterized by the occurrence of deepening differences in the level of development, and thus the phenomenon of divergence. It is worth mentioning that the ongoing globalization has meant that peripheries should also include the former and existing non-market economies. Gomułka adds other, according to him significant, stylized facts when characterizing the processes of growth in the global economy and confronts them with the proposals that Esterly and Levine (2001) put forward in this regard. Gomułka suggested the set of stylized facts, which is worth citing when considering the significance of the characteristics of modern growth for the considerations on the periods of its acceleration. This collection includes the characteristics of highly developed countries, that form an area Gomułka called the *Technology Frontier Area* (TFA), as well as underdeveloped countries outside TFA. According to Gomułka, in the area of TFA:

- The economic growth was unbalanced in the last 300 years as the growth of the sector producing qualitative changes (the innovation and education sector, which mainly includes R & D and education system) was faster than the growth of the conventional sector (involving traditional, material factors of production).
- The growth rates of the conventional and innovation-education sectors were different but stable during the technological revolution.
- Y/L ratio growth rate, where *Y* is the volume of gross domestic product (GDP) and *L* represents the number of man-hours, is quite stable in time, little differentiated between countries, and above all, little dependent on the investment rate.

However, when it comes to countries from outside the TFA, these are characterized by:

- Strong variation in Y/L ratio growth in time and between countries.
- Y/L ratio growth rate is strongly dependent on the participation of investments in national income.
- In turn, Easterly and Levine proposed the following set of facts[1]:
- These are not differences in the accumulation of physical and human capital, but the diversification of their total productivity that explains almost entirely the differences in the GDP growth rate per capita.
- There is a constant deepening of the differences in GDP levels per capita in the world, and thus divergence rather than convergence becomes the norm.
- In contrast to capital accumulation, economic growth is not durable in time.
- The flow of production factors is characterized by the same direction, which proves the existence of positive external effects there.
- The economic growth rate of a given country depends on the economic policy.

Considering the dual nature of the modern world economy system, one should pay attention to two characteristics of the growth process in the TFA area and beyond it, which fact is also mentioned by Gomułka. The first one concerns technological changes, which in the TFA countries are a consequence of the functioning of their R & D sector and education system and determine the level of total productivity of production factors. In economies outside this area, on the other hand, innovations have an imitative character and come from outside. It means that in the so-called knowledge-based economies, as opposed to peripheral economies, human capital determines decisively the level of Solow residual. The second of these characteristics are related to the role of physical capital in stimulating economic growth. According to Gomułka, recognition of high investment rate, not high innovation as a source of rapid growth is justified only in relation to countries from outside the TFA, and thus to peripheral economies. In those economies, the inflow and absorption of external technologies require investment in fixed assets and therefore accumulation in the conventional sector. Efforts were made, within the framework of the theory of economic growth, to build a growth model that takes into

[1]Adapted from Gomułka (2016, pp. 21–23).

account the functioning of the conventional and innovative sectors (Phelps 1966). The two growth characteristics presented above are also reflected in the works of other economists including (Jones 2002; Bernanke and Gürkaynak 2001). The thesis about the special significance of the process of accumulation of physical capital for the accelerated economic growth of the underdeveloped countries is widely accepted among economists. The works of Kaldor (1961), Nurkse (1962), Lewis (1978, p. 307), or Singer (1952) are the examples. It should be added that it is correct not only for market capitalist economies but also for non-market economies. The thesis is also consistent with the presented above research results of historians according to whom accelerated growth and economic miracles recorded in the periods of its occurrence involve phenomena related only to the experience of industrial economies, and the creation of such economies requires intensive accumulation of physical capital. As noted by Stojanović (1965, pp. 201–202), the unique role of the accumulation rate for growth rate in countries outside the TFA area results from its impact on GDP expansion and from the fact that its growth always shortens the time of reaching the specific volume of growth rate more than proportionally. Of course, it should be assumed that accumulation conditions growth, but it is also its result. Stojanović's opinions to adopt a stylized fact that involves the relationship between the investment rate and the rate of economic growth characteristic of non-TFA countries in the sense of Gomułka is justified. The claims are certainly confirmed by works on the theory of the growth of the socialist economy, i.e. non-market economy outside the TFA. It created particularly large opportunities for the policy of accelerated growth and the creation of the industrial economy due to institutional reasons.

The issue of economic growth in the socialist economy was of interest to Kalecki (1967, 1984). He considers various options when examining particularly the issue of accelerated growth in this system. Kalecki analyses growth acceleration at the unrestricted supply of labour and its limited resources under the conditions necessary to maintain the balance of foreign trade by means of increasing capital intensity or shortening the service life of the equipment. In addition, he considered more complex situations, such as accelerating the growth of national income at full employment by means of increasing capital intensity and shortening the life of the equipment. Kalecki also raised the issue of choosing the coefficient of capital intensity and investment structure and thus choosing the type of technical progress to be implemented in the conventional sector from the perspective of full employment. His studies focused on the analysis of changes in the rate of accumulation and, above all, the rate of investment in periods of steady and accelerated economic growth. Acceleration of the growth rate in the economy outside the TFA often leads to raising the investment rate to the level at which certain growth barriers appear, such as the barrier of labour, foreign trade, technology, and raw materials. The growth model of the socialist economy constructed by Kalecki assumed, like other models in this respect, that the increase in the national income is primarily the result of the production effect, and thus of the supply effect of the investment. Due to the institutional order existing in this type of economy, this model did not take into account the demand side. It assumed that state policy would always ensure that global demand was balanced with global supply. Given the historical experience of industrialization processes as a precondition for overcoming backwardness, this approach seemed fully justified. As shown by Kornai (1971, 1980, 1982), accelerated growth processes in the socialist economy, i.e. non-market economy, lead to the demand-side imbalance that generates permanent shortage, which is systemic due to the lack of the existing demand restriction, so characteristic of market economies. This is an extremely important observation. It shows that in a non-market economy, which, as historical experience shows, is always an economy outside the TFA and periods of accelerated growth do not lead to an economic miracle in the sense presented by Balcerowicz and Rzońca (2014), although a miracle is potentially possible in Sharma's understanding of the issue. It is worth quoting the results of Dobb's research here (Dobb 1963, ch. III), according to which the choice of production technique in the production section of consumer goods is of crucial importance in less developed countries. In his opinion, the surplus of consumer goods over the volume consumed by its producers is the necessary condition for economic growth in these countries. The surplus may be directed to satisfy the needs of the labour force producing production goods. It determines the level of the potential investment rate on which the rate of economic growth depends. The low level of this surplus in a closed economy prevents the achievement of a high rate of growth, while in the case of the opening of the economy it may lead, for example, to the so-called dependent development. A certain option may be to choose such production techniques that will ensure a constant employment ratio between the production sectors of production and consumer goods that develop at the same growth rate of growth. This, in consequence, means a steady growth rate for the whole economy. If these techniques allow an even faster increase in work efficiency, then the chance to prepare conditions for accelerating growth increases. According to Dobb, neither techniques that maximize the investment surplus nor techniques that maximize the surplus of consumption should be chosen.

On the other hand, the choice of indirect technique creates premises for accelerating growth, limiting the scale of unemployment, and a certain increase in consumption. Dobb's reflections show how difficult it is to enter the path of accelerated long-term growth in underdeveloped countries regardless of the shape of their institutional system, all the more so the extensive growth pattern usually predominates in them. This model is based on increasing the physical volume of the resources of production factors and the duplication of production technologies and systems already in production processes. Extensive growth always leads to the disclosure of various barriers that prevent the continuation of growth at the current level, which is indicated by, for example, the results of the research carried out under the Kalecki growth model. Such an increase depends primarily on increasing labour inputs. Thus, the operation of the principle of decreasing marginal work efficiency in a given production technology and inefficient institutional system lead to maintaining a relatively low growth rate in the long run (Woźniak 2004, pp. 50–51). Gomułka (2016), however, draws attention to the fact that in the period of increasing globalization, the intensification of growth processes in less-developed countries is often the result of the inflow of technologies from TFA countries. In this way, the technological barrier characteristic of non-TFA economies is overcome. As stated above, accelerated economic growth is a prerequisite for an economic miracle, but it is certainly not a sufficient condition. The theoretical and empirical analysis of the acceleration of growth processes in non-TFA economies clearly shows that. The participation of the R & D sphere in the creation of innovation is still marginal there, and innovations are mainly imitative. It turned out, however, that in certain circumstances, which occurred, for example, in the economies of China and Vietnam, the acceleration of growth in non-TFA countries may be relatively long term and stable. At the same time, it should be emphasized that the issue of recognizing China's case as an example of economic miracle is still under discussion (Best 2018; Fenby 2008; Harney 2009; Vietor 2007). The rapid growth of the Chinese economy at the turn of the twentieth and twenty-first centuries cannot certainly be fully recognized as an example of an economic miracle in the sense of Balcerowicz and Rzońca (2014), although on the other hand, it meets the conditions for the definition of this phenomenon according to Sharma (Sharma 2012). Therefore, it seems reasonable to treat separately cases of potential economic miracles in countries with non-market or quasi-market economies that are always outside the TFA.

As mentioned above, the main reasons for the growth of national income per capita in industrial economies are investments in physical capital and human capital as well as in innovations that result from investments in knowledge capital leading to productivity growth. The influence of innovation on economic development has become the subject of special interest of economists after the publication of Schumpeter's paper *Theory of Economic Development*. As stated by Clark (2008), the theory of growth shows that investments in physical and human capital explain 30–50% of growth although it is known that the impact of changes in physical capital cannot be completely separated from innovation. If that was the case, in some economies there would be a rapid growth of physical capital per capita without productivity growth and in other economies, there would be a rapid increase in productivity without an increase in physical capital per capita. Therefore, it should be recognized that these phenomena are in practice interrelated, which does not mean that trends in the theory of economic growth are assigned the same importance.

According to Gomułka (2016, p. 37), the positive relationship between the investment rate and the innovation rate may be characterized by a high strength for a low investment rate. However, a certain supply of inventions and a high level of their absorption are needed. As the investment rate is practically at the level of 15–25%, which is a small part of GDP, so the growth rate dependent on it will not exceed the spectacularly high level in the long run. This explains why cases of accelerated growth leading to the economic miracle are rare in non-TFA countries. Another important issue raised in the theory of growth concerns the manner in which the rate of investment impacts the rate of growth. Keynesian models recognize the thesis that in the capitalist economy there is no automatic guarantee of growth at the level of the natural rate determined by the resources of the labour force and technical progress. The existing rigidity of price and wage means that the actual growth rate is determined by the volume of the effective demand determined by the unstable level of investment expenditures. Stabilization of effective demand and reaching its volume at the level that guarantees the full use of production factors requires governmental activity. In contrast, in neoclassical models, the growth rate is determined by supply factors, i.e. by the population growth rate and the increase of production capacity and technical progress that determine the rate of labour productivity growth. Thus, a different weight is attached to the supply and demand side in the Keynesian and neoclassical theory of growth. Production capacities and technology are treated as data in the Keynesian theory, while the neoclassical theory treats these as variables. The demand (income) aspect of the investment is, therefore, considered in the first case, while in the other case it is the supply aspect. There is a very large number of models of economic growth referring to both Keynesian and neoclassical traditions in the economic literature. It should be emphasized that the Keynesian and neoclassical models are also characterized by significant differences as to institutional assumptions with regard to the already mentioned role of the state, the nature, and significance of competition, the economic structure of the economy, the impact of globalization, etc.

However, it is assumed that for the analysis of accelerated growth in highly developed countries, in other words, TFA countries, the best tools are growth models that derive from the neoclassical tradition or, more precisely, the Solow model sometimes referred to as the Solow-Swan model (Solow 1956; Swan 1956) and from its various mutations. It is on the basis of this model that the conclusion is drawn that the accumulation of physical capital is not able to explain the very high GDP growth per capita and its huge diversity between countries. Hence, the reasons for the observed divergence phenomenon. It is recognized that this model is based on an analysis of the production function of a general form; $Y(t) = f(K(t), L(t))$, where t is time, K—capital, L—labour, and Y—product. Constant incomes are assumed in view of scale in reference to capital and labour. Economic growth is not determined by the state policy in the Solow model. In particular, it does not depend on savings, because in the long run, the operation of the market mechanism makes growth sustainable. At this growth, capital and production grow at the rate determined by the increase in labour resources. Technical progress is exogenous in nature and is a factor compensating for the decreasing income of capital and labour. The divergence phenomena observed in the world, in particular between poorly and highly developed countries, became the reason for the modification of this model. The endogenous nature of technical progress was adopted (Romer 1986) in the alternative models and the assumption about decreasing income from the capital was repealed. However, the assumption as to decreasing income from work was maintained. Rejecting the assumption of declining incomes for both capital and labour would result in rates of increase being endogenous and constantly growing, which is contrary to empiricism. The change of assumptions meant that, by applying the concept of human capital, Mankiw, Romer, and Weil were able to explain the phenomena of divergence in the modern global economy by the occurrence of diversification of population growth rates and accumulation of capital (Mankiw et al. 1992). These authors adopted a modified form of the production function from the Solow model, i.e. $Y(t) = f(K(t), H(t), L(t))$, where H is human capital. It turned out that the model with human capital indicates a significantly higher impact of savings and population growth at the achieved level of GDP. The so-called golden rule of accumulation is adopted with reference to the Solow model, the Mankiw, Romer, and Weil model, and its generalization by Nonneman and Vanhoudt (Nonneman and Vanhoudt 1996; Tokarski 2011). The rule defines the rate of accumulation at which per capita consumption is maximized, while the economy moves along the sustainable growth path. The author of this rule was Phelps (1961). Thus, from the point of view of the condition of sustainable growth that maximizes the level of per capita consumption, there is a limit to the rate of economic growth. Endogenous growth models allow for a more in-depth analysis of the role of capital, labour, and technology in the growth process. Models of this kind also treat the issue of the impact of institutions on the course of growth to a much wider extent. Even a factor called "public order", which is created by the state as a supplier of public goods (Findlay and Wilson 1987) is introduced into these models. In turn, Sala-i-Martin (2002) presented a model of an econometric study of the institution's influence on the course of growth based on regression equations. The models of social capital impact analysis (Barro 1991; Fukuyama 1995) and creative destruction (Aghion and Howitt 1992) are also interesting in this respect.

In contrast to models assuming the endogenous nature of growth and institutions, it is extremely difficult to explain and understand the huge diversity of institutional governance in individual countries in exogenous growth models. One can only consider their impact on economic growth in the long run. This approach is, however, far from sufficient in the context of the attempts of socio-economic reforms observed in many countries undertaken to accelerate or stabilize the course of growth in the short and medium periods. Theories assuming exogenous changes in factors of production and institutions may, first of all, explain sudden and unexpected changes in the rate of growth (Clark 2008, p. 232). However, these theories are not able to answer the questions of why the industrial revolution and the rise of capitalism took place, why economic reforms in China caused a large acceleration of growth in this country and attempts to replicate these reforms in Russia failed, why the social market economy model in Germany is non-imitative, or why not all countries have reached the level of development of TFA economies, etc.

In the context of the above considerations, Rodrik's comments are of interest (Rodrik 2007). He states that there is no unambiguous relationship between the functions and the forms of the institution. There is, therefore, a wide range of freedom in the design of institutional solutions. Economic reforms in China seem to be the best example. However, in his opinion, a good institutional order is based on the economic principles of the so-called first order, i.e. protection of property rights, contract enforcement, the rule of law, effective incentives, sound money, budget liquidity, the balance of public and effective finances, and well-thought-out regulation. Acceleration of economic growth, by which Rodrik understands a situation in which GDP growth per capita by at least 2% points is maintained in an individual country's economy for at least 8 years, usually requires the implementation of a certain reform package. Experience shows that rapid economic growth is associated with a narrow range of political reforms combining institutional solutions of an orthodox nature with non-orthodox elements. However, maintaining the achieved high rate of economic growth, which is much more difficult than its acceleration, requires a much wider scope of institutional changes. Rodrik emphasizes that institutional changes introduced in some countries are difficult to implement in others. This opinion is confirmed by unsuccessful attempts to replicate by other countries the model of the German social market economy. Finally, he concludes that effective growth strategies should be based on bi-directional changes. The first direction concerns the short-term strategy, which aims to accelerate growth, while the second direction should include medium- and long-term strategies aimed at sustaining growth (Rodrik 2007, p. 68). The necessity to combine the policy of economic growth with institutional changes conducive to development and related to the so-called inclusion institutions are also highlighted by Acemoglu and Robinson (2013). It is now a widely accepted view in economics. An interesting synthesis of economic history and economics in discussion on intensive economic growth is provided by Galor (2011). His unified theory of economic growth bases on an analysis of historical process of economic changes since Malthusian regime to the state of modern sustained economic growth. The transition to sustained economic growth is always accompanied by intensive industrialization and growth of human capital accumulation resulted in individual education investments and skills improvement. Relatively to the level of development he distinguished three clubs of countries, i.e. less developed, in transition to sustainable growth, and well developed.

2.4 Conclusions

In the chapter, several concepts of economic growth were discussed from the perspective of economic history as well as theory of economics. The above considerations lead to the following conclusions:

1. There is a far-reaching consensus on the results of research conducted on the grounds of economics and economic history into the course of the economic growth process and its acceleration in the world economy system in the period of globalization. The analysis of the process of creation and functioning of the dual system of the world economy, which is the result of the historical process of the emergence and evolution of industrial capitalism, shows different mechanisms and diversification of levels of development of the centre and the periphery. The increasing divergence between the centre and the periphery should be considered as a phenomenon of a structural nature.
2. The dualism of the world economy system justifies its division into the TFA and the area outside the TFA. In the first area, economic growth is based primarily on innovations generated by the domestic R & D sector, whose development depends mainly on the resources and value of human and social capital. In the second area, however, development is determined by factors related to the rate of accumulation of physical capital, the inflow of imitative innovations, and socio-political determinants. Economics reflects the duality of the world economy

system existing in practice in the separation of the theory of the development of a poorly developed and highly developed economy.

3. Periods of accelerated economic growth in the contemporary dual system of the world economy are primarily associated with the processes of industrialization and development of the capitalist market economy in peripheral countries and the fast-paced, broadly understood innovativeness of industrial and post-industrial economies of highly developed countries. From the historical perspective, industrialization and acceleration of economic growth is the indispensable condition for overcoming the underdevelopment. This always requires the accelerated accumulation of physical capital in economically underdeveloped economies.
4. A review of the literature on the subject shows a large diversity of views of economic theoreticians on the possibilities, mechanisms, and effects of accelerating economic growth. The phenomenon of economic miracle is a consequence of rapid economic growth although not always fast growth is the same as the economic miracle. The lack of a precise definition of the economic miracle in the theory of economics, the possibility of identifying this phenomenon always only ex post and the inability to plan it, make its description and explanation mainly of a historical nature. On the other hand, the obtained research results are subject to interpretation on the grounds of economics with a fairly frequent use of statistical methods and econometric modelling methods. This leads to ordering, classifying, and grouping facts. This is the starting point for the characterization of historical paths of growth and economic development, on which economic miracles occurred. In turn, the knowledge gained on this subject is the basis for the construction of various classifications of this phenomenon.
5. Economic miracle phenomena are associated with periods of accelerated economic growth. They appeared only in times of intense industrialization and the emergence of capitalism. The industrial revolution, technological progress connected with it, the deepening specialization and concentration of manufacturing processes as well as the rapid accumulation of capital caused an increase in the productivity of production factors not seen earlier in the history of mankind and consequently instigated a rapid economic growth. Industrialization was, therefore, a necessary condition for the occurrence of economic miracles on the path of the historical development of capitalism. As it is known, the expansion of industrial capitalism led to the formation of a dual system of the world economy, divided into less-developed countries (peripheries) and highly developed countries (the centre). The relationship between the centre and the periphery is functional. It should be emphasized that both the periphery and the centre went through or have been going through the period of industrialization. The creation of the dual structure of the world capitalist economy has become the reason for the diversification of the mechanisms of development of the countries of the centre and the periphery, of the volume and structure of production there, and of the level of prosperity achieved. Identified phenomena of economic miracles in the periphery and the centre differ in their causes, mechanisms of occurrence, and the effects they cause. However, they always concern industrial economies.

6. Miracles in non-market economies, as shown by experience to date, have characteristics similar to economic miracles in peripheral countries.
7. The review of the literature on the subject indicates that ex post economic miracles identified as examples of periods of spectacularly rapid growth, may justify the adoption of the following classification in the dual system of the world economy:

   (a) miracles in highly developed countries (TFA countries):

   - caused by factors of a supply nature, such as investments of domestic and foreign capital in innovative technologies and sectors, increase in the number of inventions, organizational and product innovations, modern education, and all investments in human capital.
   - caused by factors of a demand nature, such as state intervention policy, redistribution of national income, institutional changes in the scope of taxation systems, property, applicable regulations, the degree of economic opening, preferences for the development of R & D sector, and modern education.

   (b) miracles in less-developed countries (countries outside the TFA):

   - caused by factors of a supply nature, such as investments in conventional sectors that allow rapid industrialization or modernization of existing industry, the inflow of imitative innovations, the inflow of foreign direct investment and financial capital, the increase in human capital value, the acceleration of internal capital accumulation, and the discovery of new mineral resources.
   - caused by factors of a demand nature, such as the increase in foreign demand for exported products, increase in consumer demand, access to cheap, often foreign, credit money, and institutional changes regarding the political and socio-economic system.

   (c) Miracles in non-market economies characteristic of former socialist countries and the cases of China and Vietnam, which are not fully recognized and interpreted in the context of the idea of the dual system of the global economy. These miracles may be caused primarily by raising the investment rate, similarly as it is the case in countries outside the TFA. As it is known, there is no country in the real world from the TFA with a non-market economy.

8. The classification of economic miracles proposed above is certainly one of many possible proposals in this area. Its basis is the characteristics of factors on the supply and demand side that may trigger rapid economic growth and economic miracles associated with it in the countries in the centre or the periphery. It is not possible to determine the necessary intensity and time of impact of individual factors necessary to trigger the economic miracle ex ante on the grounds of this classification, but one can determine their set, strength, and duration of impact for each case of the miracle identified ex post. Even if one assumes that a continuous and large inflow of innovations generated in the national R & D sphere is a necessary condition, though not a sufficient one, for the occurrence of a miracle in the countries of the TFA, whereas in countries outside the TFA this condition is a

high investment rate or more generally, rapid accumulation of physical capital, it is highly unlikely that in pre-selected countries the phenomenon of an economic miracle will occur. In a situation in which it is difficult to explain this phenomenon and there is a need to understand it, the proposed classification of economic miracles has significant advantages.

References

Acemoglu D, Robinson JA (2013) Why nations fail. The origins of power, prosperity and poverty. Profile Books, London

Acocella N (2002) Zasady polityki gospodarczej. Wydawnictwo Naukowe PWN, Warszawa

Aghion P, Howitt P (1992) A model of growth through creative destruction. Econometrica 60 (2):323–351

Balcerowicz L, Rzońca A (2014) Puzzles of economic growth. The World Bank, Washington, DC

Barro R (1991) Economic growth in a cross section of countries. Q J Econ 106:407–443

Barro RJ, Sala-i-Martin X (1995) Economic growth. McGraw-Hill, New York

Berger PL (1986) The capitalist revolution. Fifty propositions about prosperity, equality and liberty. Basic Books, a Division of Harper Collins Publisher, New York

Bernanke BS, Gürkaynak RS (2001) Is growth exogenous? Taking Mankiw, Romer and Weil seriously. In: Bernanke BS, Rogoff K (eds) NNBER macroeconomics annual 2001. MIT Press, Cambridge, MA, pp 11–17

Best MH (2018) How growth really happens. The making of economic miracles through production, governance, and skills. Princeton University Press, Princeton & Oxford

Cameron R (1993) A concise economic history of the world: from paleolithic times to the present. Oxford University Press, Oxford (Polish edition)

Chenery H (1979) Structural change and development policy. John Hopkins University Press, Baltimore

Clark G (2008) Farewell to alms: a brief economic history of the world. Princeton University Press, Princeton (Polish edition)

Dennison E (1967) Why growth rates differ. The Brookings Institution, Washington, DC

Desai M (1991) Human development: concepts and measurment. Eur Econ Rev 35:350–357

Dobb M (1963) Szkice z teorii wzrostu i planowania. Państwowe Wydawnictwo Naukowe, Warszawa

Dornbusch R (2000) Keys to prosperity: free markets sound money and a bit of luck. MIT Press, Cambridge (Polish edition)

Eisenstadt S (1966) Modernisation: protest and change. Prentice Hall, Englewood Cliffs, NJ

Elsner W (2012) The theory of institutional change revisited: the institutional dichotomy, its dynamic, and its policy implications in a more formal analysis. Journal of Economic Issues XLVI(1):1–44

Esterly W, Levine R (2001) It's not factor accumulation: stylized facts and growth models. World Bank Econ Rev 15(2):177–219

Fenby J (2008) The Penguin history of modern China: the fall and rise of a great power, 1850 to the present. The Penguin, London

Fiedor B, Kociszewski K (2010) Ekonomia rozwoju. Wydawnictwo Uniwersytetu Ekonomicznego we Wrocławiu, Wrocław

Findlay R, Wilson JD (1987) The political economy of lewiatan. In: Razin A, Sadka E (eds) Economic policy in theory and practice. St. Martin's Press, New York

Frank AG (1969) Capitalism and underdevelopment in Latin America. Monthly Review Press, New York

Freeman C (1984) Long waves in the word economy. Frances Pinter Publisher, London and Dover, NH

Fukuyama F (1995) Trust: the social virtues and the creation of prosperity. Free Press, New York
Furtado C (1964) Development and underdevelopment. U.C. Press, Berkeley, CA
Galor O (2011) Unified growth theory. Princeton University Press, Princeton
Gandhi L (1998) Postcolonial theory: a critical introduction. Allen & Unwin, Crows Nest
Gelei A (1974) Trendy wzrostu gospodarczego. Państwowe Wydawnictwo Ekonomiczne, Warszawa
Gerschenkron A (1962) Economic backwardness in historical perspective (A Book of Essays). The Belknap Press of Harvard, Cambridge
Golka M (2012) Cywilizacja współczesna i globalne problemy. Oficyna Naukowa, Warszawa
Gomułka S (2016) Transformacja i rozwój. Teoria i polityka gospodarcza. Wydawnictwo Naukowe PWN, Warszawa
Harney A (2009) Chińska cena. Prawdziwy koszt chińskiej przewagi konkurencyjnej. Sonia Draga, Katowice
Hobsbawm EJ (1964) Labouring man. Weidenfeld & Nicolson, London
Hobson J (2004) The eastern origins of western civilisation. Cambridge University Press, Cambridge
Jones EL (1981) The European miracle: environments, economies and geopolitics in the history of Europe and Asia. Cambridge University Press, Cambridge
Jones CI (2002) Introduction to the economic growth. WW Norton & Company, New York
Kaldor N (1961) Capital accumulation and economic growth. In: Lutz FA, Haque DC (eds) The theory of capital. St. Martin's Press, New York, pp 177–222
Kalecki M (1967) Różnice w węzłowych problemach gospodarczych między wysoko rozwiniętą i zacofaną gospodarką kapitalistyczną. In O gospodarce mieszanej w krajach "Trzeciego Świata". Państwowe Wydawnictwo Naukowe, Warszawa
Kalecki M (1984) Socjalizm, wzrost gospodarczy i efektywność inwestycji. vol 4. Państwowe Wydawnictwo Ekonomiczne, Warszawa
Kennedy P (1988) The rise and fall of the great powers. Vintage Books, New York
Kleer J, Perczyński M, Dobosiewicz Z (1989) Z doświadczeń rozwoju skokowego. Państwowe Wydawnictwo Ekonomiczne, Warszawa
Kornai J (1971) Anti-equilibrium. On economic systems theory and the tasks of research. North-Holland Publishing Company, Amsterdam
Kornai J (1980) Economics of shortage. North-Holland Publishing Company, Amsterdam
Kornai J (1982) Growth, shortage and efficiency. Basil Blackwell, Oxford
Kula M (1967) Aleksandra Gerschenkrona uwagi o zacofaniu gospodarczym. In: O gospodarce mieszanej w krajach „Trzeciego Świata". Państwowe Wydawnictwo Naukowe, Warszawa
Kurowski S (1963) Historyczny proces wzrostu gospodarczego. Państwowe Wydawnictwo Naukowe, Warszawa
Kuznetz S (1971) Economic growth of nations. Total output and production structure. The Belknap Press of Harvard University Press, Cambridge, MA
Landes DS (2000) The wealth and poverty of nations. W. W. Norton & Company, New York
Levy FD Jr (1968) Economic planning in Venezuela. Frederick A. Praeger, New York
Lewis WA (1978) Growth and fluctuations 1870–1913. George Allen & Unwin (Polish edition), London
Loomba A (2005) Colonialism/postcolonialism. Routledge, London, New York
Malaga K (2011) The main strands and dilemmas of contemporary economic growth theory. Argumenta Oeconomica 26(1):17–24
Mankiw NG, Romer D, Weil D (1992) A contribution to the empirics of economic growth. Q J Econ 107:407–437
Marks K (1951) Kapitał. Krytyka ekonomii politycznej. vol. 1. Książka i Wiedza, Warszawa
Meadows DH, Meadows DL, Randers J, Behrens WW (1972) The limits to growth. Universe Books, New York
Mishan EJ (1977) The economic growth debate. An assessment. George Allen & Unwin, London
Naisbitt J (1984) Megatrends. Ten new directions transforming our lives. Warner Books Inc, New York

Nonneman W, Vanhoudt P (1996) A further augmentation of the solow model and the empirics of economic growth for OECD countries. Q J Econ 111(3):943–953
North DC (1990) Institutions, institutional change, and economic performance. Cambridge University Press, Cambridge
North DC (2005) Understanding the process of economic change. Princeton University Press, Princeton, NJ
Nurkse R (1962) Problemy tworzenia kapitału w krajach gospodarczo słabo rozwiniętych. PWN, Warszawa
Ostrom E (1990) Governing the commons; the evolution of institutions for collective action. Cambridge University Press, Cambridge
Palma G (1978) Dependency: a formal theory of underdevelopment or a methodology for the analysis of concrete situations of underdevelopment? World Dev 6(7–8):881–924
Perroux F (1950) Economic space, theory and applications. Q J Econ 64(1):89–104
Phelps ES (1961) The golden rule of accumulation: a fable for growthmen. Am Econ Rev 51 (4):638–643
Phelps ES (1966) Golden rules of economic growth. WW Norton, New York
Polanyi K (1947) The great transformation: the political and economic origins of our time. Beacon Press, Boston, MA
Prebisch R (1963) Towards a dynamic development policy for Latin America. U.N. Publication, New York
Rodrik D (2007) One economy, many recipes. Princeton University Press, Princeton, NJ
Romer PM (1986) Increasing returns and long-run growth. J Polit Econ 94(5):1002–1037
Romer PM (1996) Advanced macroeconomics. McGraw-Hill, New York
Rosenberg N, Birdzell LE Jr (1986) How the West grew rich: the economic transformation of the industrial world. Basic Books, Inc, New York
Rosenstein-Rodan PN (1959) Uwagi o teorii "wielkiego pchnięcia". Ekonomista. 2
Rostow WW (1960) The stages of economic growth. A non communist manifesto. Cambridge University Press, Cambridge
Said EW (2003) Orientalism. Edward W. Said, New York
Sala-i-Martin X (2002) 15 years of new growth economics: what have we learnt? UPF economics and business working papers 620
Schumpeter JA (2017) The theory of economic development. Taylor & Francis, Milton Park
Sharma R (2012) Breakout nations: in pursuit of the next economic miracles. WW Norton & Company, New York
Singer HW (1952) Mechanics of economic development. Indian Economic Review, August. Reprinted in: Agarwala AN, Singh AP (eds) The economics of underdevelopment. Oxford University Press: London
Solow RM (1956) A contribution to the theory of economic growth. Q J Econ 70:65–94
Stojanović R (1965) Teoria wzrostu gospodarczego w socjalizmie. Państwowe Wydawnictwo Naukowe, Warszawa
Swan TW (1956) Economic growth and capital accumulation. Economic Record 32:334–361
Tokarski T (2009) Matematyczne modele wzrostu gospodarczego. Wydawnictwo Uniwersytetu Jagiellońskiego, Kraków
Tokarski T (2011) Ekonomia matematyczna. Modele makroekonomiczne. PWE, Warszawa
Vietor RH (2007) How countries compete: strategy, structure, and government in the global economy. Harvard Business School, Boston
Wallerstein I (1976) The modern world-system: capitalist agriculture and origins of the european world-economy in the sixteenth century. Academic Press, New York
Wallerstein I (1979) The capitalist world-economy. Cambridge University Press, Cambridge
Williamson OE (1985) The economic institutions of capitalism. Firms, markets, relational contracting. The Free Press, New York
Woźniak MG (2004) Wzrost gospodarczy. Podstawy teoretyczne. Wydawnictwo Akademii Ekonomicznej, Kraków

Chapter 3
Political Determinants of Government Structure and Economic Performance in Turkey Since 1950

Ali T. Akarca

Abstract During the last two-thirds of a century, Turkey was ruled by a wide variety of governments: single-party governments, coalitions partnered by two or more parties and by ideologically compatible and incompatible parties, minority and military governments. While single-party governments all lasted at least two terms, the rest rarely lasted even one term. The timing of these governments and the order in which they followed each other were not by chance but according to a pattern induced by coups. Typically single-party governments were ended by coups. Ideologically incompatible and then compatible coalition governments followed, usually after a brief military administration. Then once again single-party governments returned. As economic growth typically exhibits an inverted-U type of pattern over the life of a government, and declines as the number of ruling parties and the ideological distance between them increase, the coups lowered the growth rate of the country and generated political business cycles that are distinct from those induced by elections. In the chapter these assertions are explained in detail and supported using theory, history, descriptive statistics, and regression analysis. It is also shown that improving democratic institutions of the country would enhance the stability and growth of the economy greatly.

3.1 Introduction

Since 1950, when the first fair and direct election took place and the power changed hands for the first time, Turkey got ruled by a wide variety of governments: single-party governments, ideologically compatible and incompatible coalition governments partnered by two or more parties, minority and military governments. In this chapter, it will be argued that the timing and duration of these governments and the order in which they followed each other were not by chance but according to

A. T. Akarca (✉)
Department of Economics, University of Illinois at Chicago, Chicago, IL, USA
e-mail: akarca@uic.edu

M. Osińska (ed.), *Economic Miracles in the European Economies*,
https://doi.org/10.1007/978-3-030-05606-3_3

political cycles caused by *coups d'état* (or coups).[1] Furthermore, it will be shown that these cycles in turn led to parallel business cycles that are distinct from business cycles caused by elections, because economic performance varies systematically over the tenures of governments, and depend on the number of ruling parties and the ideological distance between them. To the best of my knowledge, this is the first study to tie structure of governments and business cycles to coups. Understanding this link will let us make better sense of the Turkish economic growth over the last two-thirds of a century, abandon the wrong diagnoses made about it and unnecessary and ineffective cures prescribed for them. The chapter hopes to contribute also to the literature studying how economic performance is affected by the structure and tenure of governments.

The outline of the chapter will be as follows. In the next section, historical evidence will be presented to show that in Turkey, various types of governments followed each other in a particular pattern and that military interventions were at the root of this. Then, to help us understand how the coup driven political cycles translated into business cycles, the literature studying economic performance under various kinds of governments will be reviewed in Sect. 3.3. The applicability of the findings of this literature to the Turkish case will be established in the section following that, through descriptive statistics and regression analysis. Finally, in Sect. 3.5, conclusions reached will be listed.

3.2 Political and Historical Background

As shown by Akarca (2018), Turkish electorate exhibits a tendency to gather in four camps: left-statist, right-conservative, Turkish-nationalist, and Kurdish-nationalist parties.[2] At present, the Republican People's Party (CHP), the Justice and

[1]In this chapter, coups are defined as in Powell and Thyne (2011): "illegal and overt attempts by the military or other elites within the state apparatus to unseat the sitting executive." Note that this definition allows for the possibility of coups not being led by the military, and considers overthrowing governments through threats of military intervention but without use of force as coups as well. As O'Kane (1987), a coup is considered to be to be successful if it leads to the "installation in power of a government of the conspirators' own choosing." Thus we can say that of the nine Turkish coups, the ones on 27 May 1960, 12 March 1971, 12 September 1980, and 28 February 1997 were successful, but those on 22 February 1962, 21 March 1963, 9 March 1971, 27 April 2007, and 15 July 2016 were not.

[2]The left-statist group is labeled as such, even though its leading parties cannot be considered left, because they label themselves as such at least since late sixties and occasionally small leftist parties have emerged from them. Also left-leaning people vote for them. In many studies, the Turkish-nationalist and conservative parties are grouped together and analyzed as the Turkish right wing. However, since a distinct Turkish-nationalist party existed constantly since 1950, except for brief periods when it was banned by military juntas, it is more appropriate to treat it as a separate movement. Although the rest of the right wing occasionally fragmented into several parties, they always regrouped, as will be explained below.

Development Party (AKP), the Nationalist Action Party (MHP), and the People's Democracy Party (HDP) represent these groups, respectively. Until 1946, only the first group was allowed to organize formally, except during 1924–1925 and 1930 when the Progressive Republican Party (TCF) and the Liberal Republican Party (SCF) representing the second group were permitted for about 6 and 3 months, respectively. After 1946, the second and third, and after 1995 the fourth entered the picture formally.

The right-conservative movement is the largest of the four political tendencies and usually gets more than sufficient support from the public to form a single-party government and shows a tendency to gather in one party. Since 1950, in only two elections the aggregate vote share of this bloc fell below 47%, a level more than sufficient to capture at least half of the seats in the parliament. However, after each time they came to power alone or got close to doing so, their government was toppled by the military, often with the help of the judiciary, because they were viewed as a threat to the secular and western orientation of the country. No doubt, fear of losing their influence and guardianship roles pushed the armed forces and the judiciary in that direction as well. Between 1950 and 2016, five such coups took place, four of which were successful. These involved military taking over for a few years, either directly or through a civilian government they imposed, making some institutional changes to strengthen their privileged position in the established order, and then returning to electoral democracy. We can call this type of interventions classical coups, since transitions from democracy to non-democracy typically occur this way.[3] As Acemoğlu and Robinson (2006) point out, the driving force behind such transitions is the realization by the elites that their de facto power is temporary. Before it slips away, they interfere to change political institutions toward those that give them more de jure power. Although economic crises, social unrest, political instability, and ironically threats to democracy are often cited in the literature as causes of coups, numerous memoirs written and interviews given by Turkish junta leaders reveal that the planning for the coups begin years before they take place, when the economy was performing well and there were no signs of social strife, political instability, or authoritarianism. Furthermore, economic crises far worse than the ones experienced prior to the coups and the crises while non-conservative parties were in the government have failed to trigger military interventions. Coups often overlapped with the events cited, because juntas timed them that way to make them more justifiable to the public and international community. Also, as Acemoğlu and Robinson (2006) point out, opponents of democracy are more likely to attempt coups at times of political or economic crises, when the balance of de facto power temporarily tilts in their favor. For that reason, there is a tendency for coups to occur during second or third terms of single-party governments, not during their first terms when the economy is performing well, as will be explained below.

[3]Of the coups listed in footnote 1, the ones labeled as successful, together with the one in 2007 can be considered classical coups. The rest constitute a second kind, which will be discussed later.

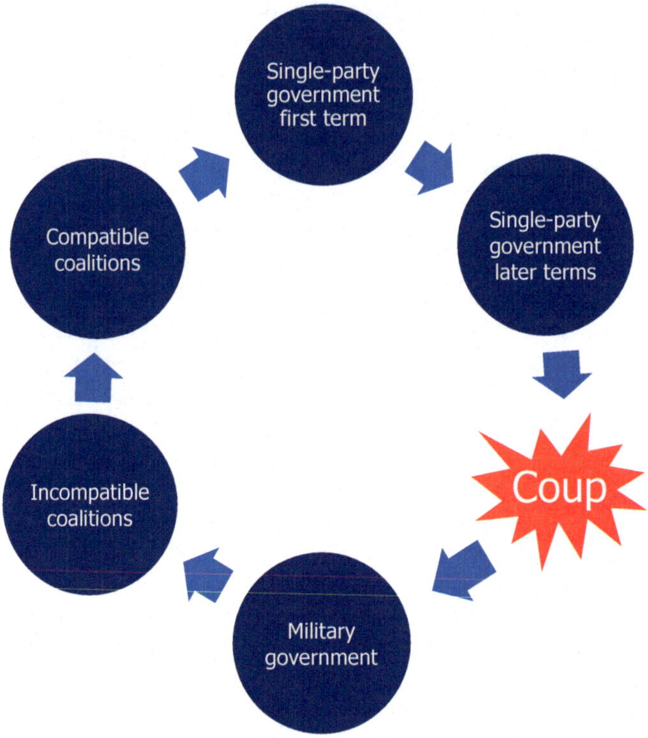

Fig. 3.1 Political cycle (own studies)

In the Turkish case, classical coups aimed also at increasing the relative de facto power of the military and making it more durable. To this end, ruling conservative parties were fragmented after each successful coup. To dilute their power even further and to be able to check it more effectively, the pieces of the fragmented conservative parties were not allowed to form a coalition government by themselves, but forced to partner with a left-statist party aligned with the military. Consequently, the governments formed after the coups were not only fragmented size wise but also ideologically. In each case however, the conservative parties eventually managed to get together again, first in a coalition government and then under the roof of a single party, which in turn led to another coup, followed by another period of coalitions. For that reason, Turkish political history can be thought of as consisting of single-party government (lasting more than one term) => coup => military rule => coalition governments (first ideologically incompatible, then compatible) => single-party government => coup cycles, as depicted in Fig. 3.1.

The five classical coups are listed in Table 3.1. After the 1960 and 1980 coups, the military took direct control. In the former the incumbent party, and in the latter all of the parties were banned. In the ones in 1971 and 1997, military forced the prime minister to resign under threat of a takeover and imposed a new government on the parliament. Although an attempt was made by the military also in 2007 to bring

Table 3.1 Political parties in power before and after coups (Tuncer 2002, 2007, 2011, 2012a, 2012b; Tuncer et al. 2003, 2015; Tuncer and Tuncer 2016)

	Ruling parties			
Coups	Immediately before the coup	Immediately after the coup	Elections	Following post-coup general elections
27 May 1960	**DP**	Military	1961	CHP + **AP** CHP + **YTP** + CKMP CHP + Ind. **AP** + **YTP** + CKMP + MP
			1965	**AP**
			1969	**AP**
12 March 1971	**AP**	CHP + **AP** + MGP **AP** + CGP	1973	CHP + **MSP** **AP** + **MSP** + CGP + MHP
			1977	**AP** + **MSP** + MHP CHP + CGP + **DP2** + Ind. **AP**
12 September1980	**AP**	Military	1983	**ANAP**
			1987	**ANAP**
			1991	**DYP** + SHP/CHP
			1995	**ANAP** + **DYP** **RP** + **DYP**
28 February 1997	**RP** + **DYP**	**ANAP** + **DSP** + **DTP**	1999	DSP + MHP + **ANAP**
			2002	**AKP**
27 April 2007	**AKP**	**AKP**	2007	**AKP**
			2011	**AKP**
			2015	**AKP**

(continued)

Table 3.1 (continued)

Coups	Ruling parties			
	Immediately before the coup	Immediately after the coup	Elections	Following post-coup general elections
			2015	**<u>AKP</u>**

The Turkish acronyms used in the table and the parties they represent are as follows: *AKP* Justice and Development Party, *ANAP* Motherland Party, *AP* Justice Party, *CGP* Republican Reliance Party, *CHP* Republican People's Party, *CKMP* Republican Peasant's Nation Party, *DP* Democrat Party (1946–1960); *DP2* Democratic Party, *DSP* Democratic Left Party, *DTP* Democrat Turkey Party, *DYP* True Path Party, *FP* Virtue Party, *MHP* Nationalist Action Party, *MSP* National Salvation Party, *RP* Welfare Party, *SHP* Social Democratic People's Party, *YTP* New Turkey Party. Of these parties, AKP, ANAP, AP, DP, DP2, DTP, DYP, FP, MSP, RP, and YTP are right-conservative; CKMP and MHP are Turkish-nationalist; and CGP, CHP, DSP, SHP are left-statist. The first two groups constitute the Turkish right wing and thus considered ideologically close. Even though its leading parties cannot be considered left, the left-statist group is labeled as such because they label themselves as left at least since late sixties, and occasionally small leftist parties have emerged from them. Also left-leaning people vote for them. The Kurdish-nationalist parties represent the fourth tendency in Turkish politics. Since they never came to power however, they do not appear in the table. The parties representing the third and fourth tendencies are usually placed in the left wing of the political spectrum. The SHP merged with the CHP shortly before the 1995 election; the right-conservative parties are bold and underlined; the largest coalition partner is listed first; the governments are listed in chronological order; governments which failed to receive a vote of confidence are ignored down the conservative government, the incumbent party thwarted it by cleverly calling a snap election and winning it handily.

Certain patterns can be discerned from Table 3.1. All of the five coups listed took place when right-conservative parties were in power. Only one party was ruling in all of them, except the one in 1997 when two parties were in a coalition but both were from the right-conservative segment. All successful coups occurred during second or third terms of single-party governments. Interestingly, the 2007 coup which took place during a conservative party's first term did not succeed. A chain of coalition governments followed each successful coup immediately, except the one in 1980 when coalitions appeared after a delay for the reasons which will be explained below. No coalitions appeared after the 2007 coup as it was unsuccessful.

The post-coup coalitions always included a statist party. The pieces of the fragmented conservative parties were not allowed to form a government by themselves, but forced to partner with a statist party so that they can be controlled more easily. Even though in 1961 the right-wing Justice Party (AP), the New Turkey Party (YTP), and the Republican Peasant's Nation Party (CKMP), which captured the votes of the Democrat Party (DP) ousted by the 1960 coup, were willing and able to form a government, the military junta forced the AP to form a government with the leftist-statist Republican People's Party (CHP) instead. Nevertheless, the planned coalition got formed later, shortly before the next general election in 1965 which brought the AP to power alone. When the 12 March 1971 coup toppled the AP government, leaders of the junta demanded a cabinet composed of AP, CHP and National Reliance Party (MGP) deputies, and a number of unelected technocrats, headed by a prime minister from the CHP.[4] The latter two parties were from the leftist-statist camp. To avoid the AP from coming to power again, the leader of an Islamist party which was banned only a year earlier, shortly after its establishment, was invited by the generals to return from self-exile abroad to establish a similar party with the aim of splitting the AP supporters. That party, named the National Salvation Party (MSP), was encouraged to form and did form a coalition government with the CHP after the 1973 election, the first one following the coup. However, as will be discussed below, when the Welfare Party (RP), which succeeded the MSP and shared with it the very same leadership and ideology, formed a coalition government in 1996 but this time with the conservative True Path Party (DYP), it got toppled by the military within a year. To erect another barrier in front of the AP's path to power, the 1971 junta engineered also separation of a faction from the party by forcing the party leadership, under threat of another coup, to table a proposal granting amnesty to the banned leaders of the DP. Those opposed to the move formed the short-lived Democratic Party (DP2). This time it took two legislative terms for the AP to acquire the power alone, but it got toppled once more in less than a year by the 1980 coup.

[4]The prime minister resigned from his party before taking office though, to appear as an independent.

By 1980, the military came to the realization that fragmenting conservative parties was futile and had harmful side effects, and changed tactics. They decided to control the right-conservative bloc directly, by establishing their own conservative party headed by a retired general they trust.[5] To make the party attractive also to voters from the Turkish-nationalist segment, they named it the Nationalistic Democracy Party (MDP). Because the leader of the CHP had taken strong stands against both the 1971 and 1980 coups, it was felt necessary to establish a new left-statist party as well.[6] That party was named the Populist Party (HP).[7] To give the MDP and HP a head start, the junta excluded from the 1983 election all parties which were continuation of the previous parties. However, the outcome of the election was a total shock for the military. The winner turned out to be not the MDP as planned but the conservative Motherland Party (ANAP), only party among the three permitted to participate in the election that was not designed by the junta. The ANAP was allowed to enter the election to give it an appearance of a true contest and to avoid the MDP from over-dominating the Turkish politics. The party was not supposed to win the 1983 election, just as the DP was not supposed to win the 1950 election. The MDP could not last even until the next parliamentary election. Although the ANAP was able to form a single-party government in 1983, its support dropped significantly by the eventual entry of other parties which were excluded from the 1983 election. The party was barely able to hold on to power for another term by calling the 1987 election before other parties could organize, by capturing some of those who left the MDP, and by benefiting from its incumbency advantage and the success of its market-oriented reforms. In 1989 local elections, the party's vote share dropped below that of the True Path Party (DYP), a conservative party formed by the leader of the defunct AP. After the 1991 parliamentary election, the third wave of coalition governments began.

One of those governments, formed by two conservative parties, the DYP and the RP, was forced by the military to give up power in 1997. To avoid formation of a new government under the same incumbent parties, one of them was split with the help of the president who was the former leader of that party. The other one and its leader got banned by the Constitutional Court for violating the secularism clause of the constitution. An ideologically compatible two-party government got replaced by an ideologically incompatible three-party coalition formed by the conservative ANAP and the Democrat Turkey Party (DTP), and the left-statist Democratic Left Party (DSP). The DTP was the party that was splintered from the DYP in 1997 as

[5]Acemoğlu and Robinson (2008) explain how elites try to offset any *de jure* power they have to give up, by increasing their de facto power (e.g., in the form of capturing political parties).

[6]It should be noted however that the leader of the CHP in 1980 was not the leader of the party in 1971 but its secretary general, and also that he supported the 1960 coup and his party cooperated with the juntas in 1960 and 1971 and nominated one of the 1971 junta leaders as their presidential candidate in 1980.

[7]All of the parties banned after the 1980 coup got legalized in 1994 but among them only the CHP regained prominence, and eventually reunited the fragmented left-statist segment. The Turkish-nationalist and right-conservative groups continued under the banners of their new parties.

mentioned above. It took not the next election but the one after that in 2002 for a new right-conservative party, the Justice and Development Party (AKP), to form a single-party government again. The AKP managed to hold on to power ever since. A coup was attempted in 2007 to change that, but as mentioned above, it failed. Ironically, the 2007 coup, rather than fragmenting, actually facilitated the consolidation of right-conservative votes under the AKP. That happened because the military inadvertently discredited the ANAP and the DYP in the eyes of their supporters by making them complicit in that coup. To stop the AKP from electing its candidate as president, the military organized a series of mass protest rallies against the party, and on 27 April 2007 posted on the Armed Forces web page a thinly veiled threat to take over if they do. A highly controversial decision was announced by the Constitutional Court 2 days later requiring participation of two-thirds of the deputies in the first round of the presidential balloting in the parliament, a rule not practiced in any of the earlier presidential elections. This took away the AKP's ability to elect its candidate without the aid of other parties. When the ANAP and DYP, under pressure by the military, decided not to participate in the presidential balloting so that the quorum required by the Constitutional Court could not be reached, they alienated many of their supporters who switched their allegiances to the AKP, which stood firm against the military and later took measures to dismantle the military tutelage system. The AKP's disavowal of political Islam no doubt facilitated this consolidation.

In short, the picture presented by Table 3.1 and the anecdotal evidence given show that coalition governments in Turkey were a consequence of political engineering by the military. Typically, ideologically incompatible coalitions followed coups first. Then came the compatible ones and eventually single-party governments again. This of course does not imply that coups are the only way coalition governments occur, but that that was the way they occurred in Turkey. Without coups coalition governments would still exist but would be much less frequent and much less fractured. Economic voting literature indicates that losses typically suffered by ruling parties as a result of strategic voting to create checks and balances against them and due to depreciation in their political capital over their tenure, usually cannot be offset by incumbency advantage unless economic performance is exceptionally good and/or it coincides with a political realignment in their favor.[8] As mentioned above and will be shown in the next two sections, economic performances of single-party governments in Turkey and other countries deteriorate after their first terms. Thus, it is reasonable to expect the vote share of the ruling party to decline eventually to a level forcing it either to lose power or to form a coalition government. However, the coup plotters in Turkey either did not realize this or did not have the patience to wait for it. Indeed, when the AKP lost its parliamentary majority in the 7 June 2015 election, after serving three terms, Turkey came very

[8]For surveys of the economic voting literature, see Lewis-Beck and Paldam (2000), Lewis-Beck and Stegmaier (2000, 2008, 2009, 2015), and Stegmaier and Lewis-Beck (2013). Akarca and Tansel (2006, 2007) and Akarca (2009, 2010, 2011a, b, 2015a, b) show that the behavior of Turkish voters is very similar to the patterns described in that literature.

close to having its first natural coalition government. Had the opposition parties in the parliament joined forces, or at least one of them agreed to partner with the AKP, the 1 November 2015 snap election would not be called and the first Turkish coalition government not created by a coup would have happened.

Before ending this section, it would be useful to briefly touch upon the non-classical coups that have taken place in Turkey. Use of classical coups as an effective tool to control the power of conservative incumbents encouraged other kind of coups. The 1960 takeover, organized by a small number of low-ranking officers and accomplished quite easily, was particularly inspiring in this regard. The leaders of that coup prepared the grounds for prospective coups also by implicitly "legitimizing" coups as a tool for removing "bad" governments, in the preamble of the 1961 constitution.[9] Marginal groups, with no hopes of achieving power through elections, tried to get it with the help of armed forces and/or the courts.[10] Also, because after each successful coup, officers who were part of the junta which accomplished it got promoted while the rest of the officers were either left behind or forced into retirement, the classical coups motivated formation of competing juntas. These eventually staged their own coups to maintain their positions or to enhance it.[11] Although the second type of coups caused a lot of damage through disruptions and instability they have created, since their goal was not to force coalitions but to grab power permanently, and because they were not successful in the first place, their impacts were short-lived and will be of less interest to us here.

Another side effect of military interventions and the guardianship system they instituted was long-lasting and should be emphasized as well. Frequent party closures and bans on political leaders hindered Turkish political parties from institutionalizing, developing democratic traditions (inter-party and intra-party), and accumulating valuable experience on good governance. It caused politicians to develop a reflex of avoiding making decisions on critical issues, passing them on to the guardianship institutions. These affected adversely not only the performances of forced coalitions but of single-party governments as well.

[9]Londregan and Poole (1990) dub such dynamics of one coup leading to another coup as a "coup-trap."

[10]For example, the 9 March 1971 coup plot, which was prevented by the March 12 1971 coup, was planned by some socialist intellectuals and leftist officers. The political parties which espoused to the views represented by the organizers of that coup received no more than 3% of the vote in various elections they contested democratically. As Can (2014) explains, the Gülen religious organization, which masterminded the 15 July 2016 takeover attempt, became an asymmetrical power center by infiltrating the armed forces and the judiciary, despite having "2-3% support at most."

[11]For example, the failed coup attempt on 22 February 1962 was organized by officers which were about to be removed from their positions by another junta. The 21 May 1963 coup attempt on the other hand was a come-back effort by those removed after the unsuccessful 1962 attempt. The 12 March 1971 coup was implemented to some extent to counter the leftist junta which planned the 9 March 1971 coup. Similarly, the 15 July 2016 coup was timed by the Gülenists to preempt the dismissal of their members from the armed forces suspected to take place in about a month.

3.3 Economic Performance Under Various Types of Government

Economic performances of governments that typically followed each other over the coup cycle were different because economic performance of a government varies depending on the number of years it was in power, number of parties in it, and the ideological distance between them. A number of reasons are offered in the literature to explain the observed differences between the performances of various governments.

Bawn and Rosenbluth (2006) point out that incumbent parties undertake projects that benefit mainly their own supporters. However, costs of these are born by everyone. Consequently, they undertake many projects for which costs to the general populace exceed benefits. Then government spending and deficits tend to be larger too, which in turn lead to higher inflation and interest rates and lower private investment. This tendency exists in every government, but to a much lesser extent in single-party governments, since larger parties encompass more interest groups and thus internalize more costs than smaller parties. The larger is the fragmentation in the government, the greater is the number of inefficient projects undertaken and investment crowding out, and smaller is the economic growth. A coalition of three parties is worse than a government including two parties, and a three-party coalition involving three equally sized parties is worse than one consisting of one large and two small parties. Besides fragmentation in size, fragmentation in ideology matters as well. When the incumbent parties have similar worldviews, the policies preferred by their constituencies overlap. Then more costs are internalized. Thus economic growth will be lower under coalitions involving parties from opposite ends of the political spectrum than those including politically coherent parties.

Bejar et al. (2011) give another reason why policy making and economic performance is likely to be poorer under multi-party governments. They point out that multi-party governments have shorter life spans than single-party governments, and consequently have shorter time horizons and lower discount factors in office. They are less concerned with future ramifications of their actions. They engage in log-rolling and pork barrel legislation to appease their constituents with more government money, and shift the burden of higher expenditures to future governments. By favoring inefficient projects, with future costs far exceeding current benefits, and by bloating budget deficits which crowd out private investment, this affects growth adversely. Bawn and Rosenbluth (2006) suggest that large parties can be thought of as coalitions of various groups too, but the commitment among these groups is much stronger and goes way beyond the next election. Thus, single-party governments have longer time horizons. Indeed in Turkey, single-party governments all lasted two or more legislative terms. The one currently in power just completed its fourth term. One was in its third and another in its second term when they were toppled by coups and could have lasted longer in the absence of military interventions. On the other hand, of the 14 coalition governments listed in

Table 3.1, only two (DYP + SHP/CHP and DSP + MHP + ANAP) were able to last as long as one legislative term.

Hall and Nishikawa (2014) approach the issue from the veto-player framework introduced by Tsebelis (1995, 1999, 2002). "Veto players" are defined as "individuals or institutions whose agreement is required for a change of the status quo." For example, each political party in a government can be considered a veto player. Hall and Nishikawa suggest that ruling party duration has an inverted U-shaped relationship with economic growth, when the number of veto players is relatively low. New governments typically make substantial changes in macroeconomic policies, which by creating uncertainty dampen investment and growth. However, this uncertainty gradually dissipates as investors observe government's policy behavior. Existence of some veto players with divergent preferences makes the policy unlikely to change. Since the largest gains in the reduction of uncertainty come with the initial observation of behavior, economic performance should improve most in the initial phases of a government's tenure. However, as the marginal returns from the stabilization of policy expectations diminish over time, pressure by special interest groups to redistribute resources rises. Market interventions to create rents for these groups distort incentives, drawing resources from efficient uses. Also, resources that can go to productive uses are diverted to lobbying efforts. Furthermore, beneficiaries of reforms instituted earlier try to lock them in and resist any attempt to alter them. This reduces government's ability to reverse policy mistakes and to respond to macroeconomic shocks in a timely fashion. Thus, extended duration in power of ruling parties eventually leads to institutional sclerosis and deteriorating economic performance.

According to Hall and Nishikawa (2014), as the number of veto players and the ideological distance among them increase, the effects which give rise to the inverted U-shaped curve relating economic growth to tenure may get moderated. Additional constraints placed on the executive enhance the credibility of policy reforms undertaken and diminish the likelihood of large deviations from the status quo. Although this makes the parties in the government less able to reverse good policies and institute harmful ones, it also reduces their ability to respond to economic shocks and to reverse prior policy mistakes. However, it is possible for large numbers of veto players to thwart institutional sclerosis by achieving productive policy cooperation over time and forestalling rent-seeking activity. The inverted U-shaped curve in question then gets flattened and may even become regular U-shaped. On the other hand, if the cooperation among the members of government come too late or take the form of log-rolling due to the reasons given by Bawn and Rosenbluth (2006) and Bejar et al. (2011), the rising portion of the regular U-curve may not be realized. In Turkey, this seems to have been the case. As mentioned above, only two out of the 14 coalition governments managed to last one legislative term but both came to an end following one of the worst economic crises the country has ever experienced. Only one coalition government (AP + MSP + MHP) was able to continue after an election, serving parts of two terms, but the partners in it were ideologically close. The growth–duration relationship under that government was shaped as an inverted U.

Too few veto players can be a problem as well. So far, we have considered only political parties as veto players and assumed that the number of veto players remains the same during a government's tenure. However, individuals and various organs of the ruling parties can act as veto players as well. Initially there are a reasonable number of veto players in single-party governments in Turkey but many of them get eliminated over their time in power. All such governments were formed by political parties which were established only a few years before taking office. The DP and the AP came to power in fourth year of their existence, the AKP in its second, and the ANAP in its first. At that stage, the ruling party's leader is really in a position of being first among equals. Other prominent politicians in the party are integral part of decision-making too. Members of cabinet have more decision-making latitude. The party's members of parliament and provincial officials are able to give their input as well. Much needed structural changes and policy actions delayed under the preceding era of coalition governments are undertaken during this period in a credible manner and economic performance improves. However, in emerging countries like Turkey, lacking strong tradition and legal framework for intra-party democracy, as the party ages the power rapidly gets concentrated in the center and in the hands of the party leader. The limited independence of regulatory bodies and the central bank is curtailed further. Competent technocrats who advise against implementation of populist policies are replaced with "Yes" men. Ruling party's members of parliament stop speaking their mind freely, as those who are too critical of the government's policies risk being removed from their party's candidate lists in the next election. Often press freedoms suffer as well. Chandra and Rudra (2015) show that higher levels of public deliberation lead to better economic performance not only in democracies but even in authoritarian regimes. With no effective veto players, when constructive criticism is halted also, policy mistakes are not noticed, and even when they are noticed, they go uncorrected. Creative ideas diminish, discretion replaces rules, policies change abruptly and arbitrarily and often not in response to changing economic conditions but due to political reasons. Corruption and rent-seeking increase which impedes dynamism and causes real resources to be shifted away from investment and toward seeking government benefits. Existence of some veto players, concerns over losing the subsequent election, and fear of providing an excuse for the military to conduct a coup may restrain the new ruling party initially, but only until it consolidates its position. Sharma (2017) argues that markets can sense the approach of the turning point. Examining stock market performance under 33 leaders in the emerging world, which reigned more than 5 years, he finds that the median stock market return for this group tends to rise faster than the emerging world average during the first 41 months of the leaders' tenures. Ninety percent of that gain occurs in the first 24 months of the new regime. After three and a half years, the markets start to move sideways.[12] This implies that in countries with weak institutions, economic performance under single-party governments begin to sour after their first terms. Documenting this process in the case of the AKP rule in Turkey, Acemoğlu and Üçer (2015) and Atiyas (2016) also pinpoint the turning point to the end of the party's first term. More evidence on this will be provided in the next section.

[12]Interestingly, running the same analysis for developed countries, Sharma (2017) finds no clear connection between stock market returns and the tenure of the political leader.

Yet another reason why economic performance is not the same under various types of governments may have to do with the incentives given to them by the electorate not being the same. According to the economic voting literature, voters assess economic performance of governments and reward or punish them through their ballots.[13] However, they base their evaluations only on the recent past, providing the politicians with an incentive to create electoral business cycles, in which economy expands right before the elections and contracts right after. Some studies, such as Powell and Whitten (1993), Whitten and Palmer (1999), Anderson (2000), Nadeau et al. (2002), Hellwig and Samuels (2008), and Hobolt et al. (2013), argue that the strength of economic voting depends on the "clarity of responsibility" for economic outcomes. Under coalition governments, especially under those fragmented in size and ideology, it becomes more difficult for voters to assign responsibility and sanction incumbent parties for their performance. Then the impact of the economy on election outcomes tends to be smaller. Fisher and Hobolt (2010), Debus et al. (2014), Duch et al. (2015), Williams et al. (2017), and Angelova et al. (2016) find further that economic voting is not only weaker in multi-party governments, but it is also not the same for all of the ruling parties. It appears that voters hold the junior members of a coalition less responsible for economic conditions than the primary incumbent party and sometimes not responsible at all. Akarca (2017) verifies these conclusions for the Turkish case and shows in addition that in coalition governments which include ideologically distant parties, incentives turn into disincentives for the junior members.

Governments that are rewarded less for a good economy and punished less for a bad one have less incentive to perform well and are more likely to sacrifice economic goals for other considerations. When voters do not hold the parties in coalition governments equally accountable, this creates conflict of interest and friction between the partners, delaying critical decisions and reducing the expected lives of the governments, which in turn generates uncertainty and instability. Parties with less or nothing to lose can drag their feet even on reforms they approve of just to deny their main coalition partner any vote gain. Furthermore, when the incumbent parties cannot get votes through good economic performance, they try to get it through populist means, such as distributing cheap credit, patronage, and transfers. Thus, governance worsens as the number of parties in the government increases and their political cohesion decreases.

In short, we should expect the coup related political cycles discussed in the previous section to generate parallel business cycles.

3.4 Empirical Results

Applicability of the assertions made in the previous section can be ascertained from Tables 3.2, 3.3, and 3.4. These show how the rate of change in per capita real GDP (henceforth, the growth rate) varied under various types of Turkish governments

[13]Note that studies surveying this literature were listed in footnote 8.

Table 3.2 Average growth rate of per capita real GDP under different types of governments (1950–2015) (%) (own calculations on the basis of TurkStat and State Planning Organization[a])

Types of Governments	Average growth rate of per capita real GDP (%)
Single-party *(36.5 years)*	3.4
Coalition *(21.25 years)*	2.6
Minority *(3 years)*	−1.2
Military *(4.75 years)*	0.8
All *(65.5 years)*	2.7

Figures reported are in percentage points and are obtained from annual data, as quarterly data is available only since 1987. In computing the averages, years in which more than one type of government prevailed are given a weight of 0.25, 0.50, or 0.75, depending on whether the regime in question ruled one, two, or three quarters. A quarter is assumed to be under the type of government which prevailed during majority of that period. First half of 1950 is treated as if it is not part of the analysis

[a]The growth rates are computed using the data provided by TurkStat for all years except 1948 and 1968. For latter 2 years, growth rates for the GNP provided by the State Planning Organization are substituted for the missing GDP-related figures. The GDP series, from which growth rates are obtained, is 1968 based for years prior to 1968, 1987 based for the years between 1969 and 1998, and 1998 based for years after 1999. The new 2009-based GDP series released by TurkStat on 12 December 2016 is not used because it goes back only as far as 1998 and is not comparable to the old series. For the period after 2010, the two series differ not only in level but growth as well. Sources listed in Table 3.1 are used to determine the periods each type of government was ruling

Table 3.3 Average growth rate of per capita real GDP under various single-party governments (1950–2015) (%) (own calculations on the basis of TurkStat and State Planning Organization[a])

	Terms			
Ruling party	1st	2nd	3rd and 4th	All
DP *(10 years)*	6.9	2.2	1.3	**3.9**
AP *(5.5 years)*	4.4	1.3	–	**3.2**
ANAP *(8 years)*	4.4	0.9	–	**2.7**
AKP *(13 years)*	5.9	1.5	2.7	**3.4**
All *(36.5 years)*	**5.4**	**1.5**	**2.2**	**3.4**

Figures reported are in percentage points and are obtained from annual data, as quarterly data is available only since 1987. In computing the averages, years in which more than one type of government prevailed are given a weight of 0.25, 0.50, or 0.75, depending on whether the regime in question ruled one, two, or three quarters. A quarter is assumed to be under the type of government which prevailed during majority of that period. First half of 1950 is treated as if it is not part of the analysis

[a]The growth rates are computed using the data provided by TurkStat for all years except 1948 and 1968. For latter 2 years, growth rates for the GNP provided by the State Planning Organization are substituted for the missing GDP-related figures. The GDP series, from which growth rates are obtained, is 1968 based for years prior to 1968, 1987 based for the years between 1969 and 1998, and 1998 based for years after 1999. The new 2009-based GDP series released by TurkStat on 12 December 2016 is not used because it goes back only as far as 1998 and is not comparable to the old series. For the period after 2010, the two series differ not only in level but growth as well. Sources listed in Table 3.1 are used to determine the periods each type of government was ruling

Table 3.4 Average growth rate of per capita real GDP under various coalition governments (1950–2015) (own calculations on the basis of TurkStat and State Planning Organization)[a]

Number of parties in government	Period	Ideological composition of government		
		Compatible *(4.5 years)*	Incompatible *(16.75 years)*	All *(21.25 years)*
Two *(7.75 years)*	1950–1983	–	2.3	**2.3**
	1984–2015	6.3	2.3	**3.2**
Three or more *(13.5 years)*	1950–1983	4.0	2.5	**3.1**
	1984–2015	–	1.2	**1.2**
All *(21.25 years)*	1950–2015	**4.6**	**2.0**	**2.6**

A coalition government is considered ideologically incompatible if at least one half of the junior parties in it are from the opposite side of the political spectrum than the primary incumbent party; Figures reported are in percentage points and are obtained from annual data, as quarterly data is available only since 1987. In computing the averages, years in which more than one type of government prevailed are given a weight of 0.25, 0.50, or 0.75, depending on whether the regime in question ruled one, two, or three quarters. A quarter is assumed to be under the type of government which prevailed during majority of that period. First half of 1950 is treated as if it is not part of the analysis

[a]The growth rates are computed using the data provided by TurkStat for all years except 1948 and 1968. For latter 2 years, growth rates for the GNP provided by the State Planning Organization are substituted for the missing GDP-related figures. The GDP series, from which growth rates are obtained, is 1968 based for years prior to 1968, 1987 based for the years between 1969 and 1998, and 1998 based for years after 1999. The new 2009-based GDP series released by TurkStat on 12 December 2016 is not used because it goes back only as far as 1998 and is not comparable to the old series. For the period after 2010, the two series differ not only in level but growth as well. Sources listed in Table 3.1 are used to determine the periods each type of government was ruling

which ruled during the 1950–2015 period. According to Table 3.2, growth was higher under single-party governments than under coalitions. Economic performance was worst under minority governments, followed by military regimes. However, a clearer picture emerges when different terms of single-party governments and different types of coalitions are distinguished. As can be seen from Table 3.3, growth was substantially higher during the first terms of single-party governments than their later terms, consistent with an inverted U-shaped relationship between economic growth and tenure. The growth in second and later terms of such governments was only one-fifth to one-half of their first terms. This pattern appears to be quite robust. It occurs (although at different degrees) under every single-party government. The fact that the same pattern has occurred under different administrations which ruled decades apart, shows that it cannot be attributed to specific factors related to a leader or a period.

No coalition government lasted more than the equivalent of one legislative term which can be taken as a sign that none of them were able to achieve a productive policy cooperation over their tenure to thwart institutional sclerosis. Table 3.4 shows that performances of coalition governments depend on the number of parties in them and the ideological distance between them. The table examines periods before and after the 1983 election separately. This enables us to check the robustness of the patterns observed. However, there are other reasons for doing this. All two-party coalitions before 1983 and all three-party coalitions after 1983 were ideologically incompatible ones (defined as at least one half of the junior parties being from the opposite wing of the political spectrum than the primary incumbent party). Also, the size fragmentation implied by the number of parties in the government was not the same in the two periods. As indicated in Sect. 3.2, by closing all of the parties, the 1980 coup caused much greater fragmentation in governments than the previous coups. This manifested itself more so in coalitions involving more than two parties. Whereas, coalitions partnered by three or more parties consisted of one large and a couple of smaller parties before 1983, only few percentage points separated the vote shares of ruling parties after 1983. Average number of effective parties, measured as suggested by Laakso and Taagepera (1979), for two-party incompatible coalitions during the two periods was quite close: 1.8 in the former and 1.9 in the latter.[14] The corresponding figures in the case of governments involving three or more parties on the other hand were 1.8 and 2.3, respectively.

For ideologically incompatible coalitions involving two parties, during both the first and second halves of the 1950–2015 period and those involving three or more parties during 1950–1983, when effective number of parties in the government was identical, average growth rates were essentially identical as well. However, the growth rate was substantially lower under ideologically incompatible three-party governments formed after 1983, when size fragmentation was much higher. The performances of ideologically compatible and incompatible governments can be compared in the case of two parties only for the post-1983 period, and in the case of three or more parties only for the pre-1983 period. In both cases growth under compatible coalitions is far higher than under incompatible ones. In short, economic performance is adversely effected by fragmentation of the government, both ideologically and size wise. Interestingly, economic performance under compatible coalitions is almost as good as that during first terms of single-party governments and far better than that during later terms of single-party governments. This shows the need for checking and balancing a party in power either through some veto players within the party or, when that is not possible, through coalition partners acting as veto players. In the case of incompatible coalition governments however, the beneficial effects of checks and balances the coalition partners provide appear to be more than offset by extra common pool problems they create.

Using the information given in Tables 3.3 and 3.4, various types of governments formed over a typical coup cycle can be ranked, according to their growth performances, as follows: (1) Single-party governments in their first terms, (2) ideologically compatible coalition governments, (3) ideologically incompatible coalition governments (4) single-party governments in their later terms, and (5) military

[14]This index, used heavily by political scientists, is really the reciprocal of the well-known Herfindahl index of industrial concentration used by the economist, but applied to the vote shares of the parties rather than the market shares of the companies. Herfindahl index sums the squared shares and varies between zero and one. Its reciprocal on the other hand can vary between one and infinity and it is easier to interpret.

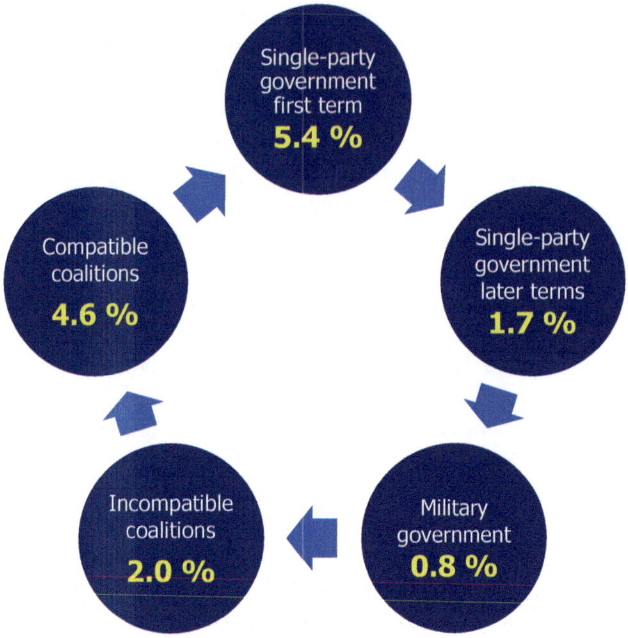

Fig. 3.2 Average growth rate of per capita real GDP over the economic cycle (own studies)

governments. This shows that coup cycles created parallel economic cycles, as demonstrated in Fig. 3.2, with economic performance going from very good, to below average, then to really bad, to closer to average, then to good and very good again.[15]

Although the descriptive tables presented provide compelling evidence, they do not control for other factors. Three omitted but important factors come to mind. First, the growth rate tends to revert to a mean. It is expected to recover after a sharp drop and return to a normal level after a spurt. Unless taken into account, these will show up as effects of the type of government ruling at those times. Second, as explained in the previous section, governments have an incentive to stimulate the economy before elections and switch to contractionary policies afterwards to offset the inflationary effects of the initial policies (unless another election is looming in the horizon). Such electoral cycles need to be separated from coup related cycles. Third, external shocks affect the economy as well and, unless accounted for, may be attributed to the administration at that time. Of course, the degree to which an external shock impacts the economy depends on the openness of the economy, which varies over time. Thus

[15]Of course the cycle following each coup was not exactly the same because coups occurred at different terms of the single-party governments, sometimes coalitions began immediately after the coup without a direct military rule first, one time a single-party government got inserted inadvertently between the coup and the coalitions, and it took increasingly longer for the conservative block to reconsolidate after a coup.

the two dimensions of the issue need to be considered jointly. Effects of these three factors and others discussed above can be measured by regressing the growth rate (G_t) on various subsections of the following variables and/or their interactions[16]:

G_{t-1}:	growth rate lagged 1 year
T_{it}:	0.25 times the number of quarters in year t which was ruled by a single-party government in its ith term ($i = 1$ during government's first term, $i = 2$ in its second term, and $i = 3$ in its third and fourth terms)
DP_{it}:	0.25 times the number of quarters in year t which was ruled by a single-party DP government in its ith term ($i = 1$ during government's first term and $i = 2$ during its second and third terms)
AP_{it}:	0.25 times the number of quarters in year t which was ruled by a single-party AP government in its ith term ($i = 1$ during government's first term and $i = 2$ during its second term)
ANAP_{it}:	0.25 times the number of quarters in year t which was ruled by a single-party ANAP government in its ith term ($i = 1$ during government's first term and $i = 2$ during its second term)
AKP_{it}:	0.25 times the number of quarters in year t which was ruled by a single-party AKP government in its ith term ($i = 1$ during government's first term and $i = 2$ during its second, third, and fourth terms)
MIXED_t:	0.25 times the number of quarters in year t which was ruled by an ideologically incompatible coalition government
MIXED2_t:	0.25 times the number of quarters in year t which was ruled by an ideologically incompatible coalition government consisting of two parties
MIXED3_t:	0.25 times the number of quarters in year t which was ruled by an ideologically incompatible coalition government consisting of three or more parties
NMIXED_t:	0.25 times the number of quarters in year t which was ruled by an ideologically compatible coalition government
MIN_t:	0.25 times the number of quarters in year t which was ruled by a minority government
MIL_t:	0.25 times the number of quarters in year t which was ruled by a military government
PRE83_t:	equals one during 1950–1983, and zero otherwise

[16]Because economic performance effects election results, one may think that an endogeneity bias would exist in the proposed regressions. However, vote share changes do not necessarily result in government changes, and not all government changes are due to elections. This can be seen from the fact that single-party governments lasted several terms and most of them came to an end not due to vote losses but due to coups. Also, many government changes occurred between elections.

POST83$_t$: equals one during 1984–2015, and zero otherwise

ELEC$_t$: $\sum_{k=1}^{4} B_{kt} - \sum_{k=1}^{4} D_{kt}$

where B_k takes on the value of 0.25 if a future parliamentary or local administrations election is within 1 year of quarter k of year t, and zero otherwise; D_k takes on the value of 0.25 if quarter k of year t is within 1 year of the last parliamentary or local administration election, unless it is also within 1 year of a future election, and zero otherwise

USG$_t$: growth rate of US per capita real GDP in year t.[17]

OPEN$_t$: ratio of exports plus imports to GNP in Turkey in year t.

More detailed explanations on the measurement of these variables and the sources of data on them are given in the notes to Tables 3.2 and 3.5.

In all of the regressions presented in Tables 3.5 and 3.6, coefficients of ELEC and USG*OPEN are positive and that of the lagged growth rate is negative. They are all statistically and numerically significant. Thus presence and importance of external factors, election related cycles, and mean reversion in the growth rate are established. However, even after controlling for these, the effects suggested in Tables 3.2, 3.3, and 3.4 remain unchanged. In Table 3.5 regressions, the constant represents growth under first terms of single-party governments. Performance under ideologically compatible coalitions turns out to be not very different from that. On the other hand, the growth rate during single-party governments' later terms is significantly lower. There appears to be no difference between second and subsequent terms of such governments. Performances of ideologically incompatible two-party coalitions is about the same as that of single-party governments in their second and third terms, but growth under incompatible coalitions involving three or more parties is somewhat worse. Military governments do as bad as the latter. Performance under minority governments is the worst.

Table 3.6 regressions allow economic performance to differ under different single-party governments.

They show that performances of the DP, AP, ANAP, and AKP governments were not the same. However, the pattern of the first term growth far exceeding that of the later terms holds true for each of these governments. The DP's first term record (given by the constants in the regressions) was the best, perhaps partially reflecting yield of returning to democracy after decades of non-democracy. The second regression in the table permits in addition the performances of incompatible governments to be different before and after 1983. It appears that such governments did considerably better in the pre-1983 period than in the post-1983 period. However,

[17] The reason for choosing the US growth rate fluctuations as a proxy for external conditions is not due to the USA being the most important trading partner of Turkey. It is not. However, American economy constitutes a large chunk of the world economy and has links to wide variety of countries including major trading partners of Turkey. Thus most shocks to the international economy effect other countries either directly or through shared trade partners with the USA. Indeed, for example trying instead British and Greek growth rates, and changes in the crude oil price proved to be unsatisfactory.

Table 3.5 Regression results I (own calculations on the basis of TurkStat, State Planning Organization and U.S. Bureau of Economic Analysis[a])

	Regressions	
Variables	1	2
Constant	4.985 (4.14)	4.956 (4.08)
G_{t-1}	−0.236 (2.19)	−0.236 (2.18)
T_{2t}	−3.483 (2.34)	−3.452 (2.30)
T_{3t}	−3.313 (2.15)	−3.307 (2.13)
$MIXED_t$	−3.987 (3.16)	
$MIXED2_t$		−3.480 (2.07)
$MIXED3_t$		−4.321 (2.95)
$NMIXED_t$	0.284 (0.15)	0.274 (0.14)
MIN_t	−8.602 (3.38)	−8.508 (3.31)
MIL_t	−4.373 (2.21)	−4.348 (2.19)
$ELEC_t$	1.480 (1.85)	1.521 (1.88)
$USG_t * OPEN_t$	2.071 (2.60)	2.100 (2.61)
F (Prob > F)	4.62 (0.00)	4.12 (0.00)
Durbin-h Prob > h	0.14 (0.44)	−0.00 (0.50)
R-square Adj. R-square	0.43 (0.33)	0.43 0.32

Dependent variable is the growth rate in per capita real GDP (G_t). For definitions of independent variables, see Sect. 3.3. Estimates are obtained using the ordinary least squares method. The numbers in parantheses, next to the parameter estimates, are the t values

[a]Sources of data are the same as in Table 3.2 for all variables except the last two, U.S. Bureau of Economic Analysis for USG, and TurkStat for OPEN. For the years 2006–2015, ratio of exports plus imports to GDP, multiplied by 1.3, is taken as the ratio of exports plus imports to GNP (the latter ratio was 1.3 times the former ratio in 2006)

the main conclusions obtained from Table 3.5, namely that compatible coalitions do better than incompatible ones and two-party coalitions do better than coalitions including three or more parties, remain unaltered.

3.5 Summary and Conclusion

As the number of parties in a government and the ideological distance between them rise, its economic performance tends to deteriorate. In Turkey, such fragmentations were caused by coups but were always followed by gradual reconsolidation of the fractured political movements. Thus military interventions not only caused economic growth to be lower but also to fluctuate in a cyclical manner. The coup-induced political business cycles were distinct from the election-induced political business cycles. Although there is an awareness of the latter in Turkey, the dynamics underlying the former, even their existence, is not recognized.

Table 3.6 Regression results II (own calculations on the basis of TurkStat, State Planning Organization and U.S. Bureau of Economic Analysis as in Table 3.5)

	Regression	
Variables	1	2
Constant	7.154 (3.97)	7.033 (3.87)
G_{t-1}	−0.254 (2.34)	−0.262 (2.38)
AP_{1t}	−2.894 (1.16)	−2.855 (1.13)
$ANAP_{1t}$	−4.394 (1.89)	−4.499 (1.92)
AKP_{1t}	−2.110 (0.92)	−2.213 (0.96)
DP_{2t}	−5.120 (2.25)	−5.001 (2.18)
AP_{2t}	−5.149 (1.65)	−5.085 (1.61)
$ANAP_{2t}$	−6.636 (2.84)	−6.593 (2.80)
AKP_{2t}	−5.585 (2.75)	−5.535 (2.70)
$MIXED_t$	−6.280 (3.34)	
$MIXED2_t$ * $PRE83_t$		−4.629 (1.53)
$MIXED3_t$ * $PRE83_t$		−5.378 (2.29)
$MIXED2_t$ * $POST83_t$		−6.348 (2.68)
$MIXED3_t$ * $POST83_t$		−8.082 (3.47)
$NMIXED_t$	−1.928 (0.81)	−1.805 (0.75)
MIN_t	−10.782 (3.74)	−10.606 (3.64)
MIL_t	−6.589 (2.76)	−6.506 (2.70)
$ELEC_t$	1.665 (2.03)	1.724 (2.06)
USG_t * $OPEN_t$	2.269 (2.84)	2.506 (3.05)
F (Prob > F)	3.24 (0.00)	2.74 (0.00)
Durbin-h (Prob > h)	−0.11 (0.46)	−0.81 (0.21)
R-square Adj. R-square	0.47 0.33	0.49 0.31

Consequently, coalitions and poor economic performance under them are viewed as natural phenomena which can be avoided only through tinkering with the electoral and governmental systems. For example, the unusually high 10% national vote threshold for a party to gain representation in the Turkish parliament was instituted in 1983 to reduce the effective number of parties and thus the likelihood of coalition governments. However, besides being undemocratic, it failed to avoid coalitions throughout the 1990s. Interestingly, a single-party government had emerged in 1965, despite the presence of an extremely proportional election system, known as "Milli Bakiye" (National Remainder), and lack of any election thresholds, nationwide or local. Putting an end to coalition governments was also used as the main justification for the recent replacement of the parliamentary system with a presidential one. Actually, the presidential system does not really eliminate coalitions but merely changes their format. When the majority of the parliament is made up of parties different from the president's, cooperation of more than one party is needed to pass the laws and the budget. The truth is that if the coups could be avoided, coalitions would be much less frequent, and when they occurred, would be formed voluntarily by ideologically compatible parties under which economic growth is reasonably good.

As there is a tendency toward a single-party government in Turkey, for good governance it is essential to have effective checks and balances to it not only from the opposition parties but also from within the ruling party itself. However, coups and the military guardianship system they have created through frequent party closures and bans on political leaders, have hindered political parties from institutionalizing, developing democratic traditions, and accumulating valuable experience on good governance. Lack of intra-party democracy caused all parties, but in particular those which rule alone, to become gradually more centralized and more authoritarian. Consequently a wide performance gap exists between the first and later terms of single-party governments. In fact, economic performance is far better under compatible coalitions than during later terms of single-party governments. Apparently lack of checks in the latter and parties acting as veto players in the former makes the difference.

In short, coups had long-lasting consequences not only politically but economically as well. Their adverse impacts in Turkey were not restricted to the periods of direct military rule but continued way into the future through the guardianship system they established, which created political fragmentation and laid coup traps. Curtailing coups will produce better economic outcomes. In that regard, failure of the last two coup attempts in 2007 and 2016 can be taken as a good sign. Especially the way the last attempt was quashed, with immediate resistance from all political parties, mainstream media, business associations, most members of the armed forces, police, judiciary, and other state institutions, and most importantly, the active involvement of ordinary people of all backgrounds, a first in Turkish history, is promising. However, using the terminology of Acemoğlu and Robinson (2006), to move from a semi-consolidated to a fully consolidated democracy, it is necessary to fill the vacuum created by the dismantling of the military-judiciary guardianship system with new political institutions that provide strong checks and balances.[18] Improving the quality of the country's democracy is of paramount importance for its economic well-being. Had the average growth rate of per capita real GDP during

[18]For example, it would be desirable to couple the newly instituted presidential system with parliamentary single-member districts for which party candidates are chosen through primaries rather than by party leaders, and winning candidates determined through two-round elections just as is the case with the president. This will empower the legislature and help them check and balance the powers of the executive which are increased and concentrated. It will also render members of parliament more responsive to their constituents than to their parties and leaders. Reforms are needed to make the judiciary independent and impartial as well, so that it neither controls the government nor is controlled by the government and sees its main role as protecting the citizens against the state and not the other way around.

1950–2015 was the same as the rate achieved during the first terms of single-party governments, Turkey's per capita real GDP today would be 5.5 times higher.[19]

Acknowledgement This work was sponsored by the Economic Research Forum (ERF) and has benefited from both its financial and intellectual support. An earlier version of this paper was presented at the 24th Annual Conference of the ERF held in Cairo, Egypt, 8–10 July 2018 and International Summer School held at Şehir University, Istanbul, Turkey, 2–4 August 2018. I have benefited greatly from the comments I have received from the audiences at these meetings. Those provided by Hoda Youssef, the discussant at the ERF conference were especially valuable. I would also like to thank Nihan Aral for her valuable suggestion concerning using diagrams to present the main arguments and findings of the study, and for her help in preparing them.

References

Acemoğlu D, Robinson JA (2006) Economic origins of dictatorship and democracy. Cambridge University Press, New York

Acemoğlu D, Robinson JA (2008) Persistence of power, elites, and institutions. Am Econ Rev 98:267–293

Acemoğlu D, Üçer M (2015) The ups and downs of Turkish growth, 2002-2015: political dynamics, the European Union and the institutional slide. Working paper no. 21608. NBER, Cambridge, MA

Akarca AT (2009) A prediction for AKP's Nationwide vote share in the 29 March 2009 Turkish local elections. İktisat İşletme ve Finans 24:7–22

Akarca AT (2010) Analysis of the 2009 Turkish election results from an economic voting perspective. Eur Res Stud J 13:3–38

Akarca AT (2011a) A prediction for AKP's Nationwide vote share in the 12 June 2011 Turkish parliamentary election. İktisat İşletme ve Finans 26:53–74

Akarca AT (2011b) Inter-election vote swings for the Turkish ruling party: the impact of economic performance and other factors. Equilibrium 6:7–25

Akarca AT (2015a) Modeling political performance of Islamist and Islamist-rooted parties in Turkey. Middle East Dev J 7:49–69

Akarca AT (2015b) Putting Turkey's June and November 2015 Election outcomes in perspective. Insight Turkey 17:81–104

Akarca AT (2017) Economic Voting under Single-party and Coalition Governments: Evidence from the Turkish Case. Working Paper No. 1128. Economic Research Forum (ERF), Giza, Egypt

Akarca AT (2018) Single party governments as a cause and coalitions as a consequence of coups in Turkey. In: Aysan AF, Babacan M, Gür N, Karahan H (eds) Turkish economy: between middle income trap and high income status. Palgrave Macmillan, Cham, pp 59–100

Akarca AT, Tansel A (2006) Economic performance and political outcomes: an analysis of the Turkish parliamentary and local election results between 1950 and 2004. Public Choice 129:77–105

Akarca AT, Tansel A (2007) Social and economic determinants of Turkish voter choice in the 1995 parliamentary election. Elect Stud 26:633–647

[19]The lesson to be drawn from this is not that term limits should be imposed but that a system needs to be established which will extend the motivation, creativity, and checks and balances of the first term to the latter terms.

Anderson CJ (2000) Economic voting and political context: a comparative perspective. Elect Stud 19:151–170
Angelova M, Konig T, Proksch S (2016) Responsibility attribution in coalition governments: evidence from Germany. Elect Stud 43:133–149
Atiyas I (2016) Replace Discretion with Rules: How Policy Reform Can Boost Economic Performance. Policy Brief No. 10. Economic Research Forum (ERF), Giza, Egypt
Bawn K, Rosenbluth F (2006) Short versus long coalitions: electoral accountability and the size of the public sector. Am J Polit Sci 50:251–265
Bejar S, Mukherjee B, Moore WH (2011) Time horizons matter: the hazard rate of coalition governments and the size of government. Econ Gov 12:201–235
Can O (2014) The structural causes of political crisis in Turkey. Insight Turkey 16:33–41
Chandra S, Rudra N (2015) Reassessing the links between regime type and economic performance: why some authoritarian regimes show stable growth and others do not. Br J Polit Sci 45:253–285
Debus M, Stegmaier M, Tosun J (2014) Economic voting under coalition governments: evidence from Germany. Polit Sci Res Methods 2:49–67
Duch R, Przepiorka W, Stevenson RT (2015) Responsibility attribution for collective decision makers. Am J Polit Sci 59:372–389
Fisher SD, Hobolt SB (2010) Coalition government and electoral accountability. Elect Stud 29:358–369
Hall S, Nishikawa M (2014) The dynamics of within-regime stability: party tenure and economic performance. Int Polit Sci Rev 35:430–447
Hellwig T, Samuels D (2008) Electoral accountability and the variety of democratic regimes. Br J Polit Sci 38:65–90
Hobolt S, Tilley J, Banducci S (2013) Clarity of responsibility: how government cohesion conditions performance voting. Eur J Polit Res 52:164–187
Laakso M, Taagepera R (1979) Effective number of parties: a measure with application to West Europe. Comp Pol Stud 12:3–27
Lewis-Beck MS, Paldam M (2000) Economic voting: an introduction. Elect Stud 19:113–121
Lewis-Beck MS, Stegmaier M (2000) Economic determinants of electoral outcomes. Annu Rev Polit Sci 3:183–219
Lewis-Beck MS, Stegmaier M (2008) The economic vote in transitional democracies. J Elect Publ Opin Parties 18:303–323
Lewis-Beck MS, Stegmaier M (2009) American voter to economic voter: evolution of an idea. Elect Stud 28:625–631
Lewis-Beck MS, Stegmaier M (2015) Economic evaluations and electoral consequences. In: Wright JD (ed) International encyclopedia of the social and behavioral sciences, vol 7, 2nd edn. Elsevier, Oxford, pp 26–32
Londregan JB, Poole KT (1990) Poverty, the coup trap, and the seizure of executive power. World Polit 42:151–183
Nadeau R, Niemi RG, Yoshinaka A (2002) A cross-national analysis of economic voting: taking account of the political context across time and nations. Elect Stud 21:403–423
O'Kane R (1987) The likelihood of coups. Aldeshot, Avebury
Powell JM, Thyne CL (2011) Global instances of coups from 1950 to 2010: a new dataset. J Peace Res 48:249–259
Powell GB, Whitten GD (1993) A cross-national analysis of economic voting: taking account of the political context. Am J Polit Sci 37:391–414
Sharma R (2017) The rise and fall of nations. W. Norton, New York
Stegmaier M, Lewis-Beck MS (2013) Economic voting. In: Valelly R (ed) Oxford bibliographies in political science. Oxford University Press, New York
Tsebelis G (1995) Decision making in political systems: veto players in presidentialism, parliamentarism, multicameralism and multipartyism. Br J Polit Sci 25:289–325

Tsebelis G (1999) Veto players and law production in parliamentary democracies: an empirical analysis. Am Polit Sci Rev 93:591–608

Tsebelis G (2002) Veto players: how political institutions work. Princeton University Press/Russell Sage, Princeton

Tuncer E (2002) Osmanlıdan Günümüze Seçimler: 1877-1999. TESAV, Ankara

Tuncer E (2007) 22 Temmuz 2007 Milletvekili Genel Seçimleri: Sayısal ve Siyasal Değerlendirme. TESAV, Ankara

Tuncer E (2011) 12 Haziran 2011 Milletvekili Genel Seçimleri: Sayısal ve Siyasal Değerlendirme. TESAV, Ankara

Tuncer E, Tuncer B (2016) 1 Kasım 2015 Milletvekili Genel Seçimleri: Sayısal ve Siyasal Değerlendirme. TESAV, Ankara

Tuncer E, Kasapbaş C, Tuncer B (2003) 2002 Milletvekili Genel Seçimleri: Sayısal ve Siyasal Değerlendirme. TESAV, Ankara

Tuncer E (2012a) 1957 Seçimleri. TESAV, Ankara

Tuncer E (2012b) 1961 Seçimleri. TESAV, Ankara

Tuncer E, Yurtseven H, Tuncer B (2015) 7 Haziran 2015 Milletvekili Genel Seçimleri: Sayısal ve Siyasal Değerlendirme. TESAV, Ankara

Whitten GD, Palmer HD (1999) Cross-national analyses of economic voting. Elect Stud 18:49–67

Williams LK, Stegmaier M, Debus M (2017) Relaxing the constant economic vote restriction: economic evaluations and party support in Germany. Party Polit 23:286–296

Chapter 4
Determinants of Economic Growth in Spain: A Historical Viewpoint

Rafael Myro

Abstract This chapter focuses on the specific factors determining Spanish economic growth from 1985 until now. After a short summary of the main features of this period, from a comparative point of view, the important structural changes are highlighted. Later, the role of labour and total factor productivity on trending growth are analysed, as are the main shocks and macroeconomic imbalances that have accompanied them. With an increase in annual per capita GDP four decimals higher than the average for the EU-15 from 1985, Spain today has an average income level equivalent to 89% of the average income of this group of countries. This formidable economic growth was facilitated in large part by the increasing openness to foreign competition achieved by integration into the EU and by incorporation into the Eurozone. It has also been favoured by considerable immigration since 1995.

4.1 Introduction

Spain managed to increase its per capita income very quickly in the second half of the twentieth century. Development in the first stage, up until the mid-1970s, was very intense. The wave of expansion of the world-wide economy was harnessed, enabling Spain to significantly close the gap between its living standards and those attained in more advanced countries. This was something that had previously seemed almost impossible during the slow process of industrialisation which began in the nineteenth century. However, led by economic integration into the EU, the final years of the twentieth century and part of the first decade of this century have also been characterised by vigorous growth, albeit with major imbalances linked to the adoption of the euro, which were revealed by the depth of the recession experienced from 2008 to 2013. Nevertheless, 2018 will probably finish being the fourth year of intense recovery at annual growth rates of over 3%.

R. Myro (✉)
Departamento de Economía Aplicada, Estructura Económica e Historia, Facultad de Economicas de la UCM, Madrid, Spain
e-mail: rmyrosan@ucm.es

M. Osińska (ed.), *Economic Miracles in the European Economies*,
https://doi.org/10.1007/978-3-030-05606-3_4

This economic growth has been accompanied by profound changes in the living and working habits of Spanish people, and changes in the way they organise and govern their society, in similar fashion to other developed countries, particularly her European Union partners. Economic progress and institutional modernisation are two inter-related, wide-reaching and long-lasting phenomena, whose continuity has found a guarantee in the gradual economic and political opening up of Spain to the rest of the world, leaving old isolationist temptations behind.

In light of the above, this chapter focuses on the specific factors determining Spanish economic growth from 1985 until now. After a short summary of the main features of this period, from a comparative point of view, the most important structural changes are highlighted. Later, the role of labour and total factor productivity on trending growth are analysed, as are the main shocks and macroeconomic imbalances that have accompanied them.

4.2 Main Features of Spanish Economic Growth Since Integration into the EU

After a period of intense and sustained economic growth for 20 years, in the expansive framework of the European Golden Age, by the early 1970s Spain had achieved a remarkable convergence in per capita income with the countries that were members of the European Economic Community (Fig. 4.1). This rapid rise in average living standards in Spain was achieved with a significant increase in physical and human capital stocks, and with significant improvements in productive efficiency, exhibited in the increase in multifactorial productivity. Industrial development was a key element in this process, as was the increasing openness to external

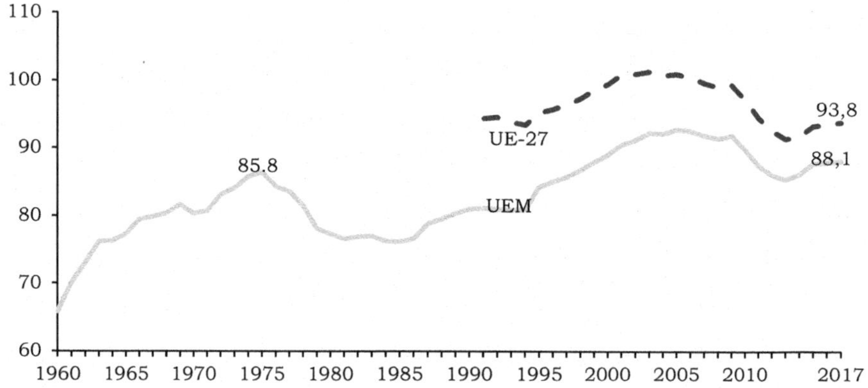

Fig. 4.1 Per capita GDP of Spain. Percentages with respect to the EU-15, in PPP of 2005 (Banco de España, Indicadores Estructurales de la Economía Española y de la UE)

competition, the construction of the welfare state and the parallel reduction in the levels of inequality in the distribution of per capita income (Lieberman 1995; García Delgado and Myro 2014).

The world economic crisis that began in the early 1970s broke this process of convergence. If, prior to this, Spain had been characterised by its highest growth yet, it was now distinguished by the stagnation of its GDP. The effects on the Spanish economy of the increase in the price of crude oil that occurred in the second half of the seventies were more acute than in other countries and they were amplified by major increases in salaries during the political transition to democracy. As a result, this crisis led to a significant increase in unemployment, a stagnation in production and high rates of inflation.

The recovery from this important crisis coincided with the accession of Spain to the European Economic Community, at a time when the integration of this area was strengthened by the creation of the European Monetary System (1979) and the Common European Market, launched through the Single Act, signed in 1986.

The positive effects of the incorporation of Spain into this select club are illustrated by its high economic growth rate in the new cycle from 1984 to the recession of 1993, the depth of which was accentuated by the contractionary effects of German unification (Salmon 1991; Martín 1997; Myro 1999). However, as it emerged from this short episode, the Spanish economy again demonstrated its high capacity for growth in the period of implementation of the single European currency, the euro, from 1994 to 2007, managing, in the last year, to surpass the average per capita income of the EU-27 and reach 93% of the EU-15 (Estrada et al. 2009).

Once again, a crisis, this time that initiated in 2007 in the USA, broke this vertiginous process of the convergence of Spanish per capita income with that of rest of the Community countries. In effect, in the period analysed here, from 1985 to 2018, as in the previous one (1961–1985), the higher comparative growth of the Spanish economy has been followed by a crisis of greater depth. Once again though, the recovery from the crisis has shown a greater economic dynamism in Spain, and this time without being able to count on the weapon of devaluation. The prospects for the next years are good, as this time the recovery has been accompanied by a surplus in external trade.

4.3 Structural Changes

The period studied here has been characterised by two important structural changes which boosted the growth of both aggregate final demand and output of Spain. They have contributed to bringing the Spanish economy more in line with that of its more developed community partners. The first was the incorporation of Spain into the European Union, following the signing of the Act of Accession in 1985. This incorporation became effective from January 1, 1986 and came with a tariff

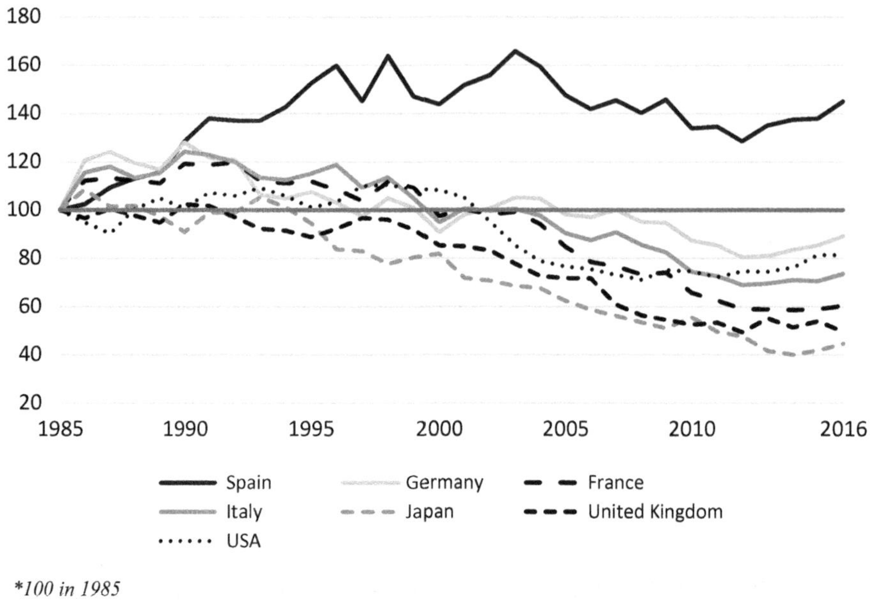

Fig. 4.2 Share of world trade in goods (WTO)

unification period of 7 years, from 1986 to 1993. In the same period, all EU countries were committed to the elimination of non-tariff barriers to trade, in response to the Single European Act, which would convert the European Economic Community into a common market. The second structural change took place from 1995 onwards and consisted of a rapid increase in immigration, a response to the growing buoyancy of the Spanish economy within the EU and to a reduction of legal barriers to the arrival of population from other countries.

4.3.1 The Export Miracle

Although the expression 'export miracle' was used during the recent crisis, when it became the only positive macroeconomic figure (Eppinger et al. 2015), the rapid increase in Spanish exports forms part of a longer-term trajectory, since entry into the EEC. The average annual increase in the volume of external sales since 1985 has been 5.3%, slightly lower than the figure for world trade of 5.8%. However, in the case of goods, the Spanish annual rate is 6.3%, higher than that of world trade (6.11%), hence between 1985 and 2017 there has been an outstanding increase in the Spanish share of world trade in goods, as shown in Fig. 4.2.

In the early years of the present century, this quota was reduced somewhat more than in other countries due to a slowdown in the external purchases of other European countries which, in the year 2000, still accounted for 75% of Spanish foreign sales.[1] Partly because of this result, Spanish companies started, from that year, an accelerated process of market diversification which allowed them to rapidly increase foreign sales during the recent crisis, giving rise to the perception of the aforementioned miracle. In fact, export growth has established an increasingly *extensive margin.*[2] The initial preference for the EU as a destination was justified by its geographical proximity, and, more importantly, by the opening up of its markets by the elimination of all tariff and non-tariff barriers that had previously hindered access.

The keys to the rapid expansion in exports since 1985 can be found in the following factors: (a) a supply of products of diverse technological composition, increasingly adapted to the structure of world demand (Myro et al. 2013), notably in the following sectors: pharmaceuticals, automobiles, agri-food, clothes, chemistry, and mechanical machinery; (b) an increasing level of sophistication of exported products following the Hausmann–Hidalgo measures (Álvarez and Vega 2016); (c) a good combination of old and new markets (Myro 2015); (d) a large group of leading companies, with relatively high efficiency, which had already embarked on the most advanced phase of internationalisation; the establishment of subsidiaries in a wide range of countries (Esteve and Rodríguez 2014) and finally (e) the increasing ability of Spanish companies to join global value chains, giving greater stability to their external sales (Gandoy 2014).

The expansion of Spanish exports has not only had a beneficial effect on aggregate final demand, output, employment and external deficit: it has also increased the size and productivity of exporting companies, improving their competitive capacity (Eppinger et al. 2015; Serrano and Myro 2017). On the other hand, as in the case of other developed countries, joining global value chains pushed up imports, particularly in the second half of the 1990s (Gandoy 2017).

The progress of internationalisation of Spanish companies is even more surprising from the perspective of investment abroad as it has taken place later but over a very short period of time. Spanish foreign FDI stock accounted for 3% of GDP in 1990. In 2007 it was already 37% and today it has reached 50%, having increased slightly during the crisis. Spanish companies have more than 10,000 subsidiaries abroad, although most of them are small sized. Service and energy companies have been the main protagonists of this process, mainly those in the banking and insurance, telecommunications, electricity and trade sectors. Its external implementation began with Latin American and EU countries; the closest, geographically and culturally. They then achieved an important presence in the United States. Today emerging countries only account for 35% of Spain's direct investment stock abroad.

[1]Some of the literature saw a deterioration in Spanish foreign price competitiveness in this slowdown in exports, partly due to a notable increase in unit labour costs. The most recent estimates regard this effect as having far less importance (Prades and García 2015; Crespo and García Rodriguez 2015).

[2]New firms, markets and products (Esteve Pérez et al. 2017).

4.3.2 Rising Immigration

In stark contrast to other European counties, there were hardly any immigrants in Spain in 1990 (0.9% of total population). However, since the date, and particularly from 1995 until the beginning of the crisis in 2008, the number of immigrants increased extremely rapidly. It reached, at the end of the period, 14% of the Spanish population, the highest level in the EU, although some other EU countries have a greater number of descendants of immigrants. From 2001 to 2007, the annual rate of increase of immigrants was 15%, the largest contribution being from Latin America (36.21%), followed by the European Union (34.45%) and North Africa (14.83%).

There were two main reasons for this increased immigration. Firstly, the rapid growth of the Spanish economy created favourable expectations of labour demand, particularly in some very expansive, low-productivity sectors, such as construction, while the incorporation of Spain into the European Union turned it into a gateway to this area, attracting immigration from its neighbours, Morocco and sub-Saharan Africa. Secondly, the demographic pressures from these areas and Latin America increased, due to the economic problems they were experiencing at the time (De la Rica 2017).

Immigration favoured increased labour force participation, and hence an increase in GDP and GDP per capita, particularly in the areas with greater concentrations of immigrants, Madrid and the Mediterranean arc. Fiscal benefits from this significant structural change appear to be higher than the associated fiscal and even social costs. In addition, immigrants occupied newly created jobs, rather than those occupied by Spanish workers, so that their arrival had little effect on the aggregate level of salaries. It also favoured the transfer of indigenous workers to more productive activities, thus increasing their productivity, an effect that has also been detected in other developed countries. Nevertheless, although the entry of immigrants does not seem to have altered the inter-industrial specialisation of the Spanish economy, there is some evidence that it has favoured the adoption of more labour-intensive techniques at the intra-industrial level (Sanromá et al. 2009; De la Rica et al. 2015). Assimilation of immigrants with the indigenous population, in terms of employment and salaries, has been higher for Latin Americans, tending to grow over time for all groups.

4.4 Factors Determining Long-Term Growth

An increase in per capita income can be achieved either by increasing the percentage of the population engaged in productive activities (the relation between workers and the total population; the employment rate in the broad sense of the term or per capita *employment*), or by increasing average labour yield or the *productivity per worker* (the relation between income and number of workers). In fact, per capita income is merely the output of these two relations, and its rate of variation can be approximated by the sum of the rate of variation of each one of them.

Table 4.1 Economic growth in selected countries—average annual rates of growth (European Commission, AMECO)

	1961–1985			1986–2017		
	GDP per capita	Labour productivity	Employment per capita	GDP per capita	Labour productivity	Employment per capita
Germany	2.8	2.9	−0.1	1.5	1.0	0.5
Spain	*3.6*	*4.9*	*−1.3*	*1.8*	*1.0*	*0.8*
France	3.2	3.6	−0.4	1.3	1.2	0.1
Greece	4.5	5.0	−0.5	0.6	0.7	−0.1
Ireland	3.1	4.0	−0.9	4.2	3.2	1.0
Italy	3.6	3.8	−0.2	0.8	0.9	−0.1
Portugal	4.0	4.5	−0.5	2.0	1.9	0.1
United Kingdom	2.2	2.4	−0.2	1.7	1.4	0.3
EU-15	2.9	3.3	−0.4	1.4	1.1	0.3
EU-28 (1)[a]				1.4	1.1	0.3
USA	2.5	1.7	0.8	1.6	1.5	0.1
Japan	5.5	5.6	−0.1	1.5	1.4	1.1

[a](1) Period 1996–2017

However, this does not mean that growth can be attained indistinctly by either of these two paths, as there are limits to increasing the employment rate of the population, arising from demographic, cultural and social factors. Moreover, this depends on increasing the capacity of production, and the more efficiently goods and services are produced, the higher the production capacity. Hence, the productivity of labour is a cornerstone of growth, explaining why the theoretical and empirical analysis of economic growth has focused on it. Only a growth based on it allows for the increase in real wages and family income.

Until 1985, economic growth in Spain had been based exclusively on increasing labour productivity (Table 4.1), the same as had occurred in many of the EU countries and in Japan. This fact translated into a moderate capacity to create employment, in contrast with the United States. This was not a serious problem while the unemployment rate was maintained at levels below 3%, in accordance with a slow increase in the working-age population. However, the economic crisis, beginning in 1970, slowed job creation, and subsequent economic growth was not enough to incorporate *baby boomers* into the labour market during the 1980s, so that the unemployment rate remained at levels close to 10% in the EU as an average, and up to 16% in the case of Spain.

As a consequence, all EU countries considered here have changed their growth patterns over the last three decades, together with their capacity to create jobs. In addition, the rate of increase of labour productivity has tended to slow down, as a result of a lower increase in the physical and human capital stock per worker, resulting from the maintenance of an invariable saving rate of around 21% on average. Spain, together with Ireland, is one of the main examples and drivers of this change. While they stand out for falling employment per inhabitant in the early years, the most notable factor in more recent years is an increase in this same value, reflecting the increase of labour share participation, first due to the *baby boom* and increasing participation of women in the labour market and then to immigration.

It must also be said that in the case of Spain, unlike Ireland, this change towards an employment generating model, accompanied as it has been by a pronounced slowdown in the growth of labour productivity, has been extremely radical. This fact is reflected by the enormous adjustment in the labour market which took place during the recent crisis, eroding part of the employment created in the early 2000s and increasing labour productivity levels.

Establishing the causes of the slowdown in labour productivity is a difficult matter which has received a lot of attention from Spanish analysts. As we know, the conventional growth theory explains an increase in labour productivity from the starting point of an aggregated output function, using two factors: the greater capitalisation of business (increase in the physical and human capital per worker, or intensification of capital) and the improvement in the joint efficiency of labour and capital applied to the productive process (or improvement in the total productivity of the factors of production—TFP), determined mainly by the factor of technological advance.

The productive capital stock per worker has grown at high rates in the period considered, from 83% of the EMU average in 1985 to 102% in 1995. This percentage fell slightly in the following years, mainly due to the expansion of employment-intensive activities, particularly those of real estate construction, but in 2012 it exceeded the value of 100 again, after the decline in the volume of employment. In fact, the investment rate of the Spanish economy, during the period considered, has been 23.5% of GDP on average, above the level of the Eurozone (21%). Inward FDI has influenced this value. Spain has the third highest level of FDI in the EU, after France and the United Kingdom, if the low-dimension countries that intermediate FDI are discounted (Fernandez-Otheo 2014).

Therefore, what is anomalous in Spain is that there is practically no increase in TFP since the beginning of the 1990s, which suggests that the efficiency levels of labour and capital applied to output have stagnated over the last 20 years. This is difficult to believe and could be due to an underestimation of the product advance rates, apart from the effect of the extraordinary progress of the construction sector.[3] Figure 4.3 shows this anomaly clearly, expressing it in comparative terms. Labour productivity in Spain, measured as a percentage of EMU, has fallen since the 1980s, and this performance has rested to a large extent on the aforementioned slowdown in

[3]Mas et al. (2015) highlight the role of the real state sector and show how not only private individuals, but companies in all sectors were investing in buildings and land. On the other hand, García-Santacana et al. (2016) find the source of negative TFP growth in the within-sector misallocation of production factors across firms. We find the phenomenon to be present in all sectors of activity, especially those in which the influence of the public sector is significant (e.g. through licensing or regulations).

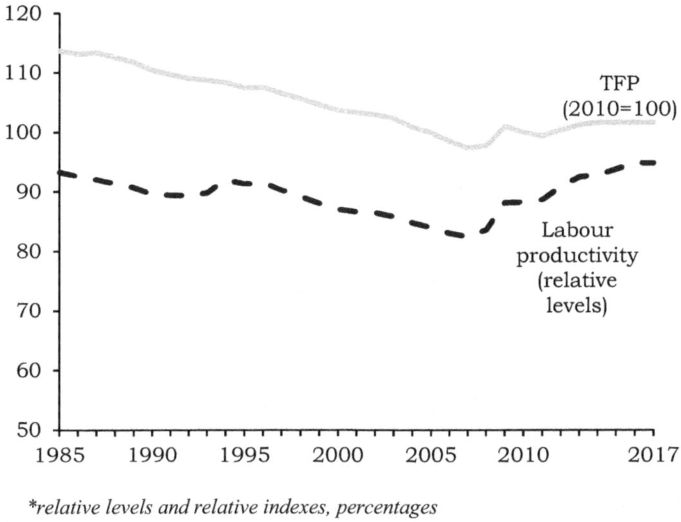

Fig. 4.3 Productivity in Spain related to EU-15 (Eurostat)

the progress of TFP. This is a distinguishing aspect of Spain that should now be addressed.

An increase in TFP, in any economy, depends on new ideas, procedures and methods being incorporated into productive processes and products. This is made feasible by the work of research teams and by enhancing the level of qualifications of workers. In the early stage of a country's development, there is ample opportunity to obtain such ideas, procedures and methods from other countries, by importing the capital goods incorporating them. This is one of the keys to the sharp increase in physical capital per worker during the industrialisation phases. It can be achieved by purchasing patents, brands and technical consulting or, more simply, by imitating technologies that are sufficiently disseminated, which are then absorbed and implemented by better trained teams of people (Jones 2016; Weil 2012). This is why human capital also plays an indirect role in technical progress, favouring the uptake, absorption and dissemination of new technologies. The location of foreign companies in the country also plays an important role in this whole process.

However, when a country reaches a high degree of development, the acquisition and assimilation of technologies from other countries becomes more difficult and costly. It is now fundamental for the country in question to make its own efforts to create new ideas and raise the skills of its workers, with a view to facilitating their absorption, dissemination and transformation into new goods and productive processes. In consonance with the process, Spain has made an appreciable effort over time to increase the number of researchers, measured here per thousand of the working population (research intensity ratio), which has advanced in parallel with the increase in the average number of years of full-time education among the

Table 4.2 Indicators of Efforts and Results of Research, 2015 (Source: OCDE, Main Science and Technology Indicators; United Nations, Development reports)

Country	R&D as a percentage of GDP	Share of business in R&D (%)	Researchers per 1000 employees	Share in total patents in EU, USA and Japan (%)[a]	Human capital[b]
USA	2.8	71.5	9.3	27.2	13.2
Japan	3.5	78.5	10.0	31.2	12.5
UE-28	1.9	63.3	7.4	24.5	11.9
Germany	2.9	67.7	8.3	8.2	13.2
France	2.2	65.1	9.8	4.6	11.6
United Kingdom	1.7	65.7	9.2	3.3	13.3
Italy	1.3	55.3	4.9	1.4	10.9
Spain	*1.2*	*52.5*	*6.6*	*0.5*	*9.8*
Sweden	3.3	68.7	14.3	1.2	12.3
Finland	2.9	66.7	15.0	0.5	11.2
Netherland	2.0	55.6	8.8	1.5	11.9
Portugal	1.3	47.1	8.7	0.1	8.9

[a]2014
[b]Average number of years of full-time education of workers

working population. The result of this trajectory is evident: in 2010, Spain is only just below the most developed countries in these indicators (Table 4.2).

Consequently, TFP stagnation cannot be attributed to differences in the numbers of researchers and level of education of the population. However, the quality of the labour force could have been lower than in other countries, having decreased from 1998 perhaps, partly compensating for the positive effect of higher educational levels (Lacuesta et al. 2008). On the other hand, the transformation of new ideas produced by research into innovation (new procedures and products) requires something more than researchers and qualified personnel. It requires greater investment in capital than we have seen, bearing in mind that R+D research spending in ratio to GDP is almost half of the French or German levels, and the gap with these countries in business spending is even wider. Business spending, a key factor in improving innovation,[4] is particularly low in Spain. Innovation also requires a system of technological organisation to ensure improvements in spending efficiency, and it would appear that not much progress has been made in this respect. If, for example, we consider the number of patents registered as an indicator, Spain lags far behind the more developed countries.

In addition to a reduced technological effort, Spain shows low 'sophistication of the business environment', which refers to the existence and functioning of

[4]Some authors find a lack of incentive to investment in R&D in the cheaper labour market created through immigration (Boldrin et al. 2010), but this seems to be contradicted by the success of the internationalisation process, not only of the largest companies but also of small and medium ones, and also by the improvement in product quality and the sophistication of exports.

innovation networks (collaboration in research between universities and companies, the development and role of clusters in the economy, external funding of R&D or patent families, etc.). It is ranked 45th out of 144 countries (for this item) in the ranking provided by the Global Innovation Index. Even an agency like the IMF has recently had to warn Spain that it stands out today as one of the countries in which less financial support is provided for innovation of private companies.

There is a clear absence of close interaction between the state and the private sector and a lack of awareness that technology is crucial to the success of an economy. The concept of the state as a mere source of finance for innovation, distant from companies and ignorant of the risks and difficulties faced by them, is a sure way to guarantee the future technological decline of a country.

In short, everything seems to suggest a predominance of marginal research in Spain with very poor results, a reflection of the relative lack of ambition and organisation in Spanish technology. It could be said that Spain has not progressed very well from the phase of imitating foreign technologies to the phase of creating its own.

The poor achievement in the field of technology makes it difficult to explain the miracle of exports (one of the two structural changes previously discussed). It is even more difficult to explain if we consider that productivity has become the key to exporting as only the most productive companies can withstand the fixed and variable costs involved in exporting (Melitz 2003; Helpman 2011), and Spain's productivity remains unimpressive too.

This therefore leads us to an apparent paradox between successful exporting on the one hand and mediocre productivity and technology on the other: Spain has embarked on a robust process of internationalisation, led by the largest companies, while its level of productivity and scientific and technological development has remained very modest. It could thus be reasonably concluded that the achievement can be explained either by the delay in the exit of companies from international markets (despite having the capacity to do so), or by high levels of human capital cohesion, resulting in good task complementarity, in line with the ideas of Ricardo Hausmann and Michael Kremer (Hausmann and Klinger 2007; Kremer 1998). However, this would be strange if our tentative hypothesis about a decrease in labour quality is correct.

4.5 Main Shocks and Macroeconomic Imbalances

So far, attention has been paid to the trend in growth. However, the Spanish economy, as any other, has experienced different supply and demand shocks, which have accelerated or slowed the long-term increase in GDP. The identification of these shocks requires a comparison between the increases in real GDP and potential GDP. This comparison shows that the increase in GDP often exceeded the increase in potential GDP, something which happened in the late 1980s, late 1990s, and 2000s (Fig. 4.4). Although there has been a mix of supply and demand

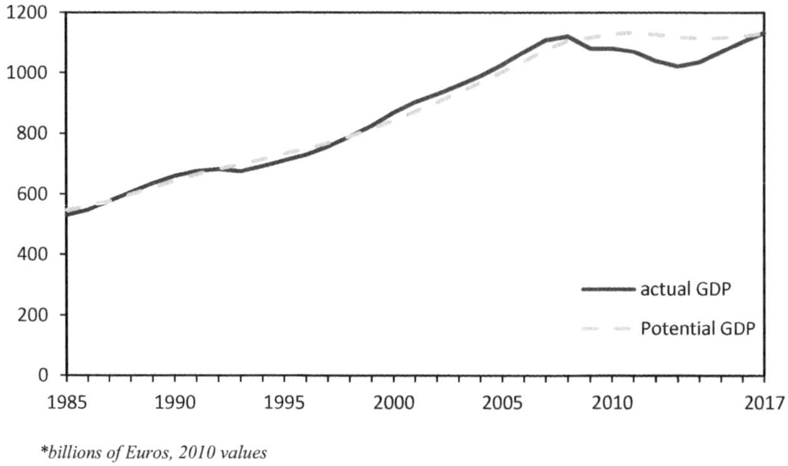

Fig. 4.4 Potential GDP and Actual GDP (Eurostat and INE)

shocks during the period considered, demand shocks have been more important in the expansive phases of Spanish economic growth, whereas supply factors have predominated in the recessive phases.

The most important positive demand shocks lasted for several years and occurred as a result of Spain's integration into Europe, initially at the time of accession, in 1986, and then with the adoption of the euro in 1998. European economic integration was gradually carried out over a period of tariff disarmament and non-tariff barrier elimination lasting 7 years, from 1986–1993, coinciding with the implementation of the Single European Act. The adoption of the euro took place over the period 1998–2002 (Martín 1997; Estrada et al. 2009).

Opening up the economy to foreign trade in times of European expansion enabled Spain to offset the rise in imports caused by trade liberalisation with greater exports. However, the growth of overseas demand in periods such as these was accompanied by a large increase in domestic demand and domestic consumption. The increase in domestic demand came from companies needing to finance gross capital formation to improve their production techniques and to increase the quality of their products, in order to adapt to a more competitive market. Domestic consumption was stimulated by the surge in real purchasing power of the population as reduced protection lowered prices and offered a greater variety of imported goods (García Delgado and Myro 2014).

In the second half of the 1980s, these increases in domestic demand were sustained by expansive monetary policies which tended to strengthen them, pushing prices up, while at the same time creating a deficit in overseas trade (Fig. 4.5). To tackle both imbalances, at the end of the decade, governments adopted monetary and fiscal containment measures; stabilisation measures which curbed economic growth and employment. They also devalued the currency in the early 1990s to recover lost

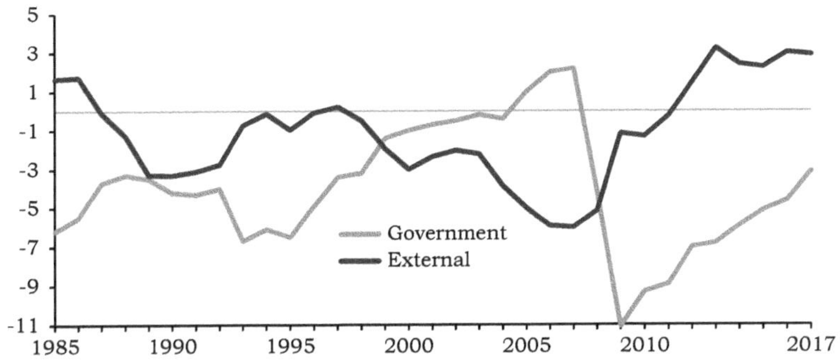

Fig. 4.5 External and Government Surplus (% of GDP) (Eurostat)

competitiveness, improve the balance on overseas accounts and prepare a new stage of expansion.

The adoption of the euro in 1998 produced a considerable reduction in interest rates by removing the risk premium (Estrada et al. 2009). In addition to this, the governments of the major developed economies decided to reduce interest rates, fearing that the dot com bubble, starting in 2001, would lead to recession. Between 1995 and 2005, the real interest rate on Spanish ten-year public debt was reduced by seven percentage points, stimulating a strong surge in domestic demand, in particular for the gross capital formation of property. The sharp increase in the number of immigrants (a positive supply shock) drove up domestic spending even further. A formidable overseas deficit increase could not be avoided. However, unlike on previous occasions, this cannot now be corrected by devaluing the currency, as Spain no longer has its own currency.

The last major demand shock was negative and occurred in 2008 and 2009, when demand for investment in construction was drastically reduced as a result of an excess of built houses, and the international financial restrictions that arose as a consequence of the crisis which originated in the USA. This shock was prolonged by the need for families and businesses to restore their balance sheets by reducing their spending. The notable increase in the public deficit (Fig. 4.5 again) partially compensated for this reduction. However, as of 2010, Spain was obliged by the European Commission to reduce this deficit, under the austerity policy, a restrictive policy common to other European countries (Banco de España 2017).

The most important supply shock in the period analysed, immigration (already discussed), has been positive and lasting, although some pressure also came in the form of rising oil prices, particularly important from 2000 to 2007. Spain is highly dependent on imported crude, although the level of dependency has gradually fallen, not so much because of the substitution of that energy source by others, but by the reduction of energy intensity. Crude oil imports accounted for 33% of total goods imports in 1985 and today represent just 11%.

Real salaries also rose, promoting an increase in unemployment during critical periods, 1993, 2008 and 2009. One of the clearest manifestations of the rigidity of the Spanish labour market is the lack of sensitivity of salaries, agreed upon in collective bargaining negotiations, to changes in the economic cycle (Jimeno 2011).

There is a difference between the large and prolonged expansive shocks mentioned (European integration and the entry of immigrants) and the derivative of wage increases. While the former are the consequence of the gradual equating of economic structure and macroeconomic policy with that of the more developed European countries, the latter is a reflection of the difficulty of achieving a parallel resemblance in the functioning and institutions regulating the labour market. This is still a pending task, which will be referred to later. Even so, Spain has approached European standards in the characteristics and functioning of its markets, and its macroeconomic management points to a future cyclical behaviour more adjusted to that of the EU's leading countries.

To conclude this section, it is worth referring to the results obtained when macroeconomic imbalances in Spain are compared with those of the European countries which have been taken as a benchmark throughout this chapter.

In the period analysed, inflation has been slightly greater in Spain as a consequence of the above-mentioned expansive shocks and the inertia stemming from the rigidity of a labour market in which wages have, as a rule, been indexed to prices (Dolado et al. 1997). Nevertheless, the entry of Spain into the Eurozone drastically reduced the growth in prices as it curbed the expectations of inflation by the trade unions, who reacted very positively to monetary integration. Today, there is no problem with inflation. As is the case with other European countries, Spain has not yet reached the ECB annual objective of 2% of increase in aggregate prices.

The balance of foreign trade in goods and services has been negative for most of the period considered here, particularly in the expansive stages, becoming very high in the years 2002–2007. However, the formidable expansion of exports and moderation of imports during the crisis years have led to an external surplus of 2% of GDP, which has remained in the years of recovery, even though production has grown at rates above 3%, something that hasn't happened since the early 1970s. The available predictions, including those of the IMF, point to the maintenance of this positive balance in the coming years. This is a very significant change in the growth model of the Spanish economy. In the past, external deficit obliged the Government to control demand growth and devalue the currency, frequently haulting GDP growth.

Public deficit increased in the crisis periods and during the enhanced infrastructure development of the late 1980s. Until the outbreak of the 2007 crisis though, Spain did not stand out among European economies for bulging public-sector deficits. However, the crisis rapidly absorbed the surplus with which it closed 2007 to reach a deficit of 11.3% of GDP by 2009. The continuation of an appreciable deficit until 2015 resulted in the cost of public debt being equivalent to 37% of GDP in 2007 and rising to 89% today. Such a high level is an impediment to public intervention and obliges moderate spending, which is serious for a country with growing spending needs in terms of education, innovation, welfare and pensions.

Unemployment, however, represents the greatest macroeconomic imbalance and it has differentiated Spain from other Community countries during the period considered here. The average unemployment rate has remained at 16% of the workforce, reaching a peak of 24% in 1994, in response to the small recession of 1993. In 2007, it fell to 8.5%, a level close to the community average, and rose to just over 27% during the recent recession.

There are four reasons for this high unemployment. First, the rapid increase in the working-age population; initially in the 1980s, due to the baby boom; and then, from 1995 to 2007, due to rising immigration. Secondly, the intense adjustment of employment that has taken place in each crisis period, with the disappearance of many low-productivity enterprises. Thirdly, the lack of mismatch between supply and demand for employment in terms of sector and skills. This helps to explain why the rate of structural unemployment in Spain is the highest among the OECD countries at 18%. This figure has increased during the crisis, mainly due to its duration, which has converted some cyclical unemployment into long-term unemployment (Bentolila et al. 2017). Finally, we have to add to these factors the effect of rigidities on the labour market.

Rigidities in the labour market exist principally in the form of high dismissal costs for workers with fixed contracts and wage agreements negotiated by sector or region, which companies are obliged to follow. These also contain renewal clauses that impede the adjustment of wages to market conditions.

In the 1980s, these rigidities favoured temporary hiring, with low dismissal costs, so that today Spain stands out for the proportion of workers with temporary contracts (27%), twice the average EU level. This contractual figure makes it easier for employment adjustments during times of crisis to be carried out through the dismissal of workers. On the other hand, it makes it difficult for companies to train workers well because of high staff turnover.

In 2012, a labour reform was carried out, to address company agreements and facilitate staff adjustments by businesses experiencing economic difficulties. This change favoured the decrease in salaries of workers with fixed contracts and the cost of firing, thus easing the market. It also favoured the adoption of measures of internal flexibility to adjust employment. The use of these measures together with an end to the application of sectoral agreements led to a slowdown in the growth of unemployment.

Today, social partners and analysts agree on the need for a new reform to make recruitment less temporary, boost training policies and facilitate labour cost adjustment through the reduction of working hours and wages, rather than by firing workers.

Nevertheless, now, during the recovery from the crisis, the most worrying issue appears to be the extension of low wage jobs, which limit the positive impact of employment on aggregate demand. In contrast with the strong recovery of company profits, and after an increase in inequality in the distribution of income during the period of crisis, this issue requires urgent intervention to avoid the deterioration of the implicit social contract which has allowed the rapid economic growth in Spain since 1960.

4.6 Conclusions

This chapter analyses the continued growth of the Spanish economy from 1985 until today. With an increase in annual per capita GDP 4 decimals higher than the average for the EU-15, Spain today has an average income level equivalent to 89% of the average income of this group of countries, having reached 77% of it in 1985. In fact, it reached even higher percentages in 2007, but through an excessive growth of spending and production, causing a considerable housing bubble and leading to a notable imbalance in the external accounts, which has been eliminated during the recent economic crisis.

This formidable economic growth was facilitated in large part by the increasing openness to foreign competition achieved first by integration into the European Union and later by incorporation into the Euro zone. It has also been favoured by considerable immigration since 1995. Both factors have contributed to bringing the Spanish economy and Spanish society more in line with those of the countries that lead the European Community.

Spanish companies have responded in an admirable and surprising way to the challenge of greater international competition, with a notable increase in exports, often described as miraculous. However, little reference is made to their increased direct investment in other countries, and this indeed has been truly miraculous.

Spain, however, is still characterised by some important peculiarities in the functioning of its labour market. These, together with the depth of the crisis it has passed through, help explain its high rate of unemployment, something which distinguishes it from the other countries of the EU. There has been a notable lack of any process of institutional convergence in this respect.

Although to a much lesser extent, the slow increase in the efficiency of Spanish production, largely attributable to the lack of a true system for scientific and technological advance, also differentiates Spain from other European Community members. In fact, there is a striking and undoubtable paradox between Spain's formidable export breakthrough and her unimpressive increase in productivity.

In 2017, Spain recovered the GDP it had had in 2007, with a lower level of employment and greater work productivity. It achieved this through a growth in GDP of more than 3% from 2015 onwards and with foreign account surpluses. It is a radical change with respect to the pattern followed up until 2007 and it justifies predictions of a favourable future, with sustained growth, free from the dark cloud of external deficits, and of convergence in per capita income with the leaders of the Eurozone.

References

Álvarez E, Vega J (2016) Promoción exterior. In: Myro R (ed) Una nueva política industrial para España. Consejo Económico y Social, Madrid, pp 153–173

Banco de España (2017) Informe sobre la crisis financiera y bancaria en España, 2008–2014. Banco de España, Madrid

Bentolila S, García Perez JI, Jansen M (2017) Are the Spanish long-term unemployed unemployable? J Spanish Econ Assoc 8(1):1–41
Boldrin M, Conde-Ruiz JI, Díaz Giménez J (2010) Eppur si muove! España: creciendo sin un modelo. FEDEA, Documento de trabajo 12
Crespo A, García Rodriguez A (2015) ¿Ha mejorado la competitividad exterior gracias a la devaluación interna? Papeles de Economía Española 150:114–126
De la Rica S, Glitz A, Ortega F (2015) Immigration in Europe: trends, policies and empirical evidence. Handbook of the Economics of International Migration, vol 24. Elsevier, Amsterdam, pp 1303–1362
De la Rica S (2017) Los efectos económicos de la inmigración: evidencia empírica. Información Comercial Española no 896(May–June):129–140
Dolado JJ, López-Salido D, Vega JL (1997) Spanish unemployment and inflation persistence: are there Phillips trade-offs?. Working Paper 9712, Banco de España
Eppinger PS, Meithaler N, Sindlinger M, Smolka M (2015) The Great Trade Collapse and the Spanish Export Miracle: firm-level evidence from the crisis. Economics Working Papers 2015–10, Aarhus University
Esteve S, Rodriguez D (2014) Características de las empresas que realizan IED. Empresas multipaís y empresas multiproducto. In: Myro R (ed) España en la inversión directa internacional, vol 7. Instituto de Estudios Económicos, Madrid, pp 301–329
Esteve Pérez S, De Lucio J, Minondo A, Mínguez R, Requena F (2017) La supervivencia exportadora, un análisis a nivel de empresa, producto y destino. Cuadernos de Información Económica 258:15–33
Estrada A, Jimeno JF, Malo de Molina JL (2009) The performance of the Spanish economy in EMU: the first ten years. Banco de España, Madrid, pp 83–149
Fernández-Otheo CM (2014) La inversión exterior directa recibida, estructura sectorial y por países. In: Myro R (ed) Rentabilidad. España en la inversión directa internacional, vol 2. Instituto de Estudios Económicos, Madrid, pp 125–158
Gandoy R (2014) La implicación española en cadenas globales de producción. In: Alonso JA, Myro R (eds) Ensayos sobre economía Española. Thomson-Reuters, Madrid
Gandoy R (2017) La dependencia importadora de la economía española. Estud Econ Apl 35 (1):111–132
García Delgado JL, Myro R (2014) The Spanish Economy. An introduction. Thomson-Reuters, Madrid
García-Santana M, Moral-Benito E, Pijoan-Mas E, Ramos R (2016) Growing like Spain, 1995–2007. Working Papers, 1619, Banco de España
Hausmann R, Klinger B (2007) The structure of the product space and the evolution of comparative advantage. CID Working Paper (146)
Helpman E (2011) Understanding global trade. Belknap Press of Harvard University Press, Cambridge, MA
Jimeno JF (2011) Collective bargaining, firm heterogeneity and unemployment. Working Papers (1131), Banco de España
Jones CI (2016) The facts of economic growth. In: Taylor JB, Uhlig H (eds) Handbook of macroeconomics, vol 2A. Elsevier, Amsterdam, pp 3–63
Kremer M (1998) The O-Ring theory of economic development. Q J Econ 108(3):551–575
Lacuesta A, Puente S, Cuadrado P (2008) Omitted variables in the measure of a labour quality index: the case of Spain. Working Papers 0835, Banco de España
Lieberman S (1995) Growth and crisis in the Spanish economy: 1940-1993. Routledge, Abingdon
Martín C (1997) España en la nueva Europa. Alianza Editorial, Madrid
Mas M, Pérez F, Uriel E (2015) Inversión y stock de capital en España (1964–2013). La salida de la crisis. Documento de Trabajo (1), Fundación BBVA
Melitz MJ (2003) The impact of trade in intra-industry reallocations and aggregate industry productivity. Econometrica 71(6):1695–1725

Myro R (1999) España en la Unión Europea: Etapas y efectos de la integración. In: García Delgado JL (ed) Economía, ante el siglo XXI. Espasa Calpe Ediciones, Madrid, pp 241–270
Myro R (2015) España en la economía global. Claves del éxito de las exportaciones españolas. RBA, Barcelona
Myro R, Álvarez ME, Fernández-Otheo CM, Rodríguez D, Vega J (2013) Fortalezas competitivas y sectores clave en la exportación española. Instituto de Estudios Económicos, Madrid
Prades E, García C (2015) Actualización de la función de las exportaciones españolas de bienes. Boletín Económico, Banco de España: 31–39
Salmon KG (1991) The modern Spanish economy. Pinter, London
Sanromá E, Ramos R, Simon H (2009) Immigrant Wages in the Spanish Labour Market: does the origin of human capital matter? Document de Treball de L'IEB, 2009/8, IEB
Serrano J, Myro R (2017) From domestic to exporter, what happens? Evidence for Spanish manufacturing firms, Mimeo
Weil D (2012) Economic growth. Routledge, Abingdon

Chapter 5
Factors of Economic Growth in Ireland

Małgorzata Szczepaniak

Abstract Irish economic growth has been an interesting phenomenon for several decades. The scale of success made the modernization process in this country known as an economic miracle. Although the dynamics of economic growth in Ireland is broadly analyzed in literature, the answer to the question of the factors is ambiguous.

The main aim of the chapter is to assess the role of such factors of economic growth in Ireland as: inflows of foreign direct investments, grants from the European Union funds, and the role of the state in the economy. The chapter also contributes to an understanding of the role of institutional system in Ireland, which is fundamental to the process of growth. Although the analysis covers the period after the accession to European Community in 1973, special attention is paid to the periods of very high dynamics of growth in the 1990s and after the crisis of the last decade.

Finally, there is question which the chapter tries to answer: if this system of specific factors of growth in Ireland that created conditions of economic success, would be the same in the context of quick recovery after the crisis.

5.1 Introduction

Ireland's economic growth observed in the second half of twentieth century is a spectacular phenomenon. During the period of membership of the European Union (the European Community at first), Ireland evolved from a country with the lowest level of development in that group into the fastest growing economy.

Ireland is a country that achieved the growth rates much exceeding the USA and European countries during the 1990s. As a result, living standards converged rapidly on EU average, GDP per capita and employment grew faster than European countries. In comparison to the dynamics of development of *Asian Tigers*, Ireland became known as the *Celtic Tiger* (Clinch et al. 2002; Kirby 2002).

M. Szczepaniak (✉)
Department of Economics, The Faculty of Economic Sciences and Management,
Nicolaus Copernicus University, Toruń, Poland
e-mail: m.szczepaniak@umk.pl

M. Osińska (ed.), *Economic Miracles in the European Economies*,
https://doi.org/10.1007/978-3-030-05606-3_5

During the last decade, Irish economic growth was admired and can be called a miracle once again. Although Ireland was among the worst hit European economies during the 2008 financial crisis, its recovery has been dramatic, leading to popular rebranding of former *Celtic Tiger* to *Celtic Phoenix* (Brazys and Regan 2018).

This chapter aims to present reflections on the factors of economic growth in Ireland with special attention to the boom period of the 1990s and recovery after the crisis in 2008, as the periods of accelerated growth. However, the main purpose is to assess the role of identified factors of economic growth in Ireland. Even though there is a widespread agreement on the enumeration of factors that played role in the economic growth in these periods, the emphasis is placed on various issues and differs across authors. Generally, the following factors are mentioned: government policy, the inflows of European Structural Funds, and the success in attracting FDI inflows, peaceful labor relations and wage moderation (Barry 1999; Leddin and Walsh 1997; O'Higgins 2002; O'Grada 1997; Szczepaniak 2015). Nevertheless, there are disagreements over the factors that have been crucial to the process of accelerated growth. FDI inflows and their pro-export character were most often analyzed and they are considered as the most important factor of growth (Barry 2004; Barry and Bradley 1997; Szczepaniak 2015). The authors proved that accelerated growth in Ireland depended on FDI. Main channels of FDI impact on economy included: technology transfer, increased investment funds, and additional marketing channels through which FDI can enhance output from the perspective of the host country (Doyle 2001; Fountas 2000). Furthermore, bi-directional relationship between economic growth and FDI was identified in Ireland (Iamsiraroj 2016). Rapid growth of GDP facilitated FDI inflows and they determined trade and accelerated growth (Szczepaniak 2015). The special attention is paid to the particular role of the state's policy. In this context, Ireland's economic growth is an example of how economic latecomers can adjust to the challenges of globalization, not only through forced withdrawal of the state, but by state intervened export-led growth model (Kirby 2002). Jobs creation as the reason for the increase in GDP per capita is analyzed by many authors (Barry 1999; Kirby 2002). Successful allocation of the European Structural Funds is also noticed as one of fundamental factors (Mac Sharry and White 2000; Kowalski 2008).

In regard to the recovery period after the crisis in the twenty-first century, there is a relative agreement that the fundamental issue is the success in attracting the FDI through maintaining the low corporate tax rates and the increase in employment in foreign owned sector (Brazys and Regan 2018; Iamsiraroj 2016).

The chapter answers the question about the list of factors of the accelerated growth during the 1990s and compares the role of identified factors in the period of quick recovery from the crisis of last decade.

5.2 The Dynamics of Economic Growth in Ireland

The dynamics of economic growth was much diversified in the period 1973–2016, but the average growth rates in characteristic periods of economic development were higher in Ireland than the EU-15 average over the entire period. However, Ireland experienced two deep crises over the entire analyzed period: the first one in the 1980s and the second one in the period 2008–2013. Ireland has experienced very high and far exceeding its European neighbors' growth rates in the 1990s. Average GDP growth over the period 1993–2000 was 7.4% while the European average was 2.1%. Nevertheless the biggest difference was observed after 2008 hence the spectacular rebuilding of the economy after the severe crisis is also worth analysis. Even though the GDP dropped dramatically in 2009, Ireland has experienced much higher GDP growth rates than the EU-15 countries since 2014. The above 25% growth rate in 2015 induced Paul Krugman to call it *Leprechaun economics* (Krugman 2017) (Fig. 5.1).

Ireland's economy is internationalized to very high extent. GDP takes into consideration the production of foreign owned companies and may be exaggerated. The example is 2015 when multinational companies (MNCs) moved their headquarters to Ireland to take advantage of its low corporate income tax (CIT) rate. That may be misleading in analyzing the economic outcomes and may overrate the results. From this point of view, it is interesting to compare GDP growth rate with the GNP growth rate in Ireland. The growth rates of GNP were lower on average by 1 percentage points than the GDP growth rate in 1973–2016. That's the reason why the GDP to GNP ratio (GDP/GNP*100%) increased from 92% in 1973 to 121% in 2016. GDP exceeded GNP in 1983 and is still higher because of high contribution of MNCs' production. This is the highest difference between GDP and GNP across

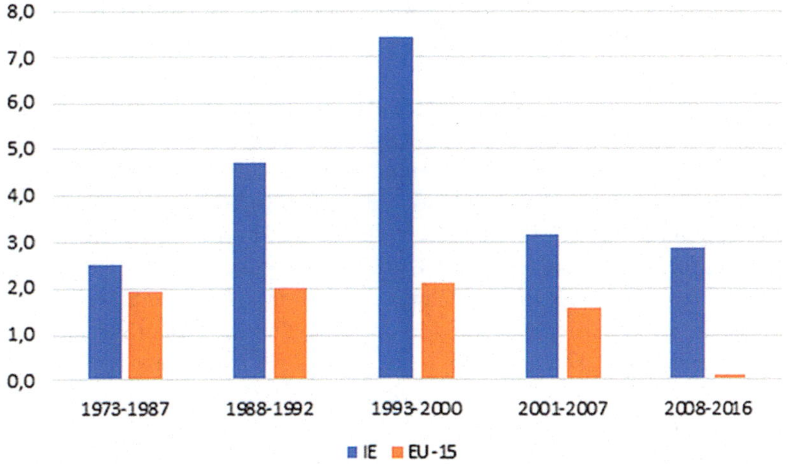

Fig. 5.1 Dynamics of GDP growth in Ireland and EU-15 (average) in the period between 1973 and 2016 (%, constant price) (own preparation on the basis of Eurostat)

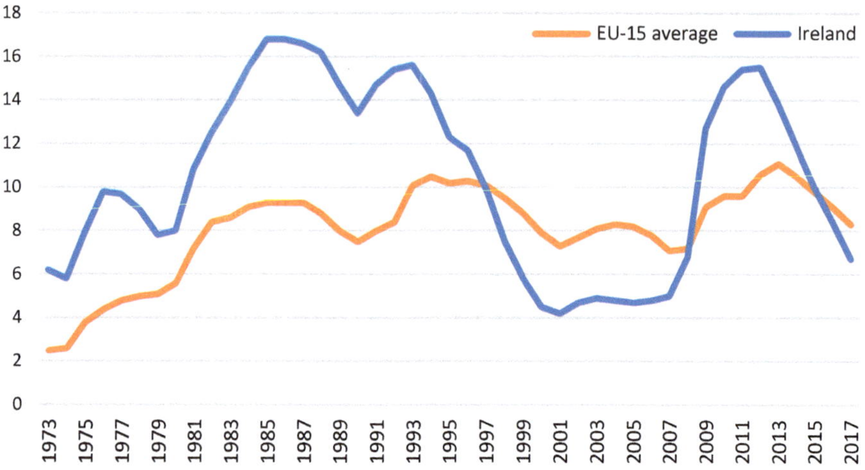

Fig. 5.2 Unemployment rates in Ireland and EU-15 in the period between 1973 and 2017 (%) (own preparation on the basis of Eurostat)

European Union countries (with the exception of Luxemburg). Hence GNP seems to be better measure of the standard of living of Irish people. It excludes globalization effects that are disproportionately impacting the measurement of the size of the Irish economy (CSO Ireland 2018).

The high dynamics of growth in the 1990s was interrelated with the remarkable performance of the labor market. Unemployment rate fell from the peak of 17% in the late 1980s to 4% in 2001. There was the rapid decrease in the unemployment in the period of accelerated growth. Situation deteriorated during the crisis. Unemployment rate was again higher than in the EU on average between 2009 and 2015. With the remarkable rebuilding after the crisis unemployment rate decreased in Ireland much more than in EU-15 on average and was lower than EU-15 average only in last 2 years (Fig. 5.2).

Ireland is characterized by relatively small population. That is why the changes in the emigration and immigration rates are mutually interrelated and sensitive to the economic changes. The highest net emigration rate of the 1980s was replaced by what is now the highest net immigration rate in the EU. Net migration reached a depression point in 1989 (−44 thousands). From the late 1990s, Ireland witnessed for the first time in its modern history the growth of population—residents who have no previous links with the country (Clinch et al. 2002). Net migration increased to 67 thousands before crisis, but started to decrease after the crisis (Statistical Yearbook of Ireland 2016). The important issue, from the point of view of labor market conditions, may be relatively high share of population at the age less than 15 years and relatively low share of productive age (15–64). These conditions of the labor market in the face of dynamic growth in the 1990s resulted in low unemployment. The shortage of workers was the reason of growing immigration. Before the crisis with the weakened demand for work, many immigrants decided to come back to home countries, but with the adverse of economic growth they can come back.

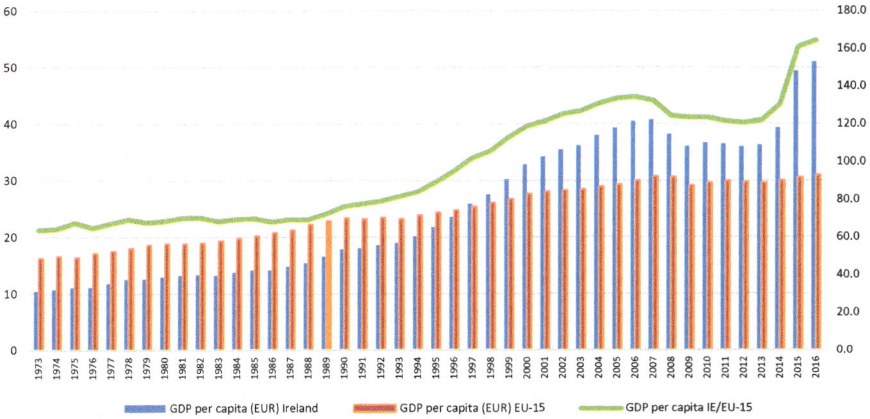

Fig. 5.3 GDP per capita in Ireland and in EU (EU-15 average; left axis) and GDP per capita in IE as a percentage of EU-15 average (GDP per capita EU-15 = 100%; right axis) (own preparation on the basis of Eurostat)

As the result of accelerated growth of GDP, the significant changes were also observed in the structure of production. There was a sharp decrease in the share of value added created in agricultural sector (from 18% in 1973 to 1% in 2016), relatively steady level of the value added created in industrial sector (from 34% in 1973 to 39% in 2016), and significant increase in the share of value added created in services sector (from 48% in 1973 to 60% in 2016) (World Bank Database 2018).

Rapid growth of GDP per person moved Ireland up the EU living standards. Nevertheless, the process of catching up was delayed. The GDP per capita in Ireland as a percentage of EU-15 average was 64% in 1973 and 77% in 1991 (Fig. 5.3). Having endured a standard of living that was only two-thirds of the EU average for almost 20 years after joining the EU, Ireland exceeded the European average in terms of the GDP per person in 1997 and was more than 160% in 2016. Paradoxically the gap between the level of development of IE and EU-15 on average increased. Ireland changed its position from the backward country to modern economy.

5.3 The Role of State in the Process of Economic Growth of Ireland

Ireland represents an interesting application for the investigation of the nature of state's role in economic growth. The role of state is considered as the fundamental factor in many frameworks: not only stabilization policy, but also creating social partnership model, creating the economic environment facilitating to run a business in Ireland, adequate use of the EU funds, selective industrial policy are important issues.

5.3.1 Stabilization Policy

The evaluation of the role of stabilization policy differs across authors. Not only the fiscal or monetary reforms should be taken into consideration but also context in which the reforms took place is undoubtedly an important issue (Honohan 1999).

The main reasons of Ireland's delayed catching up process are connected with the continuation of protectionist trade policies and irresponsible fiscal experimentation. Ireland in the mid-1980s was characterized by prolonged recession, low living standards, a negative trade balance, high unemployment of over 15%, and a hostile industrial relations condition. The positive reversal is connected with actions undertaken by the government inter alia by stabilization policy. Not only fiscal adjustment but also monetary.

First attempts of solving these problems were connected with increasing taxes, but resulted in the decrease of consumption and investment and in deterioration of the public debt to GDP ratio (112% in 1986; because of the mentioned above differences between GDP and GNP levels, debt to GNP ratio was 130% in 1987).

In 1987, political consensus stabilized the fiscal policy through a rapid cutback in government expenditures and anti-inflationary policy. Government expenditures decreased from the level of 51% GDP to 42% GDP in 1990 while budget deficit decreased from the level of −8.5% GDP to −2.7% GDP in 1990. In comparison to the period before fiscal consolidation it was on average −10% GDP (Leddin and Walsh 1997). This action allowed promised reductions in taxation and provided trade unions from wage restraint. As a result, consumption increased more than predicted. This effect was called expansionary fiscal contraction and was the reason of the broad research under the non-Keynesian effects of fiscal policy (Giavazzi and Pagano 1990; Barry and Deveraux 2003). In the 1990s mostly expansionary fiscal policy was set. The decrease in tax rates and the improvement in public finances (there were the budget surpluses observed from 1996 to 2007) created the vision of stable economy with the public debt at the level about 30% of GDP (a half of the average EU-15 level).

Liberalization of the monetary policy was undoubtedly the factor of the accelerated growth in the 1990s. The expansionary fiscal and monetary instruments were coordinated that's why the inflation rate during the period of high growth was lower than in EU-15 on average. Before the fiscal contraction, in the 1970s and 1980s, the average inflation rate was more than 9%, more than thc European average. It was also interrelated with relatively low costs of production connected with the moderate wages increase constituted in the partnership model (Kelly and Everett 2014; O'Hagan and Newman 2005). Moreover, the coincidence of stabilization program of the 1987–1989, the increase in the FDI inflow, and increase in the EU structural funds inflow occurred (Honohan 1999). However, in the period of a decade before the financial crisis (1998–2007) inflation rate was higher than in Euro area by 1 p.p. yearly on average. In the 4 years after adoption of EUR inflation rate in Ireland was two times higher than in European Monetary Union (EMU). Negative real interest rates and rapid GDP growth deteriorated the inflation before the crisis.

The facts of decrease in nominal short-term interest rates and negative real interest rates in the decade before the crisis were undoubtedly the reasons of the boom on the real estate market in Ireland. Easy access to get a credit, growing GDP per capita, and inflow of immigrants were the reasons of the dramatic increase in the demand for real estate and their prices especially in Dublin. The decrease in the real estate prices after 2008 and restrictive fiscal policy had the deflationary impact in 2009–2010 which helped to rebuild the competitiveness after crisis. The average inflation rate was 0.05% in the period 2009–2016 (Eurostat 2018).

Expansionary monetary policy conducted in the 1990s and the expansionary monetary policy set under the auspicious of European Central Bank caused that the banking system before 2008 was strongly dependent on the situation on foreign markets. Special attention should be paid to two issues: very low interest rates and the structure of assets in commercial banks. During the decade preceding the economic crisis, real interest rates in Ireland was negative. In this situation, loans granted to the private sector increased to over 200% of GDP at the end of 2008, almost twice as much as the average in the European Union (Honohan 2009). The ease of obtaining loans and low interest rates contributed to the boom in the real estate market in Ireland. The size of loans granted by banks in Ireland increased by 30% annually in 2004–2006 compared to an 8% annual increase on average in the Eurozone countries in the same period. One of the consequences was the dependence of the financial system on the domestic real estate market and the construction sector on the assets side, while on the liabilities side it was dependent on the European interbank lending markets (Kelly 2009).

In the face of the deep crisis and deteriorating economic situation in Ireland at the end of 2010, the Irish government accepted aid from the European Union and the International Monetary Fund in the amount of EUR 85 billion. However, this assistance was granted on many severe conditions (The National Recovery Plan 2010). Ireland undertook the reforms and gave the money back in 2013. Even though there was a dramatic increase in the public debt to GDP ratio in a few years of the crisis (a peak in 2013 was equal to 119% GDP). The effective economics policy enabled to decrease the ratio of the level of public debt to 72% of GDP, lower than EU average, in 2016.

5.3.2 Social Partnership Model

Social partnership model has a high contribution to an economic success of Ireland. All the severe reforms were conducted in the social consensus between employers, workers, and government. The first agreement was signed in 1987 in the answer to the fiscal imbalances problems and was called the Programme for National Recovery. It was the first of 3-year agreements and instituted the partnership approach. The first pact was so important not only because more moderate wage settlements were negotiated but also because the trade union's position was weakened. Another important issue is the increase in the awareness and understanding of the economic crisis and appropriate response to it (Honohan 1999).

In 2001, the formula of the agreement was transformed into the National Centre for Partnership and Performance, which works actively with all firms, educational institutions, and economic and advisory bodies to provide the support for organizational change (O'Higgins 2002). The most important partners are two interest groups such as the Irish Congress of Trade Unions (ICTU) and the Irish Business and Employers' Confederation (IBEC).

The negotiations were undertaken before each National Development Plan was signed. The realization of each pact enabled the severe fiscal contractions with social consensus because of high level of trust to governmental decision. That's why undertaking politically difficult reforms to decline the deficit allowed Ireland to regain its macroeconomic stability and competitiveness in the 1990s (OECD 2001).

The role of pacts was particularly important during the overcoming the economic difficulties in the 1980s. The present importance is much lower however (Hogan and Timoney 2017; O'Donell 2001). Nevertheless, social consensus and high level of trust achieved as result of the partnership model was important informal institution which undoubtedly improved the conditions of growth. Trust also affects political stability while limiting the uncertainty of entities in the economy. All these factors are not without significance for transaction costs, which may be a significant limitation of economic growth (Coase 1960).

5.3.3 Institutional Perspective

The institutions (formal—written rules and informal—i.e., trust, social consensus) can be understood as constraints imposed on human interaction and therefore shaped the way in which society and the economy works. In this meaning they are fundamental conditions of economic growth (North 2002). The institutional system in Ireland was very conducive to dynamic investment and supported business decisions to set up a company there. Low corporation tax and the low tax wedge were among the most important factors that helped to create incentives to foreign investors. The examples of liberalization and deregulation include: decrease in the number of permits, procedures to run a business, quality of the jurisdictional system guaranteeing respect of contracts and ownership, development of financial markets, and flexibility of the labor market.

A relatively low rating occurs in the area of pay and non-payroll supplements, which is in line with the liberal economic model and still a relatively low tax wedge, which is a factor ensuring competitiveness of this economy (OECD 2014).

According to Doing Business Reports, Ireland is among the top 20 countries in the aspect of easiness of doing business. In 2005 Ireland was 15, in 2007 Ireland was 10 (3 among EU countries), and 17 out of 189 countries for ease of doing business in 2016. In addition to this, the report indicates that Ireland has ranked as five for ease of trading across borders and six for ease of paying taxes and protecting minority investors (Doing Business 2017).

According to the Index of Heritage Foundation, Ireland was characterized by the highest level of freedom among the European Union countries in 2007 and was ranked three in the world. Ireland deteriorated its position during the crisis, but improved in last years. It is ranked six as one of the freest countries in the world. The very high position and the growth of freedom are associated with the improvement in the institutional conditions and are associated with the role of state (Powell 2003).

It is worth noting that Ireland still holds top positions in the aforementioned rankings among the EU countries and countries around the world. Thus, despite the deep crisis experienced by the Irish economy at the end of the first decade of the twenty-first century, Ireland is undoubtedly a country with a very high level of economic development and at the same time attractive for business.

5.3.4 The Role of European Union Funds

The membership of Ireland in the European Union had a positive impact on the dynamics of the country's economic development, also due to the inflow of funds from European Union funds.

The EU transfers were allocated mainly in such infrastructural investment as: roads, ports, airports, telecommunications but they were also concentrated on human resources (training, skill development, and education). Funds from the EU undoubtedly reduced the burden on the state budget, which helped to reduce the deficit.

In total, EUR 59.9 billion came to Ireland throughout the period 1973–2007. Ireland contributed EUR 19.5 billion to the EU budget during this period. Net income totaled EUR 40.4 billion. In the years 1973–1992, revenues from the EEC amounted to EUR 21 billion, expenses to EUR 3.9 billion, and net inflows to EUR 17.1 billion. However, in the years 1993–2007 the EU revenues amounted to EUR 38.8 billion, expenditures EUR 15.6 billion, and net inflows EUR 23.2 billion. The increase in social welfare resulted in increasing payments to the European Union. Moreover, after the very high growth rate of GDP in 2015 Ireland had to pay more to the European budget in the last years.

The inflow of capital from the European Community funds undoubtedly stimulated the development of the Irish economy and had an impact on improving the quality of economic policy in this country. Membership in this community meant participation in the structural policy of the European Union and forced entities responsible for economic policy to take advantageous decisions for development. In addition, the use of funds from the EU funds meant the need to co-finance a number of projects from national funds and planning total expenditure under the National Development Plans (NDP) and the Community Support Framework (Kowalski 2008; European Commission 2007).

Ireland allocated a significant part of the funds received from the European Structural Funds in various programs for the development of human capital.

Appropriate use of funds from the European Social Fund has enabled to create a specialist education system within 20 years, prepared for work in high-tech enterprises (the system of technological institutes and higher education at technical universities). As a result, the role of human capital in Irish growth process was dramatically positive. On the one hand, there was simultaneous effect of supply and demand side on the labor market in Ireland. The increased supply of the educated workers led to the upgrading of employment in foreign owned sectors on the one hand. On the other hand, the ability to attract the FDI led to a demand for more well-educated workers, who would otherwise emigrate (Barry 1999).

In conclusion, Ireland's membership of the European Union undoubtedly influenced the country's economic development in many aspects, but especially in the period of the 1990s. The inflow of money from the European Union funds had a direct demand effect, a short-term impact on the growth of global expenditures. The impact of European Union funds on the Irish economy should also be embedded in the wider economic and social context, because through, for example, the development of transport infrastructure or improving the quality of human capital, it undoubtedly contributed to the creation of appropriate conditions for the development of the economy and long-term impact on development processes.

5.3.5 IDA Ireland: The Role of State Agency

The Irish Industrial Development Agency (IDA), the state agency for attracting and supporting foreign owned companies' inward investment, played a key role in attracting foreign investors, when in the late 1950s Ireland, moving away from protectionist policies, adopted an export-led growth strategy.

IDA's purpose was to actively promote Ireland as a location for FDI, look for investors, offer them comprehensive assistance, good infrastructure, and in return creates a specified number of jobs within the given deadline—grants, training, and even subsidies and tax incentives. These facilities were connected with tax exemptions and breaks of profits connected with the production for export. Exemptions from the tax on the sale of exported goods were to last up to the year 1990. Although foreign companies were not directly prohibited from selling to the domestic Irish market, a high tax of around 50% was imposed on such sales, which effectively promoted exports of the entire production. Till 2003 as a result of European Commission pressures the flat CIT rate was introduced 12.5%. Nevertheless, it was one of the lowest CIT levels across the EU countries (IDA Tax Brochure 2008).

The strategy of attracting FDI was extended, in relation to the earlier period, in 1993, when the Industrial Development Act came into force, which divided the industrial development bodies into three separate units: Forfas, IDA Ireland, and Forbait. Forfas is a separate part of the Department of Entrepreneurship, Trade and Employment, which supervises the industry and scientific development and sets long-term goals for the country's development. Forbait has been transformed into Enterprise Ireland, which offers industrial enterprises a package of economic incentives. By the late 1990s, IDA Ireland began to move away from being a job-creation vehicle to win for Ireland the best in international innovation and investment (O'Higgins 2002).

The facilitating environment and IDA activities resulted in biggest world companies' decision about the location of business in Ireland (i.e., Intel, Dell, Microsoft, IBM, Apple, Google, and Facebook). It should be noted that the IDA's actions would not have been so effective if the simultaneous effective use of EU Structural Funds was made, which was intended, inter alia, to train workers recruited by foreign-invested companies investing in Ireland (Mac Sharry and White 2000).

In conclusion, the results of IDA Ireland activity include: upgraded capabilities within the foreign sector by bringing in more knowledge intensive FDI projects; cooperation between MNCs, local government, colleges, and industry; finding niche areas where Ireland has some competitive advantages like telecommunications software sector and medical device sector.

5.4 FDI: The Main Factor of Growth

5.4.1 FDI Inflows to Ireland

The size of the FDI per capita inflow to Ireland has made Ireland one of the leading countries that attract FDI not only in Europe, but also in the world. However, they were not equal during the analyzed period. It should be noticed that the outward-oriented interventionism saw the economy simultaneously becoming competitive in the market for FDI while losing competitiveness in traditional sectors that were not able to compete between 1960s and the beginning of the 1980s. Through the considerably high inflow of FDI, indigenous industry performed stronger since late 1980s—especially because of achieving cost-competitiveness (electricity, postal, telecommunication services became cheaper after the deregulation) but also because of more restrictive public procurement policies (Barry 1999).

In the period of the accelerated growth, there was an unprecedented increase in international capital flows. In the 1990s, FDI inflows grew on a global scale even 40% per year. In the beginning of the twenty-first century, however, there was a decline in FDI inflow to Ireland. The upward trend has been restored since 2007 and then 2009 continuously (Fig. 5.4). It is worth to notice that FDI inflow was higher to Ireland than to EU-15 countries on average between 1973 and 2016. In the period 1975–1986, it exceeded the EU average at about 20%. During the accelerated growth period of the 1990s, the FDI per capita inflow was more than three times higher than in EU average. But remarkable growth of FDI per capita inflows was observed in the period 2009–2016 (12 times higher than in EU-15 on average).

Ireland has been a destination of choice for FDI for many years. This fact is further substantiated by the FDI Intelligence Report for 2014 which reports that Ireland was the only country within the European top 10 to record a growth in FDI project numbers. The principle source of FDI for Ireland is from the USA, with

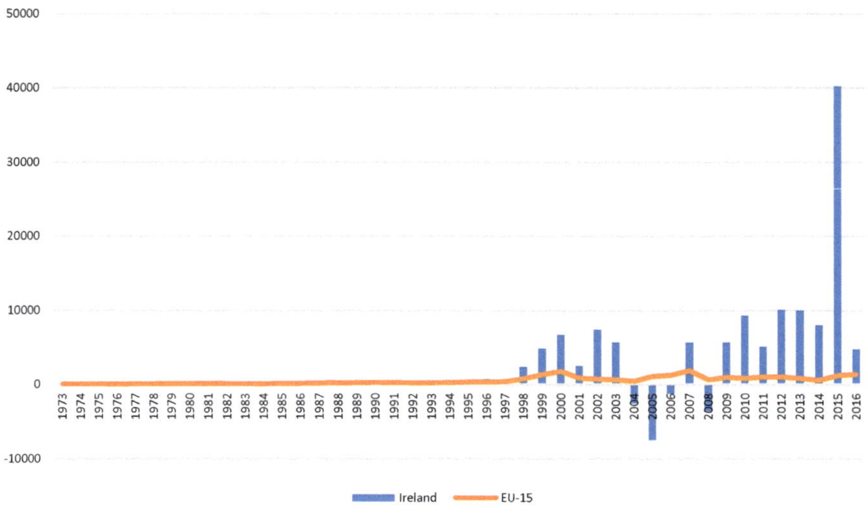

Fig. 5.4 FDI per capita inflows to Ireland and to EU-15 countries in the period between 1973 and 2016 (US Dollars at current prices per capita) (own preparation on the basis of UNCTAD)

investment of more than US$165bn. This level of investment by the USA reflects higher than the total invested in the BRIC (Brazil, Russia, India, and China) combined (FDI Intelligence 2017).

It is worth noting that the inflow of capital in the form of direct foreign investments and, in consequence, the growing number of enterprises with foreign capital in the domestic market, did not mean simultaneous progress and did not guarantee acceleration of the growth rate in the first decade after accession to the European Community. Only in the second decade of Ireland's membership, together with the development of the use of EEC structural funds and deep economic reforms, the influence of FDI undoubtedly contributed to the improvement of Ireland's economic situation. This improvement has become an accelerator for the further inflow of FDI. Nevertheless, the huge scale of the inflow and the targeted sectoral allocation of FDI supported by the Irish government's economic policy have made this factor play a huge role in the economic development of this country.

Ireland is the most internationalized country in the world after China and in Europe ranks first as the country receiving the most FDI. Its internationalization index was calculated at 63.7%, which in comparison with the majority of countries in the world, which scored less than 30%, proved the success in attracting the FDI to this country (WIR 2005). Ireland's particularly high activity in international capital flows also indicates the values of the FDI intensity index published by Eurostat. The FDI intensity index is defined as a measure of the country's activity as part of its integration with the international economy. This ratio is calculated as the ratio of the average inflow and outflow of FDI and GDP and expressed in %. Data have been available for Ireland since 1998. During the decade preceding the economic crisis, the intensity of FDI in Ireland was on average more than three times higher than the average intensity in the EU-15 countries based on Eurostat data.

Ireland's activity in the area of FDI measured with the above indicator during the crisis exceeded the average investment activity in the European Union countries several times. In the years of economic crisis, with the exception of 2008, the intensity of FDI in Ireland increased, in contrast to the downward trend in most EU countries. On average, during the crisis it exceeded the triple average value of FDI for EU-15 countries. In 2009, the intensity of FDI in Ireland was five times higher than on average in the EU-15 countries, and in 2010 this ratio was already nine times the average of the EU-15 countries (Eurostat 2018).

After the economic crisis, the Irish government has taken action to attract foreign investors again. The reason of the increase in the inflow of FDI during the financial crisis of the 2008 and later is associated with maintaining the CIT rate at 12.5%. It was not easy to Irish government because of the European Commission prosecution but was a part of a strategy of attracting FDI. That's why Ireland is still perceived as an interesting place for international corporations to locate production. This applies in particular to modern, knowledge-based departments in the economy, such as the pharmaceutical, IT, and financial services departments. Irish economy was especially beneficiary of the inflow in the computer and information services sector, which is colloquially referred to as *Dublin's Silicon Docks* (Brazys and Regan 2018). Here once again the IDA Ireland played a significant role in shaping the allocative structure of the FDI activity which was located in this special area after 2002 with Google at the beginning. After 2008, 98% of all FDI IDA activity was located in the following sectors: ICT, professional, scientific and technical activities, manufacturing, financial, and insurance. Moreover, 85% of IDA sponsored projects were high-tech production of pharmaceutical and medical equipment and computers and electrical equipment (IDA 2016).

To sum up strategy beyond the state connected with tax competition seems to be a core part of Irish recovery especially through the success in attracting FDI to high-tech service sector.

5.4.2 *Allocative Structure of FDI*

Incoming FDI was primarily located in the high technology (computer and electronic services), pharmaceutical and financial services sections. The above-mentioned sections of the economy were mainly filled by FDI from the United States. The inflow of FDI to these sections of the economy has changed the structure of the Irish industrial sector and services and stimulated economic growth. Although the inflow of FDI (most of it from the USA) has made an enormous contribution to the economy in terms of employment, export, and GDP growth, the other side has been the growing dependency on a relatively narrow production. MNCs dominated three sectors: chemicals, computers and instrument engineering and electrical engineering (Clinch et al. 2002).

American firms chose location in Ireland because of inter alia direct access to the European labor market (Brazys and Regan 2018). As a result of the huge scale of capital flows between these countries, the United States has become one of Ireland's most important trading partners. Since 1997, the balance of payments between these countries is characterized by a surplus in favor of Ireland. This shows a large, relative to the EU, dependence of Ireland's economy on the US economy. Besides, very important effect of FDI flowing to Ireland from the United States was the increase in exports of high-tech goods. Ireland has already achieved the highest in the EU index of export specialization. In 1993–2007, approximately 5% of all US FDI inflows to the European Union were reported to Ireland on average. At the same time, these investments were very pro-exported. The small Irish market was not able to guarantee the demand for the goods offered, which meant that 85% of the production of enterprises with foreign capital was exported (Barry and Bradley 1997).

In addition, it is worth noting that due to the accurate sector allocation of FDI in Ireland, the share of value added by high-technology sectors dominated by enterprises with foreign capital in GDP is much higher in Ireland than in other European countries and in the United States. The high-technology sector is highly export-oriented and enjoys higher export shares and levels of productivity—computed as net output per head—compared to indigenous Irish industry (Doyle 2001).

However, the boom was not a simple mirage caused by the foreign owned sector's behavior (like) transfer-pricing, but was connected with a dramatic job creation (Barry 1999). Unlike to other EU countries manufacturing sector employment (both indigenous and foreign owned) rose in Ireland during the 1990s, due to achieving competitiveness in internationally traded sectors.

The inflows of FDI resulted in the dramatic increase in the employment, especially in the mentioned sectors. The role of foreign sector in employment in Ireland is particularly important in Ireland because it is more than two times higher in Ireland than in EU-15 on average both in manufacturing and services. The employment in foreign owned companies has been increasing after the crisis. Cumulated increase in last 4 years was 26%. The employment in foreign owned companies reached 210,443, with the tendency to increase the share of foreign owned companies in services and decrease in manufacturing.

Considering above factors, the increase in FDI inflow and the increase in employment in enterprises with foreign capital after 2009, it can be concluded that even though they made Irish economy vulnerable to economic crisis, they were not a significant channel for the transmission of the crisis to Ireland. In this context, the dependence of the Irish economy on FDI was even anti-crisis and helped to rebuild the economy.

5.5 The Role of Trade in Economic Growth in Ireland

The increased openness of the Irish economy resulted not only in increased flows of FDI, but also the development of foreign trade in Ireland. What is more, the export-oriented inflow of FDI resulted from the actions of the Irish government's economic policy. Thus, the growth of exports and imports was the result of growth, but without any doubt it was also a factor of growth in Ireland (Szczepaniak 2015).

The role of trade was especially significant in Ireland's economic success in the 1990s, mostly in the high-tech hardware and software information technology, engineering, and pharmaceutical growth. Foreign owned firms accounted for 95% of export growth, comprising three-quarters of total goods export. Moreover, 70% of all industrial exports are accounted for by US companies.

Turnover of foreign trade increased dramatically throughout the analyzed period. In 1973 trade volume accounted for 75% GDP, between 1974 and 1992 exports and imports totaled on average 101% GDP, during the 1990s trade volume reached 140% GDP on average, reached a peak of 175% GDP in 2001, than before the crisis in 2007 it dropped to 153% GDP. Trade volume increased rapidly between 2013 and 2016 from the level of 193% GDP to 221% GDP. In addition, throughout the analyzed period, foreign trade in relation to GDP was higher in Ireland than in the EU on average. The phenomena described here confirm the relatively high dependence of Ireland's economy on foreign trade. Moreover, the share of foreign trade in GDP and, at the same time, a relatively high growth rate of GDP implies that the development of foreign trade was an accelerator of Ireland's economic development. The above statement is also reflected in the changes in the geographical structure of foreign trade, especially in the growing share of trade with the United States, with the greatest inflow of FDI.

The openness of the Irish economy and its dependence on foreign trade are evidenced not only by the volume of exports and imports, or together the growing volumes of foreign trade, but above all their share in GDP. Exports in relation to GDP grew in the entire analyzed period from 34% of GDP in 1973 to 121% of GDP in 2016. The share of imports in GDP increased from 41% of GDP in 1973 to 100% of GDP in 2016. The phenomena described here confirm the relatively high dependence of Ireland's economy on foreign trade (Fig. 5.5).

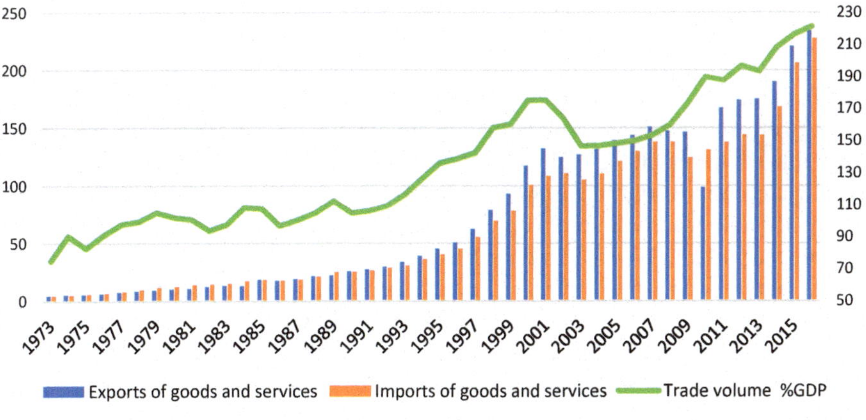

Fig. 5.5 Exports and imports (bln EUR), trade volume (%GDP) in Ireland in the period between 1973 and 2016 (own preparation on the base of AMECO database, World Bank database)

In 1973, the balance of payments was negative. Net exports as % of GDP at the time of Ireland's accession to the EU (EC at first) were −7% of GDP. Due to the processes described above taking place both due to the size and dynamics of foreign trade, from the mid-1980s the balance of payments began to be positive. It is worth notice that the accession of Ireland to the EU did not affect the automatic improvement of the trade balance. Although the foreign trade turnover grew at first, the balance of payments was negative until 1984. It was not until the 1990s that the surplus of exports over imports grew the fastest. In addition, net exports grew in the period 1991–2000 at an average annual rate of 22%, almost 3 times faster than GDP (8% pa in the same period). What is more, during the crisis, Ireland's foreign trade rate reflected by net exports as % of GDP was much higher than the average for EU countries, which on average in the EU-15 was 1% of GDP. In addition, higher export dynamics than imports resulted in the improvement of the foreign trade balance after 2008.

The above-described processes occurring in foreign trade, both in terms of volume and dynamics of both exports and imports as well as the balance of payments, indicate a significant opening of the economy and a significant importance of trade with foreign countries in the process of economic development of this country. What is more, the share of trade in GDP higher than in the European Union countries indicates that foreign trade was a factor and at the same time an accelerator of the development processes of the entire Irish economy. On the other hand, the growing importance of foreign trade was a manifestation of the development processes of the Irish economy, particularly through the growing production of enterprises with foreign capital intended for export. The above statement is also reflected in the changes in the geographical and trade structure of foreign trade, especially in the growing share of trade with the United States, from which the most FDI flowed.

5.6 Conclusions

The Irish miracle was the result of a number of interacting factors between each the synergy effect existed. Most important complimentary factors identified included: a favorable environment for FDI and high inflow of pro-export FDI as a result, state's stabilization and institutional policy, IDA's promotion of Ireland as an industrial location, stable macroeconomic environment achieved in social partnership model, and properly used EU transfers for infrastructure and training.

The analysis confirmed that the factors that determined the economic boom of the Irish economy were the simultaneous increase in the internationalization of the economy (inflow of FDI, increase in foreign trade) and state policy favorable to development processes. The export-oriented nature of FDI was fundamental to the

Irish success in economic growth. It stemmed from a series of deliberate state's actions, among which one should indicate the activities of government institutions, such as the Irish Industrial Development Agency in attracting FDI, tax incentives and tax exemptions for the production of enterprises with foreign capital. No less important was the use of EU funds adapted to development purposes. In addition, the transformation that took place in the economy during the 1990s took place under the social agreement of the government and representatives of employers and employees. The political stability achieved in this way allowed to create a climate of foreign investors' trust in the model of Irish government policy, what supported the FDI inflow to Ireland. In addition, FDI flows were of great importance to Ireland not only due to the expansion of the capital base but also caused the transfer of technologies, which undoubtedly helped in the modernization of the economy.

The example of Ireland shows that rapid economic development also raises risks. The economic policy model which was successful in accelerating the growth in the 1990s made the Irish economy vulnerable to turmoil in the international financial markets during the crisis in 2008. What is important, the inability to stabilize the economy through the monetary policy after joining the EMU in 1999 was also the factor that influenced the Irish economy. Although it is commonly pointed out that the high dependence of Ireland's economy on the inflow of foreign capital was the reason for the crisis's entry into the economy, the analysis of foreign owned sector and trade changes paradoxically showed that this characteristic structure of the economy helped to overcome the crisis. During the crisis foreign investors were well supported by institutional determinants like inter alia maintaining the low CIT rate, solid protection of property rights, and independent judiciary that enforced the rule of law. Regulatory process was very conducive to dynamic investment and supported business decisions that enhanced productivity not only during the period of accelerated growth after the crisis. Commitment to open-market policies that facilitated global trade and investment flow helped the Irish economy to overcome the crisis once again. In addition, after the crisis, the FDI inflow, production exports to the United States, and the FDI intensity index improved. Moreover, Irish plan was to facilitate the FDI connected with high-tech production. The success in attracting FDI inflow to the computer and information services sector was called *Dublin's Silicon Docks*.

In conclusion, the dynamics of growth changed over the period 1973–2016. Ireland was able to overcome two crises and achieved two periods of accelerated growth. These phenomena were caused by similar factors that worked simultaneously. Among the most important appropriate state policy reform (stabilization, structural, institutional) and success in attracting FDI to selected sectors were identified. Nevertheless during the recovery after financial crisis partnership model and the inflow of European Structural Funds played a minor importance.

References

Barry F (1999) Understanding Ireland's economic growth. Macmillan, London
Barry F (2004) Export platform FDI: the Irish experience. The EIB papers 9(2) European Investment Bank, Luxembourg
Barry F, Bradley J (1997) FDI and trade: the Irish host-country experience. Econ J 107 (445):1798–1811
Barry F, Deveraux MB (2003) Expansionary fiscal contraction: a theoretical exploration. J Macroecon 25:1–23
Brazys S, Regan A (2018) Celtic phoenix or leprechaun economics? The politics of and FDI-led growth model in Europe. New Polit Econ 23(2):223–238
Central Statistics Office in Ireland (2016) Statistical yearbook of Ireland 2016
Central Statistics Office in Ireland (2018) Modified GNI. https://www.cso.ie/px/pxeirestat/Statire/SelectVarVal/Define.asp?maintable=N1624&PLanguage=0. Accessed 24 June 2018
Clinch P, Convery F, Walsh B (2002) After the Celtic Tiger. The O'Brien Press, Dublin
Coase R (1960) The problem of social cost. J Law Econ 3:1–44
Doyle E (2001) Export-output causality and the role of exports in Irish growth: 1950–1997. Int Econ J 15:31–54
European Commission (2007) Fourth progress report on economic and social cohesion. Brussels
Eurostat database. Accessed June 2018
FDI Intelligence (2017) https://www.fdiintelligence.com/Special-Reports/2017. Accessed 23 June 2018
Fountas S (2000) Some evidence on the export-led growth hypothesis for Ireland. Appl Econ Lett 7 (4):211–214
Giavazzi F, Pagano M (1990) Can severe fiscal contractions be expansionary? Tales of two small european countries. NBER Macroecon Annu 5:75–122
Hogan J, Timoney N (2017) A discursive institutionalist approach to understanding the changes to the Irish Social Partnership Policy after 2008. J Stat Soc Inquiry Soc Ireland 45(1):67–92
Honohan P (1999) Fiscal adjustment and disinflation in Ireland: setting the macro basis of economic recovery and expansion. In: Barry F (ed) Understanding Ireland's economic growth. Macmillan, New York
Honohan P (2009) Resolving Ireland's banking crisis. Econ Soc Rev 40(2):207–231
Iamsiraroj S (2016) The foreign direct investment—economic growth nexus. Int Rev Econ Finan 42 (C):116–133
IDA Ireland Annual Report (2016) www.idaireland.ie. Accessed 2 July 2018
IDA Tax Brochure (2008) www.idaireland.ie. Accessed 2 Feb 2010
Kelly M (2009) The Irish credit bubble. Working paper no. 09/32. School of Economics, University College, Dublin
Kelly J, Everett M (2004) Financial liberalization and economic growth in Ireland. Quarterly Bulletin Autumn, National Bank in Ireland
Kirby P (2002) The Celtic Tiger in distress. Growth with inequality in Ireland. Palgrave, New York
Kowalski AM (2008) Polityka regionalna Unii Europejskiej w Irlandii i Wielkiej Brytanii w latach 1989–2006. Monografie i Opracowania 550. Szkoła Główna Handlowa, Warsaw
Krugman P (2017) Leprechaun economics. https://twitter.com/paulkrugman/status/752841032870551155. Accessed 11 Mar 2018
Leddin A, Walsh B (1997) Economic stabilization, recovery and growth: Ireland 1979–1996. Working paper series 1997. Department of Economics, University College, Dublin
Mac Sharry R, White PA (2000) The making of the Celtic Tiger. The inside story of Ireland's boom economy. Mercier Press, Dublin
North DC (2002) Understanding economic change and economic growth. Leon Koźmiński Academy of Entrepreneurship and Management, Warsaw
O'Donnell R (2001) The future of social partnership in Ireland. Discussion paper prepared for the National Competitiveness Council

O'Grada C (1997) A rocky road. The Irish Economy since the 1920s. Manchester University Press, Manchester
O'Hagan C, Newman C (2005) The economy of Ireland. National and sectoral policy issues. Gill & Macmillan, Dublin
O'Higgins E (2002) Government and the creation of the Celtic Tiger: can management maintain the momentum? Acad Manag Exec 16(3):104–120
OECD (2001) Regulatory reform in Ireland, Paris
OECD (2014) Taxing wages
Powell B (2003) Economic freedom and growth: the case of the Celtic Tiger. Cato J 22(3):431–448
Szczepaniak M (2015) Irlandia. Przemiany gospodarcze. CeDeWu, Warszawa
The National Recovery Plan 2011–2014 (2010) Department of Finance. Dublin, Ireland
World Bank (2017) Doing Business Equal Opportunity for All
World Bank (2018) https://data.worldbank.org. Accessed 20 June 2018
World Investment Report (2005) Transnational corporations and the internationalization of R&D. United Nations, New York

Chapter 6
Determinants of Economic Growth in Israel

Yochanan Shachmurove

Abstract Israel, a small country in Asia, is the start-up nation, a technology hub, the second largest start-up ecosystem in the world, a leader in innovation and cutting-edge technologies. What are the key components of the dynamic innovation culture that have made the state of Israel one of the most important entrepreneurial and technology-driven economies in the world? This chapter analyzes the basis of this miracle. It describes the huge population increase due mainly to immigration, large injections of capital, technological progress and transition from basic production of growing citrus and polishing diamonds, to current state of the art technologies.

6.1 Introduction

This chapter provides some explanations for Israel's remarkable economic growth over the past 70 years, since independence. Israel is a small country, surrounded by countries, which have not succeeded in achieving significant economic development, yet persist lunched, time and again, full-scale attack, trying to destroy, indeed to annihilate it. In May 1948, when Israel became independent, there were some 600,000 Jews in the country. By the time the battles subsided, towards the end of that year, 110,000 immigrants had arrived, 6,000 Jews had been killed in the war, and the stabilizing borders contained about 100,000 Arabs. The total population was 800–850,000. Currently, from missile-defense systems to drone technologies, from satellites to cyber warfare, Israel is a world leader in the lucrative field of military technology, as well as other innovative fields. From its inception, the history of Israel is the story of David and Goliath.

Even before its independence, Israel possesses the institutions necessary for an orderly running of a country (Williamson 1985). These institutions include the labor union as both representing the workers and the largest employer, the Jewish National

Y. Shachmurove (✉)
Department of Economics, The Faculty of Economic Sciences and Management, Nicolaus Copernicus University, Toruń, Poland

The City College and the Graduate Center, The City University of New York, New York, USA
e-mail: yshachmurove@ccny.cuny.edu

M. Osińska (ed.), *Economic Miracles in the European Economies*,
https://doi.org/10.1007/978-3-030-05606-3_6

Fund responsible for acquiring land, the Jewish Agency responsible to help the immigrants, the financial institutions, the judicial system, the political parties, the military units, all were in place before the creation of the State. Yet, Israel's economy was underdeveloped, with Purchasing Power Parity Gross Domestic Product (GDP) Per Capita of only 4,825 International Dollars, for the year 1950, expressed in 2005 prices. The year 1950 is the first year such data exist. The physical infrastructure and economic activity concentrated in a few simple industries (agriculture, diamonds, light manufacturing). At the same time, the county urgently needed infrastructure development, including massive absorption of immigrants, both Holocaust survivors and migrants/refugees from Muslim countries.

With the exception of about a dozen years following the 1973 trauma of the Yom Kippur War and the first oil crisis when a combination of defense and energy costs as well as macroeconomic mismanagement culminated in 5 years of triple digit inflation, Israel's development in the seven decades since independence has been truly remarkable. From the economic backwater of the 1950s, marked by massive, perhaps understandable, government intervention in the economy, based on Socialist ideology inherited from the early Zionist leaders who grew up in pre-Soviet Russia, Israel today is a highly advanced mixed economy, with per capita income of approximately $40,000, placing it in the middle of the world's upper income countries. Moreover, it is a hotbed of technological innovation, having become a country of innovators, inventors, entrepreneurs, visionaries, and pioneers. The country is poor in natural resources, yet blessed by human resources. Innovation is one of the most valuable resources for the State of Israel, serving as a national asset crucial to economic prosperity. One may claim that creativity is embedded in the "DNA" of the Israeli culture and way of life. The Israelis have turned their well-known thinking outside the box and chutzpah to innovation and creativity in defending and prospering themselves.

This chapter details the factors that are the basis of this miracle. It describes the huge population increase due mainly to immigration, large injections of capital, technological progress and transition from basic production (local infrastructure, basic industries such as citrus and diamonds), to current cutting-edge technology.

Israel currently has the greatest concentration of high-tech start-up companies anywhere outside of the Silicon Valley in the United States (USA). High-tech industry now accounts for more than 54% of Israel's industrial exports, and over 26% of the country's exports. In Israel, 135 out of every 10,000 workers are scientists and engineers, compared to the United States (second place), where 85 out of every 10,000 workers are so employed. Moreover, in Israel, 9 out of every 1,000 workers are engaged in Research and Development (R&D), nearly double the rate of the USA and Japan.

Israel has achieved worldwide recognition for pioneering fields such as regenerative medicine and stem cell research, tissue engineering, aerospace, microelectronics, communications, computer science, superconductivity, fiber optics, optoelectronics, quantum engineering, water resource development and management, catalysis, nanotechnology, biotechnology, the life sciences, and more. What are the key components of the dynamic innovation culture that have made the state of

Israel one of the most important entrepreneurial and technology-driven economies in the world?

Israel is the start-up nation (Gordis 2017; Katz and Bohbot 2017; Jorisch 2018; Senor and Singer 2011; Wesfeld 2015; Siegel 2017), the miracle place of innovation. Since the 1980s, over 250 Israeli companies have had an initial public offering on the NASDAQ. As of August 2017, one Israeli company is listed on the NASDAQ-100 index: Check Point Software. As of April 22, 2018, 107 Israeli companies are listed on Wall Street stock exchanges, i.e., the NASDAQ, NYSE, and AMEX. Ninety-five of these companies are registered on the NASDAQ, with total capitalization of more than 88 billion dollars.[1] The Israeli companies concentrate in the following sectors: Basic Industries, Capital Goods, Consumer Durables, Consumer Non-Durables, Consumer Services, Finance, Health C are, Public Utilities, and the High-Technology sector.

Many of these companies either are founded by or are led by graduates of the Technion – Israel Institute of Technology. An institution founded in 1912, 36 years before the founding of the state of Israel. The Technion, Israel's first university, consistently ranked among the world's top science and technology research universities. It has been the primary source of technological manpower and the largest comprehensive academic center for advanced science and technology education, as well as applied research. Frenkel et al. (2012) estimate that the annual output of only the Technion graduates in high-tech, communications, and research and development exceeds $20 billion, a figure that is greater than the gross domestic product of 85 countries.

Israel has brought to the world a few innovations such as smart drip and micro-irrigation, cherry tomato, electric car, the Disk-on-Key, geothermal power plants, clean geothermal power, solar windows, a device to prevent crib death, and so on. For more innovations made in Israel, the reader is referred to: https://www.israel21c.org/israels-top-45-greatest-inventions-of-all-time-2/.

As mentioned, currently, Israel is the second largest start-up ecosystem in the world, after Silicon Valley. Almost every multinational tech firms have Research and Development centers in Israel. These include Intel, IBM, Microsoft, Google, Facebook, and Apple. Many of these multinational corporations have also acquired Israeli start-ups.

Israel strives itself to form strategic partnerships between its institutions of higher education and industry, particularly with multinational corporations, in a wide range of high-tech fields including pharmaceuticals, information and communications technologies (ICT), biomedical engineering, energy, defense, and environmental protection. Multinational corporations have established labs or research centers on or near Israeli university campuses in order to benefit from proximity to its students (e.g., Microsoft, *Hewlett Packard*, and Intel to name a few). Collaboration with

[1]See: https://www.nasdaq.com/screening/companies-by-region.aspx?region=Middle+East&country=Israel

industry is also interweaved with educational programs—including research grants and internships for students.

Before turning to the challenging question of the possible causes of the Israeli economic development, Sect. 6.2 provides a brief description of the Israeli economy since 1990. Section 6.3 looks at the general picture as for the causes for the development of the economy. Sections 6.4 and 6.5 devolve more deeply into the real and monetary aspects of the sources of economic growth. Section 6.4 reports on the real sector and the labor market in Israel. Section 6.5 presents the monetary and financial dominants that have led to the economic growth. Section 6.6 describes the future challenges facing the Israel economy. Section 6.7 briefly concludes.

6.2 Description of the Israel Economy

This section provides a brief description of the Israeli economy. Figure 6.1 presents the Israeli GDP in constant 2010 US$. The figure vividly shows the progress the small country of Israel has achieved in a relatively short period.

Figure 6.2 shows GDP growth in annual percent. The figure points to the fact that Israel has never had a recession as usually defines. Moreover, despite of many wars, the Israeli economy rebounded quickly. Observe, for example, the GDP growth rate following the Six Day War that reached above 16%. An important feature of the Israeli economy, which is relevant for this paper, is the fact that the 2000–2002 Information Technology (IT) bubble affected the Israeli economy more than the financial crisis of 2007–2008. The drop in GDP growth was twice as big in 2000–2002 versus 2007–2008.

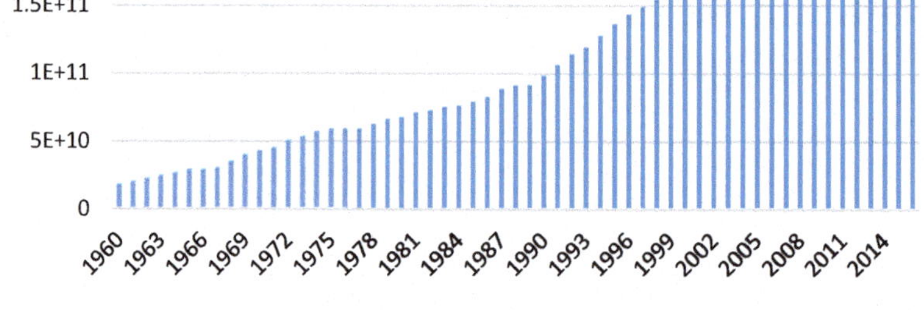

Fig. 6.1 Israel gross domestic product (Constant 2010 US Dollar) (http://www.cbs.gov.il/ts/)

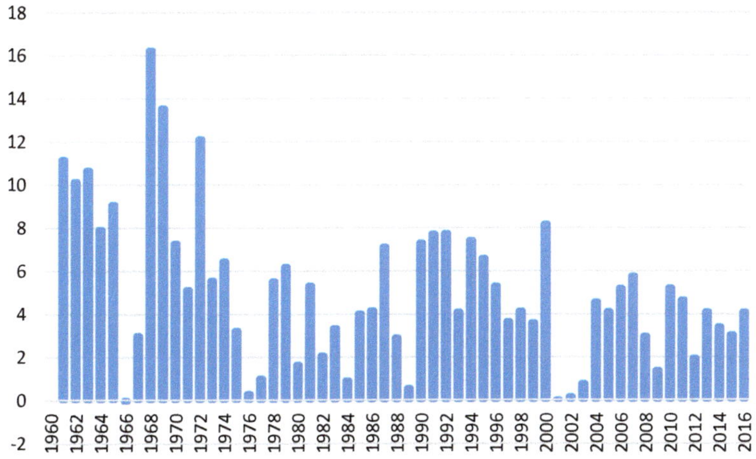

Fig. 6.2 Israel GDP growth rate in 1960–2016 [annual %] (http://www.cbs.gov.il/ts/)

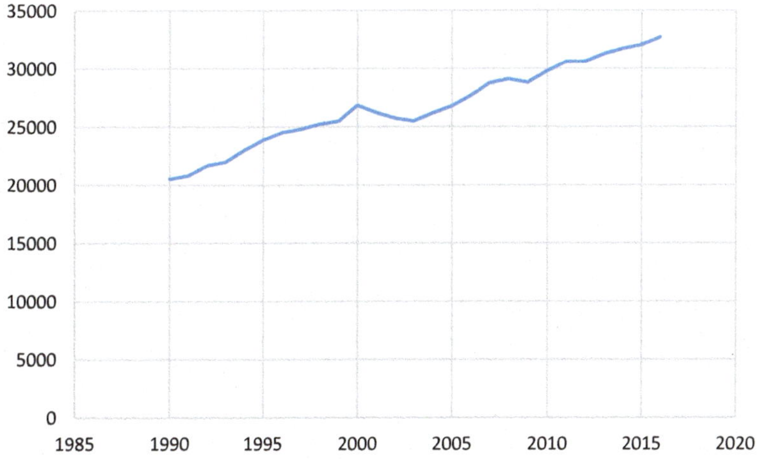

Fig. 6.3 Israel GDP per capita PPP (Constant 2011 International $) (http://www.cbs.gov.il/ts/)

Figure 6.3 shows the GDP per capita in constant 2011 international dollar. It shows, in general, an upward increase from 20,000 in 1990 to almost 36,000 international dollar in 2016.

Next, Fig. 6.4 below presents GDP per person employed expressed in constant 2011 Purchasing power Parity (PPP) dollars. From about 60,000 in 1990, reaching above 76,000 in 2016. Again, one observes constant increase in return to labor input, which points out that the capital per laborer and the technological innovations lead to such an increase.

Table 6.1 presents some key macroeconomic variables for the years 2014–2017 and provides forecasts by the Organization for Economic Co-operation and

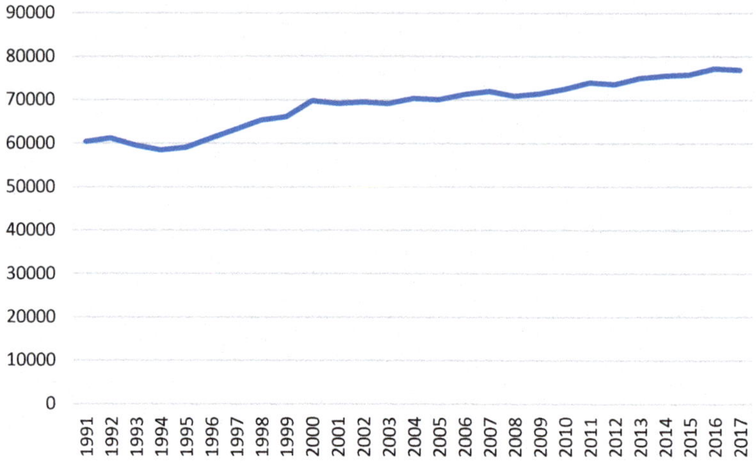

Fig. 6.4 Israel GDP per person employed (Constant 2011 PPP $) (http://www.cbs.gov.il/ts/)

Development (OECD) for the years 2018–2019. The macroeconomic figures include a ray of indicators of the Israeli economy. Among these indicators, Table 6.1 shows the key components of the Gross Domestic Product, i.e., private consumption, investment, government expenditures, exports and imports. The table also provides statistics for potential GDP of the Israeli economy. Additionally, Table 6.1 presents a summary of other crucial macroeconomic variables such as employment, unemployment rate, various indicators of the price level, such as GDP deflator, consumer and producer price indexes, different measures of nominal wages, short and long run interest rates as well as government debt.

As it can be seen from Table 6.1, all the macroeconomic indicators show positive current and forecasted outcomes for the Israeli economy.

6.3 Israeli Economic Miracle: A General Picture

Although it is hard to pinpoint the causes of the Israeli miracle, one may start with the often used Hebrew word of "Ein Breira"—that can be translated to "we do not have a choice, but . . ." This deeply rooted idiom tells each Israeli not to accept the current state of affairs, but to actively pursue to improve the situation.

One may start with history. For generations, Jews run, hide and fight to survive. This ability to be satisfied with what you have and trying to make the best out of it has saved the Jews in their wandering in the Diaspora outside of Israel and in the first few generations as the country needed to overcome outside and inside enemies which surrounded it, aiming to total annihilate the young state. The outside enemies have been the countries surrounding Israel. This forces Israel to develop technology that will allow it to win and deter wars. It has directed the Israelis to excel under

Table 6.1 Macroeconomic indicators and projections (OECD 2018) (*Economic Outlook No.102*, November, updated)

	2014	2015	2016	2017	2018	2019
	Current prices NIS billion	Percentage changes, volume (2010 prices)				
GDP	1103.5	2.6	4.0	3.3	3.5	3.4
Private consumption	614.3	4.1	6.1	3.3	3.6	3.4
Government consumption	250.6	3.1	3.9	2.9	3.0	2.0
Gross fixed capital formation	219.3	−0.8	11.9	2.5	4.1	8.4
Of which: Housing	74.3	1.5	8.1	1.3	−0.4	4.0
Non-residential and government	145	−1.9	13.9	3.1	6.3	10.4
Final domestic demand	1084.2	2.9	6.7	3.0	3.6	4.1
Stockbuilding[a]	3.7	0.6	−0.7	0.5	0.5	0.0
Total domestic demand	1087.9	3.5	6.0	3.5	4.1	4.1
Exports of goods and services	355.5	−2.4	2.5	3.2	4.7	3.9
Imports of goods and services	339.9	0.0	9.4	4.0	6.3	6.4
Net exports[a]	15.6	−0.9	−2.0	−0.2	−0.7	−0.7
Other indicators (% change, unless otherwise specified)						
Potential GDP		3.3	3.3	3.3	3.2	3.3
Output gap2		0.3	0.9	0.9	1.1	1.2
Employment		2.6	2.7	2.2	2.0	1.9
Unemployment rate[b]		5.3	4.8	4.2	4.2	4.2
GDP deflator		2.7	1.0	0.1	0.9	1.9
Consumer price index		−0.6	−0.5	0.2	1.0	1.7
Core consumer prices		0.4	0.0	0.0	1.1	1.7
Average wage per employee		3.0	3.2	2.9	3.7	4.0
Unit labor cost		2.5	1.4	2.7	2.1	2.6
Current account balance[c]		4.9	3.5	2.7	2.0	1.3
General government fiscal balance[c]		−2.1	−2.1	−2.0	−2.9	−2.9
Underlying government fiscal balance[d]		−2.4	−2.6	−2.4	−3.5	−3.5
Underlying government primary fiscal balance[d]		0.5	0.0	0.1	−0.9	−0.9
General government gross debt[c]		64.1	62.3	61.1	61.6	61.6
General government net debt[c]		60.3	58.7	57.5	58.0	58.0
Three-month money market rate, average		0.1	0.1	0.1	0.2	1.0
Ten-year government bond yield, average		2.1	1.9	1.9	2.1	2.8

[a]Contributions to changes in real GDP, actual amount in the first column
[b]As a percentage of the labor force
[c]As a percentage of GDP
[d]As a percentage of potential GDP

pressure, to maneuver, to circumvent, to challenge current accepted methods of performing tasks.

The Jewish tradition, going back to biblical and Talmudic times, encourages, indeed requires, questioning and thinking differently, always creating hypothetical circumstances that challenge the current wisdom and question accepted techniques. One of the inside enemy is the fact that most of the land is arid, subject to the infrequent rain from heaven. This leads the Israelis to excel in water and agricultural technology. Today, quite amazingly, Israel is water-independent as far as its drinking requirements. The country is poor in natural resources, for example, there is no coal. Consequently, Israel became a leading force in using the sun and other alternatives to coal energy.

The ability to turn a disadvantage to advantageous successes is found in the population size of Israel. A small, some would say tiny country with a population of eight million, forces Israeli researchers and entrepreneurs to look outside, to think globally and reach out to foreign markets. The small domestic market dictates developing products that the world at large demands, willing to fund projects through the entrepreneurial process.

Another factor that may explain the Israeli miracle is the mandatory service for both men and female that brings together as a melting pot different parts of the Israeli population. Whereas on the surface, one may consider a compulsory military service of 3 years as a waste of human resources, Israelis use the time to learn skills that will take many more years to develop in a civilian setting. The lessons one learns, the friendship and comrade one acquires, the ability to cooperate and train in peacetime and under fire, the teamwork, all contribute to the leadership skills and entrepreneurial characteristics of the Israeli society. A person of age 18–19 gets a huge responsibility on state-of-the-art military equipment, installations, camps, and humans. Not only the Israeli young needs to make sure the equipment is when and where it is needed, but also to attend to the welfare of her or his soldiers, merely a year younger than them. This places a responsibility and opportunity to practice leadership and to draw from different skills of the member of your group. Moreover, the army shows Israelis that failures are only preludes to trying all over again and yet again until the "mission" is accomplished. No matter the efforts, the time required, etc., the mission is the important aim.

Moreover, at age 16, the army reaches out to hackers and math prodigies inviting them to elite training units. In these units, the teenagers acquire extensive knowledge and experience in state of the art technologies, still under development. The trainees are exposed to developers and inventors who work with them, hand in hand mentoring, as well as learning from them. This, in turn, encourages these young teenagers to open their mind for inventions. Furthermore, the army reaches out to a very large segment of the population for initial screening; not just hackers and prodigies, inviting them to elite training units. They are invited for initial screening; some prefer combat units and only go to high tech or whatever, much later.

Naturally, many of the skills developed and encouraged in the army are applied to civilian areas. For examples, engineers who developed missiles to shot targets use similar technology to invent the camera pill. Some of these army unites are so unique that the friendship developed through many sleepless nights turned to teams establishing start-up companies.

Another crucial factor explaining the development of the Israeli economy is the role of immigration (Lucas 2014). Israel is a nation of immigrants. The Israeli Law of

Return, which was passed in 1950, imposes no barriers to immigration. Israel offers both free immigration and grants Jewish immigrants immediate citizenship, regardless of origin or skill. This Law of Return applies only to Jews or those descended from at least one Jewish grandparent. All other immigrants are subject to temporary status of a few years before being able to request citizenship.

Immigrants are almost by definition risk takers. You cannot survive if you are not. Such an ability to adapt, to get away under difficult unpredictable circumstances are the milk and butter of the newcomers. Furthermore, Jews immigrants who are subject to the law of returns are eligible for an envelope of financial assistance which is composed of learning the Hebrew language through an innovative program aimed at all ages of immigrants (Ulpan), providing housing and offering seed money to start their own enterprises.

Between the years 1948 and 2016, Israel absorbed in a short time more than 3.1 million immigrants, among them 1.22 million from the Former Soviet Union, 138,000 from North America, and close to 92,000 from Ethiopia (Table 6.2). These immigrants have injected new blood to the innovation engines of the country. Many of the new immigrants are highly educated and strongly motivated to succeed in the newfound land. Furthermore, the immigrants, once settled, keep ties with their country of birth and open markets accesses and diversification of talents unprecedented to the World. The reason for the immigration from the Former Soviet Union was the Russian economic depression which caused the Russian GDP to fall between 37 and 50 percent between 1989 and 1998 (Rosefielde and Hedlund 2009). The full Russian economic recovery was reached only in 2006. For more details, see Razin and Sadka (2017) and Razin (2018a, b).

Observing the second input of a country's production function, after human resources, is capital. Israel has benefitted from capital transfer from the Diaspora, from the reparation by Germany and by foreign aid from other countries, most notably in recent years from the USA.

An important factor is the policies by the state of Israel early on to encourage foreign direct investment and domestic entrepreneurship. Since, as early as 1993, the Israeli government has offered tax-incentive to foreign venture capital investment in Israel, matching their investment one to one, i.e., doubling the investment. As a result, annual venture capital investment in Israel rose from 58 million dollars in 1993 to 3.3 billion dollars by 2000. The number of start-ups backed by the government program, called YOZMA ("Initiative"), has risen from 100 to 800 by the year 2000.

Another important factor helping the Israeli economic miracles is new technologies in oil and gas drillings. These new discoveries are going to change the international status of the country, making it a significant exporter of oil and gas, boasting its revenues as well as political power.

Another factor, which is aiding the Israeli economy, is the rate of birth. Israel birth rate is 3.1 children, whereas the Organization for Economic Co-operation and Development (OECD) average, for example, is only 1.7. The average birth rate in the OECD in 1963 was 3.3. According to the World Bank, the number of children per female in the World decreased from 4.8 in 1960 to 2.4 in 2016. This problem is

Table 6.2 Immigrants to Israel (Israeli Statistical Office)

	Total immigrants to Israel	Immigrants from F.S.U.	Total immigration from North America	Total immigration from Ethiopia
1948	101,828	1175	336	40
1949	239,954	3255	659	1
1950	170,563	290	888	5
1951	175,279	196	618	1
1952	24,610	74	353	40
1953	11,575	45	234	3
1954	18,491	30	349	13
1955	37,528	139	380	25
1956	56,330	470	209	1
1957	72,634	1324	313	5
1958	27,290	729	409	4
1959	23,988	1362	379	3
1960	24,692	1923	462	3
1961	47,735	224	348	2
1962	61,533	194	677	11
1963	64,489	314	968	17
1964	55,036	541	1122	8
1965	31,115	895	1016	9
1966	15,957	2054	826	21
1967	14,469	1403	739	13
1968	20,703	224	1035	17
1969	38,111	3019	6419	14
1970	36,750	992	7158	13
1971	41,930	12,839	8122	7
1972	55,888	31,652	6034	40
1973	54,886	33,477	4786	41
1974	31,979	16,816	3393	24
1975	20,028	8531	3065	19
1976	19,754	7279	2979	10
1977	21,429	8348	2906	90
1978	26,394	12,192	3285	37
1979	37,222	17,614	3273	45
1980	20,428	7570	2550	259
1981	12,599	1770	2670	650
1982	13,723	782	2934	950
1983	16,906	399	3806	2393
1984	19,981	367	2827	1886
1985	10,642	362	2090	8327
1986	9505	202	2179	236
1987	12,965	2096	1986	231
1988	13,034	2283	1700	595

(continued)

Table 6.2 (continued)

	Total immigrants to Israel	Immigrants from F.S.U.	Total immigration from North America	Total immigration from Ethiopia
1989	24,050	12,932	1533	1448
1990	199,516	185,227	1546	4121
1991	176,100	147,839	1703	20,014
1992	77,057	65,093	2068	3648
1993	76,805	66,145	2280	863
1994	79,844	68,079	2398	1197
1995	76,361	64,848	2503	1312
1996	70,919	59,048	2262	1411
1997	66,221	54,621	2057	1661
1998	56,730	46,032	1788	3110
1999	76,766	66,848	1697	2290
2000	60,201	50,817	1735	2201
2001	43,473	33,601	1653	3274
2002	33,570	18,508	2040	2656
2003	23,273	12,383	2385	3029
2004	20,899	10,130	2640	3695
2005	21,183	9431	2987	3571
2006	19,269	7469	3201	3595
2007	18,131	6643	2957	3607
2008	13,701			1570
2009	14,574	6948	2554	243
2010	16,633	7158	2505	1652
2011	16,892	7225	2662	2666
2012	16,557	7234	2525	2432
2013				450
Total	**3,108,678**	**1,223,723**	**138,161**	**91,825**

currently acute in Germany where the government is aware of the need for qualified labor force in order to support its social security and payments to it pensioners. Another country facing such a problem is Japan that has both a declining population and anti-immigration policy.

In contrast, in Israel, the average fertility rate for orthodox (Charedim) Jews is 6.8, religious Jews 4.4, for Muslim families 3.3, and for secular Jews 2.1, more than the replacement rate. Moreover, these fertility rates have almost not declined since the 1960s, in contrast to other world's economies. Among the factors leading to the high fertility rates are the security situation and government policies aimed at encouraging births. Additionally, the fact that Israel did not suffer from deep economic crises because of both the subprime crises in the USA and the Euro crisis contributes to this high fertility phenomenon.

When one studies the declining fertility rates all over the world, Muslim countries such as Iran, Saudi Arabia, Egypt, Pakistan, and countries in Africa, such as Kenya, Ghana, and South Africa, the Israeli fertility rate is a miracle. This miracle, if not channeled and encouraged by policy, may have its effects on congestions, inadequate infrastructure, misallocation of resources, and an increase in the share of low paying occupations—all challenges that the Israeli authorities need to consider. More on the challenges to the Israeli economy are discussed in Sect. 6.6.

6.4 Sources of Economic Growth in Israel: Real Sector and Labor Markets

For nearly the entire first century of the Zionist endeavor, socialist, almost Bolshevik, outlook dominated both thinking and practice of economic development. The key movers in economics and politics were emigrated from Russia during the first decade of the twentieth century (the Second Aliyah) and were critically influenced by the economic philosophies that also brought about the Russian revolution of 1917. Members of the Second Aliyah developed the kibbutz movement and were the main functionaries who developed the Histadrut, the pre-state quasi-governmental, local economic umbrella organization. Founded in 1920, the Histadrut combined both a federation of labor unions, ownership, and/or virtual control of various enterprises ranging from natural monopolies (public transport, naval and air ports) to core industrial firms (Tnuva—a dairy cooperative, Kur—an industrial mega-cooperation) and public service enterprises (sick funds, health care, sports teams, and more).

Arguably, this highly centralized and politicized organization was the appropriate option for those early years. In that period, the Jewish settlement was exceedingly small, required major infrastructure and other development and had to deal with violent opposition to its mere existence. Additionally, Israel had to absorb massive immigrants relative to the size of the native Jewish population and poorly developed institutional infrastructure required for well-functioning markets (e.g., preservation of property rights) despite the existence of many necessary institutions for a modern nation.

During the first years of independence, Israel's basic economic circumstances did not change much, with immigration now unencumbered by international geopolitics and infrastructure development, including basic housing for immigrants, still the major priority for more government control. As immigration tapered off and development progressed, forces advocating an increased role for the private sector have emerged.

This situation combined with more than a decade of macroeconomic mismanagement culminated in a major economic crisis at both the macro and micro levels. The macro situation was largely resolved by the Economic Stabilization Program of July 1985, whereby a heterodox approach of both fiscal austerity and a coordinated nominal-side "freeze" succeeded in drastically reducing rampant inflation and eliminating Israel's massive twin deficits. At the time, there was broad awareness that returning the economy to health would require a broad range of structural reforms that would essentially transform the economy to a modern, mixed-capitalist regime.

While the basic direction and thrust of the reform process that transpired over two decades were understood, the timing and institutional details of the various segments of the reforms were not part of an overall program designed at the outset. Instead, the process was the result of initiatives undertaken by various governments and other public and quasi-public institutions as well as reactions to exogenous developments, especially the massive immigration following the collapse of the Soviet Union at the end of the 1980s and the large-scale discrediting of socialism that accompanied that traumatic event.

The first steps in real sector reform included a major change in the government policy of bailing out large, inefficient, failing enterprises (for example, ATA—a textile company, Israel Aircraft, and Tadiran) and legislated, phased-in foreign trade liberalization. At about the same time, the massive wave of immigration from the Former Soviet Union (FSU) described above began, bringing about an initial phase of required fiscal expansion for immigrant absorption with large, supply-side benefits expected to follow in the medium and long run.

This led to the gradual adoption of longer-term fiscal planning, culminating in the adoption of a series of fiscal rules. While the specific rules were often broken and changed, the notion that fiscal policy must first conform to some sound, "top-down," macro framework became over the years a policy mantra that has been accepted and adhered to by various governments. Consequently, the government debt to GDP ratio has declined over two decades from approximately 200% to below 60%.

Many of the determinants of growth in Israel have been a reaction to exogenous forces. In the labor market, for example, the massive immigration led to a weakening of the Histadrut—the worker union that in Israel was also the largest employer next to the Government employees, where competition for jobs by unorganized immigrants (many for ideological reasons) reduced the effectiveness of collective bargaining. In the first decade of the 2000s, the Internet introduced most welcomed "disruptions" in the functioning of the labor market (that led to a large leftward shift of Beveridge curve), with websites largely replacing the highly inefficient government labor exchanges, especially for low-skilled workers. In addition, the Likud party that came into power began a process of privatizations that makes labor markets more competitive.

To sum up this section: The successful resolution in the mid-1980s of a largely self-made crisis along with the immigration wave of the early 1990s have brought about an enduring metamorphosis in Israel's approach to economic management. Realization hit that massive government management and control of large sectors of the economy is not conducive to the development and growth of an advanced economy. Transition to date has been accomplished gradually, for the most part with political legitimacy and very limited protest; this in spite of a significant increase in income inequality that only recently is beginning to be reversed.

In spite of very impressive achievements that have resulted in Israel attaining advanced economy status for the past decade, per capita income in Israel still remains significantly below the levels typifying the highest per capita income group. While this is due in part to idiosyncratic social anthropology (viz. Jewish Haredim and Arabs), there is still a very important residual share of glaring inefficiency (low productivity, excessive regulation and its implementation, etc.) in important sectors of the economy. The next section analyzes monetary policy as a determinant of the Israeli economic growth.

6.5 Monetary and Financial Determinants of the Israeli Economic Growth

While development of the monetary and financial sectors of an economy are correctly regarded as a "means" towards promoting economic development and growth, rather than "ends" in their own right, there is a large literature emphasizing the critical importance of ensuring that monetary and financial development is commensurate with that of the real sector (Jovanovic and Greenwood 1990).

For the first few decades of Israel's independence, the combination of the need to absorb massive waves of immigration and to improve basic infrastructure (roads, electricity, water, etc.) along with some tenuous features of Israel's institutional infrastructure (e.g., status of property rights) led to massive government involvement in the monetary and financial sectors. The largest financial institutions were owned and dominated by the government or by quasi-government entities. These include, for example, the Histadrut—the national labor union, the Jewish Agency, and a few major and influential political parties. The government and the Central Bank of Israel, Bank of Israel, determined the terms and conditions of most short-, medium- and long-term savings instruments, credit availability and costs. Large public sector borrowing requirements led to policies that provided relatively favorable terms to government sponsored financial instruments relative to privately sponsored ones. By the late 1980s, Israel's monetary and financial systems were essentially nationalized and highly repressed.

The first stages of reform (late 1980s and 1990s) concentrated on a drastic reduction of government involvement in the financial sector, including the following key elements:

1. Reduction of budget deficits and, hence, of financing needs.
2. Privatization of banks that had been nationalized in the early 1980s, following the collapse of a bank stock price manipulation scheme by the banks themselves.
3. Gradual elimination of inflation differentials between Israel and the major advanced economies via the gradual adoption of the inflation targeting monetary policy framework.
4. Gradual capital account liberalization.

5. Transformation of foreign exchange regime and market from adjustable peg to fully floating regime and development of forex market by eliminating the Central Bank's role as market-maker.
6. De-regulation and development of markets for domestic financial instruments—government bonds, Tel-Aviv Stock Exchange (TASE), forex and other options such as, Israel Central Bank Bills (Makam).

The Makam are short-term securities (up to 1 year) issued by the Bank of Israel to affect the level of the interest rate in the money market. They are issued to the public. Their rate of return is determined in trading on the stock exchange.

By the first few years of the current millennium (2000–2003) Israel had established credibility for price stability by moving to a full-fledged flexible inflation targeting regime and was steadily reducing the government debt ratio, albeit from a very high level. Successful management of the combined dot.com crash and the second intifada crisis set the stage for a second round of major financial reforms.

The second intifada was the second Palestinian uprising against Israel—a period of intensified Israeli–Palestinian violence. It started in September 2000 until February 8 2005. The death toll, including both military and civilian, is estimated to be about 3,000 Palestinians and 1,000 Israelis, as well as 64 foreigners.

These financial reforms included: major pension reform in 2003 establishing principles for an actuarially sound system over the long term, establishment of Makam as a market-based monetary policy instrument, reform and significant extension of capital market taxation, legislated divestiture by banks of subsidiaries dealing in long-term contractual savings and investment banking, strengthening of the Israel Securities Authority (ISA) and, later on, regulation of long-term savings institutions.

This lengthy and comprehensive reform process has had some significant positive results. Most notably, in the wake of Israel's impressive real sector achievements, it has enabled the significant expansion of foreign financing of Israeli enterprises including both Foreign Direct Investment (FDI) and portfolio investment by foreign institutional investors, large and small portfolio investors, and some money center banks. In general, the heightened and visible presence of sophisticated foreign financial institutions in Israel appears to have beneficial knock-on effects, incentivizing both the government and private entities to conduct their business in accordance with the more prudent international norms.

6.6 The Future Challenges for the Israeli Economy

Where does all this leave us in terms of the role over time and the current status of the monetary/financial sector in Israel's economic development? In particular, it is appropriate to ask whether non-financial businesses and households in Israel have access to monetary and financial products and services with quantity and quality commensurate with the state of the real sector. To what extent does the domestic financial industry provide the products and services and innovate and to what extent do foreign entities do this?

On the monetary front, Israel has clearly achieved price stability and a domestic currency based monetary regime that provides a credible nominal anchor for the economy. Naturally, it remains to be seen whether the recent period of Israel's ultra-easy monetary policy during a long period of high real growth and very low unemployment, yet sub-target inflation will result in a renewed bout of higher inflation and, if so, how this will be dealt with. In the area of monetary and payment services, however, the facilities available to the household sector clearly lag behind standards established in most advanced countries, for example there are no local internet banking services available.

Regarding credit and finance in general, on the household side, in spite of recent rapid growth of credit, various ratios of household debt (e.g., total, residential mortgages) to GDP ratios are still quite low compared with advanced economies. On the corporate side, both non-bank financial institutions and foreign banks are increasing their presence in markets for business finance but the system as a whole still could use improvement.

Furthermore, Israel has some challenges. According to the Women at Work Index 2018 compiled by PwC, Israel ranks 14 among all 33 OECD countries. The gender wage gap, i.e., the shortfall of female relative to male wages, in 2016 was 18.7%. For a comparison, the corresponding wage gap is 6.8% in Poland. In order to close the wage gap, PwC estimates that it will require a 23% increase for women's wages and will generate $12 billion US dollars increase in female wages. The Gross Domestic Product (GDP) impacts of increasing female employment rates to Swedish levels will increase GDP by 8.3% ($26 billion!). Moreover, female boardroom representation in Israel stands at only 22%. However, this index shows that next to Luxembourg, Israel is the second biggest movers from the year 2000 to 2016.

The IMD World Competitiveness Center (https://www.imd.org/wcc/world-competitiveness-center/) has ranked countries for 29 years. The ranking strives to measure the extent to which a country is able to foster an environment in which enterprises can generate sustainable value. The ranking recognizes the factors that facilitate prosperity. The last available ranking published as Competitiveness Yearbook 2017 is for the year 2017 covering 63 economies. As part of this index, the Digital Competitiveness Ranking (https://www.imd.org/wcc/world-competitiveness-center-rankings/world-digital-competitiveness-rankings-2017/) analyzes and ranks countries' ability to adopt and explore digital technologies leading to transformation in government practices, business models, and society in general. Israel is ranked 13. Singapore, Sweden, and the USA rank first three places, respectively.

In terms of knowledge, know-how necessary to discover, understand, and build new technologies, Israel was ranked 5 in 2016 and 7 in 2017 with Singapore, Sweden, and Canada at the lead. In technology, overall context that enables the development of digital technologies, Israel ranks only 27. As far as the category of Future Readiness, the level of a country preparedness to exploit digital transformation, Israel ranks only 11 in 2017 while it was ranked 9 in 2016.

Table 6.3 World Digital Competitiveness Rankings 2013–2017 (https://www.imd.org/wcc/world-competitiveness-center-rankings/world-digital-competitiveness-rankings-2017/)

Israel	2013	2014	2015	2016	2017
Overall	12	11	10	13	13
Factors					
Knowledge	7	7	4	5	7
Technology	23	23	22	24	27
Future readiness	5	9	7	9	11
Knowledge					
Talent	26	26	25	23	21
Training and Education	12	10	7	6	11
Scientific concentration	2	2	2	2	2
Technology					
Regulatory framework	32	32	26	26	26
Capital	16	18	18	20	27
Technological framework	21	22	25	26	28
Future readiness					
Adaptive attitudes	14	13	17	17	18
Business agility	7	12	11	11	9
IT integration	3	3	2	3	7
Digital	12	11	10	13	13
Competitiveness	19	24	21	21	22

Looking at subsectors (Table 6.3), Israel excel in digital and technological skills (ranked number 1), in percent of total expenditures on R&D out of GDP (ranked 1). In cyber security, Israel is ranked 2. In total R&D personnel per capita, and in scientific research legislation, Israel is ranked 4. Despite the bright picture, Israel is ranked low in R&D productivity by publication (ranked 51), in Enforcing contracts (48), and in immigration laws of non-Jews (53). In wireless broadband, Israel rank is 50.

As far as Doing Business, as conducted by the World Bank, (Table 6.4), not everything is shining in the start-up nation, Israel again needs to improve its practices where it is currently ranked at 54. Table 6.4 provides some rethinking by Israeli policy makers, to avoid, using past achievements in areas, which require constant innovations and rejuvenations. To save space, only data for the year 2018 is presented in Table 6.4. Further details are available at the World Bank site.

To provide a few statistics, according to the ranking of Economics departments by Tilburg University, the Department of Economics at Tel-Aviv University was ranked number 18 in the years 1995–1999, whereas it ranks 73 in the years 2010–2016. The Department of Economics at the Hebrew University was ranked 32 in 1995–1999, but only 78 in 2010–2016. The ranking is based on the number of papers published in 74 leading economic journals. As far as full-time faculty, the Hebrew University had 29 such positions in the academic year 1997–1998.

Table 6.4 Doing Business in Israel (The World Bank)

Year	2018
Rank global (DB18)	54
Rank—Starting a business (DB18)	37
Rank—Dealing with construction permits (DB18)	65
Rank—Getting electricity (DB18)	77
Rank—Registering property (DB18)	130
Rank—Getting credit (DB18)	55
Rank—Protecting minority investors (DB18)	16
Rank—Paying taxes (DB18)	99
Paying taxes—DTF-Postfiling index (0–100) (DB17–18 methodology)	61.36
Rank—Trading across borders (DB18)	60
Rank—Enforcing contract (DB18)	92
Rank—Resolving insolvency (DB18)	29

The number of full-time faculty shrinks at that institute to 20. The situation at Tel-Aviv University is even worse, from 24.75 full-time position in the Department of Economics in 1997–1998 to mere 14.5 full-time positions (https://www.themarker.com/news/education/1.6028553).

In this context, it is alarming that all Israeli universities are losing their competiveness, losing faculty members and lagging in scientific publications. In particular, the shrinking number of full-time faculty members for all economic departments in Israel is alarming. The decrease represents a reversal of what was the most important sector in Israel, feeding a labor force that is highly educated, internationally known, and well respected. Moreover, the number of scientific publications has been steadily declining.

The Enterprise Surveys of the World Bank (Table 6.5) ranked Israel according to different criteria. This table summarizes Enterprise Surveys data for Israel and highlights the biggest obstacles experienced by private sector firms in Israel. The 12 sub-tables summarize key factual indicators at the country and regional levels for each of the business environment topics. A few subjective indicators are also available.

Table 6.6 presents the average number in thousands of salaried employees in sophisticated sectors of the Israeli economy for the years 2012–2016.

The table details seven sophisticated industries of the Israeli economy, such as human health, education, etc. The table shows the number of sophisticated salaried employees out of the total labor force in these sectors. One observes a steady increase in employment in these sectors. This, as mentioned above, leads to an increase in inequality and may hamper future development of the state of Israel.

Table 6.5 Enterprise Surveys—Israel (http://www.enterprisesurveys.org/data/exploreeconomies/2013/Israel)

Indicator	Israel	Middle East and North Africa	All countries
Corruption			
Bribery incidence (percent of firms experiencing at least one bribe payment request)	0.1	21.4	18
Bribery depth (% of public transactions where a gift or informal payment was requested)	0	18.4	14.1
Crime			
Percent of firms paying for security	55.7	35.9	55.1
Finance			
Percent of firms with a checking or savings account	99	79.1	86.8
Percent of firms with a bank loan/line of credit	55.1	28.6	33.7
Proportion of loans requiring collateral (%)	56.7	77.4	79.1
Value of collateral needed for a loan (% of the loan amount)	120.9	183	205.8
Percent of firms whose recent loan application was rejected	0.3	10.2	11
Percent of firms using banks to finance investments	46.4	25.9	26.2
Proportion of investments financed internally (%)	63.8	71.1	71
Proportion of investments financed by banks (%)	31.6	15.6	14.9
Percent of firms using banks to finance working capital	34.3	24.3	30.3
Percent of firms identifying access to finance as a major constraint	3	31.9	26.3
Firm characteristics			
Age of the establishment (years)	22.4	18.8	16.5
Proportion of private domestic ownership in a firm (%)	96.3	95.1	87.7
Percent of firms with at least 10% of foreign ownership	4.9	5.7	11.7
Percent of firms with at least 10% of government/state ownership	0.2	0.3	0.9
Gender			
Percent of firms with female participation in ownership	27.3	23.3	35.3
Percent of firms with majority female ownership	3.1	3.4	14.5
Percent of firms with a female top manager	10.1	5.4	18.6
Infrastructure			
Percent of firms experiencing electrical outages	18.2	53.4	59.1
Average duration of a typical electrical outage (hours) if there were outages	4	9.1	4.5
Days to obtain an electrical connection (upon application)	55.3	42.6	32.4
Percent of firms identifying electricity as a major constraint	5.9	35.3	31.3
Percent of firms experiencing water insufficiencies	0.5	19	14.9
Innovations and technology			
Percent of firms having their own web site	67.2	47.2	44.4

(continued)

Table 6.5 (continued)

Indicator	Israel	Middle East and North Africa	All countries
Percent of firms using e-mail to interact with clients/suppliers	98.9	64.9	71.7
Percent of firms that introduced a new product/service	17.1	26	36.7
Performance			
Capacity utilization (%)*	75.7	64.7	72.1
Real annual sales growth (%)	2.6	−6	1.5
Annual employment growth (%)	5	3.4	5
Regulations and taxes			
Senior management time spent dealing with the requirements of government regulation (%)	4.3	9	9.6
Percent of firms visited or required to meet with tax officials	52.2	52	57.2
Trade			
Days to clear direct exports through customs	4.6	6.4	7.4
Percent of firms identifying customs and trade regulations as a major constraint	6.5	21.1	17.8
Workforce			
Proportion of production workers (out of all permanent workers)	55.9	70.8	72.7
Proportion of skilled workers (out of all production workers) (%)	88.8	68.2	74.8
Percent of firms identifying labor regulations as a major constraint	1.1	11.8	10.9
Percent of firms identifying an inadequately educated workforce as a major constraint	12.2	20.3	21.1

6.7 Conclusions

This chapter describes the Israeli miracle, provides some explanation to the growth of the economy, and shed lights for some of the challenges the Israel economy is facing. What are the most important factors of growth that distinguish Israel from other countries? Some of these factors are rooted in Jewish history and tradition. The current and potential inhabitants of Israel cherish learning from an early age and throughout life. The long-held traditions are always to question, to think differently. Speaking openly is encouraged, even demanded from an early age. The custom is to avoid accepting the opinions or the directives of any higher authority that pertain to know better. Israelis respect and respond to other people based on their knowledge and wisdom, rarely on their formal rank in the organizations' hierarchy. Israeli society in general appreciates and respects inventors and innovators.

Another important factor is the mindset of Ein Breira, i.e., "there is no other way, but..." To these factors, one adds the huge influx of immigrants, from literally all over the world who have immigrated to Israel with an utmost desire to contribute to

Table 6.6 Monthly average in thousands salaried employees (http://www.cbs.gov.il/)

Year	Human health and social works activities	Education	Local, public and defense administration and social security	Administrative and support service activities	Professional, scientific, and technical activities	Financial and insurance activities	Information and communications	Total in sophisticated industries	Total labor force
2012	351.4	422.8	122.4	271.6	202.5	102.1	161.2	1633.948	**3139.50**
2013	363.7	445.6	124.6	280.3	207.3	102.7	155.6	1679.777	**3204.90**
2014	376	457	127.6	286.1	213.9	106.2	157.8	1724.719	**3293.40**
2015	385.5	472	131.2	287.2	223.2	107.4	164.8	1771.256	**3386.10**
2016	395.4	489	133.7	294.4	233.5	107.7	174	1827.647	**3493.80**

its development and prosperity, to become an integral contributing part of its multifaceted society. Moreover, even before the State achieved its independence, there existed the necessary institutions to encourage individuals to excel.

Another significant factor in creating the innovative state is the Israeli army with its compulsory service for about 3 years, where all layers of society are forced to integrate, to learn from each other and when necessary literally save each other's life. Another factor is the geographic small size of the country that allows people to meet face-to-face, debate and exchange opinions, brainstorm and test their ideas against those of other. Another important factor is the realization by the Israeli government that its population has many alternatives outside of the country. Accordingly, the Israeli government is obligated to increase the population's standard of living. It requires adequate fiscal, monetary, and income policies. These factors detailed in this chapter are some of the keys to the success of the innovative state that turns Israel to become the hub for innovations, the cradle of start-ups.

The chapter also discusses in details some of the obstacles to the Israeli economy. Despite these obstacles, the author is optimistic and confident that Israel and Israelis will find the proper policies to lead the country to stardom.

Acknowledgement I am highly indebted to the generous insights provided by Edward (Akiva) Offenbacher from the Bank of Israel. I would like to thank Professor Yaffa Machnes from Bar-Ilan University for her comments and insights on the Israeli economy, Professor Magdalena Osińska from Nicolaus Copernicus University in Toruń, the editor of this book and Tomer Shachmurove for many discussions on this chapter.

References

Frenkel A, Maital S, DeBare I (2012) Technion nation: Technion's contribution to Israel and the World. Technion – Israel Institute of Technology, Haifa

Gordis D (2017) Israel: a concise history of a nation Reborn. Ecco, New York (reprint edition)

Jorisch A (2018) Thou Shalt innovate: how Israeli ingenuity repairs the world. Gefen Publishing House, Jerusalem

Jovanovic B, Greenwood J (1990) Financial development, growth, and the distribution of income. J Polit Econ 98(5):1076–1107

Katz Y, Bohbot A (2017) The weapon wizards: how Israel became a high-tech military superpower. St. Martin's Press, New York

Lucas REB (ed) (2014) International handbook on migration and economic development. Elgar, Edward

OECD (2018) OECD economic outlook, Volume 2018 Issue 1: preliminary version. OECD Publishing, Paris. Accessed 9 Aug 2018

Razin and Sadka (2017) Migration-Induced redistribution with and without migrant voting CEPR discussion paper no. DP12175

Razin A (2018a) Israel's immigration story: winners and losers. Israel Econ Rev 15(1):73–106

Razin A (2018b) Israel and the world economy: the power of globalization. MIT Press, Boston

Rosefielde S, Hedlund S (2009) Russia since 1980: wrestling with westernization. Cambridge University Press, Cambridge

Senor D, Singer S (2011) Start-up nation: the story of Israel's economic miracle. Twelve, New York

Siegel SM (2017) Let there be water: Israel's solution for a water-starved world. Thomas Dunne Books/St. Martin's Griffin, New York
The marker. https://www.themarker.com/news/education/1.6028553. Accessed 30 May 2018
Wesfeld T (2015) How did Israel become a hub for innovation? Creator by WeWork
Williamson OE (1985) The Economic Institutions of Capitalism. Free Press, New York
World Digital Competitiveness Yearbook (2017) https://www.imd.org/wcc/world-competitiveness-center-rankings/world-digital-competitiveness-rankings-2017/

Part II
Statistical Identification and Econometric Modelling of Economic Miracles in Selected Economies

Chapter 7
Testing for Structural Breaks in Macroeconomic Processes of Growth

Marcin Fałdziński

Abstract This chapter investigates structural changes in economic growth, using the sample of four countries, i.e. Ireland, Spain, Turkey and the Netherlands, and covers the time period 1980–2016. In this case, structural breaks are interpreted as large, infrequent shocks switching the economy from one regime to another. In order to search for structural changes, the unit-root and the structural breaks testing methodology is applied. Specifically, a pure structural change model with the Andrews–Zivot test and the Bai–Perron test are employed. The paper's findings suggest that most of the structural breaks for these four countries are specific to their situation. Nevertheless, the financial crisis of 2007–2009 is indicated as common for all of them.

7.1 Introduction

A structural change is viewed as a dominant aspect of economic growth. In the steady state growth the economy still achieves positive growth, but at a low level. One of the remedies of such a situation is to reallocate resources from sectors of low productivity to those of higher, which is an equivalent to structural change. There have been many studies dealing with structural changes and economic growth: Lewis (1954), Clark (1957), Kaldor (1966), Kuznets (1966, 1979), Denison (1967), Syrquin (1988), Lin (2009, 2012a, b), Lin and Monga (2010), Harada (2015) and Vu (2017). In most cases, empirical evidence proves that the effect of structural change on growth is positive, but not always. McMillan et al. (2014) show that structural change in productivity growth was negative for Latin America in the

Financial support from research project no. 2015/17/B/HS4/01000 supported by the National Science Centre in Poland is gratefully acknowledged.

M. Fałdziński (✉)
Department of Econometrics and Statistics, The Faculty of Economic Sciences and Management, Nicolaus Copernicus University, Toruń, Poland
e-mail: marf@umk.pl

M. Osińska (ed.), *Economic Miracles in the European Economies*,
https://doi.org/10.1007/978-3-030-05606-3_7

years 1990–2005, and for Africa in the years 1990–2000. A structural change may be an endogenous or exogenous phenomenon.

One possible method of identifying structural changes is testing for unit root and structural breaks. Different characteristics of the data-generating process of an economic time series have great implications for modelling and economic theories. A non-stationary process, a process that has a unit root, does not return to long-run deterministic path and current shocks have a permanent effect of the long-run level of the series. On the contrary, shocks in stationary time series have transitory effects and the series exhibit the trend-reversion property. Moreover, ignoring structural breaks in the long-run trend, when testing for the underlying trend, can result in dubious statistical outputs and further economic implications. The idea of structural breaks and their impact on the long-run properties of output series has attracted attention of researchers: Nelson and Plosser (1982), Perron (1989), Rudebusch (1992), Ben-David and Papell (1995, 1988), Startz (1998), Noriega and Ramírez (1999), Ben-David et al. (2003), Smyth and Inder (2004), Carrion and German (2007). A unit-root property with or without a structural break has a significant impact on the correctness of econometric models and economic frameworks. Testing for structural breaks can identify some extraordinary events and can help derive more information on the behaviour of the tested series. In addition, testing for breaks may lead to finding structural breaks which occur simultaneously across different economic processes.

7.2 Testing for Structural Breaks

The standard linear regression model assumes that the parameters of the model do not vary across observations. Despite this assumption, the structural changes at some dates in the sample period play an empirically relevant role in the applied time series analysis. The parameters of a typical time series do not remain constant over time. This causes paradigm shifts at irregular intervals. The time of such a shift is a structural break and the period between two break points is known as a regime. There have been several studies aimed at measuring break points. The first group of studies was able to detect only one unknown structural break point. Perron (1990), Hansen (1990, 1992), Banerjee et al. (1992), Perron and Vogelsang (1992), Chu and White (1992), Andrews (1993), Andrews and Ploberger (1994), Perron (1997) did some major works in this area. Studies by Nelson and Plosser (1982), Perron (1989), Zivot and Andrews (1992) tested for unit root in the presence of a structural break. Bai (1994, 1997) considered the distributional properties of the break dates. The second group of studies was an improvement over the first, since it was able to detect multiple structural breaks, most importantly endogenous break points. Significant contributions were made by Zivot and Andrews (1992), Perron (1989), Bai and Perron (2003a, b), Lumsdaine and Papell (1997) tests for unit root allowing for two breaks in the trend function. Hansen (2001) considers multiple breaks, although he considers the breaks to be exogenously given.

Tests for parameter instability and a structural change in regression models have been an important part of applied econometric work dating back to Chow (1960), who tested for a regime change at a priori known dates. To relax the requirement that the candidate break date is known, Quandt (1960) modified the Chow framework to consider the F-statistic with the largest value over all possible break dates. Andrews (1993) and Andrews and Ploberger (1994) derived the limiting distribution of the Quandt and related test statistics. More recently, Bai (1997) and Bai and Perron (1998, 2003a, b) provide theoretical and computational results that further extend the Quandt–Andrews framework by allowing for multiple unknown break points.

The detection of structural changes is significant in the context of analysing and forecasting time series. Tests in the study of structural changes can be divided into the following categories (cf. Maddala and Kim (1998)):

- Testing the existence of a change without modelling this change
- Known or unknown date of the collapse occurrence
- One or multiple structural changes
- One-dimensional or multi-dimensional dependence between the variables
- Stationary or non-stationary variables

Let us begin with a unit-root testing methodology without a break using the Augmented Dicky–Fuller (ADF) (1979) test. First of all, we say that a series is weakly stationary (in short stationary) if the mean and autocovariance do not vary with respect to time. If the series does meet these criteria, then it is said to be non-stationary. The ADF test takes into account a higher-order correlation by assuming that the series follows autoregressive process of the forms:

$$\Delta y_t = \alpha y_{t-1} + \sum_{i=1}^{p} \beta_i \Delta y_{t-i} + \varepsilon_t, \tag{7.1}$$

$$\Delta y_t = \text{const} + \alpha y_{t-1} + \sum_{i=1}^{p} \beta_i \Delta y_{t-i} + \varepsilon_t, \tag{7.2}$$

$$\Delta y_t = \text{const} + \alpha y_{t-1} + \beta t + \sum_{i=1}^{p} \beta_i \Delta y_{t-i} + \varepsilon_t, \tag{7.3}$$

where $\Delta y_t = y_t - y_{t-1}$ are first differences of y_t and ε_t is the white noise. Equations (7.1) and (7.2) refer to a mean-stationarity and Eq. (7.3) refers to a trend-stationarity. The null and alternative hypotheses may be written as: $H_0 : \alpha = 0$, $H_1 : \alpha < 0$ and evaluated using the standard t-statistic $t_\alpha = \hat{\alpha}/S(\hat{\alpha})$, where $\hat{\alpha}$ is the estimate and $S(\hat{\alpha})$ is the standard error of the estimate. Dickey and Fuller (1979) show that a test statistic does not follow the t-distribution but its critical values are simulated for range of sample sizes and different tests. MacKinnon (1996) provides a wide array of simulations for the ADF test and allows for approximation of critical values and p-values for arbitrary sample sizes. Another issue is to choose the lag order for the lagged first differences. Ng and Perron (1995) show that the selection of the lag length through the significance of the testing statistic t_α gives better properties in terms of size and power of the test than based on the information criteria.

Phillips and Perron (1988) propose an alternative method for dealing with serial correlation when testing for stationarity. Phillips and Perron derive the t-statistic where serial correlation does not affect the asymptotic distribution of the test. The Phillips and Perron test (PP test) is based on the statistic:

$$\check{t}_\alpha = t_\alpha \sqrt{\left(\frac{\gamma_0}{f_0}\right)} - \frac{T(f_0 - \gamma_0)(S(\hat{\alpha}))}{2f_0^{1/2}\mathrm{SE}}, \tag{7.4}$$

where SE is the standard error of the regression, γ_0 is a consistent estimate of the error variance in Eqs. (7.1)–(7.3), and f_0 is an estimator of the residual spectrum at frequency zero. The asymptotic distribution of the PP test is the same as the ADF test.

Contrary to the ADF and the PP test, Kwiatkowski et al. (1992) propose the KPSS test which assumes that the series is trend-stationary under the null hypothesis against the alternative of a unit root.

The three mentioned tests, i.e. the ADF, the PP and the KPSS tests, do not allow for a structural break. Perron (1989) shows that the power to reject the null hypothesis (a unit root) decreases when the stationary alternative is true and a structural break is ignored.

Zivot and Andrews (1992) modified the Perron test in order to incorporate the fact that the time of the break is unknown. We assume that a structural break occurs at time T_b, i.e. $1 < T_\mathrm{b} < T$ and is an endogenous phenomenon, unlike Perron (1989) who view a structural break to be exogenous. Following Perron (1989) and Zivot and Andrews (1992) notation, we are considering three models:

$$\Delta y_t = \mathrm{const} + \alpha y_{t-1} + \beta t + \gamma \mathrm{DU}_t + \sum_{i=1}^{p} \beta_i \Delta y_{t-i} + \varepsilon_t, \tag{7.5}$$

$$\Delta y_t = \mathrm{const} + \alpha y_{t-1} + \beta t + \delta \mathrm{DT}_t + \sum_{i=1}^{p} \beta_i \Delta y_{t-i} + \varepsilon_t, \tag{7.6}$$

$$\Delta y_t = \mathrm{const} + \alpha y_{t-1} + \beta t + \delta \mathrm{DT}_t + \gamma \mathrm{DU}_t + \sum_{i=1}^{p} \beta_i \Delta y_{t-i} + \varepsilon_t, \tag{7.7}$$

where $\varepsilon_t \sim$ i. i. d. $(0, \sigma^2)$, $\mathrm{DU}_t = \begin{cases} 1 & \text{if } t > T_\mathrm{b} \\ 0 & \text{otherwise} \end{cases}$ and $\mathrm{DT}_t = \begin{cases} 1 & \text{if } t > T_\mathrm{b} + 1 \\ 0 & \text{otherwise} \end{cases}$.

Model (7.5) permits a one-time change in the level of the series, model (7.6) allows for a one-time change in the slope of the trend function, and model (7.7) allows for a one-time change in the slope and the trend function of the series. Additional p lagged Δy_{t-i} variables are to eliminate possible nuisance parameter dependencies in the limit distribution of the test statistic. The null hypothesis for all three models is $\alpha = 0$ which means that the series y_t contains a unit root without a structural break (in the intercept, in the trend and in both respectively for model (7.5)–(7.7)). The alternative hypothesis, i.e. $\alpha < 0$, means that the series is a trend-stationary process with one-time break occurring at an unknown point in time. Andrews and Zivot propose an explicit algorithm for selecting the break point, i.e. that every point is a possible break point and test all of them. The proposed algorithm chooses the break point as a one which minimizes the one-sided t-statistic for testing $\breve{a} = 1$. Following Andrews and Zivot notation let $\hat{\lambda}_{\text{inf}}$ denote such a minimizing value of a break fraction $\lambda = T_b/T$ for models (7.5)–(7.7). The corresponding test statistic is then

$$t\left[\hat{\lambda}_{\text{inf}}\right] = \text{inf}_{\lambda} t(\lambda), \tag{7.8}$$

where $\lambda \in (0, 1)$. In order to reject the null of a unit root then $\text{inf}_{\lambda} t(\lambda) < C_\alpha$ where C_α denotes the left-tail α critical value from the asymptotic distribution of the test. Some end points of the sample must be excluded due to the issue that they cause the asymptotic distribution of the statistics to diverge towards infinity. A common trimming region is specified as $(0.15T, 0.85T)$.

Bai and Perron (1998, 2003a, b) propose a test for multiple unknown break points. Following notation of Bai and Perron let assume a multiple linear regression model with T periods and m potential breaks which means we have $m + 1$ regimes. In regime i with T_i observations, we have the following linear regression:

$$y_t = X_t'\beta + Z_t'\delta_i + \varepsilon_t, \tag{7.9}$$

where y_t is the dependent variable, X_t and Z_t are vectors of independent variables, β and $\delta_i\,(i = 1,\ldots,m + 1)$ are the vectors of parameters and ε_t is the innovation process. There are two groups of independent variables. The X_t vector contains variables whose parameters are the same across regimes. On the other hand, the Z_t vector contains variables whose parameters vary across regimes. When in regression (7.9) there are no variables in the vector X_t then we obtain model where all of the parameters vary across regimes. In order to estimate parameters of the regression (7.9), Bai and Perron consider the least-squared method of estimation which constitutes in minimizing the sum-of-squared residuals for a set of m break points. Bai and Perron (2003a, b) propose algorithms for the global optimizers for multiple break points regression due to the numerical complexity. Bai and Perron (1998) generalize the Quandt and Andrews test (Andrews 1993). They test for equality of the δ_i across multiple regimes. The null hypothesis states no break points against the alternative hypothesis of k breaks. The F test statistic is derived as

$$F(\lambda_1, \ldots, \lambda_k) = \frac{1}{T}\left(\frac{T - (k+1)q - p}{kq}\right)\left(R\hat{\delta}\right)'\left(R\hat{V}\left(\hat{\delta}\right)R'\right)^{-1}R\hat{\delta}, \tag{7.10}$$

where $\lambda_i = T_i/T$ for $i = 1,\ldots,k$, $\left(R\hat{\delta}\right)' = \left(\delta_1' - \delta_2', \ldots, \delta_k' - \delta_{k+1}'\right)$, $\hat{V}\left(\hat{\delta}\right)$ is the variance covariance matrix of the $\hat{\delta}$, q is the minimal length of a segment, i.e. $T_i - T_{i-1} \geq q$, p is the number of variables in X_t. Then the sup$F$ type test statistic is defined as

$$\sup F(\lambda_1, \ldots, \lambda_k) = \sup_{\lambda_1, \ldots, \lambda_k} F(\lambda_1, \ldots, \lambda_k). \tag{7.11}$$

This version of the test (global k breaks vs. no breaks) assumes that k breaks is known before. It is possible to assume that there are unknown number of breaks to some upper bound but it means that maximization of the statistic is made for a given k breaks and across different values of the test statistic.

Another possible procedure to test for multiple breaks is a sequential testing which involves a test of parameter constancy with unknown break. If there is no constancy of parameter (rejection of the null), then the sample is divided into two samples in regard to the break date. For these two samples, the break point is determined whenever the null is rejected for a single unknown break point test. The procedure is repeated for all cases where the null is rejected.

Bai and Perron (1998) provided another approach to test k break points under the null. This approach boils down to testing $k + 1$ breaks versus k breaks where global approach and sequential testing are combined.

7.3 Structural Breaks and Economic Growth: Empirical Analysis

We examine the unit-root properties for four countries, i.e. Ireland, Spain, Turkey and the Netherlands, using macroeconomic annual time series. The sample period for each variable ranges from 1980 to 2014 for Ireland, from 1980 to 2015 for Spain, from 1980 to 2016 for Turkey and from 1981 to 2016 for the Netherlands. The description of the data is given in Table 7.1. In addition, for GDP and GNP, a standard Hodrick–Prescott (HP) filter has been employed to remove the trend and the cyclical components of growth (Hodrick and Prescott 1997; Durlauf and Temple 2005).

The first step of the analysis is to ascertain the integration properties of the series. We use the Phillips–Perron test for three models, where there is no constant, with constant and with a linear trend. As was mentioned before, a stationarity property is important when we deal with economic time series and underlying trends. In the second step, the Andrews–Zivot test was carried out in order to test for unit root with possible one break. In this case, the regressions (7.5)–(7.7) were estimated. The third step is to use the Bai and Perron test to identify multiple breaks for all given time series. For the Bai and Perron test it is assumed that model (7.9) consists of exogenous variables in the X_t vector (it is a pure structural change model), but the breaking regressors in the vector Z_t are in the first case only constant and in the

Table 7.1 Variable names and units (own summary)

Short name	Country	Full name	Variable unit
GDP	I, S, T, N	Gross Domestic Product	Billions of euro (I, S), millions of dollars (T, N)
HP_GDP	I, S, T, N	Gross Domestic Product	Billions of euro (I, S), millions of dollars (T, N) (Hodrick–Prescott filter)
FDI	I, S, T, N	Foreign Direct Investment	Millions of euro (I, S), millions of dollars (T), % of GDP (N)
NI_EU	I, S	Net income from EU	Millions of euro
EMP	I, S	Employment	Thousands
EXR	T, N	Exchange Rate	Turkish lira/USD (T), EUR/USD (N)
PD	I, S, T, N	Public Debt	Billions of euro (I, S), % of GDP (T, N)
DEFLATOR	I, S, T, N	GDP deflator	[%] of GDP
INV	I, S, T, N	Investments	Billions of euro (I), % of GDP (T), millions of US dollars (N)
IMF_L	T	Loans from the IMF	Thousands SDR
MFP	N	Multifactor productivity	Index (constant price)
N_Ex	I, S, T, N	Net Export	Billions of euro (I, S), millions of US dollars (T, N)
SR	I, S, T, N	Short-term interest rate	[%]
LR	I, S, T, N	Long-term interest rate	[%]
TFP	I, S, T	Total factor productivity	Index (constant price)
UNEM	T, N	Unemployment Rate	[%]
WB_L	T	Loans from the World Bank	USD
FDI/GDP	I, S		[%]
NI_EU/GDP	I, S		[%]
I/GDP	I, S		[%]
HP_GNP	I	Gross National Product	Billions of euro (Hodrick-Prescott filter)

In column labelled County, "I" stands for Ireland, "S" for Spain, "T" for Turkey and "N" for Netherlands. The data were downloaded from http://www.economywatch.com/, http://www.cso.ie/en/statistics/ and http://stats.oecd.org, https://data.worldbank.org/, https://www.imf.org/en/data, https://ec.europa.eu/eurostat/data/database, financial reports of the European Union, https://www.ilo.org/global/statistics-and-databases/lang%2D%2Den/index.htm, https://www.bde.es/webbde/en/estadis/infoest/bolest17.html, https://fred.stlouisfed.org/

second linear trend. Moreover, it is assumed that error distributions may differ across breaks, which provide robustness of the test to error distribution variation (see Bai and Perron 2003b). White standard errors are computed which are robust to heteroscedasticity. We have to keep in mind that time series are quite short (less than 40 observations) and that could affect the results. In the next empirical parts of this chapter, all calculations were carried out using the EViews software.

7.3.1 Empirical Application: A Case of Ireland

Based on the PP test results (Table 7.2), almost all series have a unit root, whereas three series, i.e. FDI, FDI/GDP (levels and logarithms) and SR, are stationary. Interestingly, some series are integrated of order two, i.e. GDP and GNP, after Hodrick–Prescott filter is applied. Tables 7.3 and 7.4 present the Andrews and Zivot test results and the Bai and Perron test results along with break years.

We can observe structural breaks in the 1980s and the 1990s. The growth fundamentals were laid by the publication of Economic Development programme in 1958. This programme focused on the policies such as, for example, reorientation from import towards export, where foreign direct investment (FDI) is a key to success. This resulted in an increase of manufacturing export from 30% in 1960 to 69% in 1990 (O'Sullivan 1995; Doyle 2001). The policy of foreign direct investment and high-tech industry played a significant role in economic growth in Ireland. The 1990s is the period when Ireland experienced growth rates far exceeding other European countries. The average GDP grew over 4 years—up to 1997 it was 8.4%, where exports in 1996 represented 76% of GDP in constant prices (Cassidy 2004). The year 2008 is another break point due to the financial and economic crisis, which had a detrimental effect on growth in Ireland. This fact is consistent with other general findings and implies nonlinearity, as, for instance, in Woo and Kumar (2015).

7.3.2 Empirical Application: A Case of Spain

The PP test results for Spain are presented in Table 7.5. Most of the series have unit root. The following time series: NI_EU/GDP (logarithms), PD (logarithms) and GDP with Hodrick–Prescott filter have two unit roots. Tables 7.6 and 7.7 present the Andrews and Zivot test results and the Bai and Perron test results along with break years.

The common break year which can be identified is 1985, which is the year when Spain joined the European Union. Before the economic integration with the EU, Spain had witnessed rapid growth in its living standards due to the increase in physical and human capital stocks and significant improvements in productive efficiency (Lieberman 1995) in the early 1970s. That was slowed down by the

Table 7.2 Results of the Philips and Perron (PP) test for Ireland (own calculations)

	PP test (no constant)		PP test (constant)		PP test (linear trend)	
Variable	Level data	First differences	Level data	First differences	Level data	First differences
DEFLATOR	2.295	−1.955**	−1.822	−2.457	−1.389	−2.504
EMP	1.416	−2.602**	−0.514	−2.871*	−1.846	−2.820
FDI	−2.642***	−7.711***	−3.063**	−7.477***	−3.869**	−7.391***
FDI/GDP	−2.431**	−7.363***	−3.075**	−7.174***	−3.750**	−7.077***
GDP	2.315	−1.755*	−0.172	−2.532	−1.789	−2.503
GNP	2.963	−2.039**	0.407	−2.975**	−2.150	−3.074
HP_GDP	2.874	−0.742	−0.114	−1.275	−1.973	−0.592
HP_GNP	3.758	−0.570	0.333	−1.511	−2.264	−0.719
HP_ln_GDP	3.850	−0.717	−0.781	−0.950	−1.124	−0.898
INV	−0.159	−1.999**	−1.239	−1.982	−1.565	−1.928
I/GDP	−1.116	−2.467**	−1.740	−2.476	−1.722	−2.482
LR	−2.393**	−5.602***	−1.240	−6.124***	−2.065	−6.429***
N_EX	1.522	−2.954***	−0.536	−2.997**	−2.010	−2.910
NI_EU	−0.661	−5.127***	−1.198	−5.042***	−1.428	−5.703***
NI_EU/GDP	−0.792	−5.055***	−0.723	−4.973***	−1.859	−5.172***
PD	1.925	−1.837*	0.791	−2.038	−0.270	−2.216
SR	−2.284**	−6.629***	−0.981	−9.521***	−3.608**	−11.185***
TFP	0.238	−8.797***	−3.187**	−8.647***	−3.128	−8.454***
ln_DEFLATOR	2.721	−3.537***	−3.86***	−3.614**	−2.851	−3.312*
ln_EMP	1.773	−2.371**	−0.465	−2.771*	−1.785	−2.714
ln_FDI	−0.786	−9.843***	−3.545**	−9.782***	−3.819**	−9.667***
ln_FDI/GDP	−0.768	−9.674***	−3.667***	−9.548***	−3.649**	−9.423***
ln_GDP	3.216	−1.489	−0.675	−2.410	−1.289	−2.416
ln_ INV	0.511	−2.336**	−0.993	−2.314	−1.621	−2.278

(continued)

Table 7.2 (continued)

Variable	PP test (no constant)		PP test (constant)		PP test (linear trend)	
	Level data	First differences	Level data	First differences	Level data	First differences
ln_I/GDP	0.765	−2.354**	−1.700	−2.336	−1.699	−2.352
ln_LR	−1.711*	−3.762***	−0.583	−3.912***	−2.330	−3.863**
ln_N_EX	0.991	−4.926***	−1.129	−5.491***	−1.394	−5.967***
ln_NI_EU	−0.350	−4.949***	−1.018	−4.874***	−1.605	−5.162***
ln_NI_EU/GDP	−0.968	−4.763***	−0.261	−4.774***	−1.828	−5.012***
ln_PD	1.495	−2.617**	−0.375	−2.863*	−1.081	−2.878
ln_SR	−1.151	−5.061***	1.767	−5.545***	−1.741	−6.065***
ln_TFP	0.292	−8.777***	−3.193**	−8.397***	−3.134	−8.432***

ln and HP suffix denote natural logarithm and Hodrick–Prescott filter applied, respectively. *, ** and *** denote statistical significance at 10%, 5% and 1% level, respectively

Table 7.3 Results of Andrews and Zivot (AZ) test for Ireland (own calculations)

	AZ test (no constant)		AZ test (constant)		AZ test (linear trend)	
Variable	*t*-stat	Break year	*t*-stat	Break year	*t*-stat	Break year
DEFLATOR	−3.769	2000	−3.575	2007	–	–
EMP	−3.721	2009	−2.981	2007	−3.026	2004
FDI	−3.365	2004	−3.669	2009	−5.285**	2005
FDI/GDP	−4.208	2004	−3.657	2009	−5.145**	2005
GDP	−3.133	1999	−2.701	2007	–	–
GNP	−3.305	1999	−2.793	1992	−3.144	1996
HP_GDP	−4.611*	2008	–	–	–	–
HP_GNP	−4.557	2008	−4.511	2006	−4.537	2005
HP_ln_GDP	−3.383	2008	−3.047	1999	−3.522	2009
INV	−3.742	2002	−3.152	2007	–	–
I/GDP	−3.649	2008	−3.347	2006	−3.251	2003
LR	−3.294	2007	−3.359	1987	−3.171	1997
N_EX	−3.730	2001	−2.789	1992	–	–
NI_EU	−2.939	1990	−3.843	1992	−4.452	1990
NI_EU/GDP	−3.145	1998	−3.409	1991	−3.485	1990
PD	−9.625***	2008	−5.734***	2007	−5.322**	2004
SR	−4.993**	1994	−4.263	2000	−4.933**	1994
TFP	−5.245**	2001	−4.117	1996	−5.282**	2001
ln_DEFLATOR	−4.318	2008	−3.988	2006	−4.307	2000
ln_EMP	−3.913	2009	−3.025	2007	−2.804	1998
ln_FDI	−5.468***	2004	−4.214	2009	−9.271***	2004
ln_FDI/GDP	−5.270**	2004	−4.072	2009	−9.403***	2004
ln_GDP	−3.951	2008	−3.357	2006	−2.949	2004
ln_INV	−3.408	2008	−2.988	2006	−2.493	2004
ln_I/GDP	−3.569	2009	−3.264	2006	−3.029	2003
ln_LR	−5.276**	2009	−4.136	2006	−4.386	2001
ln_N_EX	−2.775	1987	−3.817	2001	−3.707	2001
ln_NI_EU	−3.246	2005	−3.056	1992	−3.103	1990
ln_NI_EU/GDP	−2.933	2005	−3.082	1992	−3.072	1990
ln_PD	−7.815***	2008	−3.854	2006	−3.585	2000
ln_SR	−0.942	2009	−3.169	2009	−3.822	2007
ln_TFP	−5.220**	2001	−4.119	1996	−5.251**	2001

ln and HP suffix denote natural logarithm and Hodrick–Prescott filter applied, respectively. *, ** and *** denote statistical significance at 10%, 5% and 1% level, respectively

economic crisis later in that decade. The recovery from that crisis was paired with the European Economic Community accession. The period of 1986–1993 is the time of high economic growth in Spain. Similar to Ireland, Spain's rapid increase in export created a path for growth in the long run (Eepinger et al. 2015). The huge FDI increase in the share of GDP for Spain played a similar role as in the case of Ireland. The time period from 1993 to 1995 exhibited other breaks which stand out from

Table 7.4 Results of Bai and Perron (BP) test for Ireland (own calculations)

	BP test (constant as breaking regressor)	BP test (linear trend as breaking regressor)
Variable	Break year	Break year
DEFLATOR	1985, 1993, 1998, 2003	1985, 1998, 2004, 2009
EMP	1994, 1999, 2004	1985, 1994, 2009
FDI	2009	1989, 1994, 1999, 2004, 2009
FDI/GDP	2009	1994, 1999, 2004, 2009
GDP	1985, 1990, 1995, 2000, 2005	1987, 1995, 2000, 2009
GNP	1990, 1995, 2000, 2005	1988, 1997, 2009
HP_GDP	1988, 1993, 1998, 2003, 2008	1989, 1995, 2003, 2008
HP_GNP	1989, 1994, 1999, 2004, 2009	1988, 1994, 2006
HP_ln_GDP	1986, 1991, 1996, 2001, 2006	1988, 1993, 2002, 2007
INV	1998, 2004, 2009	1989, 1994, 2005, 2010
I/GDP	1985, 1998, 2009	1988, 2009
LR	1985, 1991, 1997	1998
N_EX	1986, 1992, 1997, 2002, 2009	1994, 2004, 2009
NI_EU	1985, 1990, 1999, 2005	1990, 1997, 2002, 2009
NI_EU/GDP	1985, 1999, 2005	1991, 1999, 2009
PD	1985, 2010	1987, 1995, 2000, 2005, 2010
SR	1985, 1994, 1999, 2009	1988, 1993
TFP	1987, 1995, 2001	2001
ln_DEFLATOR	1985, 1993, 2001	1985, 1990, 1996, 2004, 2009
ln_EMP	1994, 1999, 2004	1989, 1998, 2009
ln_FDI	2009	1985, 1990, 1998, 2004, 2009
ln_FDI/GDP	1990, 1998, 2004, 2009	1985, 1990, 1998, 2004, 2009
ln_GDP	1989, 1995, 2000, 2005	1989, 1994, 2001, 2009
ln_INV	1997, 2003, 2009	1988, 2008
ln_I/GDP	1985, 1997, 2009	1989, 1995, 2009
ln_LR	1986, 1993, 1998	No breakpoints selected
ln_N_EX	1987, 1992, 1997, 2002, 2009	1986, 2001
ln_NI_EU	1985, 1990, 2001, 2007	1991, 2005, 2010
ln_NI_EU/GDP	1985, 1999, 2006	1994, 2009
ln_PD	1985, 2000, 2009	1987, 1995, 2000, 2008
ln_SR	1994, 1999, 2009	1994, 2004, 2009
ln_TFP	1987, 1995, 2001	2001

Tables 7.6 and 7.7. These years are connected with a short recession period in Spain and with the implementation of the single currency, the euro (Estrada and Malo de Molina 2009). In Spain, starting from 1995 there has been a huge increase in immigration mainly due to rapid growth and the demographic pressures from sub-Saharan Africa and Latin America. Immigration strengthened an increase in GDP and increase in productivity (De la Rica et al. 2015). Exactly as Ireland, Spain was influenced deeply by the financial crisis in 2007–2009, which is evident from the AZ test and the BP test results.

Table 7.5 Results of the Philips and Perron (PP) test for Spain (own calculations)

	PP test (no constant)		PP test (constant)		PP test (linear trend)	
Variable	Level data	First differences	Level data	First differences	Level data	First differences
DEFLATOR	−2.392**	−6.957***	−2.053	−7.628***	−2.486	−7.911***
EMP	0.891	−2.333**	−0.840	−2.526	−1.874	−2.349
FDI	−1.386	−9.411***	−2.717*	−9.796***	−3.421*	−10.636***
FDI/GDP	−1.142	−9.513***	−3.007**	−9.599***	−3.234*	−10.119***
GDP	2.494	−1.636*	−0.752	−2.514	−1.569	−2.518
HP_GDP	3.350	−0.825	−1.108	−0.442	−0.652	−0.708
INV	0.166	−2.835***	−1.371	−2.875*	−1.418	−2.865
I/GDP	−0.418	−2.979***	−1.701	−2.931*	−1.544	−2.870
LR	−1.877*	−2.610**	0.255	−2.532	−1.983	−2.764
N_EX	−1.767*	−7.591***	−2.080	−7.469***	−1.987	−7.864***
NI_EU	0.331	−6.193***	−1.039	−6.877***	−2.951	−6.729***
NI_EU/GDP	3.257	−3.073***	−2.238	−4.209***	−2.033	−4.375***
PD	−1.174	−4.903***	1.841	−5.342***	−1.460	−6.206***
SR	0.247	−2.288**	−1.649	−2.264	−3.092	−2.115
TFP	−2.708***	−4.387***	−0.738	−4.929***	−2.162	−4.876***
ln_DEFLATOR	−1.656*	−2.818***	−1.633	−2.769*	−1.247	−2.914
ln_EMP	−1.212	−6.019***	−1.699	−5.928***	−1.498	−5.953***
ln_FDI	−1.232	−6.262***	−1.695	−6.167***	−1.504	−6.198***
ln_FDI/GDP	5.552	−3.587***	2.653	−4.590***	−0.091	−5.278***
ln_GDP	−2.247**	−7.115***	−0.867	−8.792***	−3.077	−8.930***
ln_hp_GDP	0.193	−2.354**	−1.634	−2.402	−3.066	−2.215
ln_INV	−2.173**	−6.853***	−1.944	−7.537***	−2.498	−7.730***
ln_I/GDP	1.130	−2.112**	−0.781	−2.358	−1.926	−2.504
ln_LR	0.022	−7.758***	−2.374	−7.976***	−2.874	−8.717***

(continued)

Table 7.5 (continued)

	PP test (no constant)		PP test (constant)		PP test (linear trend)	
Variable	Level data	First differences	Level data	First differences	Level data	First differences
ln_NI_EU	−0.844	−8.268***	−3.001**	−8.291***	−3.232*	−8.988***
ln_NI_EU/GDP	3.357	−1.405	−1.261	−2.526	−0.721	−2.759
ln_PD	4.629	−0.940	−2.160	0.284	2.248	−1.049
ln_SR	0.855	−2.643***	−1.352	−2.757*	−1.311	−2.788
ln_TFP	0.058	−2.970***	−1.699	−2.920*	−1.545	−2.908

ln and HP suffix denote natural logarithm and Hodrick–Prescott filter applied, respectively. *, ** and *** denote statistical significance at 10%, 5% and 1% level, respectively

Table 7.6 Results of Andrews and Zivot (AZ) test for Spain (own calculations)

Variable	I-stat	Break year	*t*-stat	Break year	*t*-stat	Break year
DEFLATOR	−4.252	1987	−3.891	1988	−4.254	1987
EMP	−3.630	1999	−3.127	1992	−3.697	2003
FDI	−5.021**	2009	−4.327	2008	−6.041***	2000
FDI/GDP	−4.653*	2009	−4.223	2003	−5.760***	2000
GDP	−3.506	2009	−3.467	2007	−3.893	2003
HP_GDP	−3.450	2009	−2.041	2006	−2.418	2009
INV	−4.347	2009	−3.722	2007	−4.134	2003
I/GDP	−4.431	2009	−4.111	2007	−4.409	2003
LR	−4.562	1996	−4.176	2004	−5.211**	1996
N_EX	−3.683	2003	−4.648*	2008	−5.982***	2004
NI_EU	−4.237	2005	−3.174	2003	−4.308	1995
NI_EU/GDP	−3.903	2005	−3.208	1999	−5.089**	1995
PD	−3.480	2009	−4.582*	2007	−4.812*	2005
SR	−4.796*	1994	−3.949	2002	−4.670*	1994
TFP	−3.596	2001	–	–	–	–
ln_DEFLATOR	−4.117	1987	−3.763	1988	−4.121	2000
ln_EMP	−3.784	1999	−3.288	2006	−3.797	2002
ln_FDI	−5.056**	2009	−4.317	2003	−5.053**	2000
ln_FDI/GDP	−5.075**	2009	−4.445	2002	−5.057**	2000
ln_GDP	−4.297	2009	−4.567	2007	−4.600*	2005
ln_hp_GDP	−1.597	1996	−2.848	2010	−2.825	2009
ln_INV	−4.483	2009	−4.280	2007	−4.401	2003
ln_I/GDP	−4.474	2009	−4.142	2007	−4.336	2003
ln_LR	−4.630*	1996	−3.312	1990	−4.594*	1996
ln_NI_EU	−4.182	2006	−4.286	2003	−4.699*	1995
ln_NI_EU/GDP	−7.246***	1993	−3.293	1997	−7.866***	1993
ln_PD	–	–	−3.736	1987	–	–
ln_SR	−1.334	1989	−2.753	2009	−3.358	2007
ln_TFP	−3.580	2001	–	–	−2.862	2008

ln and HP suffix denote natural logarithm and Hodrick–Prescott filter applied, respectively. *, ** and *** denote statistical significance at 10%, 5% and 1% level, respectively. "–" denotes cases where test was not able to carried out

7.3.3 Empirical Application: A Case of Turkey

In Table 7.8, the Phillips and Perron test results are presented. A great number of the series have unit root, but there are some stationary series as well, i.e. N_EX, IMF_L, WB_L, EXR (logarithms) and TFP (logarithms). The series GDP with Hodrick–Prescott filter have two unit roots. Tables 7.9 and 7.10 present the Andrews and Zivot test results and the Bai and Perron test results along with break years.

In the case of Turkey, the AZ test and the BP test results indicate that there are many possible years as breaks. Nevertheless, some of the years stand out more than

Table 7.7 Results of Bai and Perron (BP) test for Spain (own calculations)

Variable	BP test (constant as breaking regressor) Break year	BP test (linear trend as breaking regressor) Break year
DEFLATOR	1987, 1993, 2009	1987, 1993, 2001, 2009
EMP	1988, 1999, 2004, 2011	1997, 2009
FDI	1988, 2000, 2009	1985, 1990, 1997, 2003, 2009
FDI/GDP	1988, 2000, 2009	1986, 1991, 1998, 2003, 2009
GDP	1988, 1995, 2000, 2005	1996, 2009
HP_GDP	1988, 1995, 2000, 2005	1985, 1992, 1997, 2005, 2010
INV	1988, 1999, 2004, 2009	1988, 1996, 2009
I/GDP	2000, 2009	1993, 2009
LR	1985, 1992, 1997	1985, 1990, 1995, 2000, 2011
N_EX	1988, 2004, 2011	1985, 1993, 2002, 2008
NI_EU	1995, 2006	1995, 2005
NI_EU/GDP	1995, 2005	1995, 2005
PD	1987, 1994, 2003, 2009	1985, 1995, 2002, 2009
SR	1985, 1994, 1999, 2009	1989, 2000
TFP	1985, 1998, 2003, 2008	1988, 1994, 2011
ln_DEFLATOR	1987, 1993, 2009	1987, 1993, 2009
ln_EMP	1988, 1999, 2004, 2011	1987, 1993, 2009
ln_FDI	1987, 1999	1993, 2000
ln_FDI/GDP	1986, 1998	1990, 1998, 2003, 2009
ln_GDP	1988, 1998, 2003	1985, 1990, 1995, 2000, 2009
ln_hp_GDP	1987, 1993, 1999, 2004	1985, 1990, 1996, 2004, 2009
ln_INV	1988, 2000, 2011	1987, 1993, 2009
ln_I/GDP	1999, 2010	1993, 2009
ln_LR	1985, 1992, 1997, 2003	1997, 2005, 2011
ln_NI_EU	1995, 2006	1995, 2004, 2010
ln_NI_EU/GDP	1993, 2006	1993, 2006
ln_PD	1985, 1990, 1995, 2003, 2009	1986, 1996, 2002, 2009
ln_SR	1993, 1998, 2009	1994, 2007
ln_TFP	1985, 1998, 2003, 2008	1985, 1990, 1997, 2011

others. The first such a period is 1985–1987. It should be emphasized that prior to that period Turkey had been struck by economic crisis in 1979 followed by the coup d'état of 1980. In that time the Turkish lira was devaluated by 77% and the sovereign risks increased implied by the military takeover and the abolishment of political parties. The period of 1980–1987 is known as the post-coup time (Bilgel and Karahasan 2016). The year 1987 is also a year of elections in Turkey. The change of ruling parties and coups are believed to be inductive to business cycles in Turkey (Akarca 2018). The next discernible period is 1993–1995. This period is called "the dollarization" of the economy. By the end of 1994, about 50% of the domestic assets base was held in the foreign-currency deposits. In 1994 local elections took place,

Table 7.8 Results of the Philips and Perron (PP) test for Turkey (own calculations)

	PP test (no constant)		PP test (constant)		PP test (linear trend)	
Variable	Level data	First differences	Level data	First differences	Level data	First differences
DEFLATOR	−1.861*	−8.328***	−2.239	−8.354***	−2.626	−8.633***
EXR	2.849	−2.382**	1.686	−3.006**	−0.921	−3.563**
N_EX	−2.450**	−10.264***	−4.225***	−10.049***	−4.260***	−9.943***
FDI	−0.645	−4.758***	−1.255	−6.152***	−2.258	−5.797***
GDP	15.421	−3.142***	5.597	−5.210***	0.149	−6.849***
HP_GDP	30.207	3.538	10.452	1.055	3.225	−1.661
IMF_L	−5.148***	−14.515***	−5.419***	−14.256***	−5.372***	−14.217***
INV	−0.001	−8.573***	−2.392	−8.627***	−3.671**	−8.875***
LR	−0.782	−9.146***	−1.601	−9.023***	−2.235	−9.112***
PD	−0.476	−5.776***	−2.045	−5.696***	−1.849	−5.727***
SR	−1.206	−9.137***	−1.915	−9.015***	−2.580	−9.599***
TFP	0.297	−7.733***	−3.043**	−7.757***	−3.302*	−7.725***
UNEM	1.573	−5.671***	−1.722	−8.348***	−2.449	−8.675***
WB_L	−2.208**	−8.182***	−2.938*	−8.077***	−3.417*	−8.430***
ln_DEFLATOR	−1.377	−6.819***	−1.104	−6.916***	−1.770	−6.959***
ln_EXR	−3.447***	−1.471	−2.167	−2.469	−0.284	−3.275*
ln_FDI	1.583	−6.898***	−1.991	−7.632***	−3.135	−7.694***
ln_GDP	10.594	−3.714***	−0.625	−8.126***	−3.262*	−8.093***
ln_HP_GDP	14.234	−2.149**	−2.242	−3.375**	−3.998**	−2.562
ln_INV	0.125	−8.660***	−2.419	−8.626***	−3.713**	−8.813***
ln_LR	−0.458	−7.119***	−0.850	−7.096***	−2.431	−7.634***
ln_PD	0.205	−5.821***	−2.213	−5.751***	−1.909	−5.827***
ln_SR	−0.548	−6.477***	−0.799	−6.460***	−2.305	−6.626***
ln_TFP	−2.383**	−7.860***	−3.074**	−7.886***	−3.341*	−7.857***

(continued)

Table 7.8 (continued)

	PP test (no constant)		PP test (constant)		PP test (linear trend)	
Variable	Level data	First differences	Level data	First differences	Level data	First differences
ln_UNEM	1.561	−5.924***	−1.703	−8.568***	−2.406	−8.891***

ln and HP suffix denote natural logarithm and Hodrick–Prescott filter applied, respectively. *, ** and *** denote statistical significance at 10%, 5% and 1% level, respectively

Table 7.9 Results of Andrews and Zivot (AZ) test for Turkey (own calculations)

	AZ test (no constant)		AZ test (constant)		AZ test (linear trend)	
Variable	*t*-statistics	Break year	*t*-statistics	Break year	*t*-statistics	Break year
DEFLATOR	−4.522	2002	−4.805*	1995	−7.000***	1999
EXR	−2.189	1989	−2.844	1995	−2.888	1999
N_EX	−4.993**	1998	−4.642*	2002	−5.180**	1998
FDI	−7.310***	2005	−3.636	1997	−6.966***	2005
GDP	−2.396	2010	−3.907	2003	−4.361	2001
HP_GDP	−2.139	2003	−5.819***	1999	−5.141**	1998
IMF_L	−3.881	1999	−2.978	2001	−6.707***	1999
INV	−4.789*	2004	−4.136	2002	−4.638*	2004
LR	−4.035	2003	−3.315	1995	−3.583	1994
PD	−2.960	2000	−2.488	2005	−6.507***	2002
SR	−3.886	2003	−3.356	1995	−4.221	1994
TFP	−3.991	2004	−3.482	2008	−4.523	2004
UNEM	−4.379	2001	−3.954	1999	−4.637*	2001
WB_L	−3.203	2011	−4.134	2011	−4.161	2010
ln_DEFLATOR	−4.336	2003	−3.602	1995	−4.218	2003
ln_EXR	−3.295	1992	−4.623*	2002	−4.268	1994
ln_FDI	−3.706	2005	−3.537	2009	−5.072**	2005
ln_GDP	−4.413	1999	−3.643	1988	−4.255	1999
ln_HP_GDP	−3.707	2002	–	–	–	–
ln_ INV	−4.661*	2004	−4.073	2002	−4.499	2004
ln_LR	−4.256	2004	−4.003	1997	−4.210	1994
ln_PD	−3.163	2000	−2.478	2005	−5.018**	2002
ln_SR	−4.146	2002	−3.193	1995	−3.723	2002
ln_TFP	−4.015	2004	−3.537	1987	−4.499	2004
ln_UNEM	−4.168	2001	−3.560	1999	−4.371	2001

ln and HP suffix denote natural logarithm and Hodrick–Prescott filter applied, respectively. *, ** and *** denote statistical significance at 10%, 5% and 1% level, respectively

the austerity programme was announced, and the value of the Turkish lira started to fall rapidly from the end of 1993 (Feridun 2008, 2009). The Turkish economy was influenced by the economic crisis of 2007–2009, but between 2002 and 2007, the average annual growth rate was 6.9%. Taşkın (2014) argues that GDP growth in Turkey was inclusive between 2002 and 2011, but there is significant heterogeneity in inclusiveness of economic growth across regions and over time. Bozkurt (2015) found that in the period of 1998–2013 there is causality from economic growth to R&D. As the real economic activities and growth rate increase, R&D must also increase for sustainability.

Table 7.10 Results of Bai and Perron (BP) test for Turkey (own calculations)

	BP test (constant as breaking regressor)	BP test (linear trend as breaking regressor)
Variable	Break year	Break year
DEFLATOR	2003	1985, 1999, 2004
EXR	2001, 2012	1991, 1996, 2001, 2007, 2012
N_EX	No breakpoints selected	No breakpoints selected
FDI	1989, 2000, 2005, 2010	2005
GDP	1987, 1996, 2005, 2011	2001, 2009
HP_GDP	1988, 1995, 2002, 2007, 2012	1987, 1997, 2002, 2007, 2012
IMF_L	No breakpoints selected	No breakpoints selected
INV	2005	1986, 2004
LR	1985, 1994, 1999, 2004, 2009	2000
PD	2002, 2007, 2012	1986, 1991, 2002
SR	1985, 1994, 2002, 2007	1986, 1994, 2001, 2006, 2011
TFP	1986, 2004, 2009	1987, 2004
UNEM	1987, 1996, 2002	1996, 2011
WB_L	1999, 2011	1991, 1997, 2002, 2011
ln_DEFLATOR	2004	1998, 2005
ln_EXR	1985, 1990, 1995, 2000, 2012	1994, 2002, 2009
ln_FDI	1988, 2000, 2005	1988, 1993, 2005
ln_GDP	1987, 1996, 2004, 2011	1987, 2001, 2008
ln_HP_GDP	1986, 1993, 2002, 2009	1985, 1990, 1995, 2002, 2010
ln_INV	2005	1986, 2004
ln_LR	1991, 2004, 2009	1994, 2004, 2009
ln_PD	2002, 2008	1986, 1991, 2002
ln_SR	1985, 2004, 2009	2002, 2010
ln_TFP	1986, 2004, 2009	1987, 2004
ln_UNEM	1987, 1996, 2002	1996, 2011

7.3.4 Empirical Application: A Case of the Netherlands

In Table 7.11, the Phillips and Perron test results are presented. Almost all of the series have one unit root. The series GDP (levels and logarithms) with Hodrick–Prescott filter have two unit roots. Tables 7.12 and 7.13 present the Andrews and Zivot test results and the Bai and Perron test results along with break years.

The early 1980s are the years of stagnation where the large supply of labour acted as a drag on the economy, causing a high unemployment rate and breaking overall productivity performance. The early 1980s are characterized by privatization of the economy, creation of competition, and government debt removal. The first breaks period was identified in the years 1986–1988; this was the time of the growth in technology and the R&D stack (Ark and Jong 1996). The GDP growth of that period is also attributed to the global economic recovery. Another break years which stand out are 1997–1998. These were the years before introduction of the single currency,

Table 7.11 Results of the Philips and Perron (PP) test for the Netherlands (own calculations)

	PP test (no constant)		PP test (constant)		PP test (linear trend)	
Variable	Level data	First differences	Level data	First differences	Level data	First differences
DEFLATOR	5.731	−2.024**	−0.071	−3.300**	−1.600	−3.304*
EXR	−0.721	−4.259***	−1.822	−4.609***	−2.126	−6.187***
FDI	−1.883*	−11.179***	−2.595	−13.292***	−3.238*	−12.936***
GDP	4.219	−2.214**	−0.573	−3.895***	−1.461	−3.814**
HP_GDP	4.680	−0.468	−0.906	−1.207	−0.729	−1.646
INV	−0.401	−4.233***	−1.501	−4.161***	−2.247	−4.177**
LR	−2.869***	−4.203***	−1.457	−4.869***	−3.007	−4.925***
MFP	2.699	−3.765***	−1.415	−4.543***	−1.294	−4.601***
N_EX	2.517	−6.095***	−0.117	−6.469***	−2.541	−9.644***
PD	−0.627	−2.926***	−1.727	−2.865*	−1.702	−3.353*
SR	−1.756*	−5.047***	−1.448	−5.052***	−2.707	−5.132***
UNEM	−0.763	−5.497***	−1.271	−5.445***	−1.773	−5.437***
ln_DEFLATOR	5.910	−2.448**	−0.862	−3.866***	−1.300	−3.780**
ln_EXR	−1.351	−4.424***	−1.874	−4.345***	−1.968	−4.480***
ln_FDI	0.009	−6.072***	−1.279	−10.252***	−2.819	−12.123***
ln_GDP	5.068	−1.806*	−1.503	−3.672***	−0.398	−4.244**
ln_HP_GDP	5.717	−0.647	−2.053	−0.578	0.967	−2.346
ln_INV	0.262	−4.214***	−1.507	−4.141***	−2.295	−4.107**
ln_LR	−1.264	−1.438	4.148	−1.911	3.281	−2.410
ln_MFP	2.893	−3.673***	−1.576	−4.481***	−1.362	−4.593***
ln_PD	−0.351	−3.155***	−1.662	−3.082**	−1.622	−3.439*
ln_SR	−1.123	−4.582***	0.807	−4.724***	−1.265	−5.352***
ln_UNEM	−0.575	−3.542***	−1.224	−3.488**	−1.095	−3.321*

ln and HP suffix denote natural logarithm and Hodrick–Prescott filter applied, respectively. *, ** and *** denote statistical significance at 10%, 5% and 1% level, respectively

Table 7.12 Results of Andrews and Zivot (AZ) test for the Netherlands (own calculations)

Variable	*t*-stat	Break year	*t*-stat	Break year	*t*-stat	Break year
DEFLATOR	−4.798*	2000	−2.863	2011	−2.665	2011
EXR	−3.448	1990	−4.184	1991	−4.346	1996
FDI	−4.358	2004	−3.831	2008	−5.095**	2005
GDP	−4.209	2009	−3.649	2007	−3.554	2006
HP_GDP	−3.294	2009	−3.398	2000	−3.279	2009
INV	−4.068	2009	−4.019	1989	–	–
LR	−4.693*	1989	−3.834	2011	−4.373	1989
MFP	–	–	–	–	–	–
N_EX	−3.109	2010	–	–	–	–
PD	–	–	–	–	–	–
SR	−4.309	1989	−3.627	1990	−4.319	1993
UNEM	−3.494	2009	−5.029**	2002	−4.866*	2000
ln_DEFLATOR	−3.782	2000	−3.231	2009	−3.030	2011
ln_EXR	−3.059	1990	−3.516	1991	−3.895	1996
ln_FDI	−4.326	1998	−4.182	2008	−4.924*	2004
ln_GDP	−3.743	2009	−3.928	2005	−3.879	2005
ln_HP_GDP	−2.980	2008	−5.319**	1998	−4.636*	1998
ln_INV	−4.147	2009	−3.949	1989	–	–
ln_LR	1.916	2011	−1.273	2011	−1.815	2011
ln_MFP	–	–	–	–	–	–
ln_PD	–	–	–	–	–	–
ln_SR	–	–	−3.131	2008	−3.589	2007
ln_UNEM	−4.016	2009	−4.610*	2002	−5.170**	2000

ln and HP suffix denote natural logarithm and Hodrick–Prescott filter applied, respectively. *, ** and *** denote statistical significance at 10%, 5% and 1% level, respectively. "–" denotes cases where test was not able to be carried out

the euro. The 1990s and early 2000s are the years of slow and steady growth in the Netherlands. The financial crisis was also prominent in the Netherlands which resulted in not only GDP decrease but also a housing crisis (Masselink and van den Noord 2009).

7.4 Conclusions

There has been a growing interest in structural changes in economic literature. In the study we have focused on structural changes which can be captured by the structural breaks testing methodology and unit-root testing. We examined structural breaks of four countries, i.e. Ireland, Spain, Turkey and the Netherlands. Structural breaks were tested using the Andrews-Zivot test and the Bai-Perron test. We also tested for unit root employing the Phillips–Perron test. As it turns out, for all four countries we can observe structural breaks which are mainly specific to their own economic history including both internal policy changes and external factors. One common break for

Table 7.13 Results of Bai and Perron (BP) test for the Netherlands (own calculations)

	BP test (constant as breaking regressor)	BP test (linear trend as breaking regressor)
Variable	Break year	Break year
DEFLATOR	1991, 1996, 2001, 2006, 2012	1987, 2001, 2008
EXR	1987, 1999, 2004	1986, 1997, 2003, 2008
FDI	1989, 1998, 2004, 2009	No breakpoints selected
GDP	1990, 1998, 2006	1995, 2002, 2009
HP_GDP	1988, 1993, 1998, 2003, 2008	1987, 1993, 2003, 2008
INV	1986, 2002, 2010	1988
LR	1986, 1997, 2003, 2012	1987, 1992, 2000, 2007
MFP	1989, 1994, 1999, 2005	1995, 2002, 2009
N_EX	1993, 2004, 2012	1987, 1993, 1999, 2009
PD	1999, 2010	2000, 2005, 2008, 2014
SR	1989, 1994, 2009	1989, 1994
UNEM	1990, 1998, 2012	1986, 1994, 2002
ln_DEFLATOR	1991, 1996, 2001, 2006, 2012	1987, 2001, 2009
ln_EXR	1987, 1999, 2004	1986, 1997, 2003, 2008
ln_FDI	1988, 1998, 2004	1991, 2002, 2008
ln_GDP	1989, 1997, 2005	1996, 2002, 2009
ln_HP_GDP	1987, 1992, 1997, 2002, 2007	1986, 1991, 2000, 2005, 2010
ln_INV	1986, 2002, 2010	1988
ln_LR	1996, 2003, 2012	1989, 2007, 2012
ln_MFP	1989, 1994, 1999, 2005	1995, 2002, 2009
ln_PD	1999, 2010	2003, 2008, 2014
ln_SR	1995, 2009	1989, 1994, 2007, 2011
ln_UNEM	1990, 1998, 2011	1986, 1994, 2003, 2010

all countries in the study was found, i.e. the financial crisis of 2007–2009. This period had very immense influential power so that detrimental effects are easily observable and it is also a significant focus in the literature, including the Chaps. 3–5, presented in the first part of this book.

7.5 Databases

http://www.economywatch.com/
http://www.cso.ie/en/statistics/
http://stats.oecd.org/
https://data.worldbank.org/
https://www.imf.org/en/data/
https://ec.europa.eu/eurostat/data/database/
https://www.ilo.org/global/statistics-and-databases/lang%2D%2Den/index.htm

https://www.bde.es/webbde/en/estadis/infoest/bolest17.html
https://fred.stlouisfed.org/

References

Akarca AT (2018) Coup induced political business cycles in Turkey. Economic Research Forum Papers. http://erf.org.eg/wp-content/uploads/2018/02/Ali-Akarca.pdf. Accessed 12 May 2018

Andrews DWK (1993) Tests for parameter instability and structural change with unknown change point. Econometrica 61:821–856

Andrews DWK, Ploberger W (1994) Optimal tests when a nuisance parameter is present only under the alternative. Econometrica 62:1383–1414

Ark BV, Jong HD (1996) Accounting for economic growth in the Netherlands since 1913. GGDC Research Memorandum 199626. Groningen Growth and Development Centre, University of Groningen. https://ideas.repec.org/p/gro/rugggd/199626.html. Accessed 10 Mar 2018

Bai J (1994) Least squares estimation of a shift in linear processes. J Time Ser Anal 15:453–472

Bai J (1997) Estimation of a change point in multiple regression models. Rev Econ Stat 79:551–563

Bai J, Perron P (1998) Estimating and testing linear models with multiple structural changes. Econometrica 66:47–78

Bai J, Perron P (2003a) Computation and analysis of multiple structural change models. J Appl Econ 6:72–78

Bai J, Perron P (2003b) Critical values for multiple structural change tests. Econometrics J 18:1–22

Banerjee A, Lumsdaine RL, Stock JH (1992) Recursive and sequential tests of the unit-root and trend-break hypotheses: theory and international evidence. J Bus Econ Stat 10(3):271

Ben-David D, Papell DH (1988) Slowdowns and meltdowns: post war growth evidence from 74 countries. Rev Econ Stat 80:561–571

Ben-David D, Papell DH (1995) The great war, the great crash and steady state growth: some new evidence about an old stilized fact. J Monet Econ 36:453–475

Ben-David D, Lumsdaine RL, Papell DH (2003) Unit roots, poswar slowdowns and long-run growth: evidence from two structural breaks. Empir Econ 28(2):303–319

Bilgel F, Karahasan BC (2016) Thirty years of conflict and economic growth in Turkey: a synthetic control approach. London School of Economics, 'Europe in Question' Discussion Paper Series, Paper No. 112/2016. https://ssrn.com/abstract=2801525. Accessed 22 Nov 2017

Bozkurt C (2015) R&D expenditures and economic growth relationship in Turkey. Int J Econ Finan Issues 5(1):188–198

Carrion J, German V (2007) Stochastic convergence amongst Mexican states. Reg Stud 41 (4):531–541

Cassidy M (2004) Productivity in Ireland: trends and issues. Central Bank of Ireland Quarterly Bulletin, pp 83–106

Chow G (1960) Tests of equality between sets of coefficients in two linear regressions. Econometrica 28:591–605

Chu CSJ, White H (1992) A direct test for changing trend. J Bus Econ Stat 10:189–199

Clark C (1957) The conditions of economic progress, 3rd edn. Macmillan, London

De la Rica S, Glitz A, Ortega F (2015) Immigration in Europe: trends, policies and empirical evidence. In: Handbook of the economics of international migration. Elsevier, p 1303–1362

Denison EF (1967) Why growth rates differ. Brookings, Washington, DC

Dickey DA, Fuller WA (1979) Distributions of the estimators for autoregressive time series with a unit root. J Am Stat Assoc 74:427–431

Doyle E (2001) Export-output causality and the role of exports in Irish growth: 1950–1997. Int Econ J 15:31–54

Durlauf SJ, Temple JP (2005) Growth econometrics. In: Aghion P, Durlauf S (eds) Handbook of economic growth. North Holland, Amsterdam, p 555–677

Eepinger PS, Meithaler N, Sindlinger M, Smolka M (2015) The great trade collapse and the Spanish export miracle: firm-level evidence from the crisis. Economics Working Papers 2015–10. Aarhus University. https://onlinelibrary.wiley.com/doi/abs/10.1111/twec.12530. Accessed 23 June 2017

Estrada J, Malo de Molina JF (2009) The performance of the Spanish economy in EMU: the first ten years. In: Jimeno JF (ed) Spain and the Euro. The first ten years. Banco de España, p 83–149

Feridun M (2008) Currency crises in emerging markets: the case of post-liberalization Turkey. The developing economies. Int J Econ Finan Issues 5(1):188–198

Feridun M (2009) Determinants of exchange market pressure in Turkey: an econometric investigation. Emerg Mark Financ Trade 45(2):65–81

Hansen BE (1990) Lagrange multiplier tests for parameter instability in non-linear models. University of Rochester, Rochester. http://www.ssc.wisc.edu/*bhansen/paper/LMTests.pdf. Accessed 21 Sept 2017

Hansen BE (1992) Test for instability with I(1) processes. J Bus Econ Stat 10:321–335

Hansen BE (2001) The new econometrics of structural change: dating breaks in U.S. labor productivity. J Econ Perspect 15(4):117–128

Harada T (2015) Structural change and economic growth with relation-specific investment. Struct Chang Econ Dyn 32:1–10

Hodrick R, Prescott EC (1997) Postwar U.S. business cycles: an empirical investigation. J Money Credit Bank 29(1):1–16

Kaldor N (1966) Causes of the slow rate of economic growth of the United Kingdom. Cambridge University Press, London

Kuznets S (1966) Modern economic growth: rate structure and spread. Yale University Press, London

Kuznets S (1979) Growth and structural shifts. In: Galenson W (ed) Economic growth and structural change in Taiwan. The Postwar experience of the Republic of China. Cornel University Press, London

Kwiatkowski D, Phillips PC, Schmidt P, Shin Y (1992) Testing the null hypothesis of stationarity against the alternative of a unit root: how sure are we that economic time series have a unit root? J Econ 54:159–178

Lewis WA (1954) Economic development with unlimited supplies of labour. Manch Sch Econ Soc Stud 22:139–191

Lieberman S (1995) Growth and crisis in the Spanish economy 1940–1993. Routledge, London

Lin JY (2009) Economic development and transition. Cambridge University Press, Cambridge

Lin JY (2012a) New structural economics: a framework for rethinking development and policy. The World Bank, Washington, DC https://openknowledge.worldbank.org/handle/10986/2232. Accessed 4 Jan 2018

Lin JY (2012b) The quest for prosperity: how developing economies can take off. Princeton University Press, Princeton

Lin JY, Monga C (2010) The growth report and new structural economics. Policy Research Working Paper 5336. The World Bank. http://hdl.handle.net/10986/3821. Accessed 17 May 2017

Lumsdaine RL, Papell DH (1997) Multiple trend breaks and the unit root hypothesis. Rev Econ Statistics 79:223–230

MacKinnon JG (1996) Numerical distribution functions for unit root and cointegration tests. J Appl Econ 11:601–618

Masselink M, van den Noord P (2009) The global financial crisis and its effects on the Netherlands. Economic analysis from the European Commission's Directorate-General for Economic and Financial Affairs, 6(10). http://ec.europa.eu/economy_finance/.../pages/publication16339_en.pdf. Accessed 15 May 2017

Maddala GS, Kim IM (1998) Unit roots, cointegration, and structural change. Cambridge University Press, Cambridge

McMillan M, Rodrik D, Verduzco-Gallo Í (2014) Globalization, structural change, and productivity growth, with an update on Africa. World Dev 63(1):11–32

Nelson CR, Plosser CI (1982) Trends and random walks in macroeconomic time series. J Monet Econ 10:139–162

Ng S, Perron P (1995) Unit root tests in ARMA models with data dependent methods for the selection of the truncation lag. J Am Stat Assoc 90:268–281

Noriega AE, Ramírez A (1999) Unit roots and multiple structural breaks in real output: how long does an economy remain stationary. Estud Econ 14(2):163–188

O'Sullivan M (1995) Manufacturing and global competition. In: O'Hagan JW (ed) The economy of Ireland: policy and performance of small European country. Gill and Macmillan, Dublin

Perron P (1989) The great crash, the oil-price shock and the unit-root hypothesis. Econometrica 57:1361–1401

Perron P (1990) Testing for a unit root in a time series with a changing mean. J Bus Econ Stat 8:153–162

Perron P (1997) Further evidence on breaking trend functions in macroeconomic variables. J Econ 80(2):355–385

Perron P, Vogelsang TJ (1992) Nonstationarity and level shifts with an application to purchasing power parity. J Bus Econ Stat 10:301–320

Phillips PCB, Perron P (1988) Testing for a unit root in time series regression. Biometrika 75:335–346

Quandt RE (1960) Tests of hypotheses that a linear system obeys two separate regimes. J Am Stat Assoc 55:324–330

Rudebusch G (1992) Trends and random walks in macroeconomic time series: a reexamination. Int Econ Rev 33:661–680

Smyth R, Inder B (2004) Is Chinese provincial real GDP per capita nonstationary? Evidence from multiple trend break unit root tests. China Econ Rev 15:1–24

Startz R (1998) Growth states and shocks. J Econ Growth 3(3):203–215

Syrquin M (1988) Patterns of structural change. In: Chenery H, Srinavasan TN (eds) Handbook of development economics. North Holland, Amsterdam

Taşkın T (2014) GDP growth in Turkey: inclusive or not? Cen Bank Rev 14:31–64

Vu KM (2017) Structural change and economic growth: empirical evidence and policy insights from Asian economies. Struct Chang Econ Dyn 41:64–77

Woo J, Kumar MS (2015) Public debt and growth. Economica 82:705–739

Zivot E, Andrews DWK (1992) Further evidence on the great crash, the oil price shock, and the unit-root hypothesis. J Bus Econ Stat 10:251–270

Chapter 8
Threshold Error Correction Model: A Methodological Overview

Maciej Gałecki and Magdalena Osińska

Abstract In this chapter, the methodology related to threshold error correction models is discussed. The aim of the chapter is to summarize several approaches to time series modelling using both a univariate case and a multivariate case. The concept of stationarity is crucial when a model specification is projected. When time series are stationary, then threshold autoregression models or threshold distributed lag models can be estimated. These models represent a framework for flexibly and describe associations showing potentially non-linear and delayed effects in time series data. On the other hand, however, when data exhibit non-stationarity, the non-linear cointegration approach is applied. In this case, the threshold effects around the long run path present in the Threshold Error Correction Model (TECM) are discussed. A modified method for testing for a threshold in TECM based on the Enders and Siklos approach is proposed. Furthermore, methods of statistical inference in the case of a threshold in both stationary and cointegrating spaces are discussed.

8.1 Introduction

The concept of cointegration and error correction mechanism (ECM) introduced by Engle and Granger in 1987 has dramatically changed the picture of econometric modelling. Applied hitherto econometric time series models were questioned because of the following two reasons: spurious regression (due to non-stationarity) as well as impossibility of modelling long and short run dynamics at the same time. Engle and Granger procedure allowed modelling a system where only one

Financial support from research project no. 2015/17/B/HS4/01000 supported by the National Science Centre in Poland is gratefully acknowledged.

M. Gałecki · M. Osińska (✉)
Department of Econometrics and Statistics, The Faculty of Economic Sciences and Management, Nicolaus Copernicus University, Toruń, Poland
e-mail: mgalecki@umk.pl; emo@umk.pl

M. Osińska (ed.), *Economic Miracles in the European Economies*,
https://doi.org/10.1007/978-3-030-05606-3_8

cointegrating vector was present. Johansen (1988) extended the procedure of testing for cointegration for multivariate time series models such as vector autoregression (VAR) and developed a multivariate modelling framework called vector error correction model (VECM). Following these publications, abundant literature arose on both econometric methodology and macroeconomic applications.

The novelty of the cointegration idea lied in that once a long run equation (or equations in the multivariate case) was established, a short run dynamics and the adjustment to the long run could be observed. Yet this approach assumed that the speed of the economic system adjustment to the long run was symmetric.

Balke and Fomby (1997) applied the idea of non-linear threshold modelling developed by Chan (Chan 1993) and by Tong (Tong 1990) and put it together with the concept of cointegration. Enders and Siklos (2001) developed the scheme of testing for both non-linear cointegration and asymmetry assuming that the reaction of the system is asymmetric around lagged ECM or lagged momentum ECM. As the ECM is stationary, the threshold value was naturally assumed to be zero. Stigler (2010) provided a broad overview of different methods related with threshold error correction modelling including both univariate and multivariate models.

Many authors found that economic and financial processes often exhibited non-equal reaction when the stimulus was either positive or negative. Granger and Lee (1989) using a threshold model with a sign function revealed asymmetries in sales, production and inventories in the USA. The most frequent asymmetric relationships are those related with the price transmission. Frey and Manera (2007) provided a wide overview of the existing literature on asymmetries in price transmission finding that a threshold-type asymmetry is quite likely in a wide range of markets. The examples to support price asymmetry come mainly from the financial markets, see Martens et al. (1998); gasoline markets, see Ghassan and Banerjee (2013); Leszkiewicz-Kędzior and Welfe (2014); wheat market, see Hassouneh et al. (2017) as examples. Piłatowska and Włodarczyk (2017) showed a threshold error correction relationship between CO_2 emission and economic growth.

The subject of this book is related with discussing, identifying and modelling accelerated economic growth in selected economies. Thus, we decided to apply the Threshold Error Correction (TECM hereafter) approach to find out the mechanism of the intense economic growth and fluctuations around it. In this chapter, we present the methodology that was used in the next ones for empirical analysis and economic interpretation. The purpose of this chapter is to summarize several approaches to time series modelling using both a univariate case and a multivariate case as well as to provide a sequential procedure of testing for possible threshold variables. The chapter is organized as follows: in the first section the idea of threshold model building has been shown, and in the second one the procedure of Enders and Siklos as well as its extensions are briefly described. In this part, a modified testing approach using a TECM basis has been discussed. In the third section, some information on the methods used for parameters estimation are presented, while in the fourth section other tests based on variance-covariance approach are shown. Two of them were used for comparison and validation of the empirical results presented in the sequent chapters of this book. The conclusions sum up the proposed methodology.

8.2 The Idea of Threshold Model Building

The point of the threshold models is the assumption of local states approximation and passing from one state (regime) to another via threshold parameter (see Tong 1990). It allows analysing economic systems through their decomposition into simpler subsystems. Threshold models can be included into a wider class of switching regression models with a sharp switching function of the Heaviside form. The simplest form for the switching econometric model can be defined as follows (see Maddala 1983).

$$\text{Regime 1}: y_i = \beta_1' X_{1i} + u_{1i} \quad \text{if } \gamma' Z_i \geq a_i \tag{8.1}$$

$$\text{Regime 2}: y_i = \beta_2' X_{2i} + u_{2i} \quad \text{if } \gamma' Z_i \geq a_i \tag{8.2}$$

where $\gamma' Z_i \geq a_i$ defines a set of conditions, u_{1i}, u_{2i} and a_i are normally distributed, with zero mean and following variance–covariance matrix Σ:

$$\Sigma = \begin{bmatrix} \sigma_1^2 & \sigma_{12} & \sigma_{1a} \\ & \sigma_2^2 & \sigma_{2a} \\ & & 1 \end{bmatrix}. \tag{8.3}$$

This simple model (8.1)–(8.3) serves as an illustration of switching regression idea widely known in econometrics because it was primarily dedicated to cross-section type of data. In the case of time series models, situation complicates due to:

- non-stationarity of the series
- univariate or multivariate scope of analysis

Let us start with a brief discussion of a threshold model for stationary time series. Let Y_t denotes a k-dimensional random vector. The model

$$Y_t = B^{J_t} Y_t + A^{J_t} Y_{t-1} + H^{J_t} \varepsilon_t + C^{J_t}, \tag{8.4}$$

where J_t is a random variable taking values of finite set of natural numbers $\{1, 2, 3, \ldots, p\}$, B^{J_t}, A^{J_t}, H^{J_t} are $k \times k$-dimensional matrices of the coefficients, ε_t is k-dimensional white noise, C^{J_t} is a vector of constant Eq. (8.4) is called a canonical form of the threshold model. It defines a wide class of the models depending on the value of J_t (Tong 1990). Threshold models defined by Tong typically have an autoregressive structure considered in all regimes. Thus they are called threshold autoregression models (TAR). The general TAR model is given as:

$$\begin{aligned} Y_t = {} & \alpha_0^1 + \alpha_1^1 Y_{t-1} + \cdots + \alpha_k^1 Y_{t-k} + I(Z_{t-d} \leq r) \\ & \cdot \left(\alpha_0^2 + \alpha_1^2 Y_{t-1} + \cdots + \alpha_l^2 Y_{t-l}\right) + \varepsilon_t \end{aligned} \tag{8.5}$$

- d, k and l are non-negative integers,

- $0 \leq l \leq k$
- ε_t is the residual white noise,
- r is the threshold parameter such as

$$I(Z_{t-d} \leq r) = \begin{cases} 1 & \text{if } Z_{t-d} \leq r \\ 0 & \text{otherwise} \end{cases} \tag{8.6}$$

The threshold variable in (8.5) can be lagged endogenous variable or an exogenous variable, letting $Z_t = [Y_{t-i}, X_{t-i}]$ where $i = \{1, 2, \ldots, d\}$. When J_t is the function of Y_t, then a self-exciting threshold autoregressive (SETAR) model is specified (see Chan 1993). The SETAR(p; k_1, k_2,..., k_p) model is defined in the following way:

$$Y_t = \alpha_0^j + \sum_{i=1}^{k_j} \alpha_i^j Y_{t-i} + h^j \varepsilon_t \tag{8.7}$$

conditionally on $Y_{t-d} \in R_j$, where $j = 1, \ldots, p$ denotes the number of regimes. A more convenient form of (8.7) is the following:

$$Y_t = \begin{cases} \alpha_0^1 + \alpha_1^1 Y_{t-1} + \cdots + \alpha_{k_1}^1 Y_{t-k_1} + \varepsilon_{1t} & \text{for } Y_{t-d} \leq r_1 \\ \alpha_0^2 + \alpha_1^2 Y_{t-1} + \cdots + \alpha_{k_2}^2 Y_{t-k_2} + \varepsilon_{2t} & \text{for } r_1 < Y_{t-d} \leq r_2 \\ \cdots\cdots\cdots\cdots\cdots\cdots\cdots\cdots\cdots\cdots\cdots\cdots & \\ \alpha_0^p + \alpha_1^p Y_{t-1} + \cdots + \alpha_{k_p}^p Y_{t-k_p} + \varepsilon_{pt} & \text{for } Y_{t-d} > r_{p-1} \end{cases} \tag{8.8}$$

For two regimes, we have the following $I(y)$ function

$$I(y) = \begin{cases} 0 & \text{when } y \leq 0 \\ 1 & \text{when } y > 0 \end{cases}. \tag{8.9}$$

and the corresponding SETAR(2, k, l) model

$$\begin{aligned} Y_t = \alpha_0^1 + \alpha_1^1 Y_{t-1} + \cdots + \alpha_k^1 Y_{t-k} + I(Y_{t-d} \leq r) \\ \cdot \left(\alpha_0^2 + \alpha_1^2 Y_{t-1} + \cdots + \alpha_l^2 Y_{t-l}\right) + \varepsilon_t \end{aligned} \tag{8.10}$$

When all $\alpha_i^2 (i = 0, 1, 2, \ldots, 1)$ parameters are zeros, then (8.10) becomes the linear autoregressive model.

TAR and SETAR models are formulated for stationary autoregression processes. Unless stationarity of the process can always be ensured at the level of each regime, it is more complicated at the level of the entire system. Niglio et al. (2012) analysed the problem basing on the papers by Petruccelli and Woolford (1984) and Chan et al. (1985). Sufficient and necessary conditions for stationarity of a 3-regimes SETAR model, where the residual term is assumed to be i.i.d., were derived by Chan et al. (1985). It corresponds to the case when only one lag is present in each regime.

However, conditions for stationarity of a SETAR process with more than one lag are still not known (Stigler 2010).

It is worth noting that if the time series in interest satisfied stationarity condition, then TAR/SETAR models of the form (8.5) and (8.7) can be completed by exogenous variables in the regimes, such that the model can be then called a TAR-X or a SETAR-X model, or as it has been proposed by Gasparrini—a distributed lags non-linear model (Gasparrini 2011). By analogy to ARMAX model we suggest using a TAR-X (SETAR-X) model or a distributed lags threshold model (DLTM)

$$Y_t = \alpha_0^1 + \alpha_1^1 Y_{t-1} + \cdots + \alpha_k^1 Y_{t-k} + \mathbf{B}^{1'}\mathbf{X}_{t-i} + I(Z_{t-d} \leq r) \cdot \left(\alpha_0^2 + \alpha_1^2 Y_{t-1} + \cdots + \alpha_l^2 Y_{t-l} + \mathbf{B}^{2'}\mathbf{X}_{t-i}\right) + \varepsilon \tag{8.11}$$

where $\mathbf{X}_{t-i}$ is a vector of stationary exogenous variables $i = \{0,1,2\ldots\}$ and $\mathbf{B}^{1'}, \mathbf{B}^{2'}$ are corresponding vectors of parameters.

8.3 Threshold Error Correction Models

In the empirical research on modelling intense economic growth periods a threshold error correction model (TECM) approach is applied, with a central assumption that there exists a long run path describing the direction of the economic development but in the short run temporal asymmetry is possible. It is argued that in the short run the dynamics is non-linear and concentrated around a certain threshold variable, which is a subject of testing. The magnitude of threshold is a subject of estimation. The TECM idea comes from seminal papers by Balke and Fomby (1997) as well as from Enders and Siklos (2001). Stigler (2010), in his review of characteristics and techniques of threshold models construction, emphasized that testing for threshold cointegration is particularly difficult because it involves two problems: the presence of cointegration and that of non-linearity. Hence, the following cases are possible: cointegration and threshold effects (1); cointegration and no threshold effects (2); no cointegration and no threshold effects (3); and no cointegration and threshold effects (4).

In this chapter, the following three versions of the TECM are discussed in detail. The first one was originally proposed by Enders and Siklos (2001). At the beginning it is assumed that a linear cointegrating equation exists under the conditions defined in Engle and Granger (1987)

$$Y_t = \alpha_0 + \sum_{i=1}^{k} \alpha_i X_{it} + u_t \tag{8.12}$$

Then the testing regression is estimated as

$$\Delta u_t = I_t\rho_1 u_{t-1} + (1 - I_t)\rho_2 u_{t-1} + \sum\nolimits_{i=1}^{p} \beta_i \Delta u_{t-1} + \varepsilon_t \tag{8.13}$$

where

$$I_t = \begin{cases} 1 & \text{for } u_{t-1} \geq \gamma \\ 0 & \text{for } u_{t-1} < \gamma \end{cases} \quad \text{or} \quad I_t = \begin{cases} 1 & \text{for } \Delta u_{t-1} \geq \gamma \\ 0 & \text{for } \Delta u_{t-1} < \gamma \end{cases} \text{ and } \gamma = 0.$$

In Eq. (8.13), it is assumed that the threshold is defined in terms of error correction mechanism u_{t-1}.

The set of two null hypotheses to be tested is as follows:

$$H_0^1 : \rho_1 = \rho_2 = 0 \tag{8.14}$$

$$H_0^2 : \rho_1 - \rho_2 = 0 \tag{8.15}$$

H_0^1 is for the case of no threshold cointegration then the Engle-Granger linear cointegration (Engle and Granger 1987) is confirmed, while H_0^2 assumes a symmetric reaction, so that it is again the argument for linear cointegration. If both hypotheses are rejected, i.e. the Enders and Siklos procedure indicates threshold type of cointegration around the long run equilibrium it means that the short run adjustment is asymmetric respectively for positive and negative changes. The precise interpretation of the set of hypotheses to be tested (8.14 and 8.15) was given by Balke and Fomby (1997). This interpretation is given in Table 8.1.

The results of testing using the Ender and Siklos approach allows identifying asymmetric reaction around the entire cointegrating vector (which can be unknown) but they do not indicate the individual threshold variable, responsible for the asymmetric mechanism of the system. In such a case, a reasonable solution is to ask about single variables that diversify the mechanism of a short run adjustment. Two possible cases are considered: first, when a threshold variable enters the cointegrating vector and, second, where it is not present in the long run. In the first case the threshold variable is responsible for both long run and short run dynamics, while in the second one—the cointegrating vector remains independent of the threshold, since it works in the short run only. The approach that fits the above idea partially was proposed by Kapetanios et al. (2006) and was modified by Bruzda

Table 8.1 Possible models under the no-TECM hypotheses (based on Balke and Fomby (1997)

System characteristics	Linearity	Non-linearity
No cointegration	H_0^1 :No linear cointegration (3)	H_0^2 :No cointegration. Non-linear residual process (4)
Cointegration	H_0^2 :Linear cointegration (2)	H_0^2 :Non-linear cointegration (1)

The numbers 1–4 correspond to the cases specified by Stigler (2010))

(2007). Having (8.12) unchanged, the testing Eq. (8.13) is a subject of re-formulation to the form

$$\Delta Y_t = I_t \rho_1 u_{t-1} + (1 - I_t)\rho_2 u_{t-1} + \omega \Delta X_t + \sum\nolimits_{j=1}^{p} \psi_{yj} \Delta Z_{t-j} + e_t \tag{8.16}$$

where indicator functions I_t remain the same as defined above and $\gamma = 0$. This test can be extended by allowing for other than $u_{t-1} = 0$ and $\Delta u_{t-1} = 0$ threshold variables. The set of possible threshold variables is defined in the vector Z_t

$$Z_t = (Y_t, X_{1t}, X_{2t}, \ldots, X_{kt})', X_t = (X_{1t}, X_{2t}, \ldots, X_{kt})'.$$

Then the threshold value (empirical level of γ) is a subject of estimation where

$$I_t = \begin{cases} 1 & \text{for } Z_{t-i} \geq \hat{\gamma} \\ 0 & \text{for } Z_{t-i} < \hat{\gamma} \end{cases} \tag{8.17}$$

or

$$I_t = \begin{cases} 1 & \text{for } \Delta Z_{t-i} \geq \hat{\gamma} \\ 0 & \text{for } \Delta Z_{t-i} < \hat{\gamma} \end{cases} \tag{8.18}$$

and

$$-\infty < \hat{\gamma} < \infty; \hat{\gamma} = \arg\min_{\gamma} \text{AIC}(\gamma) \tag{8.19}$$

This approach allows identifying asymmetric reaction around the long run but individual variable is allowed to be a threshold. Thus, the number of observations in the short run remains unchanged in both regimes.

At the third stage we proposed a new testing procedure based on the entire set of variables available in both long run and short run equations. This procedure extends the set of possible thresholds and determines the way of their impact on the identification of periods of intense economic growth within the observed sample. It has been described in Boehlke et al. (2017). The long run Eq. (8.12) remains the same as previously. The testing equation is however modified to the form:

$$\begin{aligned} \Delta Y_t = {} & I_t \rho_1 u_{t-1} + (1 - I_t)\rho_2 u_{t-1} + I_t \omega_1 \Delta X_t + (1 - I_t)\omega_2 \Delta X_t \\ & + \sum\nolimits_{j=1}^{\max\{p;q\}} I_t \psi_{1j} \Delta Z_{t-j} + \sum\nolimits_{j=1}^{\max\{p;q\}} (1 - I_t)\psi_{2j} \Delta Z_{t-j} + e_t \end{aligned} \tag{8.20}$$

where

$$I_t = \begin{cases} 1 & \text{for } Z_{t-i} \geq \hat{\gamma} \\ 0 & \text{for } Z_{t-i} < \hat{\gamma} \end{cases} \quad \text{or} \quad I_t = \begin{cases} 1 & \text{for } \Delta Z_{t-i} \geq \hat{\gamma} \\ 0 & \text{for } \Delta Z_{t-i} < \hat{\gamma} \end{cases}$$

and

$$-\infty < \hat{\gamma} < \infty; \hat{\gamma} = \arg\min_{\gamma} \mathrm{AIC}(\gamma)$$

remain as defined above, symbols p and q correspond to maximum lag numbers for Y_t and X_t, respectively.

In the proposed model, the short term equations differ between the regimes taking three elements: the vector of explanatory variables, number of observations and parameters estimate. Thus, this approach seems to be most complex because it shows asymmetries not only around the long run but also in the short run dynamics. The advantage of such an approach is that in the final TECM a different set of variables can act in different regimes having the long run relationship unchanged. Its limitation is however related to the number of observations; if the times series in interest is short, then some results cannot be tested.

Three approaches to TECM specification described above should be considered as nested. The last one nests the second approach and the second nests the first one. The sequence of testing from the simplest to the widest approach validates the results. If they can be confirmed by Enders and Siklos, Kapetanios et al. and our approaches, the non-linear mechanism underlying the relationship in interest is very likely.

8.4 Remarks on Estimation Procedures

The parameters of TAR/SETAR (or TAR-X/SETAR-X) models can be estimated by conditional least squares (LS) or maximum likelihood (ML) methods. Typically all the parameters in (8.5) or (8.6) are unknown and need to be estimated. The objectives of model selection are Akaike Information Criterion (AIC) or Bayesian Information Criterion (BIC).

The parameters of the TAR/SETAR models are estimated, conditionally on whether the parameters d, r and k are known or not. The parameters are usually not known and have to be estimated. Let us consider the following version of a SETAR model:

$$Y_t = \begin{cases} a_0^1 + a_1^1 Y_{t-1} + \cdots + a_{k_1}^1 Y_{t-k_1} + \varepsilon_{1t} & \text{for } Y_{t-d} < r \\ a_0^2 + a_1^2 Y_{t-1} + \cdots + a_{k_2}^2 Y_{t-k_2} + \varepsilon_{2t} & \text{for } Y_{t-d} \geq r. \end{cases} \tag{8.21}$$

The estimation proceeds in two variants (Tong 1983 and Tong 1990). The estimation of parameters standing with lagged variables with fixed d, r, k_1, k_2 is simply OLS in regimes. On the other hand, however, the estimation of all parameters including thresholds assumes sequential procedure starting with initial values of the delay and threshold d and r fixed at d_0 and r_0, respectively. Then, the numbers of lags are determined within the regimes and parameters $a_p^i$are estimated. Finally, the values of the delay parameter and threshold parameter (d and r respectively) are estimated. The objective of model selection is typically AIC or BIC, although other functions like SSR or log-likelihood can be taken, too. A solution is obtained through concentration of the objective function conditional on the value of r. For Akaike information criterion, it can be written as:

$$\mathrm{AIC}(r) = \left\{ \arg\min_{r} \mathrm{AIC}(r) \right\}, \tag{8.22}$$

where r means a threshold parameter in the model (8.21). Minimization of (8.22) is done through a grid search: the values of the threshold variable are sorted, a certain percentage of the first and last values is excluded to ensure a minimum number of observations in each regime, the AIC is estimated for each selected value $\hat{r}$ and the one that minimize the AIC is taken as the estimate. This method is called conditional least squares or concentrated least squares (see Stigler 2010). The properties of the conditional LS estimator of a threshold were examined by Chan (1993) and in Gonzalo and Pitarakis (2002). He found that the distribution of $\hat{r}$ is a compound Poisson process with nuisance parameters, which cannot be computed easily. He also found that the estimator of the threshold $\hat{r}$ was super-convergent (allows taking the threshold value as given and making standard inference), whereas the estimator of the slope coefficients, $\hat{a}_p^i$, was convergent (Stigler 2010). The significance of a threshold can be justified through the procedure of inference described in the next section.

When a Threshold Error Correction Model (TECM) is to be estimated, two ways are possible. The first one suggested by Balke and Fomby (1997) is a two-step procedure, assuming that the cointegrating vector is estimated in the first step and then treated as constant. Balke and Fomby indicated that the super-convergence of the OLS estimator in the long run equation holds when the residuals follow a SETAR process. This concept refers to the single equation case with one cointegrating vector. In a system case the Threshold Vector Error Correction Model (TVECM) is required. Hansen and Seo (2002) derived a maximum likelihood estimator, suggesting the procedure of searching for sequent parameters values. The details are presented in Hansen and Seo (2002), Seo (2011), and Stigler (2010).

8.5 Statistical Inference in Threshold Models Framework

It has already been shown that threshold models belong to the non-linear class of models. Together with smooth transition regression (STR) models and Markov switching models, they constitute a group of piecewise regressions. Their usefulness to economic time series data lies in describing and forecasting the dynamics that changes (switches) from one regime to another with a switching variable. The regimes describe asymmetric relationships conditional on the threshold value. It is closely connected with structural breaks in the threshold variable. While structural breaks are identified in the time series data, the question arises whether a linear econometric model properly describes the relationships analysed. The first solution to a structural break case is adding a dummy variable for the period of break. Better results can be however obtained using threshold models. They help identifying threshold variables and allow for intuitive interpretation of the results.

8.5.1 Threshold Models and Structural Changes

Structural changes in the single equation form have been a subject widely discussed and implemented in Chap. 7 of this book. In addition to single-equation threshold models, structural changes can be described by multi-equation models. Most often we use VAR or VECM class models. If we want to take into account a structural change in modelling, an important element of statistical inference is testing the occurrence of structural change. In the case of a multidimensional error-correction model with a standard form (Johansen 1995), testing of the occurrence of structural change is based on several statistics:

1. LR (Johansen 1995)—testing the change in the absolute term and trend in the case of a known switching point.
2. LM and its modifications: Sup LM, Mean LM and Exp LM (Seo 1998)—in the case of an unknown moment of disturbance.
3. When testing for the stability of model parameters, we use our own values determined on the basis of recursive estimation (Hansen and Johansen 1999).

If the process generating data is the sum of the deterministic and stochastic components (Lütkepohl 2005), then a structural change can occur in each of them. This requires separate testing. If the deterministic component in the data-generating process contains only the absolute term, then the structural change can be represented by the alteration of the absolute term. If we know the break period, then we propose Wald's statistics to test the structural change in the deterministic component, and sup*WALD* statistics (Gosińska 2015) for the unknown moment of break.

Let us assume that the vector $y_t = [y_{1t}, \ldots, y_{Mt}]^T$ represents M variables integrated to the first degree. If the dimension of the cointegration space is R, $0 < R < M$, then for the VAR model of the form: $\Pi(L)y_t = \varepsilon_t$, where $\varepsilon_t = [\varepsilon_{1t}, \ldots, \varepsilon_{Mt}]^T$ is a vector $M \times 1$ of white-noise random components, there is a VECM representation (Johansen 1995; Majsterek 2008):

$$\Delta y_t = \Pi y_{t-1} + \sum\nolimits_{s=1}^{S-1} \Gamma_s \Delta y_{t-s} + \varepsilon_t \tag{8.23}$$

where

$$\Pi = \sum_{s=1}^{S} \Pi_s - I$$

$$\Gamma_i = -\sum_{s=i+1}^{S} \Pi_s = -(\Pi_{i+1} + \Pi_{i+2} + \cdots + \Pi_S)$$

$$\Pi = \mathrm{AB}^T$$

The A and B matrices of the dimension $M \times R$ have a standard interpretation. For the model (8.23) we can introduce variables 0–1 both into the cointegration space and outside it. The presence of 0–1 variables may result from atypical observations or from structural changes. Let us assume that the data-generating process consists of a deterministic element and a stochastic element (Lütkepohl 2005; Gosińska 2015):

$$v_t = y_t + Hd_t \tag{8.24}$$

where

$y_t = [y_{1t}, \ldots, y_{Mt}]^T$—vector of variables integrated to the first degree with the dimensions $M \times 1$,
$d_t = [d_{1t}, \ldots, d_{Zt}]^T$—vector of deterministic variables with the dimensions $Z \times 1$,
$H = [h_1; \ldots; h_z]$—matrix of parameters with the dimensions $M \times Z$ related to deterministic components, $h_z = [h_{z1}, \ldots, h_{zM}]^T$.

The presence of a structural change in the VECM model may refer to the stochastic or deterministic part of the process generating data. Depending on the nature of the break, this results in different VECM threshold models.

Let us assume that the structural change concerns only the deterministic component of the data-generating process and consists only of a constant. If the presence of a structural change in the generating process can be taken into account by introducing the variable 0–1 in the appropriate period t_0, $d_t = [1\ u_t]^T$, then the data-generating process will take the form (Gosińska 2015):

$$v_t = y_t + h_1 + h_3 u_t \tag{8.25}$$

where

$$u_t = \begin{cases} 0, & \text{for } t < t_0 \\ 1, & \text{for } t \geq t_0 \end{cases} \tag{8.26}$$

Only one structural change in the period t_0 corresponds to the defined variable u_t. If there are more structural changes, the Eq. (8.24) should be multiplied by $\Pi(L)$ (cf. Gosińska 2015):

$$\Pi(L)v_t = \Pi(L)y_t + \Pi(L)h_1 + \Pi(L)h_3u_t \tag{8.27}$$

After appropriate transformations (Gosińska 2015), we obtain a representation of the VECM model with the absolute term and the change of the absolute term

$$\Delta v_t = A\left[B^T v_{t-1} + g_1 + g_3 u_{t-1}\right] + \sum\nolimits_{s=1}^{S-1} \Gamma_s \Delta v_{t-s} + \sum\nolimits_{s=0}^{S-1} f_3^s \Delta u_{t-s} + \varepsilon_t \tag{8.28}$$

for $t = S + 1, S + 2, \ldots,$

where $g_1 = -B^T h_1$, $g_3 = -B^T h_3, f_3^s = \begin{cases} h_3, & \text{dla } s = 0 \\ -\Gamma_s h_3, & \text{dla } s = 1, 2, \ldots, S-1 \end{cases}$.

If we define matrices (Gosińska 2015):

$$G = [g_1\ g_3],$$

$$d_{t-1} = \begin{bmatrix} 1 \\ u_{t-1} \end{bmatrix},$$

$$\Delta d_{t-s} = \begin{bmatrix} 0 \\ \Delta u_{t-s} \end{bmatrix},$$

$$F_s = \left[f_1 f_3^s\right],$$

where f_1 is a vector with the dimensions $M \times 1$, then the equation of the form (8.28) can be expressed as:

$$\Delta v_t = \mathrm{AB}^{*T} v_{t-1}^* + \sum\nolimits_{s=1}^{S-1} \Gamma_s \Delta v_{t-s} + \sum\nolimits_{s=0}^{S-1} F_s \Delta d_{t-s} + \varepsilon_t \tag{8.29}$$

where

$v_{t-1}^* = \begin{bmatrix} v_{t-1} \\ d_{t-1} \end{bmatrix}$—vector with the dimensions $N \times 1$, $N = Z + M$,

$B^{*T} = [B^T\ G]$—matrix of cointegrating vectors with the dimensions $R \times N$,

G—matrix of parameters related to deterministic variables in the cointegrating space of the dimensions $R \times Z$,

F_s—parameter matrix for deterministic variables outside the cointegrating space of the dimensions $M \times Z$.

The simplest form of the model (8.28) is to include only the deterministic component of the absolute term. This is equivalent to the lack of structural change. This means that h_3 is a zero vector. The VECM model for the data-generating process $v_t = y_t + h_1$ can be written as (Gosińska 2015):

$$\Delta v_t = \mathrm{AB}^{*T} v_{t-1}^* + \sum\nolimits_{s=1}^{S-1} \Gamma_s \Delta v_{t-s} + \varepsilon_t \tag{8.30}$$

where
$v_{t-1}^{*} = \begin{bmatrix} v_{t-1} \\ 1 \end{bmatrix}$,
$B^{*T} = [B^T \; g_1]$,
$g_1 = -B^T h_1$.
Accepting the restriction $g_1 = -B^T h_1$ allows the absolute term in the model (8.30) not to generate a linear trend.

The introduction of the 0–1 variable in the cointegration space in period t means that in the data-generation process the given structural change occurred in the period $t-1$. If the structural change is the cause of introducing the variable 0–1 into the cointegration space, then the corresponding variables 0–1 must be found also outside the cointegrating space (Gosińska 2015).

Testing the structural change in the absolute term in the known period of t_0 is performed with the use of Wald's statistics (cf. Gosińska 2015). The determination of its value is based on a two-stage procedure, in which the parameters of the stochastic part are estimated first, assuming the cointegration order R, and then the parameters of the deterministic part. In the null hypothesis we assume no structural change:

$$H_0 : h_3 = 0$$
$$H_1 : h_3 \neq 0$$

With the valid H_0 (no structural change), the vectors of the parameters related to the variables that describe the structural change in the cointegration space are equal to zero ($g_3 = 0$). Similarly, all short-term parameters related to the deterministic variable u_t are equal to zero.
If the moment of the structural change is unknown, we apply an appropriate generalization of Wald's statistics (Andrews 1993; Gosińska 2015):

$$\text{supWALD} = \max_{0<\tau<1}\text{WALD}(\tau) \tag{8.31}$$

where τ characterizes the moment of structural change defined as $t_0 = \tau T$, where T represents the number of observations in the sample. The highest value of Wald's statistics corresponds to the most significant structural change. Testing a structural change only in the absolute term consists in verifying the hypothesis H_0: $h_3(\tau) = 0$, where $h_3(\tau)$ is a vector of parameters for the variable:

$$u_t = \begin{cases} 0, & \text{for } t < [\tau T] \\ 1, & \text{for } t \geq [\tau T] \end{cases}$$

The distribution of the *supWALD* statistics is non-standard. Critical values must be determined by means of a simulation.

8.5.2 Testing for Non-linearity in Threshold Models Using Tsay Test

Tsay test (Tsay 1998) indicates whether variable is generated by linear or non-linear process. In null hypothesis it is assumed that Y_t is linear versus the alternative hypothesis that it follows the multivariate threshold model in (8.32).

$$Y_t = c_j + \sum\nolimits_{i=1}^{p} \varphi_i^{(j)} Y_{t-i} + \sum\nolimits_{i=1}^{q} \beta_i^{(j)} X_{t-i} + \varepsilon_t^{(j)} \quad \text{if } r_{j-1} < Z_{t-d} \leq r_j \qquad (8.32)$$

where

$j = 1, \ldots, s$
$t = 1, \ldots, n$
c_j are constant vector,
Y_t are k-dimensional time series, $Y_t = (Y_{1t}, \ldots, Y_{kt})'$,
X_t are v-dimensional exogenous variables, $X_t = (X_{1t}, \ldots, X_{vt})'$,
Z_{t-d} are threshold variable with delay d
$-\infty = r_0 < r_1 < \cdots < r_{s-1} < r_s = \infty$
p and q are non-negative integers.

The innovations satisfy $\varepsilon_t^{(j)} = \Sigma_j^{1/2} a_t$. $\Sigma_j^{1/2}$are symmetric positive definite matrices and a_t is a sequence of serially uncorrelated random vectors with mean 0 and covariance matrix I, which is the identity matrix. The threshold variable Z_t have a continuous distribution and it is assumed to be stationary. Model (8.32) has s regimes and it is non-linear in time when $s > 1$ but is a piecewise linear model in the threshold space Z_{t-d}. For model (8.32), we assume that the threshold variable Z_t is known, but the delay d, the number of regimes s, and the thresholds r_i are unknown.

Let us assume that

$$Y_t' = x_t'\Phi + \varepsilon_t', \quad t = h+1, \ldots, n \qquad (8.33)$$

where $h = \max(p, q, d)$,

$x_t' = \left(1, Y_{t-1}', \ldots, Y_{t-p}', X_{t-1}', \ldots, X_{t-q}'\right)$ is a $(pk + qv + 1)$—dimensional regressor,
Φ—is the parameter matrix,
the notation u' denotes the transpose of u.

If the null hypothesis holds, then the least squares estimates of (8.33) are useful. The arranged regression (8.34) based on the increasing order of the threshold variable Z_{t-d} is

$$Y_{t(i)+d}' = x_{t(i)+d}'\Phi + \varepsilon_{t(i)+d}', \quad i = 1, \ldots, n-h \qquad (8.34)$$

where

$t(i)$ is the time index of $z(i)$,
$z(i)$ is the ith smallest element of S,
S is the threshold variables with regression (2), $S = \{Z_{h+1-d}, \ldots, Z_{n-d}\}$.

If Y_t is linear process, then the recursive least squares estimator of the arranged regression (8.34) is consistent, so that the predictive residuals approach white noise. In effect, predictive residuals are uncorrelated with the regressor $x'_{t(i)+d}$. If Y_t follows a threshold model, then the predictive residuals are no longer white noise, because the least squares estimator is biased. In this case, the predictive residuals are correlated with the regressor $x'_{t(i)+d}$.

Let $\hat{\Phi}_m$ be the least squares estimate of Φ of Eq. (8.34) with $i = 1, \ldots, m$. It means the estimate of arranged regression (8.34) using data points associated with the m smallest values of Z_{t-d}.

Let

$$\hat{e}_{t(m+1)+d} = Y_{t(m+1)+d} - \hat{\Phi}'_m x_{t(m+1)+d} \tag{8.35}$$

be the predictive residuals and

$$\hat{\eta}_{t(m+1)+d} = \frac{\hat{e}_{t(m+1)+d}}{\left[1 + x'_{t(m+1)+d} V_m x_{t(m+1)+d}\right]^{1/2}} \tag{8.36}$$

where

$$V_m = \left[\sum_{i=1}^{m} x_{t(i)+d} x'_{t(i)+d}\right]^{-1}$$

is the standardized predictive residuals of regression (8.34). These quantities can be efficiently obtained by the recursive least squares algorithm. Next, consider the regression

$$\hat{\eta}'_{t(l)+d} = x'_{t(l)+d}\Psi + w'_{t(l)+d}, \quad l = m_0 + 1, \ldots, n - h \tag{8.37}$$

where m_0 means the starting point of the recursive least squares estimation.
The testing hypotheses refer to Eq. (8.37).

$$H_0 : \Psi = 0$$
$$H_1 : \Psi \neq 0$$

Tsay used the following test statistic:

$$C(d) = [n - h - m_0 - (kp + vq + 1)]\{\ln[\det(S_0)] - \ln[\det(S_1)]\} \tag{8.38}$$

where the delay d means that the test depends on the threshold variable Z_{t-d}, det (A) indicates the determinant of the matrix A, and

$$S_0 = \left[\frac{1}{n - h - m_0}\right] \sum_{l=m_0+1}^{n-h} \hat{\eta}_{t(l)+d} \hat{\eta}'_{t(l)+d}$$

and

$$S_1 = \left[\frac{1}{n - h - m_0}\right] \sum_{l=m_0+1}^{n-h} \hat{W}_{t(l)+d} \hat{W}'_{t(l)+d}$$

where $\hat{w}_t$ stands for the vector of the least squares residuals in (8.37). If the null hypothesis that Y_t is linear is true and under some regularity conditions, $C(d)$ is asymptotically a chi-squared random variable with k(pk + qv + 1) degrees of freedom. Tsay had conducted a simulation study to examine the finite-sample performance of the proposed test statistic $C(d)$ in (8.38). For performance under the null hypothesis, he had considered three models. Two of them were stationary and the third represented a cointegrated system with two unit-roots (Engle and Yoo 1987). Tsay had excluded the constant term from the non-linearity test in (8.38) for model (8.37) and use a larger m_0 to start the recursive estimation. The sample sizes used are $n = 150$ and 300, and the number of replications is 10,000. In the test author assumed that $y_{1,t-d}$ is the threshold variable, $d \in \{1, 2, 3, 4\}$. For stationary models as it was anticipated, the empirical distributions of the test statistic $C(d)$ are close to their asymptotic chi-squared distributions and do not depend on the choice of the delay d. Limited experience shows that for a unit-root nonstationary series, a small m_o may introduce bias in the empirical distributions of $C(d)$, resulting in larger empirical percentiles. Tsay used $m_0 \approx 5\sqrt{n}$ for the unit-root series and $m_0 \approx 3\sqrt{n}$ for the stationary case, where n is the sample size. In an application, the choice of m_0 is a compromise between stable starting estimation and good power in testing.

To study the power of the test, Tsay used a two-dimensional threshold autoregressive model as well as a three-dimensional threshold autoregressive model. The innovations are independent multivariate normal with mean 0 and variance $\sum_j$. The results are based on 10,000 replications of sample sizes 150 and 300. Furthermore, to see the stability of the results, the simulation is repeated three times. The starting point m_0 of the recursive least squares is 50 for the first simulation, which is approximately $3\sqrt{300}$, and 40 for the second and third simulations. The results showed a satisfactory power of the test when the delay d is both correctly specified and misspecified. The power of the test deteriorates when the specified delay moves away from the true d.

8.5.3 Threshold Cointegration Testing: The Hansen–Seo Test

In 2002, *Journal of Econometrics* published an article entitled 'Testing for two-regime threshold cointegration in vector error-correction models'. The authors of the article, Bruce E. Hansen and Byeongseon Seo, proposed a new test for threshold cointegration. The test statistic depends on the covariance structure of the processes under examination and has an asymptotic distribution. The p value is determined using the bootstrap procedure. The starting point for the test is the linear VECM model for p of the first differences in endogenous processes with l lags. We assume that each process is integrated to the first degree. There is only one cointegrating vector in the model. The VECM linear model takes the following form (8.39):

$$\Delta x_t = A' X_{t-1}(\beta) + u_t \tag{8.39}$$

where

$$X_{t-1} = \begin{pmatrix} 1 \\ w_{t-1}(\beta) \\ \Delta x_{t-1} \\ \Delta x_{t-2} \\ \dots \\ \Delta x_{t-l} \end{pmatrix}$$

$x_t - p$—dimensional vector of processes $I(1)$
$w_t(\beta) = \beta' x_t$—cointegration vector—$I(0)$
X_{t-1} (β)—vector of explanatory variables with dimensions $k \times 1$
A—parameter matrix with dimensions $k \times p$
$k = \mathrm{pl} + 2$
$\Sigma = E(u_t \; u_t')$—a matrix of variance-covariance of residual processes.

The residual processes vector takes the form (8.40):

$$\tilde{u}_t = \Delta x_t - \tilde{A}' X_{t-1}(\tilde{\beta}) \tag{8.40}$$

Parameters $(\beta, A, \sum)$ are estimated using the highest probability method, so that the residual processes u_t are Gaussian white noise. If $p = 2$ one should apply one normalizing restriction on the matrix β, in the form of equating one of the elements of the matrix to one. For $p > 2$ a normalizing restriction should be imposed on variables coming into the cointegrating vector, preferably on those that adapt to the long-term equilibrium. The imposition of restrictions is necessary for the model to be identifiable.

Let us convert the model (8.39) into a two-regime threshold model with TVECM cointegration described by the following Eq. (8.41):

$$\Delta x_t = \begin{cases} A_1' X_{t-1}(\beta) + u_t, & \text{if } w_{t-1}(\beta) \leq \gamma \\ A_2' X_{t-1}(\beta) + u_t, & \text{if } w_{t-1}(\beta) > \gamma \end{cases} \tag{8.41}$$

or equivalently

$$\Delta x_t = A_1' X_{t-1}(\beta) d_{1t}(\beta, \gamma) + A_2' X_{t-1}(\beta) d_{2t}(\beta, \gamma) + u_t \tag{8.42}$$

where

$$d_{1t}(\beta, \gamma) = l(w_{t-1}(\beta) \leq \gamma)$$
$$d_{2t}(\beta, \gamma) = l(w_{t-1}(\beta) > \gamma)$$

$l(.)$—indicator function.
Switching between equations in regimes depends on the cointegration vector (the error-correction component does not have to be the only threshold variable). Matrices of coefficients A_1 and A_2 determine dynamics in regimes, both long-term and short-term.
The null hypothesis takes the form:

$$H_0 : A_1 = A_2$$
$$H_1 : A_1 \neq A_2$$

In the null hypothesis we assume a linear model with cointegration, in the alternative one, a threshold model with cointegration. Let us assume that parameters (β and γ) are known and constant. The model compatible with H_0 takes the form:

$$\Delta x_t = A' X_{t-1}(\beta) + u_t, \tag{8.43}$$

and we will save the H_1 compliant model as:

$$\Delta x_t = A_1' X_{t-1}(\beta) d_{1t}(\beta, \gamma) + A_2' X_{t-1}(\beta) d_{2t}(\beta, \gamma) + u_t \tag{8.44}$$

With

$$X_1(\beta, \gamma) = X_{t-1}(\beta)\, d_{1t}(\beta, \gamma)$$

a matrix of observations on explanatory variables was determined in the regime below the threshold variable, and with

$$X_2(\beta, \gamma) = X_{t-1}(\beta)\, d_{2t}(\beta, \gamma)$$

a matrix of observations on explanatory variables in a regime above the threshold variable.

In the next step, the Kronecker product was created for the matrix of explanatory variables ordered in ascending order according to the threshold variable and the residual vector from the linear VECM model.

$$\begin{aligned}\xi_1(\beta,\gamma) &= \tilde{u}_t \bigotimes X_{t-1}(\beta) d_{1t}(\beta,\gamma)\\ \xi_2(\beta,\gamma) &= \tilde{u}_t \bigotimes X_{t-1}(\beta) d_{2t}(\beta,\gamma)\end{aligned} \tag{8.45}$$

where

$\tilde{u}_t$—residual vector from linear VECM.

With $M_1(\beta,\gamma)$ i $M_2(\beta,\gamma)$ we designated the matrices determined as follows:

$$\begin{aligned}M_1(\beta,\gamma) &= I_p \bigotimes X_1(\beta,\gamma)' X_1(\beta,\gamma)\\ M_2(\beta,\gamma) &= I_p \bigotimes X_2(\beta,\gamma)' X_2(\beta,\gamma)\end{aligned} \tag{8.46}$$

where

I_p—unit matrix with dimensions $p \times p$.

Then, the matrices $\Omega_1(\beta,\gamma)$ and $\Omega_2(\beta,\gamma)$ were determined:

$$\begin{aligned}\Omega_1(\beta,\gamma) &= \xi_1(\beta,\gamma)' \xi_1(\beta,\gamma)\\ \Omega_2(\beta,\gamma) &= \xi_2(\beta,\gamma)' \xi_2(\beta,\gamma)\end{aligned} \tag{8.47}$$

Based on the matrices $M_1(\beta, \gamma)$, $M_2(\beta, \gamma)$ and $\Omega_1(\beta, \gamma)$, $\Omega_2(\beta, \gamma)$, we determined the Eicker–White estimator of the variance-covariance $\hat{V}_1(\beta,\gamma)$ and $\hat{V}_2(\beta,\gamma)$ for the evaluation vectors of the parameters $\hat{A}_1(\beta,\gamma)$, $\hat{A}_2(\beta,\gamma)$:

$$\begin{aligned}\hat{V}_1(\beta,\gamma) &= M_1(\beta,\gamma)^{-1} \Omega_1(\beta,\gamma) M_1(\beta,\gamma)^{-1}\\ \hat{V}_2(\beta,\gamma) &= M_2(\beta,\gamma)^{-1} \Omega_2(\beta,\gamma) M_2(\beta,\gamma)^{-1}\end{aligned} \tag{8.48}$$

Determination of the statistic

$$\begin{aligned}&\mathrm{LM}(\beta,\gamma)\\ &= \mathrm{vec}\left(\hat{A}_1(\beta,\gamma) - \hat{A}_2(\beta,\gamma)\right)' \left(\hat{V}_1(\beta,\gamma) - \hat{V}_2(\beta,\gamma)\right)^{-1} \mathrm{vec}\left(\hat{A}_1(\beta,\gamma) - \hat{A}_2(\beta,\gamma)\right)'\end{aligned} \tag{8.49}$$

takes place provided that the parameters β and γ are known (e.g. from the economic theory) or estimated (only single equation models). Otherwise, the test statistic takes the form:

$$\mathrm{supLM} = \sup_{\gamma L \leq \gamma \leq \gamma U} \mathrm{LM}(\tilde{\beta},\gamma) \tag{8.50}$$

The obtained LM statistic is heteroskedastically resistant. Both LM and SupLM statistics do not have a staged distribution with critical values. In order to verify the null hypothesis, the bootstrap *p value* was determined as a percentage of simulated LM statistics that exceed the current value of the LM statistics. The bootstrap can be built by randomizing residuals in regimes or by randomizing observations of explanatory variables in regimes. The selection of LM statistics was dictated by the possibility of implementation to the bootstrap.

The search area of the threshold variable value $[\gamma_L, \gamma_U]$ is constructed in such a way that γ_L is Π_0 percentile of the cointegrating vector, and γ_U is $1-\Pi_0$ percentile. Π_0 should not represent a value that is too close to zero. Andrews (1993) showed that this reduces the test power and claims that it is desirable for Π_0 to be contained between 0.05 and 0.15.

Using the Monte Carlo method and bootstrap, Hansen and Seo determined the size and power of the test. For the purpose of the experiment, they used a two-equation VECM and TVECM with a lag of 2 (the lag for variable levels). Obviously one cointegrating vector was assumed. The process generating the data (VECM, with the validity of the hypothesis H_0) is given by (8.51):

$$\Delta x_t = \begin{pmatrix} \mu_1 \\ \mu_2 \end{pmatrix} + \begin{pmatrix} \alpha_1 \\ \alpha_2 \end{pmatrix} (x_{1t-1} - \beta x_{2t-1}) + \Gamma \Delta x_{t-1} + \begin{pmatrix} u_{1t} \\ u_{2t} \end{pmatrix} \tag{8.51}$$

$$x_t = (x_{1t}, x_{2t})'$$

The switching between the regimes results from the value of the cointegrating vector (in the case of rejecting H_0):

$$(x_{1t-1} - \beta x_{2t-1}) \leq \gamma$$

or

$$(x_{1t-1} - \beta x_{2t-1}) > \gamma$$

Two samples with numbers of 100 and 250 were considered. Two variants were assumed for the residual processes. In the first case, the vector u_t was generated by a process with a normal distribution $N(0, 1)$, i.e. with homoscedastic variance, in the second by the GARCH process (1, 1). For the residual process generated by a process with a normal distribution, the rejection rates H_0 (the test size) are similar regardless of the adopted parameterization. Randomizing the bootstrap implementation of set explanatory variables in the regimes, for the 100 element test, with the rejection level of 5%, the test slightly rejects H_0. The rejection rate ranges from 0.71 to 0.108. In the case of randomizing a residual process to the bootstrap, the test behaves slightly better, the test ranges from 0.048 to 0.084. For a sample with a count of 250, the test size is improved significantly. For determined regressors it ranges from 0.067 to 0.080, and for randomized residuals, from 0.052 to 0.058. The generation of the residual process through the GARCH process (1, 1) does not interfere with the size of the test. Similarly, better results were obtained in the case of randomizing the bootstrap. To determine the test power, it was assumed that the process generating the data is expressed by the following formula (8.52):

$$\Delta x_t = \begin{pmatrix} 1 \\ 0 \end{pmatrix} (x_{1t-1} - x_{2t-1}) + \begin{pmatrix} \delta \\ 0 \end{pmatrix} (x_{1t-1} - x_{2t-1}) I(x_{1t-1} - x_{2t-1} \le \gamma) + u_t \tag{8.52}$$

where $u_t \sim N(0, I_2)$.
If $\delta = 0$, the process that generates the data becomes linear. For values different from zero, the generating process is two-regime. For $\delta \neq 0$, it was assumed that it takes four values (0.2; 0.4; 0.6; 0.8). The test power increases as the threshold effect of the sample size increases. The power of the test is higher in the case of randomizing residual processes than in the case of randomizing predefined regressors. Moreover, it is slightly higher when we estimate the parameters of the cointegrating vector before the bootstrap procedure (we calculate the LM statistics in the form (8.49) and not (8.50)).

8.6 Conclusions

In this chapter, some remarks on specification of threshold models with a special respect to threshold error correction models are presented. What comes from this analysis is that the identification the threshold mechanism underlying economic relationships is not an easy task. The reasons of departures from the assumed statistical characteristics are as follows: insufficient number of observations in empirical time series, structural instability in economic processes due to presence of outliers, structural breaks, asymmetry of information in the markets, discontinuities in economic policies, globalization and other processes that destabilize steady state of economic growth. On the other hand, the advantages of TECM are obvious. TECM approach allows modeling both long and short run dynamics of economic processes including the information about asymmetry in the adjustments to the long run.

As has been indicated, the procedure of testing for threshold can be considered from different viewpoints. One perspective is related to differences in the model specifications across given thresholds. This perspective is represented by the Enders and Siklos approach, Kapetanios et al. approach and our proposal. The second perspective is related to variance–covariance matrix of residuals. This approach is represented by the Tsay test. The Hansen and Seo test allows considering jointly the results coming from the first and the second. It is worth noting that structural breaks cannot be ignored while identification of threshold is made.

Each procedure discussed in this chapter has its own pros and cons. The careful sequential application of the methods for identification and estimation of threshold-type models allows validating the results and interpreting the results. However, deeper simulation-based studies on the comparison of the methods are still required.

References

Andrews DWK (1993) Tests for parameter instability and structural change with unknown change point. Econometrica 61(4):821

Balke NS, Fomby TB (1997) Threshold cointegration. Int Econ Rev 38:627–645

Boehlke J, Fałdziński M, Gałecki M, Osińska M (2017) Dynamics of economic growth in Ireland in 1980–2014. St. Petersburg State Polytechnical University Journal. Economics 10(2):7–20

Bruzda J (2007) Procesy nieliniowe i zależności długookresowe w ekonomii. Analiza kointegracji nieliniowej. Wydawnictwo UMK, Toruń

Chan KS (1993) Consistency and limiting distribution of the least squares estimation of a threshold autoregressive model. Ann Stat 21:520–533

Chan KS, Petruccelli JD, Tong H, Woolford SW (1985) A multiple-threshold AR(1) model. J Appl Probab 22(2):267–279

Enders W, Siklos PL (2001) Cointegration and threshold adjustment. J Bus Econ Stat 19 (2):166–176

Engle RF, Granger CWJ (1987) Cointegration and error correction: representation, estimation, and testing. Econometrica 55(2):51–276

Engle RF, Yoo S (1987) Forecasting and testing in a cointegrated system. J Econ 35:143–159

Frey G, Manera M (2007) Econometric models of asymmetric price transmission. J Econ Surv 21 (2):349–415

Gasparrini A (2011) Distributed lag linear and non-linear models in R: the package DLNM. J Stat Softw 43(8):1–20

Ghassan HB, Banerjee PK (2013) A threshold cointegration analysis of asymmetric adjustment of OPEC and non-OPEC monthly crude oil prices. Empir Econ 49:305–323

Gonzalo J, Pitarakis J-Y (2002) Estimation and model selection based inference in single and multiple threshold models. J Econ 110(2):319–352

Gosińska E (2015) Testowanie zmiany strukturalnej w modelu VEC. Bank i Kredyt 46(6):579–600

Granger CWJ, Lee TH (1989) Investigation of production, sales and inventory relationships using multicointegration and non-symmetric error correction models. J Appl Econ 4:145–159

Hansen H, Johansen S (1999) Some tests for parameter constancy in cointegrated VAR-models. Econometrics J 2(2):306–333

Hansen BE, Seo B (2002) Testing for two-regime threshold cointegration in vector error-correction models. J Econ 110:293–318

Hassouneh I, Serra T, Bojnec S, Gil JM (2017) Modelling price transmission and volatility spillover in the Slovenian wheat market. Appl Econ 49(41):4116–4126

Johansen S (1988) Statistical analysis of cointegration vectors. J Econ Dynam Control 12 (2–3):231–254

Johansen S (1995) Likelihood-based inference in cointegrated vector autoregressive models. Oxford University Press, Oxford

Kapetanios G, Shin Y, Snall A (2006) Testing for cointegration in nonlinear smooth transition error correction models. Economet Theor 22(6):279–303

Leszkiewicz-Kędzior K, Welfe A (2014) Asymmetric price adjustments in the fuel market. Central European J Econ Modelling Economet (CEJEME) 6(2):105–127

Lütkepohl H (2005) New introduction to multiple time series analysis. Springer Verlag, Berlin

Maddala G (1983) Limited-dependent and qualitative variables in econometric. Econometric Society Monographs No. 3. Cambridge University Press, New York

Majsterek M (2008) Wielowymiarowa analiza kointegracyjna w ekonomii. Wydawnictwo Uniwersytetu Łódzkiego, Łódź

Martens M, Kofman P, Vorst TCF (1998) A threshold error-correction model for intraday futures and index returns. J Appl Econ 13(3):245–263

Niglio M, Giordano F, Vitale CD (2012) On the stationarity of the threshold autoregressive process: the two regimes case. In: Giommi A (ed) 46th Scientific Meeting of the Italian Statistical Society

Petruccelli JD, Woolford SW (1984) A threshold AR(1) model. J Appl Probab 21(2):270–286

Piłatowska M, Włodarczyk A (2017) The environmental Kuznets curve in the CEE countries-the threshold cointegration approach. Argumenta Oeconomica 39(2):307–340
Seo B (1998) Tests for structural change in cointegrated systems. Economet Theor 14:222–259
Seo M (2011) Estimation of nonlinear error correction models. Economet Theor 27(2):201–234
Stigler M (2010) Threshold cointegration: overview and implementation in: R. Revision 5: April 2013. https://cran.r-project.org/web/packages/tsDyn/vignettes/ThCointOverview.pdf.
Tong H (1983) Threshold models in non-linear time series analysis. Lecture notes in statistics Vol. 21. Springer-Verlag, New York
Tong H (1990) Non-linear time series: a dynamical system approach. Oxford University Press, Oxford
Tsay RS (1998) Testing and modeling multivariate threshold models. J Am Stat Assoc 93 (443):1188–1202

Chapter 9
Econometric Analysis of Economic Miracles in Selected Economies Using TECM Approach

Jerzy Boehlke, Marcin Fałdziński, Maciej Gałecki, and Magdalena Osińska

Abstract Empirical results of econometric models for selected growth economies, i.e. Ireland, Spain, Turkey, and the Netherlands, obtained in the years 1980–2016 are discussed in detail. The purpose of the research is to answer the question whether periods of intense economic growth in different types of economies took place and how long they really lasted. The factors playing the crucial role in the periods of intense economic growth and their strength and direction are tested. The threshold error correction approach is used to both testing and modelling of long-term growth and fluctuations around it in short run. The results of econometric procedure allowed identifying both periods of economic miracles and crucial factors of growth acceleration. The economic miracles are evident in Ireland and the Netherlands.

9.1 Introduction

This chapter presents empirical results of econometric models for selected growth economies, i.e. Ireland, Spain, Turkey, and the Netherlands obtained in the years 1980–2016. The purpose of the research is to identify possible periods of intense economic growth in different types of economies, which are defined in Chap. 2 of the book. Also, the factors playing the crucial role in the periods of intense economic growth, their strength and direction, as well as similarity across the economies in

---

Financial support from research project no. 2015/17/B/HS4/01000 supported by the National Science Centre in Poland is gratefully acknowledged.

J. Boehlke
Department of Economics, The Faculty of Economic Sciences and Management, Nicolaus Copernicus University, Toruń, Poland
e-mail: jurekbo@umk.pl

M. Fałdziński · M. Gałecki · M. Osińska (✉)
Department of Econometrics and Statistics, The Faculty of Economic Sciences and Management, Nicolaus Copernicus University, Toruń, Poland
e-mail: marf@umk.pl; mgalecki@umk.pl; emo@umk.pl

M. Osińska (ed.), *Economic Miracles in the European Economies*,
https://doi.org/10.1007/978-3-030-05606-3_9

interest are studied. In this part, we applied the threshold error correction approach to both testing and modelling of long-term growth and fluctuations around it. The rationale for threshold error correction modelling in application to intense economic growth is such that we are looking for the periods of intense economic growth, the periods when the growth rates are faster than 'normal' (faster than expected) due to intentional policy of the macroeconomic authorities. Such periods do not last forever, but taking into account the definition formulated by Balcerowicz and Rzońca (2014), discussed in Chap. 1 of the book, they can either move the economy towards stable effective, innovated, and productive path (the Core economy) or improve economic performance of the country but only temporarily (the Periphery). In the latter, the economy is characterized by ups and downs, but it does not manage to break the limit of the technology frontier area (TFA). Casselli and Coleman (2006) explain this fact by the proportion of skilled and unskilled labour. Growiec (2012) supported previous findings by developing a broad and profound study on the distribution of the world technology frontier across space.

Coming back to the analysis of intense economic growth, the key issue of the research is to model an aggregate category that serves as a measure of economic output in chosen economies (e.g. GDP or GNP) in both the long run and short run. The selection of countries was not random. According to the classification made in Chap. 2 of this book (Boehlke 2019), it is clear that among European market economies we selected one economy inevitably coming from the Core (from the Technological Frontier Area), i.e. the Netherlands, and one economy definitely coming from the Periphery (outside the TFA), i.e. Turkey. We also selected two important European economies that made great progress and entered the Core but still have some problems and typically they are classified as peripheral cases. However, the division between the Core and Periphery is subject of discussion. As Toussaint (2011) states, 'the Periphery is subjected to decisions made by this hegemonic Core'. Looking at the evidence given in Growiec (2012), one can easily notice that the technical efficiency changed over time. For example, in the Netherlands and in Spain, it decreased between 1970 and 2000, while in Ireland it significantly increased. Looking at the GDP per worker indicator in 2017, its values (in USD, PPP constant for 2011) were as follows: Ireland 152,197; Spain 83,606; the Netherlands 94,978 and Turkey 68,676. Taking into account that Ireland's GDP is significantly higher due to the transfers of multinational companies abroad the GDP/employment ratio still remains among the world leaders (see: https://data.worldbank.org).

To our knowledge, the econometric models intended to detect factors of economic miracles were not the subject of analysis. However, switching regression concepts were used for modelling business cycles. Three types of nonlinear models are widely used in empirical applications, i.e. smooth transition regression models (Teräsvirta 1994), threshold models (Tong 1990), and Markov switching models (Hamilton 1989). Teräsvirta and Anderson (1992) applied STAR models in quarterly logarithmic production indices for 13 countries and Europe to describe the responses of production to large negative shocks such as oil price shocks. Granger et al. (1993) used STAR models to describe the relations between GNP and the Index of Leading

Indicators. They found that nonlinearity should be taken with care because in case of nonlinear model there is a possibility of overfitting due to data mining. That is why it is very important to check if the data exhibit nonlinearity before the model is estimated. TAR models have been used to describe the asymmetry observed in the quarterly US real GDP by Tiao and Tsay (1994), Potter (1995), and Proietti (1998) to mention a few. Osińska et al. (2018) applied the TAR/SETAR approach to investigate the mechanisms of business cycles in the EU economies. On the other hand, Hamilton (1989) had a great impact on business cycle modelling. He introduced and then applied a Markov switching model for econometric analysis of business cycle in the USA measured by the real GNP data (in logs and in differences). The results supported the two different regimes in the US economy: slow and fast economic growth. Another important example of MS modelling is the publication by Krolzig (1997) who compared MS models with a different number of regimes for business cycle in Germany and other market economies. Billio et al. (2013) compared both MS models and S ETAR models in application to the Industrial Production Index and Unemployment Rate in Euro area, observed monthly. They concluded that both specifications stem signals that do not vary sensibly. However, MS models seem better for noisy time series with high heteroscedasticity, whereas SETAR models are more sensitive for any recession episodes showing even non-existing recession periods. The *ex-post* signals coming from MS models are delayed when compared with SETAR.

The above examples, apart from Granger et al. (1993), did not include an error correction principle. Applied econometrics methods including models based on the concept of linear error correction mechanism and the selected theoretical models of growth have been widely adopted since the late 1980s. Theoretical models of economic growth have been repeatedly implemented in linear and nonlinear error correction models, both uni-dimensional and multi-dimensional. These models have become a basis for the construction of both the equilibrium paths for economic subsystems and for the construction of the so-called models of the national economy (Bergheim 2008; Welfe 2013). Currently, these models are widely implemented for modelling economic growth in post-communist countries and developing countries. The examples of the models include Dungey and Vehbi (2011); Ekanayake (1999); Hagemejer (2018). They are an alternative for DSGE models preferred by central banks which are not always able to respond adequately to the needs of statistical data.

This chapter is organized as follows. In the next section, the model hypotheses are specified based on theoretical models of growth as well as model specifications are explained. In the third section, the characteristics of the data used for analysis and the methodological outline of the research are provided. The cases of intense economic growth in Ireland, Spain, Turkey, and the Netherlands are empirically analysed in the fourth section. The results consist of testing for threshold error correction nonlinearity and estimated empirical TECM models in both the long and short run. In the fifth section, the robustness of the results based on the Tsay test and the Hansen and Seo test is checked. The conclusions are summarized in the sixth section.

9.2 Remarks on Model Specifications

9.2.1 Theoretical Basis of the Model

Theoretical analysis relatively assumes that the neoclassical economic paradigm is one of the possible cases of interpretation and evaluation. The literature on various problems of real economic growth is abundant. A complete and at the same time comprehensive overview of this literature can also be found in *the Handbook of Economic Growth* (Aghion and Durlauf 2005; Acemoglu 2009; Tokarski 2009, 2011). Due to the fact that the economic miracles in market economies in the twentieth and twenty-first centuries are defined as a result of constructivist actions of the state (government) aimed to accelerate periodically the pace of economic growth faster than expected, the use of endogenous growth models referring to the Solow-Swan model (Solow 1956; Swan 1956) seems to be obvious. These are models employing L.S. Pontryagin's maximum principle and based on the Mankiw–Romer–Weil model (Mankiw et al. 1992) in the following form:

$$Y = K^{\alpha}H^{\beta}(\mathrm{AL})^{1-\alpha-\beta}$$

where Y—total output, H—human capital, AL—effective labour resource, K—physical capital, and $\alpha > 0$, $\beta > 0$, $\alpha + \beta < 1$.

In addition, their extension is considered in the form of Nonneman–Vanhoudt model (Nonneman and Vanhoudt 1996). It extends the previously mentioned models by introducing n-capital input. Within these models the rate of investment in the resources of different types of production factors is indigenized. The endogenous nature of technical progress is also assumed. The choice of the above-mentioned models is justified by their assumption of the new classical economics of long-term behaviour rationality of economic entities.

As follows from the definitions of an economic miracle (see Chap. 1), economic miracles are not only constructivist (planned), but are also short term. Decisions of the state (government) as to the manner, time, and effects of their generation are always burdened with short-term factors, sometimes contrary to the assumption of rationality, usually incremental rather than systemic. The *ex-post* assessment of the effects generated by the miracles within the reported study is conducted in the light of the above-mentioned models of economic growth based on the assumption of the long-term rationality. An additional advantage of the choice of endogenous growth models of the Mankiw–Romer–Weil and Nonneman–Vanhoudt type, which are based on the production function of the Cobb-Douglas type, is their suitability to different types of economic miracles observed in the twentieth and twenty-first centuries. The advantages of the Cobb-Douglas function as the basis for modelling results from its presence in the models of growth, universality, and availability of statistical data.

As is known, the economic institutions are difficult to be modelled econometrically; therefore, such analysis will take place while attempting to interpret the causes of the success or failure of economic miracles policy in selected economies. This approach creates opportunities for applying the methodological concepts for the study of the historical process of economic growth developed on the basis of the new economic history, located in the mainstream of new institutional economics. These methodological concepts are important both from the point of view of the theory and economic policy and are continuously developed. As is shown in Chap. 10, the concept of Imperfect Knowledge Economics is also useful as regards the interpretation of different cases of economic miracles.

9.2.2 Threshold Error Correction Model Specification

The theoretical models mentioned are particularly useful for formulating a long run equation in the growth modelling. The endogenous variable is the level of the real aggregate measure of total production, such as GDP or GNP. As has already been mentioned in the introduction part, there are several discrepancies between the measures of growth since none of them covers all important elements generated by what should be captured by the economic growth term. The GDP measures total value of production in the economy expressed in monetary units, while GNP (or Gross National Income—GNI) is used for measuring the total income in the national economy. Furthermore, there is no direct relationship between the level of GDP and the economic welfare. To capture the latter, GDP per capita is widely applied. Malaga (2011) provides a brief discussion on the economic growth measurement issue. Apart from GDP and GDP p.c., he mentions other indicators, such as, for instance, the Green Gross Domestic Product (GGDP), the Index of Sustainable Economic Welfare (ISEW), or the Genuine Progress Indicator (GPI). However, what comes out from this discussion is that the advantages of these indicators are arguable, thus GDP and GDP p.c. are widely used.

Having in mind the above, in our further considerations the GDP level is assumed as a proper measure of what is observed as economic potential and its rate of growth as the measure of growth. The main reason is that GDP is the first indicator observed when growth is intensified (or slowed down).

We focus on most likely factors that are responsible for the level of real GDP in the long run and for the fluctuations around it in the short periods. One more thing needs explaining. Despite the fact that the concept of modelling economic miracles can seem very close to the theory of economic convergence (Barro and Sala-i-Martin 1992), it is not considered. Catching up the process is perceived here as a consequence of the miracle in the peripheral economies, while in the core ones it is thought as a part of economic competition.

We assumed that in the short run the dynamics of fluctuations can be symmetric or asymmetric. This depends on stability of the growth mechanism that is observed. If, however, intentional policy is implemented to eliminate barriers of growth and the growth starts to accelerate, one should realize that in such a period the observed hitherto relationships change. This idea explains the possible asymmetry in adjustment to the growth pattern and/or a change in the long run slope. Such a characteristic allows identifying the economic miracle, but its consequences can be observed with some delay. The first evidence of the miracle is that the output increases significantly. If it is so, further consequences are visible, too. One can easily guess that not each level of growth means that the economic miracle has started. It must be higher than expected in a specified time period and/or accompanied by the reforms that eliminate at least one barrier of growth. As a consequence, many elements should act together when an intense growth is put into motion, with particular role of economic governance (Best 2018). Such a line of reasoning brings us to the model specification. We assumed a threshold error correction specification since, due to a sharp mechanism of switching; it allows identifying two (or more) different regimes. One may ask why one equation approach has been selected instead of a system approach. The simplest and true reason is related to the limited number of observations. However, the most important argumentation comes from the comparability of the results across countries under investigation. We assumed a time series approach individually to each country and applied a similar set of variables (factors of growth). Considering a system (or subsystem), more complicated relationships within the system occur, thus we decided to limit the analysis with the primary intention of empirical identification of the periods of economic miracles. It needs emphasizing that in this research we focused on growth measured in terms of aggregate GDP (or GNP) and we attempt at identifying the most likely mechanism of generating intense growth, particularly in the short run.

The models are specified for one sector economy considered in time. The specification of the long run path was based on the Cobb-Douglas type of the model. Standard model linearization through using logarithmic transformation of the function was made when being applied. Having GDP as an endogenous variable, all variables presented in Table 7.1 in Chap. 7 were taken into account as potentially exogenous in the long run of the form:

$$Y_t = \alpha_0 + \sum_{i=1}^{k} \alpha_i X_{it} + u_t \tag{9.1}$$

We considered the following division of the growth factors: (1) internal variables within the country, i.e. the Employment and Unemployment rates, Public debt, GDP deflator, Domestic Investment, Multifactor productivity, Short and Long interest rates and (2) external factors such as Foreign Direct Investment, Net income from the EU, Exports, Imports and Net Export, the Exchange rate. A special role in the second group is assigned to the interventional and external source of funds represented by loans from international financial institutions (the International Monetary Fund and the World Bank), which were important in the case of Turkey. The internal variables are simply resources of the given economy or are naturally created by the market and economic policy created by the government and economic authorities (such as interest rates or public debt). Multifactor productivity incorporates economic efficiency coming not only from the technology and human capital skills but also from the cultural and organizational factors. The external factors can be divided into sources of growth (FDI, Net income from the EU, the Exchange rate) and the consequences of growth, for example, the relationship between Exports and Imports. But the feedback implies exports and imports to act as a source of growth. Institutions are rather difficult to be observed as a time series. Thus, FDI, Net income from the EU, loans from international institutions, and multifactor productivity are proxies showing some institutional progress (or regress). Referring to the Nonneman–Vanhoudt growth model, implementing Investments, FDI, Net Income from the EU, and/or loans from international institutions allows considering the *n*-capital expenditures. Although the same variables can be observed in almost each economy they, however, possess different level, different structure, and contribute in growth path in a different way. Sala-i-Martin (2002) summarized the most important lessons from the empirical literature on growth. Among most powerful factors of growth one can find the initial level of income, the 'quality of government', institutions (such as free markets, property rights, and the rule of law) and openness of the economy. He also mentioned that the relation between most measures of human capital and growth is weak, but some measures of health, such as life expectancy are robustly correlated with growth. He also states that a simple determinant of growth does not exist.

Periods of intense economic growth can be specified by testing for a threshold variable and statistical significance of the short-term relationships observed in the regimes. Then, the proposed model takes the following form:

$$\begin{aligned}\Delta Y_t &= I_t\rho_1 u_{t-1} + (1-I_t)\rho_2 u_{t-1} + I_t\omega_1\Delta X_t + (1-I_t)\omega_2\Delta X_t + \\ &\sum_{j=1}^{\max\{p;q\}} I_t\psi_{1j}\Delta Z_{t-j} + \sum_{j=1}^{\max\{p;q\}} (1-I_t)\psi_{2j}\Delta Z_{t-j} + e_t\end{aligned} \tag{9.2}$$

where

$$I_t = \begin{cases} 1 & \text{for} \quad Z_{t-i} \geq \hat{\gamma} \\ 0 & \text{for} \quad Z_{t-i} < \hat{\gamma} \end{cases} \quad \text{or} \quad I_t = \begin{cases} 1 & \text{for} \quad \Delta Z_{t-i} \geq \hat{\gamma} \\ 0 & \text{for} \quad \Delta Z_{t-i} < \hat{\gamma} \end{cases}$$

and

$$-\infty < \hat{\gamma} < \infty; \hat{\gamma} = \arg\min_{\gamma} \mathrm{AIC}(\gamma)$$

where $\hat{\gamma}$ is estimated value of the threshold and $Z_t = (Y_t, X_{1t}, X_{2t}, \ldots, X_{kt})'$, $X_t = (X_{1t}, X_{2t}, \ldots, X_{kt})'$, $u_{t-1}$is an error correction term (ECM) whereas it can be alternatively changed into Δu_{t-1}, which is called momentum ECM, symbols p and q denote maximum lag numbers for Y_t and X_t, respectively.

9.3 Data Characteristics and Methodology Outline

In the research, a time series approach was assumed. Thus, the key factor of the data was comparability of observed time series. That is why yearly data were used. The advantage of yearly data is that they are not a subject of noise due to heterogeneity of minor shocks, while the disadvantage is short time series data. The sources of data include Eurostat, OECD, the World Bank, the International Monetary Fund, the International Labour Organization, Central Bank of Spain, Federal Reserve Bank of St. Louis, financial reports of the EU, financial reports of the EU, and the statistical offices of the analysed countries. The data cover the period starting from 1980 though the economies experienced the periods of economic miracles in different years starting from 1950. We recall them when describing the individual economies. The entire period of data observation covers the years 1980–2016. This period is relatively short in terms of the number of observations and that is why we assumed only two regimes in the observed path of economic growth extracted from the original series. In the analysis both forms, i.e. level and logs, were applied; however, the presentation relates only to logarithmic transformations. The full set of variables in interest with symbols and sources of the data is given in Table 7.1 (Chap. 7 of this book).

In market economies, the growth is uneven and it is characterized with fluctuations of real GDP around a long run growth path. These fluctuations are cyclical and repeatable. These are obviously due to the business cycles (Burns and Mitchell 1946). It is interesting that in the case of searching economic miracles business cycles are not helpful. This is because not each growth pattern (e.g. phase of prosperity) should be considered as miraculous. It requires further conditions, as was discussed in Chaps. 1 and 2. Thus, cyclical fluctuations must be removed from the series of GDP (or GNP). It was done using the standard Hodrick and Prescott (HP) filter (Hodrick and Prescott 1997).

The TECM methodology applied while conducting empirical research is widely discussed in Chap. 8 of this book. Below we only summarize the plan of the research. It consists of the following steps:

1. Data analysis:
   (a) At this step, the long-term trend was extracted from the real GDP series observed in Spain, Turkey, and the Netherlands and in the case of Ireland—real GNP using the HP filtering procedure. Such a long-term trend allows modelling the long run without business cycles. Original and extracted series (in logs) are presented in Fig. 9.1.
   (b) The series were checked for presence of the unit roots and structural breaks. The Augmented Dickey Fuller and Philips and Perron tests as well as the Andrews and Zivot and Bai and Perron tests were used, as was described in Chap. 7 of this book.

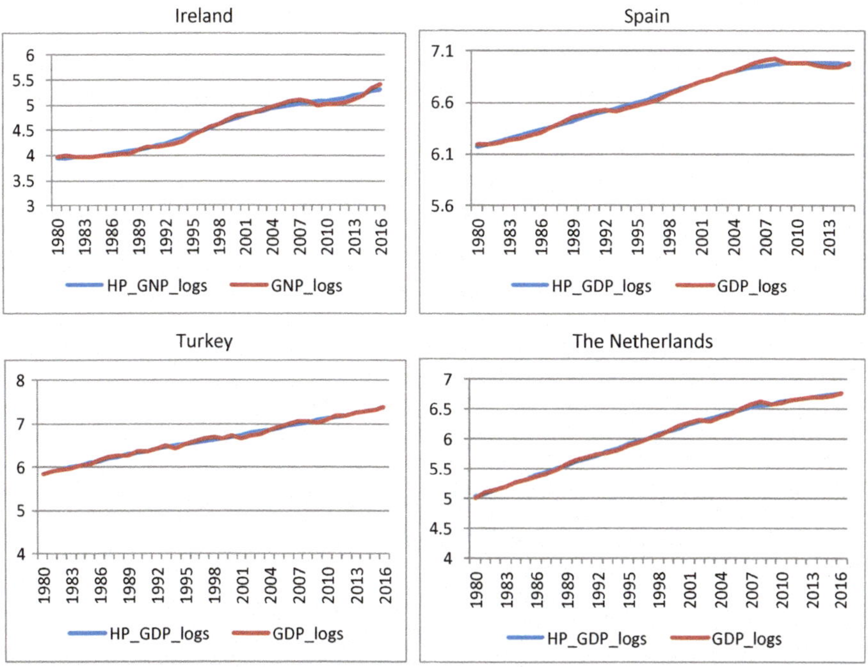

Fig. 9.1 Log (GDP) and a long run trend extracted using the Hodrick-Prescott filter (for Ireland GNP was used, for Spain data end in 2015) (own computations)

2. Estimation of long run relationships using OLS and testing for structural breaks in residuals using the Quandt test (Quandt 1960).
3. Testing for threshold error correction form vs. linear cointegration (Linear ECM) or vs. the threshold stationary model (TAR-X/SETAR-X) in a sequence of tests:

   (a) The Enders and Siklos (2001) original approach,
   (b) The Kapetanios et al. (2006) and Bruzda (2007) approach,
   (c) Our approach (see: Boehlke et al. 2017 and Chap. 8).

   This approach is summarized in Fig. 9.2.

1. Checking for the robustness of the results using the Tsay test and Hansen and Seo test.
2. Model estimation using the full information maximum likelihood (FIML) method with the Chan procedure (Chan 1993) for estimating the value of threshold.

One important remark is required to explain the relationships between threshold models and structural breaks. If a structural break is detected in the error correction term, it can be a strong argument for existence of nonlinear mechanism around the linear long run growth. In this case, a standard testing procedure presented in Quandt (1960) is satisfactory. A wide survey on structural breaks detecting is presented in Chaps. 7 and 8.

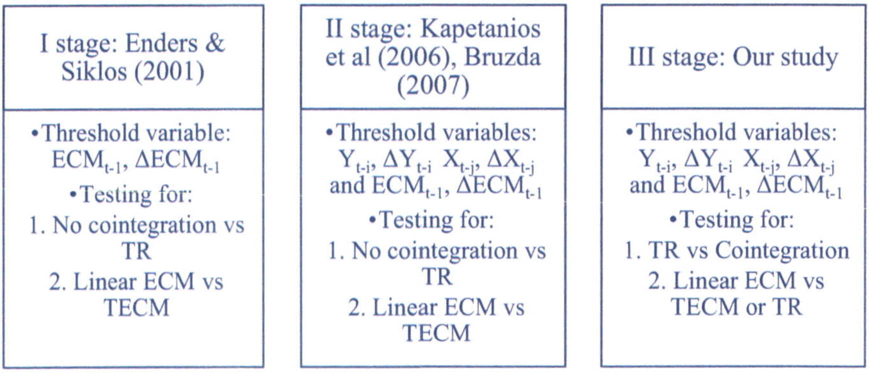

Fig. 9.2 Sequent steps of testing for threshold cointegration using TECM framework. TR denotes a threshold type regression model, for example, TAR, SETAR, or TAR-X/SETAR-X (own study)

9.4 Econometric Analysis of Economic Miracles in Selected Economies: Empirical Results

In this subchapter, we present the results of testing for thresholds in four selected economies using both the TECM approach based on the parameters asymmetry idea and the *ex-post* idea based on the residual variance-covariance matrix. Further, threshold error correction models are estimated and analysed in the context of intense economic growth.

9.4.1 Economic Miracle in Ireland in 1980–2016

The economy of Ireland as an example of economic miracle has been a subject of a wide economic and statistical analysis in the last several years. The most recent book by O'Leary (2015) developed a multi-aspect discussion on such factors as technology, exports, as well as taxation system and policy of the government as very important determinants of growth of the country called 'Celtic Tiger'. Barry et al. (2001) analysed, among others, the role of structural funds in Ireland's recent economic growth and concluded that neither the Single Market nor the Structural Funds are likely to account fully for this increase in Ireland's share. It has been emphasized that another factor of success is related to the social partnership agreements and the timing of the structural funds use. As concerns the growth factors as the source of an economic success of the Irish economy, some economists emphasized the role of the Irish economic policy, especially the stabilization policy and since the middle of the last decade of the twentieth century institutional reforms (changes in economic law, tax system, education) (Honohan and Walsh 2002), others focused on the influence of FDI and financial support from EU founds (Barry 2002) or explaining the Irish case as effective industrialization of the 1990s

(Piński 2013) and the combination of economic policy, institutional reforms (especially regulatory reforms) and EU membership (Szczepaniak 2015). According to Cassidy (2004), there are five important considerations in discussion about the Irish economy: solid macroeconomic fundamentals, general regulatory environment supporting and encouraging business and entrepreneurship development, good access to risk capital, educational attainment of the workforce, and conditions to R&D activity. The overview of the factors of the Irish economic success is presented in Chap. 5 of this book (Szczepaniak 2019).

What are the main characteristics of the Irish economy within the observed period? The average GDP annual growth rate of 1980–2008 was at 6.6%. The highest GDP level, i.e. 274.71 billion of USD, was achieved by Ireland in 2008. In the same period, GDP per capita PPP in 1980 started from the level 13,434 USD, it reached 37,276 USD in 2008 and finally 46,633 USD in 2014. According to the World Bank Group, the GDP value of Ireland in 2014 represented 0.40% of the world economy amounting to 250.81 billion US dollars. Ireland could be characterized as a rapidly growing economy before the last financial crisis and incredible GDP decrease after 2008. In the 2008–2010 period, the average GDP growth rate was at minus 3.5%. The situation started to improve after 2013. Comparing it with other developed economies, it is necessary to treat it as quite typical in the period of 2008–2014.

Figure 9.3 shows the GDP and GDP growth rate in 1980–2016 and in Fig. 9.4 the GDP and GNI (formerly: GNP) levels are compared.

The Gross National Income (GNI) (formerly: GNP) level is deliberately lower and its dynamics is also smaller due to transfers from foreign companies abroad. Other important indicators gained spectacular results. For example, HDI of Ireland in 1980 was of 89% HDI of the USA and it was still improving reaching 0.923 in 2015, which ranked Ireland eight in the world. In 2014, the Index of Economic Freedom and Heritage Foundation Index ranked Ireland ninth in the world 'economically free' economies category.

Ireland has considerably benefited from the large number of foreign companies that have chosen it as a location for European expansion—mainly due to an incredibly low corporate tax rate of 12.5%. The export-dominated economy has also been lifted by a relatively weak euro and a strong resumption of domestic demand from its once heavily indebted consumers. However, the structure of the economy of Ireland is quite complicated, and the overall picture is much more diversified. The multinational companies (MNE hereafter) are included in the GDP which growth rate exceeds not only the GNI growth rates but other indicators as well. This is particularly visible when compared with the individual consumption and the government consumption growth rates. The statistics revealed in 2016 by the Central Statistics Office of Ireland caused a real concern about the state of national accounts in Ireland. It happened that after restructuring the assets and other operations the GDP year-to-year growth rate was equal to 26.3% in 2015 in comparison to 2014. The CSO representative commented on this fact that it had increased the capacity for production in the economy and impacted the accounts for 2015 in the increase of exports and imports. Due to the large GDP growth rates observed in the

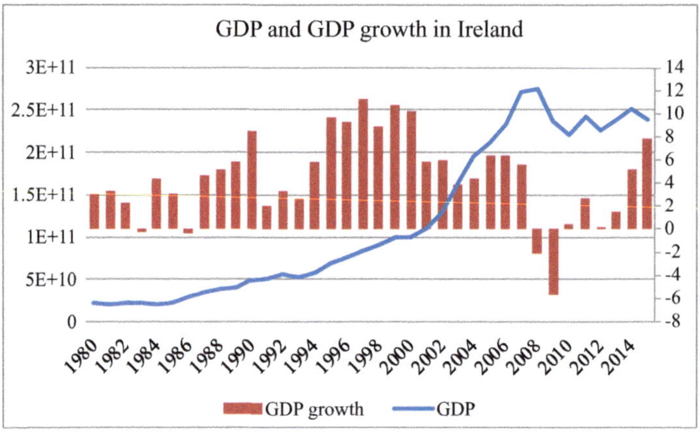

Fig. 9.3 GDP and GDP growth rate (PPP) in Ireland in 1980–2015 (Based on the World Bank http://databank.worldbank.org/data/)

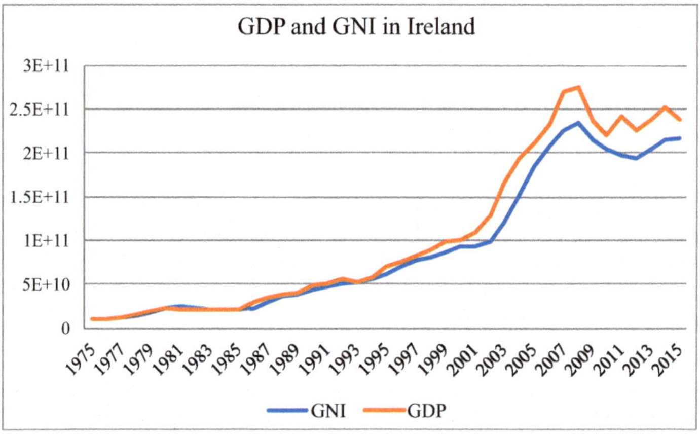

Fig. 9.4 Levels of the GDP and GNI in Ireland in 1975–2015 (Based on the World Bank http://databank.worldbank.org/data/)

last years which were not accompanied with respective growth rates of the Irish households' income, it is recommended to use the GNP as a measure of economic growth in the case of Ireland. The initial results, considering the GDP analysis, were published in Boehlke et al. (2017). In Boehlke et al. (2018), we analysed the Irish GNP in the years 1980–2014. In this section, we deepen the research by extending the sample up to 2016 and including the Hansen and Seo test for validation of the results.

The econometric analysis of the Irish economy has started with the testing for unit roots as well as structural breaks which was reported in Chap. 7. Following the

Table 9.1 Long run equation in the case of the Irish GNP trend (in logs, extracted with HP filter) (own computations)

Variable name	Coefficient	Standard error	*p*-Value
Const	2.23958	0.56596	0.0051
lnFDI	−0.00230	0.00115	0.0550
lnEMP	0.34169	6.68E-02	<0.0001
lnPD	−0.05284	0.02235	0.0253
lnDEFLATOR	−0.22750	0.03203	<0.0001
SR	−0.49167	0.15904	0.0045
LR	0.43131	0.16916	0.0165
TFP	0.43292	0.07738	<0.0001
Time	0.03906	0.00340	<0.0001
R^2	0.999	AIC	−210.705
DW	1.376	BIC	−196.206
QLR test (*p*-value)	8.36E-11	Year of break	2000

QLR test represents Quandt test for structural breaks (Quandt 1960)

results, testing for threshold type cointegration was proceeded according to the steps presented in the previous section. Tables 9.1, 9.2, 9.3, 9.4, 9.5, 9.6, and 9.7 present the results of the analysis.

It can be seen that many variables contribute to the long run growth in Ireland. The main impact of such growth factors as employment and total factor productivity is clear. The respective parameters estimates 0.34169 and 0.43292 are significant and positive. Coming back to the Nonneman–Vanhoudt model—FDI can be included into *n*-capital resource. The FDI surprisingly negatively contributes to the long run growth, which can be caused by different factors. One possible explanation comes from the relationship between the inflows of direct investment and outflows from the multinational companies located in Ireland. If this difference is negative, the impact of FDI on growth can be negative due to the correlation with the mentioned outflows of profits. The Quandt test indicates a significant structural break in ECM in 2000. In Tables 9.2 and 9.3, the results of testing for a threshold variable in three tests are presented: the Enders and Siklos test, Kapetanios test, and our approach.

Thus, the best result for Ireland is obtained when the GDP deflator was taken into account. It is evident due to the elimination of inflationary process in Ireland after the political consensus in 1987. However, higher than the EU average inflation rate in Ireland accompanied the intense economic growth (see: Chap 5 of this book). The second best model is related to the first difference of FDI lagged by 1 year, which has been indicated as one of the main factors of intense economic growth. In Table 9.5 below, we present two best estimated TECMs for the economy of Ireland.

Validation of the results has been made on two levels. The first one is the distinction between linear and nonlinear (threshold type) model with the Tsay test (Tsay 1998; comp. Chap. 8). The second one was made using the Hansen and Seo test (Hansen and Seo 2002: comp. Chap. 8). The tests were calculated for thresholds identified in Table 9.3.

Table 9.2 Enders and Siklos test results for HP_lnGNP in original and Kapetanios et al. versions (constant number of observations) (own computations)

Threshold variable	Threshold value	H[1]: $\rho_1 = \rho_2 = 0$ p-value	H[2]: $\rho_1 - \rho_2 = 0$ p-value	Remark
Original Enders–Siklos test				
ECM(t-1)	0	0.0005	0.628	Linear cointegration
ΔECM(t-1)	0	0.0005	0.370	Linear cointegration
Kapetanios et al. test				
ECM(t-1)	0	0.0000	0.0014	Partial cointegration TAR-X
ΔECM(t-1)	0	0.0003	0.4543	Linear cointegration
ΔlnFDI(t-1)	−0.27408	0.0002	0.1876	Linear cointegration
ΔlnDEFLATOR (t-1)	0.05193	0.0003	0.5915	Linear cointegration
ln DEFLATOR (t-2)	**4.172848**	**0.0000**	**0.0749**	**Threshold cointegration**
ΔlnI(t-2)	**0.16464**	**0.0000**	**0.0070**	**Threshold cointegration**
TFP(t-2)	**0.989182**	**0.0003**	**0.0500**	**Threshold cointegration**
ΔTFP(t-2)	0.02321	0.0000	0.0272	Partial cointegration TAR-X
ΔlnN_Ex(t-2)	0.044306	0.0003	0.0213	Partial cointegration TAR-X
lnFDI(t-3)	**10.00247**	**0.0000**	**0.0107**	**Threshold cointegration**
lnPD(t-3)	3.843299	0.0000	0.0013	Partial cointegration TAR-X
LR(t-3)	**1.0729**	**0.0001**	**0.0542**	**Threshold cointegration**
lnEMP(t-4)	**7.572812**	**0.0000**	**0.0092**	**Threshold cointegration**
lnI(t-4)	**3.383271**	**0.0000**	**0.0453**	**Threshold cointegration**
ΔlnNI _UE(t-4)	**−0.15654**	**0.0019**	**0.0535**	**Threshold cointegration**
ΔlnPD(t-4)	0.050598	0.0019	0.0010	Partial cointegration TAR-X
ΔSR(t-4)	0.0058	0.0004	0.9516	Linear cointegration
HP_lnGNP(t-5)	**4.996166**	**0.0007**	**0.0460**	**Threshold cointegration**
lnNI_UE(t-5)	6.338849	0.0000	0.0401	Partial cointegration TAR-X
SR(t-5)	1.0625	0.0002	0.0618	Partial cointegration TAR-X
lnN_Ex(t-5)	0.12392	0.0001	0.2384	Linear cointegration

(continued)

Table 9.2 (continued)

Threshold variable	Threshold value	H^1: $\rho_1 = \rho_2 = 0$ p-value	H^2: $\rho_1 - \rho_2 = 0$ p-value	Remark
ΔHP_lnGNP(t-5)	**0.025508**	**0.0000**	**0.0721**	**Threshold cointegration**
ΔlnEMP(t-5)	0.00523	0.0000	0.0004	Partial cointegration TAR-X
ΔLR(t-5)	−0.0005	0.0002	0.2510	Linear cointegration

Significant thresholds in the case of threshold cointegration are in bold

Table 9.3 Our version of the Enders and Siklos test (variable number of observations) (own computations)

Threshold variable	Threshold value	H^1: $\rho_1 = \rho_2 = 0$ p-value	H^2: $\rho_1 - \rho_2 = 0$ p-value	Remark
ECM(t-1)	0	0.2602		No cointegration
ΔECM(t-1)	**0**	**0.0001**	**0.0000**	**Threshold cointegration**
ΔlnFDI(t-1)	**−0.27408**	**0.0002**	**0.0000**	**Threshold cointegration**
ΔlnDEFLATOR (t-1)	0.05193	0.0716	0.0000	Partial cointegration TAR-X
lnDEFLATOR (t-2)	**4.17284**	**0.1467**	**0.0253**	**Threshold cointegration**
TFP(t-2)	0.98918	0.1488	0.0000	Partial cointegration TAR-X
lnFDI(t-3)	10.00247	0.1672		No cointegration
LR(t-3)	**1.07290**	**0.0000**	**0.0000**	**Threshold cointegration**
lnI(t-4)	3.38327	0.0317	0.0000	Partial cointegration TAR-X
ΔlnPD(t-4)	0.05059	0.0959	0.0000	Partial cointegration TAR-X
ΔSR(t-4)	0.00580	0.0008	0.0000	Partial cointegration TAR-X
SR(t-5)	1.06250	0.4252		No cointegration
Δhpt_lnGNP(t-5)	0.02550	0.0157	0.0000	Partial cointegration TAR-X
ΔlnEMP(t-5)	**0.00523**	**0.0036**	**0.0000**	**Threshold cointegration**
ΔLR(t-5)	−0.00050	0.7095		No cointegration

Significant thresholds in the case of TECM are in bold

Table 9.4 Best estimated TECM models according to AIC and BIC with respect to a threshold value (own computations)

Threshold variable	AIC	BIC
lnDEFLATOR(t-2)	−318.612	−304.044
ΔlnFDI(t-1)	−296.466	−285.335
LR(t-3)	−269.45	−255.831
ΔECM(t-1)	−265.514	−251.836
ΔlnEMP(t-5)	−237.908	−228.686

Table 9.5 Two best TECM models for GNP in Ireland in 1980–2016 (own computations)

Dependent variable	Threshold variable		Value of threshold		Threshold variable		Value of threshold	
ΔHP_lnGNP	lnDEFLATOR (t-2)		4.172848		ΔlnFDI(t-1)		−0.27408	
	N1 =	18	N2=	15	N1 =	23	N2 =	11
	BIC =		−304.044		BIC =		−285.335	
Variable name	I regime	I*p*-value	II regime	II *p*-value	I regime	I *p*-value	II regime	II *p*-value
Const	0.005	0.004	0.007	0.000	0.012	0.000	0.035	0.000
ΔSR			−0.047	0.000	−0.100	0.032		
ΔLR	−0.109	0.002	0.153	0.000	−0.190	0.041		
ΔlnFDI							0.002	0.000
ΔlnNI_UE	0.000	0.096					−0.002	0.000
ΔlnI	0.035	0.000	−0.009	0.001			−0.063	0.000
ΔlnPD	0.013	0.032	−0.011	0.014			−0.174	0.000
ΔTFP	0.134	0.000			−0.014	0.047	1.228	0.000
ΔlnEMP	−0.034	0.096			0.138	0.001	−0.350	0.000
ΔlnN_Ex	0.056	0.000	−0.030	0.001				
ECM(t-1)	−0.088	0.060	−0.078	0.000	−0.155	0.021	−1.361	0.000
ΔHP_lnGNP (t-1)	0.773	0.000	0.958	0.000	0.692	0.000		
ARCH LM(4)	(0.744)		(0.983)		(0.836)		(0.626)	
Ljung-ox Q(1)	(0.607)		(0.642)		(0.884)		(0.315)	
Q(2)	(0.409)		(0.399)		(0.327)		(0.602)	
Q(3)	(0.355)		(0.601)		(0.510)			

For ARCH LM and Ljung-Box tests, *p*-values are given in brackets

It should be noted that in the case of the Tsay test all of the thresholds identified in the earlier testing procedure, i.e. ΔECM(t-1), ΔlnFDI(t-1), ln DEFLATOR (t-2), LR (t-3), and ΔlnEMP(t-5), were confirmed. Additionally, ΔHP_lnGNP(t-5) was indicated as a threshold variable.

Considering the above, we can state that the increase in FDI lagged by 1 year is responsible for the mechanism of generating intense economic growth periods.

The results of the Hansen and Seo test seem to be most robust for the reason that this test accounts for both residual variance-covariance matrix and model parameters

Table 9.6 The results of the Tsay test for selected thresholds (own computations)

Threshold variable	*C*(*d*)	*p*-Value	Decision
ECM(t-1)	17.638	0.0241	TAR-X
ΔECM(t-1)	14.081	0.0497	**Threshold cointegration**
ΔlnFDI(t-1)	44.199	0.0000	**Threshold cointegration**
ΔlnDEFLATOR(t-1)	1.198	0.9770	Linear cointegration
lnDEFLATOR(t-2)	24.872	0.0031	**Threshold cointegration**
TFP(t-2)	1.865	0.9849	Linear cointegration
LR(t-3)	23.454	0.0092	**Threshold cointegration**
lnI(t-4)	3.723	0.9773	Linear cointegration
ΔlnPD(t-4)	4.747	0.7842	Linear cointegration
ΔSR(t-4)	3.437	0.8418	Linear cointegration
ΔHP_lnGNP(t-5)	60.593	0.0000	**Threshold cointegration**
ΔlnEMP(t-5)	17.602	0.0073	**Threshold cointegration**

Significant thresholds in the case of TECM are in bold

Table 9.7 The results of the Hansen and Seo test for selected thresholds (own computations)

Threshold variable	LM	*p*-Value	Decision
ECM(t-1)	2.932	0.002	TAR-X
ΔECM(t-1)	2.022	0.143	Linear cointegration/Threshold cointegration
ΔlnFDI(t-1)	**25.617**	**0.068**	**Threshold cointegration**
ΔlnDEFLATOR(t-1)	39.129	0.000	TAR-X
lnDEFLATOR(t-2)	0.681	1.000	Linear cointegration
TFP(t-2)	6.728	0.181	Linear cointegration
LR(t-3)	2.467	0.123	Linear cointegration/Threshold cointegration
lnI(t-4)	3.436	1.000	Linear cointegration
ΔlnPD(t-4)	3.500	0.778	Linear cointegration
ΔSR(t-4)	130.641	0.334	Linear cointegration
ΔHP_lnGNP(t-5)	35.947	0.994	Linear cointegration
ΔlnEMP(t-5)	27.372	0.163	Linear cointegration

Significant thresholds in the case of TECM are in bold

estimates. In this test, ΔlnFDI(t-1) was fully confirmed as a threshold variable and additionally ΔECM(t-1) and LR(t-3) seem to be close to confirmation. It is interesting that in the period of intense economic growth (regime I above the threshold value) a strong positive first-order autoregression with a parameter estimate equal to 0.692 was present. Comparing the adjustment coefficient in the first regime, it was equal to -0.155 while in the second it was -1.361. It shows a strong asymmetry in the short run adjustment towards the long run trend. The adjustment coefficient in the intense growth regime was not very strong, so the tendency to return to the long run level was slow. In the case of the second regime, it can be observed that the economy adjusts much faster to the long run trend (in a period shorter than 1 year). Thus, a tendency towards growth accelerating has been fully confirmed.

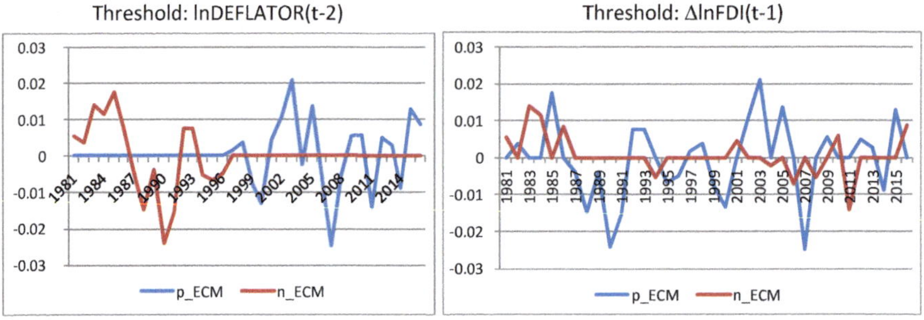

Fig. 9.5 Regimes indicated by thresholds: lnDEFLATOR(t-2) and ΔlnFDI(t-1) (own computations). Symbols: p_ECM denotes regime I and n_ECM denotes regime II

In Fig. 9.5, the ECM processes in two regimes for the best models reported in Table 9.5 are presented.

It can be seen that the regime of intense economic growth in Ireland identified by ΔlnFDI(t-1) threshold variable covered the following years: 1982; 1985; 1987–1993; 1995–2000; 2002–2003; 2005; 2007; 2009 and 2012–2015. The second regime covered: 1981; 1983–1984; 1986; 1994; 2001; 2004; 2006; 2008; 2010–2011. The years 1995–2000; 2002–2003; 2005; 2007 correspond to the economic miracle case.

9.4.2 Economic Miracle in Spain in 1980–2015

According to Tortilla (2000), the modern economic history of Spain is poorly understood, even by people from that country. It is a very interesting case for researchers because of a successful transition from dictatorship to democracy and from a controlled economy and autarky (1939–1959) to a liberal and open system. To explain and understand that phenomenon, we need to adopt a long-term view. The Spanish economy is described and analysed as one of the examples of an economic miracle of the twentieth century. In Chap. 3 of this book, Myro (2019) characterized Spain's economic growth from the perspective of economic history. To understand this case, it is necessary to remember that the twentieth century in Spain was marked by political instability and a war that led to the situation in which this country was lagging far behind the developed European economies. Political instability returned again in the 1920s, which was made worse by the Great Depression culminating in the Spanish Civil War since 1936–1939. The war was won by the fascist regime of Francisco Franco who was installed as a dictator. Franco's regime pursued a policy of autarky (Anserson 1970). The Spanish government started to modernize the national economy by public investment in infrastructure, especially in a highway network and in car industry. The Spanish economic miracle began in the mid-1950s due to the political and economic stabilization resulting from US aid and former Franco's infrastructure projects which were implemented during the 1940s. It was initiated by the reforms promoted by the so-called technocrats. During the 1950s and 1960s, Spain's level of industrialization grew rapidly. The economic expansion was heavily based on public investment in infrastructure development but also on the opening of Spain as a tourist destination (Tisdell 2013). It took Spain only 20 years to transform from an unindustrialized country before the 1960s to an economy that could easily adapt to become a part of the European Economic Community (Dowrick, Nguyen 1989). The miracle ended also the period of autarky. It originated from the Stabilization Program introduced in1959 (Prados de la Escosura et al. 2010), which made it possible for a high number of agricultural workers to migrate from the villages to the big Spanish cities at that time. This rural exodus created a new class of industrial workers in the cities. The economic boom led to an increase in the construction of largely unplanned, cheaply constructed suburbs on the peripheries of many urban areas. Prados de la Escosura and Sanz (1996, p. 379) mentioned that liberalization and structural reforms in post-1959 Spain were gradual but financial stabilization was radical. The economic history of Spain describes its model of economic transition in a closed-economy framework. Before the transition, the Spanish economy could be characterized by an over-dimensioned public sector, very low interest rates and high government debt. The transition reduced the size of the public sector which was gradually replaced by a growing private sector. In Spain, a series of economic reforms undertaken between 1957 and 1959 set the Spanish economy in the path of high growth.

Between 1976 and the mid-80s Spain had also some of the best leaders in power. The King Juan Carlos had the loyalty of the army and he really guided the country into democracy. Generally, the post-war political and economic history of Spain shows the gradual liberalization of that country. It should be noted that Spain went through a minor economic recession in the late 1970s. A major factor in Spain's economic growth since the 1980s is also its entry into the NATO and the EU structures. The EU's subsidies really encouraged a massive investment in Spain. In 2008, Spain had a huge bubble on the property market. There was no other country in the world at that time with an equivalent number of ongoing construction projects. As a result of path dependence, Spain also has a problem that there is no productive model based on industry, the Internet or in any private sector, except for the tourist sector (Llopis, Teresa 2006). Despite that Spanish living standards keep increasing and the development of a large middle class in this country has been observed.

Prados de la Escosura and Sanz (1996) distinguished two spectacular periods in Spain's political and economic history following the period of Franco's dictatorship. The first one is a transition to democracy and liberal economy (1975–1985) and the second one is the recession of the early 1990s. Explaining this economic transition entails many challenges. Spain has historically been a poor country if compared with the rich countries of Europe, but after the development initiated in the 1960s and having gone through the process of full incorporation of the country into developed capitalism even if cut across by many specific elements and with its integration in the European Economic Community, gradually Spain started to be a member of the rich part of the world. The evolution of the Spanish economy since the 1960s may be briefly described as follows. There is a first industrialization and urbanization drive in the 1960s. Internal demand was growing due to industrialization, urbanization, and the corresponding increased incomes. The country could export thanks to low wages and a submitted labour force. The key points in the economic policy of that period were to implement political democracy, achieve macroeconomic stability and public financial discipline. The reform in Spain was successful because it targeted three goals concerning the institutional order at once. It would have not been possible in other way. Spain before the 1960s of the twentieth century was a country with a strong government with a high control of the economy, very limited access to financing and a low taxation capacity, and the ambition to improve the country's situation. The plan of 1959 and the previous fiscal reform of 1957 targeted the macroeconomic instability and the unsustainability of the public debt. The consequence of these two problems was a depressed private initiative with barriers to access credit and low incentives to invest. The public sector, by scaling down the amount of debt, allows economic entrepreneurs to save more and to start new firms and investment projects. In this period, the government was choosing the interest rates setting them by law and controlling inflation by issuing debt and printing money. These two tools allowed the government to influence the amount of private investment in the economy. In such a situation, government bonds with very low interest rates could compete for funds with other investment options like holding the money in bank deposits. This made it possible for the government to capture a big share of the savings.

Since 1986 Spain has been integrated into the EU but still relies on a productive model based on low labour costs and low level technology. The country has increasingly become an interesting market for the central countries of the EU. In the context of great expansion of world trade and EU integration processes, the Spanish productive system shows the weakness of its productive specialization, where the most competitive sectors have been losing weight in front of other activities leading its growth. Spain has had no solid and permanent productive development but has been surviving through a model of low productivity, low wages, high labour precariousness, and enormous ecological deterioration. With a few strategic modern sectors (automobile, chemistry, and agro-industry) at the hands of foreign capital and very few advanced technological sectors, with the main part of enterprises very small and at the hands of native entrepreneurs only used to very traditional managing ways, mainly directed to exert pressure and if in difficulty dismiss workers (Prados de la Escosura and Rosés 2009). Only a few firms have become powerful global undertakings and other few ones of advanced technology have developed but they are from being enough to drive the country behind them. An interesting comparison of economic growth in Europe is provided by Timmer et al. (2012).

In the first period after the accession in 1986 the fact that Spain belonged to the EEC gave security to the European investors more interested in buying existing industries than expanding or improving the productive capacity, while many Spanish entrepreneurs took the opportunity to sell their industries. An important number of small industries disappeared and a dual structure of the economy was emerged: few modern corporations and many small traditional ones struggling to absorb advanced technology in order to produce competitively for the internal market and export. A high external deficit that could only be solved with four devaluations in 2 years (1992–1994) developed. The Maastricht Treaty (1992) and its conditions together with the strong will of the Spanish government to be among the first group of countries in the EMU led to a though adjustment programme during the early 1990s. The macroeconomic conditions for taking part in the euro zone were fulfilled attaching the country to the euro area but the economy did not recover before 1995. In 1994, unemployment was at 24.1% of the working population. Pressure upon wages increased and working precariousness, determined by submerged economy, temporality, short-term labour contracts (that accounted for more than 33% of labour contracts according to official statistics and to more than 50% according to other estimates that decreased internal demand), occurred. At the same time, the beginning of the building bubble had been started.

The productive structure of the country at the beginning of the twentieth century consists of a few great firms owned by foreign transnational holdings (Telefonica, Repsol, Banco Santander, Banco Bilbao, Abertis) and a lot of small companies working either for the first ones or for the internal market. The weakness of internal demand and the pressure of economic facts have also led to the development of quite a number of firms dedicated to exports, which are increasing. However, the country suffers a permanent foreign dependency on capital, technology, and knowledge. Even the sectors making for prosperity were sectors of a medium level of technology, like the building construction and car industry. Locally owned capital, in general terms, remained uncompetitive internationally. The economy was driven by internal demand, tourism, and thanks to the EU Structural and Cohesion Funds, investment in infrastructures was possible beyond the capacity of the Spanish state. Yet, in the late 1990s and the early 2000s, this receipt for failure was transformed into the 'Spanish Economic Miracle'. This so-called miracle was sustained by two major set of events. The first one was the housing bubble and the second one the internationalization of a few Spanish-based holdings created from the privatization of state companies and monopolies.

In 2000, unemployment rate was 20.4% and in 2004 it was 12.2%. But to participate in the Eurozone another adjustment programme was established and, without devaluation which was impossible after taking a common currency, competitiveness (internal and external) became more difficult. Nevertheless, the euro permitted to keep a greater external trade deficit. In front of the problems of this model, capitals looked for non-tradable sectors where competition was not relevant (building industry, commercial big areas) or oligopolistic sectors being privatized (energy, communications) or financial speculation. On the side of demand, the willingness to reach the European level of consumption was maintained and even increased through cheap credit, especially to buy apartments and the building industry boom was established. A number of elements existed and developed that led to an enormous expansion of the construction industry all over the world. In Spain, that expansion was spectacular. During the period from 2000 to 2007, the Spanish economy was booming. Unemployment in 2007 was at the lowest, since democracy even after absorbing more than four million economic immigrants in a decade. The housing market was highly dynamic and prices surged. Even after the USA experience on that market, Spanish authorities and even the financial sector reacted with a rather optimistic outlook (Cable 2009).

Spanish banks did not seem to be significantly involved in the American mortgage problems and due to a bank crisis Spain had suffered. In the 1980s, Spanish banks had tighter regulations and reserves than the rest of western banks (Roubini and Mihm 2010). During the financial crisis, the IMF and especially the EU started compelling the Spanish government to implement and respect the well-known adjustment programmes and in 2010 an important change in policy took place. In January 2010, the Spanish Government started enacting some adjustment measures but in May 2010 the Government was compelled to approve a very tough austerity programme. From this year, the only objective of economic policy became the reduction of public deficit and control of public debt. Spanish total debt reached about 400% of GDP but public debt is about 60%, thus the problem seemed to rest on the external private debt and not on the public debt. In sum, during the period of 2008–2010 deficit and debt of the Spanish economy increased rapidly, and it was a strong dependence on external credit. It was severely revealed that the credit was at the basis of the prosperity and growth of the Spanish economy of the first decade of the 2000s. On the other hand, the high deficit was due on the side of expenditures to the generous help given to the financial sector as well as to the other programmes to face the crisis, among them the very high expenditure due to unemployment subsidies; but also to the deterioration of the revenues resulting from the lower economic activity (Etxezarreta et al. 2011). The crisis deteriorated the financial situation of the government but the deterioration is also due to the political will to maintain and improve the fiscal system in favour of the richest; not only increase of taxes on profits of enterprises and returns to capital have been extremely low, if any, but taxation on Wealth and Inheritance have been eliminated, while Value Added Tax and others on consumption have increased.

Recapitulating, the case of economic miracle in Spain happened in a country in which the complex interrelationship between economics and politics influenced the modernization process and economic growth in the twentieth and twenty-first centuries so historical path dependency must be taken into consideration more deeply and carefully than in other countries. In Fig. 9.6, one can see the GDP and GDP growth rate in Spain in the years 1980–2015.

The econometric analysis of the Spanish economy started with the testing for unit roots as well as structural breaks, which was reported in Chap. 7. Following the results, testing for threshold type cointegration was proceeded according to the steps presented in Sect. 9.3 of this chapter. The time series analysed were transformed into logs when necessary. Tables 9.8, 9.9, 9.10, 9.11, 9.12, and 9.13 present the results of the analysis.

Table 9.8 shows the equation describing the long run trend (HP_lnGDP). It is worth noting that all the regressors, i.e. employment (EMP), public debt (PD), total factor productivity (TFP), investment (I), net income from the EU (NI_EU), and net export (N_Ex), contribute positively in the long-term path of growth in Spain. It is

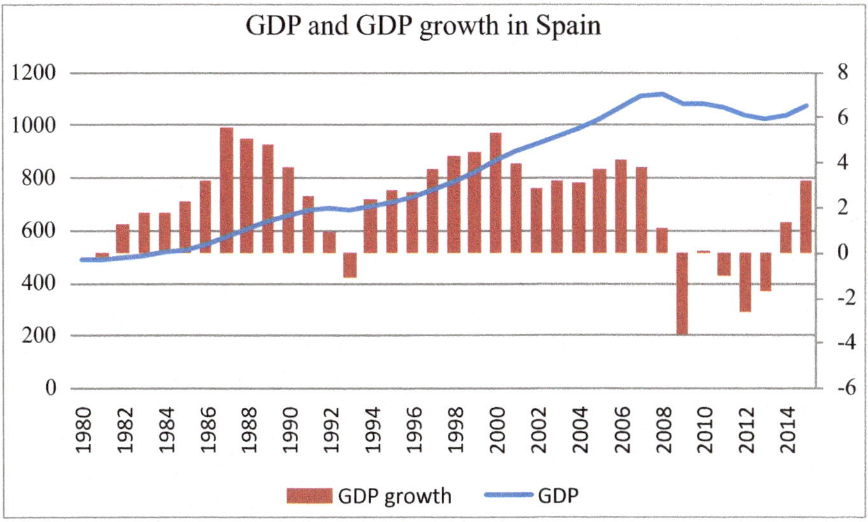

Fig. 9.6 GDP and GDP growth rate (PPP) in Spain in 1980–2015 (Based on the World Bank http://databank.worldbank.org/data/)

Table 9.8 Long run equation in the case of the Spain GDP trend (in logs, extracted with HP filter) in 1980–2015[a] (own computations)

Variable name	Coefficient	Standard error	*p*-Value
lnEMP	0.098	0.027	0.0010
lnPD(t-1)	0.044	0.002	<0.0001
lnTFP	0.127	0.005	<0.0001
lnI(t-1)	0.064	0.016	0.0004
lnNI_EU(t-1)	0.003	0.001	0.0041
lnN_Ex	0.083	0.009	<0.0001
R^2	0.999	AIC	−260.592
DW	1.574	BIC	−251.260
QLR test (*p*-value)	1.86E-27	Year of break	1993

QLR test represents Quandt test for structural breaks (Quandt 1960)
[a]It should be noted that in the case of Spain the final date is 2015

known that in the long run relationship is independent on time. However, results of some incentives are visible after a certain lag (t-1). For example, investment in real economy starts to contribute after the entire process is put into motion. The same concerns net incomes from the EU, which are assigned to different periods of time after payment and are in a great share allocated in public infrastructure and human capital development. Lagged public debt depends upon the way of the money utilization but it is not so obvious. The possible lags can also result from the transformation of GDP (we look at the long-term trend here). However, such growth factors as employment and TFP contribute to growth in the same period in which the

Table 9.9 Enders and Siklos test results for HP_log_GNP in original and Kapetanios et al. versions (constant number of observations) (own computations)

Threshold variable	Threshold value	H[1]: $\rho_1 = \rho_2 = 0$ *p*-value	H[2]: $\rho_1 - \rho_2 = 0$ *p*-value	Remark
Original Enders–Siklos test				
ECM(t-1)	0	0.00023	0.690	Linear cointegration
ΔECM(t-1)	0	0.00015	0.215	Linear cointegration
Kapetanios et al. test				
ECM(t-1)	0	0.707		No cointegration
ΔECM(t-1)	0	0.558		No cointegration
lnPD(t-1)	**6.109**	**0.000**	**0.004**	**Threshold cointegration**
ΔlnPD(t-1)	0.112	0.020	0.626	Linear cointegration
SR(t-1)	1.117	0.584		No cointegration
lnI(t-2)	5.586	0.342		No cointegration
ΔlnEMP(t-2)	−0.016	0.540		No cointegration
ΔSR(t-2)	−0.017	0.024	0.366	Linear cointegration
ΔlnFDI(t-3)	0.017	0.360		No cointegration
ΔlnGDP(t-3)	−0.010	0.464		No cointegration
lnGDP(t-4)	**6.974**	**0.009**	**0.015**	**Threshold cointegration**
lnDEFLATOR (t-4)	4.663	0.002	0.002	Partial cointegration TAR-X
ΔlnNI_EU(t-4)	−0.630	0.657		No cointegration
Δhp_lnGDP(t-4)	0.008	0.689		No cointegration
ΔlnI(t-4)	−0.046	0.673		No cointegration
ΔlnTFP(t-4)	−0.002	0.074	0.897	Linear cointegration
lnFDI(t-5)	3.433	0.451		No cointegration
lnNI_EU(t-5)	0.374	0.517		No cointegration
lnEMP(t-5)	**2.870**	**0.000**	**0.000**	**Threshold cointegration**
lnN_Ex(t-5)	−0.050	0.000	0.000	Partial cointegration TAR-X
hp_lnGDP(t-5)	1.458	0.027	0.431	Linear dependence
lnTFP(t-5)	4.686	0.000	0.631	Linear dependence
ΔlnN_Ex(t-5)	−0.022	0.002	0.080	TAR-X
ΔlnDEFLATOR (t-5)	−0.002	0.037	0.435	Linear dependence
LR(t-5)	1.087	0.017	0.446	Linear dependence
ΔLR(t-5)	−0.004	0.225		No cointegration

Significant thresholds in the case of threshold cointegration are in bold

Table 9.10 Our version of the Enders and Siklos test (variable number of observations) (own computations)

Threshold variable	Threshold value	H^1: $\rho_1 = \rho_2 = 0$ p-value	H^2: $\rho_1 - \rho_2 = 0$ p-value	Remark
ECM(t-1)	0.00	0.418		No cointegration, TAR-X
ΔECM(t-1)	0.00	0.220		No cointegration, TAR-X
ΔlnPD(t-1)	0.112	0.060	0.000	Partial cointegration TAR-X
SR(t-1)	1.117	0.313		No cointegration, TAR-X
ΔlnFDI(t-3)	0.017	0.135	0.000	Partial cointegration TAR-X
lnDEFLATOR (t-4)	**4.663**	**0.073**	**0.000**	**Threshold cointegration**
ΔlnTFP(t-4)	−0.002	0.551		No cointegration, TAR-X
lnNI_EU(t-5)	0.374	0.496		No cointegration, TAR-X
lnN_Ex(t-5)	−0.050	0.000	0.000	Partial cointegration TAR-X
hp_lnGDP(t-5)	**1.458**	**0.000**	**0.000**	**Threshold cointegration**
lnTFP(t-5)	4.686	0.990		No cointegration, TAR-X
ΔlnN_Ex(t-5)	−0.022	0.122	0.000	Partial cointegration TAR-X
ΔlnDEFLATOR (t-5)	−0.002	0.072	0.000	TAR-X
LR(t-5)	1.087	0.599		No cointegration, TAR-X
ΔLR(t-5)	−0.004	0.253		No cointegration, TAR-X

Significant thresholds in the case of threshold cointegration are in bold

output is calculated. TFP contributes most in the long run trend of growth with the parameter 0.127. The Quandt test indicates a significant structural break in ECM in 1993.

In Tables 9.9 and 9.10, the results of testing for threshold variables in three tests are presented: the Enders and Siklos test, Kapetanios et al. test and our approach.

In the case of the Enders and Siklos original test, the linear cointegration was confirmed. It means that there is no asymmetry in the short run adjustment around the long run. However, a deeper analysis allows revealing asymmetric relation on both sides of individual thresholds.

Table 9.11 Two best TECM models for GDP in Spain in 1980–2015 (own computations)

Dependent variable	Threshold variable		Value of threshold		Threshold variable		Value of threshold	
d_HP_lnGNP	HP_lnGDP(t-5)		1.458		lnDEFLATOR (t-4)		4.663	
	N1=	11	N2=	19	N1=	11	N2=	20
	BIC =		−362.838		BIC =		−350.853	
Variable name	I regime	I *p*-value	II regime	II *p*-value	I regime	I *p*-value	II regime	II *p*-value
Const	0.002	0.000	0.007	0.000	0.008	0.000	0.003	0.000
ΔLR	0.046	0.082	−0.007	0.082				
ΔlnFDI			0.001	0.001	0.001	0.006		
ΔlnNI_UE			0.000	0.055				
ΔlnEMP	0.050	0.000	0.005	0.163			0.067	0.000
ΔlnTFP	−0.127	0.000	0.022	0.028			−0.178	0.000
ΔlnN_Ex			−0.002	0.032	−0.003	0.000		
ECM(t-1)	−0.169	0.007	−0.016	0.172	−0.010	0.130	−0.179	0.024
ARCH LM(4)	(0.188)		(0.067)		(0.895)		(0.771)	
Ljung-Box max Q(1)	(0.406)		(0.248)		(0.869)		(0.178)	
Q(2)	(0.541)		(0.303)		(0.680)		(0.350)	
Q(3)			(0.264)				(0.392)	

For ARCH LM and Ljung-Box tests, *p*-values are given in brackets

Table 9.12 The results of the Tsay test for selected thresholds (own computations)

Threshold variable	*C*(*d*)	*p*-Value	Decision
ECM(t-1)	22.413	0.008	TAR-X
ΔECM(t-1)	14.054	0.120	TAR-X
ΔlnPD(t-1)	5.315	0.379	Linear cointegration
SR(t-1)	3.109	0.960	Linear cointegration
ΔlnFDI(t-3)	16.253	0.039	TAR-X
lnDEFLATOR(t-4)	5.384	0.371	Linear cointegration
ΔlnTFP(t-4)	14.896	0.037	TAR-X
lnNI_EU(t-5)	28.532	0.001	TAR-X
lnN_Ex(t-5)	21.484	0.000	TAR-X
HP_lnGDP(t-5)	**29.491**	**0.000**	**Threshold cointegration**
lnTFP(t-5)	4.442	0.815	Linear cointegration
ΔlnN_Ex(t-5)	40.207	0.000	TAR-X
ΔlnDEFLATOR(t-5)	32.917	0.000	TAR-X
LR(t-5)	10.383	0.109	TAR-X
ΔLr(t-5)	33.721	0.000	TAR-X

Significant thresholds in the case of threshold cointegration are in bold

Table 9.13 The results of the Hansen and Seo test for selected thresholds (own computations)

Threshold variable	LM	*p*-Value	Decision
ECM(t-1)	27.499	0.000	TAR-X
ΔECM(t-1)	61.087	0.000	TAR-X
ΔlnPD(t-1)	34.901	0.000	TAR-X
SR(t-1)	48.084	0.000	TAR-X
ΔlnFDI(t-3)	96.828	0.000	TAR-X
lnDEFLATOR(t-4)	**25.923**	**0.000**	**Threshold cointegration**
ΔlnTFP(t-4)	28.469	0.592	Linear cointegration
lnNI_EU(t-5)	37.688	0.000	TAR-X
lnN_Ex(t-5)	49.013	0.003	TAR-X
HP_lnGDP(t-5)	49.336	0.735	Linear cointegration
lnTFP(t-5)	75.4806	0.024	TAR-X
ΔlnN_Ex(t-5)	140.697	0.000	TAR-X
ΔlnDEFLATOR(t-5)	61.989	0.000	TAR-X
LR(t-5)	20.762	0.888	Linear cointegration
ΔLr(t-5)	1.102	0.011	TAR-X

Significant thresholds in the case of threshold cointegration are in bold

While analysing the results of TECM model estimation, one can notice that the parameters estimated related to short run adjustments should be significant. Due to a small number of observations, we decided to show the results with higher than 5% *p*-values. It can be observed that when the deflator is playing the role of a threshold variable, the departure from 5% significance level is in the regime I and it equals 0.130. In the second model (divided according to GDP), the parameter of adjustment in the second regime is significant only at 0.172 level.

Validation of the results was made on two levels. The first one is the distinction between the linear and nonlinear (threshold type) model with the Tsay test (Tsay 1998; see Chap. 8). The other consists in using the Hansen and Seo test (Hansen and Seo 2002). The tests were calculated for thresholds identified in Table 9.10.

The results shown in Tables 9.10, 9.12, and 9.13 allow to state that our approach indicated two thresholds for TECM models in Spain. These are GDP deflator lagged by 4 years and GDP trend lagged by 5 years. On the other hand, the Tsay test confirmed HP_lnGDP(t-5) as a threshold for the TECM model and deflator as a threshold for the nonlinear TAR-X model while the Hansen and Seo test indicated only lnDEFLATOR(t-4) as a threshold. Thus, we discuss both cases as thresholds for Spanish growth and fluctuations around it in 1980–2015.

In Fig. 9.7, the ECM processes in two regimes for the models presented in Table 9.11 are illustrated.

It can be seen that the regime of intense economic growth in Spain identified by HP_lnGDP(t-5) corresponds to the following years: 2004–2015, while lnDEFLATOR(t-4) indicated the years 1983–1990 and 1992–1995. Comparing the years of Spain's economic miracle with the growth rate, it can be noticed that GDP deflator allows more precise division because the years 1983–1990 and 1994–2000

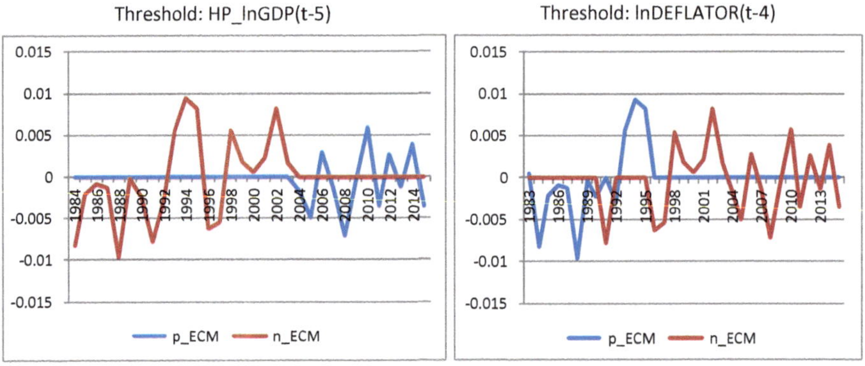

Fig. 9.7 Regimes indicated by thresholds:HP_lnGDP(t-5) and lnDEFLATOR(t-4) (own computations). Symbols: p_ECM denotes regime I and n_ECM denotes regime II

can be noticed as faster growth rates. One should remember that we are working with filtered out data, i.e. we use trend series extracted with HP filter thus the dynamics of growth can differ when compared with untransformed data. As Myro (2019) mentioned before entering the euro area in 1999, the inflation rate in Spain exhibits a tendency to be higher than in the EU. The division made by HP_lnGDP(t-5) threshold is simpler, and it seems to be related with 2004 as the year of the EU extension or of important increases in the house prices (a housing bubble). One can interpret this as evidence that the economy was growing rather systematically before 2003 and then the situation changed due to the incremental increase in real estate prices, and unsustainable indebtedness of both households and construction companies accompanied by the EU enlargement.

9.4.3 *Is Turkey Really Able to Generate an Economic Miracle?*

The case of the economic miracle in Turkey is extremely interesting because of the relationship between economic and political factors influencing the performance of the national economy. When describing and analysing Turkey's economic history of the twentieth and twenty-first centuries, it is necessary to emphasize that the economy of this country is one of emerging market economies.

In economic literature, Turkey is usually defined as a developed country or as a newly industrialized country. Since 1961 Turkey has been a member of OECD and since 1999 has been in the G-20 major economies. Turkey is also an important world producer of TV sets, consumer electronics, white goods, automobiles, ships, steel, and clothing. Other sources of the country's GDP are tourism, financial services, and traditionally production and export of agricultural products. Turkey's population exceeds 75 million people and is still growing.

To understand the historical path to modernity and the process of the economic development of Turkey, it is necessary to characterize their basic features. The economic history of Turkey could be described by four main periods signified with major changes in economic policy and institutional order (Akalin 1995):

1. 1923–1929, a period of private accumulation
2. 1929–1950, a period of state accumulation
3. 1950–1980, a period of state-guided industrialization based on import substituting protectionism
4. 1980 onwards, a period of opening the Turkish economy to international liberal trade and financial market transactions.

Akalin (1995) indicates that the Turkish backward economy developed into a modern industrial economy between 1923 and 1985. The path of the Turkey's development was not smooth. As Yeldan and Unuvar reported (Yeldan and Unuvar 2015), by the late 1970s, Turkey's economy had reached a deep economic crisis. Unemployment was about 15%, industry was using only 50% of its capacity. Disequilibrium of public finance was very deep so the government could not even pay the interest on foreign loans. Because of these facts, in 1980 the reform programme was implemented. Its main idea was to shift the Turkish economy towards export-led growth. The government pursued it by means of economic package including devaluation of the Turkish lira, flexible exchange rates, maintenance of positive real interest rates, very restrictive control of the money supply and credit, tax system reform, subsidies and other public expenditures reduction, freeing of prices for goods and services offering by state enterprises, and opening the economy for foreign investments. The results of these reforms were both significant and noticeable. Between 1981 and 1985 the real GNP grew 3% per year, industrial output raised by an average over 9% per year, lira devaluation resulted in higher export. Export of manufactured goods increased by an average of 45% per year. The relatively high inflation rate and unemployment rate were still a very important socio-economic problem (Boratav et al. 2001). All those positive economic indicators helped Turkey to achieve high marks from credit-rating agencies and after that to cover its budget deficits in a period of 1993–1996 by foreign credit (Gazioglu 2003, pp. 189–195). The interest rate was relatively low so the demand for money and credit offered by foreign banks and financial institutions increased rapidly under the regime of fixed exchange rate of the Turkish lira. In effect, the rate of interest increased. Lira was devaluated by implementing flexible exchange rates and as usually in these circumstances, the process of 'dollarization' was commenced (Feridun 2012). It was a standard mechanism of debt and currency crisis for developing countries implementing a neo-liberal economic policy in the opened economy. In 1994, about 50% of total deposit base was in foreign currency (in 1993 only 1%). It was a very hard time for the Turkish economy. The deep currency crisis in Turkey was then strongly associated with fiscal imbalances, capital outflows, and liberal liquidity conditions of course banking sector performance (Nurhan 1999, pp. 89–113). The government had to implement a new programme of economic reforms and an economic policy. Main changes in economic policy concerned the large public debt reduction, increase in prices offered by the public enterprises, increase in taxes, privatization of state-owned enterprises and lira devaluation. In 1994, real wages fell very sharply (20% below the rate of consumer price inflation) (Feridun 2008, pp. 386–427). The period between 1994 and 2001 in Turkish economic history is often defined as the successive crisis. One of the important crises was in 2000 and it was followed by the second in 2001, as a result of IMF disinflation programme assuming devaluation of lira, reduction state subsidies for agriculture, privatization of state enterprises, and reduction of the public sector in the national economy. It was marked by corrupted governments, political instability, foreign divestment, budgetary deficit, and hyperinflation.

The reforms implemented in the beginning of the 2000s were based on the economic deregulation replacing discretions and protectionism in the social and economic spheres of the Turkish economy. The Central Bank independence, public expenditures control, fiscal restrictions, establishing the Bank Supervisory and Regulation Agency, and fight with corruption were the most important elements of these reforms. The period of 2002–2007 is often defined as 'the Turkish economic miracle' despite that in 1987–1989 the Turkish economy grew about 9% per year. Following the crises of 2000 and 2001, the political arena had witnessed the rise to power of the Justice and Development Party (AKP). It is very interesting that after the election in 2002 it was observed the withdrawal from its populist discourse as an anti-IMF and anti-liberal reactionary movement and turned to implementing the neo-liberal economic policy. Atiyas (2016, pp. 1–6) stated that Turkey in 2000–2007 went through a period when the scope of bargaining powers of government due to the financial crisis, and the fact that Justice and Development Party (AKP) embraced reforms and found them consistent with their prevailing political objectives such as the EU membership and political and socio-economic internal stability. What is obvious, there are difficulties to measure the real impact of all institutional changes on economic performance. Nevertheless, one can note that between 2002 and 2007, Turkey experienced one of the highest sustained growth rates of income per capita in its history. Atiyas reported that macroeconomic stability was achieved relatively quickly and inflation was reduced to single digits. The reforms created an environment more conducive to expect the benefits of competition and creative destruction. He also argued that the major lesson from the reforms programme shows that if a reform-minded government decided to adopt pro-competition institutional reforms, for example, to increase policy credibility and enhance the degree of competition, there is a good chance that reforms will prove very effective. Typically, this involves delegation of considerable policy-making authority to relatively independent agencies insulated from short-term challenges.

Significant features of the AKP governments over the post-2003 period (AKP won the political election also in 2007, 2011, June and November 2015) was that they had successful adoption of the neo-liberal policy under the domination of strong government without confronting any strong political opposition. It seems reasonable because voters usually hold coalition governments less responsible for economic performance than single party governments (Akarca 2017). Over this period, Turkey continued to specialize in standard technologies and low labour cost production in line with an export-based growth strategy, within the international division of labour. Despite that Subasat (2014, pp. 137–160) emphasizes that Turkey is one of the leading countries in terms of the increase in current account deficit. Although external debt to GDP ratio has declined since 2003, the International Investment Position (an indicator which shows the total financial resources externally borrowed to GDP ratio) has increased very rapidly. Subasat concludes by arguing that although Turkey has attracted substantial financial resources, only a small portion of them has been invested into the productive economy, which is evident from declining investment to GDP ratios. This opinion is supported by Yeldan and Unuvar (2015). According to them, an increase in external debt before 2008 was generated by the real economy in about 65% and after that year only in 1.6%. Turkey's economy signifies another bubble economy where economic growth is led by domestic demand which is supported by external resources. Turkey's economy is, therefore, neither a miracle nor even a mild success story. The period after 2008, despite the intense growth rates 2010 and 2011, was entering with severe disequilibriums and fast increased debt burdens (Nurhan et al. 2009, pp. 739–751). Feridun (2008) made an interesting analysis of this period in the Turkish economy.

The literature review on economic history shows that the case of the Turkish economy is investigated and interpreted in two different theoretical perspectives. In the light of the theory of economic development of peripheral economies with internal savings deficit and extractive institutions (Acemoglu and Robinson 2013, pp. 73–83), domestic economic policy enforcing the high rate of economic growth is usually limited by fluctuations in a global economic system and effect of domination of high developed countries. The final result is an increase in external financial debt, so correction of the domestic economic policy is needed by implementation of a (liberal or authoritarian) programme of reforms. A comprehensive disinflation programme under the guidance and supervision of the International Monetary Fund from 1999 is a good example of this way of thinking. In this approach, the economic performance of Turkey must be interpreted as a result of changes in external circumstances.

The second point of view emphasizes the internal factors like political cycles, economic and social reforms, changes in formal institutional order, and informal institutions as the most decisive factors influencing the process of economic growth. According to Yeldan and Khakimzhanov (2005, p. 110), from this perspective the macroeconomic disequilibrium of the 1990s must be interpreted as a direct outcome of the endogenously driven cycles of economic growth, stagnation, destabilization, and crisis. They concluded that adjustment periods are usually strictly connected with the state apparatus reorganization. It is an important condition to achieve a balance between economic rationale and realities of the market and political forces. Following that approach, the concept of the political cycle analysing by Akarca (2019, Chap. 4) gives an opportunity for explaining the impact of political powers, army, economic performance, and economic policy. It could be treated as an interesting base for understanding the phenomenon of the 'Turkish miracle' case.

In spite of the differences between those two approaches, both of them characterize usually a very similar mechanism of changes in emerging market economies. These changes are cyclical and it is always a shift from liberal to anti-liberal or from anti-liberal to liberal economic policy. In the case of Turkey, the exposition of the internal political and economic factors is very reasonable but it must be remembered that the economic miracle happened in a special period 2002–2007 in which financialization processes influenced very much the global economy so the question how to investigate and interpret the relationship between external and internal factors of its economy performance is very important. It seems that the assumption concerning high costs of the liberal economic policy in an opened economy as a reason for accepting the most influencing role of internal factors in economic performance of Turkey is compatible with the experience in global economic system in that time. As Yeldan and Unuvar (2015, p. 17) stated, the generally favourable global conditions that were intensively conductive to the rapid growth performance of the economy under the AKPs first rule of administration are not present after the global financial crisis in 2008. Generally, securing stability of the national economy under very turbulent external environment must be evaluated as too costly and dangerous. It is necessary to emphasize that significant political and socio-economic changes in Turkey have been widely supported by the army (1960, 1971, 1980, 1993, 1998, 2015). The reasonable final conclusion from the investigation of the Turkish economic miracle case is that the rapid economic growth of this country depended on political cycles in which political powers and the army influenced the goals and instruments of the economic policy being implemented by the government. The Turkish economic miracle finished in 2007 but after 2009 economic growth in this country started to increase very fast again but the discretional economic policy replaced regulation. This conclusion means that the state is regarded as an active agent which is the policy maker mainly in shaping, leading and supervising socio-economic policy using its political power. It is worth adding that in 2016 HDI report ranked Turkey in 71st position in the world. Turkey's GDP and GDP growth rate in observed in 1980–2016 are shown in Fig. 9.8.

The econometric analysis of the Turkish economy started with the testing for unit roots as well as structural breaks which was reported in Chap. 7. Following the results, testing for threshold type cointegration was proceeded according to the steps presented in the previous section. Tables 9.14, 9.15, 9.16, 9.17, 9.18, 9.19, 9.20, and 9.21 present the results of the analysis.

Having in mind that in Turkey the deficit of the balance of payment characterized the observed period, we introduced two variants of the long run equations consequently in further steps of testing. In the first one (Variant I), net export was included (as in other countries) and, in the second one (Variant II), exports and imports were included as two separate variables, EXP and IMP, respectively. Hagemejer (2018) argues that exports often perform better while growth modelling than net exports. The long run equations are presented in Table 9.14.

It seems clear from the results presented in Table 9.14 that including exports and imports separately into the long run equation gave more reasonable results and that better values of such indicators and statistics as AIC, BIC, R^2, and DW were obtained in comparison to the variant of net export. It should be noted that in the case of Turkey as a peripheral economy, another set of variables acts in comparison to advanced economies. These are loans from the IMF, the unemployment rate, and

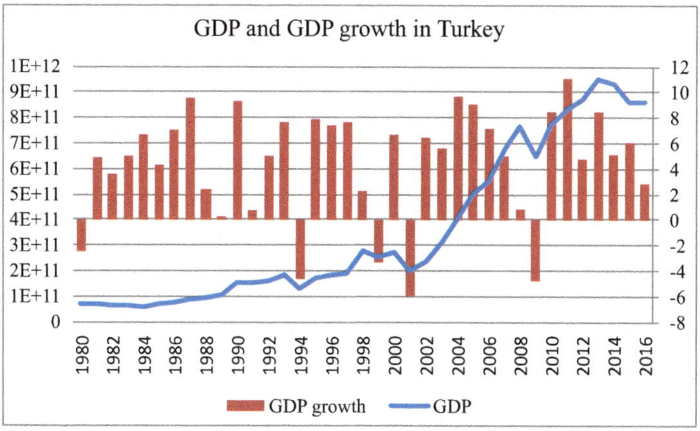

Fig. 9.8 GDP and GDP growth rate (PPP) in Turkey in 1980–2016 (Based on the World Bank http://databank.worldbank.org/data/)

Table 9.14 Long run equations in the case of the Turkish GDP trend (in logs, extracted with HP filter) (own computations)

Variable name	Coefficient	Standard error	*t* Stud. *p*-values
Variant I			
Const	2.30330	1.29112	0.0849
lnN_Ex	0.35500	0.08677	0.0003
PD	−0.53090	0.09946	<0.0001
I	1.82071	0.49386	0.0009
UNEMP	2.70054	0.98945	0.0107
SR	−0.22414	0.05817	0.0006
lnIMF_L	−0.02672	0.01209	0.0351
lnEXR	0.10943	0.00425	<0.0001
R^2	0.986	AIC	−99.771
DW	1.288	BIC	−86.884
QLR test (*p*-value)	<0.0001	Year of break	1999
Variant II			
lnEXP	0.21938	0.04301	<0.0001
lnIMP	0.15307	0.05734	0.0121
ln_DEFLATOR	0.18709	0.02902	<0.0001
I	1.28296	0.26564	<0.0001
UNEM	1.93443	0.24128	<0.0001
lnEXR	−0.02611	0.00792	0.0025
Time	0.01736	0.00309	<0.0001
R^2	0.999	AIC	−150.816
DW	1.450	BIC	−139.540
QLR test (*p*-value)	<0.0001	Year of break	1986

QLR test represents Quandt test for structural breaks (Quandt 1960)

Table 9.15 Enders and Siklos test results for HP_log_GDP in original and Kapetanios et al. versions (constant number of observations) (own computations)

Threshold variable	Threshold value	H^1: $\rho_1 = \rho_2 = 0$ *p*-value	H^2: $\rho_1 - \rho_2 = 0$ *p*-value	Remark
Original Enders–Siklos test				
ECM I	0	0.0007	0.237	Linear cointegration
ΔECM I	0	0.0011	0.351	Linear cointegration
ECM II	0	0.0001	0.418	Linear cointegration
ΔECM II	0	0.0001	0.604	Linear cointegration
Kapetanios et al. test				
Variant II				
ECM(t-1)	0	0.1492		No cointegration
ΔECM(t-1)	0	0.2196		No cointegration
lnEXP(t-4)	4.76	0.0220	0.0245	Partial cointegration TAR-X
lnIMP(t-5)	4.46	0.0000	0.0000	Partial cointegration TAR-X
ΔlnEXP(t-5)	**0.02**	**0.0022**	**0.0034**	**Threshold cointegration**
ΔlnIMP(t-5)	0.14	0.0000	0.0000	TAR-X

Significant thresholds in the case of threshold cointegration are in bold

exchange rate. The last factor appears not due to the level of economic advancement but due to the fact that Turkey has its own currency, the Turkish lira (TLY), whose rate was observed vs. the US dollar. It should be noted that the loans from the International Monetary Fund were taken in the years 1983, 1984, 1994, 1999, 2000, 2002, and 2005, while leveraging from the World Bank has been systematic since 1989. In Tables 9.15 and 9.16, the results of testing for thresholds are presented.

In Table 9.15, one can see the results of the Enders–Siklos test in its original version and in the Kapetanios et al. version. While looking at the original test—only linear (symmetric) cointegration in the Engle and Granger (1987) sense was confirmed for both cases: net export (I) as exports and imports (II). In the case of the Kapetanios et al. test for net exports, there were no evidence for threshold cointegration, that is why this case is not reported in the table. While considering exports and imports separately, threshold cointegration was detected for ΔlnEXP (t-5). This fact is quite clear when a developing export-oriented economy is considered. It is worth noting that in the case of levels (not presented here), the Kapetanios et al. test was able to detect much more threshold (such as TFP, IMF_L, WB_L, N_EX, DEFLATOR, PD, LR, I, SR, and FDI with the lags from 2 to 5), although the levels are typically more sensitive for structural breaks and threshold type of model is the one that indicates even very short changes in the regimes (Billio et al. 2013).

Considering our approach, there were no thresholds confirmed for logs, so that the indication of no TECM must be formulated. Only in the case of levels, ΔEXP (t-5) was indicated as a threshold. However, our test indicated that the proper

Table 9.16 Our version of the Enders and Siklos test (variable number of observations) (own computations)

Threshold variable	Threshold value	H[1]: $\rho_1 = \rho_2 = 0$ p-value	H[2]: $\rho_1 - \rho_2 = 0$ p-value	Remark
Variant I				
ECM(t-1)	0	0.0021	0.0000	Partial cointegration TAR-X
ΔECM(t-1)	0	0.0001	0.0000	TAR-X
lnFDI(t-1)	6.846	0.1091	0.0000	TAR-X
lnI(t-1)	1.262	0.0003	0.0000	Partial cointegration TAR-X
TFP(t-1)	0.962	0.0025	0.0000	TAR-X
lnEXR(t-1)	4.134	0.0100	0.0000	TAR-X
ΔlnEXR(t-1)	0.400	0.0000	0.0000	TAR-X
hpt_lnGDP(t-4)	6.606	0.0116	0.0000	TAR-X
LR(t-5)	1.435	0.0015	0.0000	TAR-X
lnWB_L(t-5)	5.147	0.0010	0.0000	TAR-X
Variant II				
ECM(t-1)	0	0.0000	0.0000	TAR-X
ΔECM(t-1)	0	0.0230	0.0000	Partial cointegration TAR-X
lnEXP(t-4)	4.76	0.6395		TAR-X
lnIMP(t-5)	4.46	0.0300	0.0000	Partial cointegration TAR-X
ΔlnIMP(t-5)	0.14	0.1804		TAR-X

The case of partial cointegration denotes that only one adjustment coefficient was negative and significant. TAR-X denotes a short-term threshold type mechanism

Table 9.17 Real GDP yearly average growth rates in Turkey (own computations)

Period	GDP HP trend Growth rates-avg. [in %]	GDP Growth rate-avg. [in %]
1981–2016	4.367	4.432
1981–1988	5.528	5.370
1989–1995	4.033	3.742
1996–2001	3.597	2.556
2002–2007	4.383	6.793
2008–2016	4.098	3.811

mechanism of growth in Turkey is a nonlinear threshold type one. It suggests that short run asymmetries are present. They result from strong policy activities towards generating growth but the policy succeeds only in the short-term periods. The full range of test results is reported in Table 9.16.

When analysing Turkey, the results seem not to confirm the hypothesis of systematic intense economic growth which can be considered as an economic miracle, despite the fact that spectacular GDP growth rates and increase in exports were observed. As is mentioned in Akarca (2017) and Chap. 4 in this book, short

Table 9.18 The best TECM models for ΔlnGDP in Turkey in 1980–2016, Kapetaniuos et al. case (own computations)

Dependent variable	Threshold variable		Value of threshold	
ΔHP_lnGDP	ΔlnEXP(t-5)		0.02	
	N1=	31	N2=	31
	BIC=		−264.262	
Variable	I regime	I p-value	II regime	II p-value
Const	0.043	<0.0001	0.043	<0.0001
ΔlnFDI	0.008	0.0001	0.008	0.0001
ΔlnEXP	0.025	0.029	0.025	0.029
ΔlnEXP(t-1)	−0.069	<0.0001	−0.069	<0.0001
ΔlnIMP	0.070	0.0003	0.070	0.0003
ΔlnIMP(t-1)	−0.048	<0.0001	−0.048	<0.0001
ΔlnDEFLATOR	0.015	0.0119	0.015	0.0119
ΔPD(t-1)	−0.016	0.0252	−0.016	0.0252
ΔUNEM	0.575	<0.0001	0.575	<0.0001
ΔUNEM(t-1)	−0.205	0.0022	−0.205	0.0022
ΔTFP	−0.134	0.0049	−0.134	0.0049
ΔTFP(t-1)	0.130	0.0003	0.130	0.0003
ΔLR	0.028	0.0008	0.028	0.0008
ΔlnIMF_L	0.004	0.0007	0.004	0.0007
ΔlnIMF_L(t-1)	0.005	0.0001	0.005	0.0001
ΔlnWB_L(t-1)	−0.002	0.0002	−0.002	0.0002
Δln_EXR	−0.009	0.0003	−0.009	0.0003
ECM(t-1)	**−0.091**	**0.0061**	**−0.301**	**0.0002**
ARCH LM(4) p-values	(0.283)		(0.283)	
Ljung-Box p-values Q(1)	(0.720)		(0.720)	
Q(2)	(0.517)		(0.517)	
Q(3)	(0.642)		(0.642)	

For ARCH LM and Ljung-Box tests, p-values are given in brackets. The short run parameters are the same in regimes, only the coefficient ECM(t-1) differs across regimes

periods of intense growth are related with the election cycles, which are the main characteristics in the economic growth in Turkey.

The case of Turkey is most diversified since it is hard to find a rationale to estimate a TECM model, unless variables are in logs. However, when sub-periods are observed, quite diversified growth rates are observed. Table 9.17 shows the growth rates in the entire period and specified sub-periods.

One can easily confirm that the years 2002–2007 were the concentration of the highest growth rates on average, when measured using the GDP growth rate. When the first differences of trend extracted by the HP filter are considered, the rates of growth are typically lower apart from the period 1981–1988. More precisely, the years when the GDP growth rate exceeded 8% in Turkey were the following: 1987,

Table 9.19 The results of the Tsay test for selected thresholds (own computations)

Threshold variable	$C(d)$	p-Value	Decision
Variant I			
ECM(t-1)	4.638	0.947	Linear cointegration
ΔECM(t-1)	8.599	0.855	Linear cointegration
lnFDI(t-1)	4.087	0.995	Linear cointegration
lnI(t-1)	1.183	0.999	Linear cointegration
TFP(t-1)	5.984	0.741	Linear cointegration
lnEXR(t-1)	5.783	0.954	Linear cointegration
ΔlnEXR(t-1)	4.665	0.946	Linear cointegration
hpt_lnGDP(t-4)	10.492	0.312	Linear cointegration
LR(t-5)	39.255	0.000	TAR-X
lnWB_L(t-5)	17.767	0.087	TAR-X
Variant II			
ECM(t-1)	7.585	0.817	Linear cointegration
ΔECM(t-1)	19.564	0.34	TAR-X
lnEXP(t-4)	10.443	0.403	Linear cointegration
lnIMP(t-5)	20.281	0.088	TAR-X
ΔlnEXP(t-5)	NA	NA	
ΔlnIMP(t-5)	10.562	0.393	Linear cointegration

Table 9.20 The results of the Hansen and Seo test for selected thresholds (own computations)

Threshold variable	LM	p-Value	Decision
Variant I			
ECM(t-1)	19.488	0.0001	TAR-X
ΔECM(t-1)	11.099	0.0001	TAR-X
lnFDI(t-1)	1.020	0.999	Linear cointegration
lnI(t-1)	35.182	0.999	Linear cointegration
TFP(t-1)	4.240	0.0001	TAR-X
lnEXR(t-1)	7.173	0.0001	TAR-X
ΔlnEXR(t-1)	62.845	0.084	TAR-X
hpt_lnGDP(t-4)	0.778	0.999	Linear cointegration
LR(t-5)	34.510	0.001	TAR-X
lnWB_L(t-5)	12.161	0.022	TAR-X
Variant II			
ECM(t-1)	0.631	1.000	Linear cointegration
ΔECM(t-1)	0.471	1.000	Linear cointegration
EXP(t-4)	0.046	0.814	Linear cointegration
IMP(t-5)	0.224	1.000	Linear cointegration
ΔIMP(t-5)	2.536	0.001	TAR-X

Table 9.21 Ranking of best estimated TECM models according to AIC and BIC with respect to a threshold value (Kapetanious et al. case, variables in levels) (own computations)

Threshold variable	AIC	BIC
ΔIMF_L(t-3)	12.808	42.738
WB_L(t-5)	15.165	43.014
ΔTFP(t-2)	16.066	45.067
ΔI(t-5)	**18.526**	**45.772**
ΔWB_L(t-3)	20.346	47.283

The result confirmed by Tsay and Hansen and Seo tests are in bold

1990, 2004, 2005, 2010, and 2011. On the contrary, negative values were observed in 1994, 1990, 2001, and 2009.

Validation of the results was made on two levels. The first one is the distinction between a linear and nonlinear (threshold type) model with the Tsay test (Tsay 1998; see Chap. 8). The second one was made using the Hansen and Seo test (Hansen and Seo 2002). The tests were performed for thresholds identified in Table 9.16.

The results of the Tsay test do not confirm a threshold cointegration case for any threshold. However, they support a threshold mechanism in the long run for such thresholds as LR, WB_L, ΔECM, and IMP with respective lags.

The results of the Hansen and Seo test are summarized in Table 9.20. They show that a nonlinear (threshold) mechanism has been detected in the short run for such thresholds as ECM and ΔECM, TFP, EXR, LR, and WB_L and for IMP with respective lags. For exports, a linear cointegration has been indicated.

It is worth noting that when comparing testing for thresholds, the Tsay test supported the results obtained by the Kapetanious et al. test, while the Hansen and Seo test results were closer to our approach. To sum up, both tests (Tsay and Hansen and Seo) indicated LR and WB_L lagged by 5 years as thresholds. Both variables indicated the indebtedness of the Turkish economy and its solvency in the long term. This is in line with the remarks made by Yeldan and Unuvar (2015).

Figure 9.9 presents the ECM processes in two regimes for the model demonstrated in Table 9.18.

It can be noted that the regime of intense economic growth in Turkey identified by **Δ**lnEXP(t-5) threshold variable covers the following years: 1984–1987, 1990–1991, 1993–2011, and 2014–2015. It is clear that this threshold features one regime and outperforms it over the second one which covers the years: 1988–1989, 1992, 2002, and 2012–2013. The results of the Kapetanious et al. test are confirmed by the Hansen and Seo test. These two are supported by estimated values of parameters. In the regime I, the adjustment parameter was equal to −0.091, while in the second it was −0.0301. It indicates a higher speed of adjustment in the second regime (below the equilibrium), when compared to the first one (above the equilibrium). It can be seen that the empirical study provided some indications about the asymmetry in the short run adjustment to the long run one.

It has already been mentioned that in case of data observed in levels, more evidence for threshold cointegration case have been indicated. We skip them for

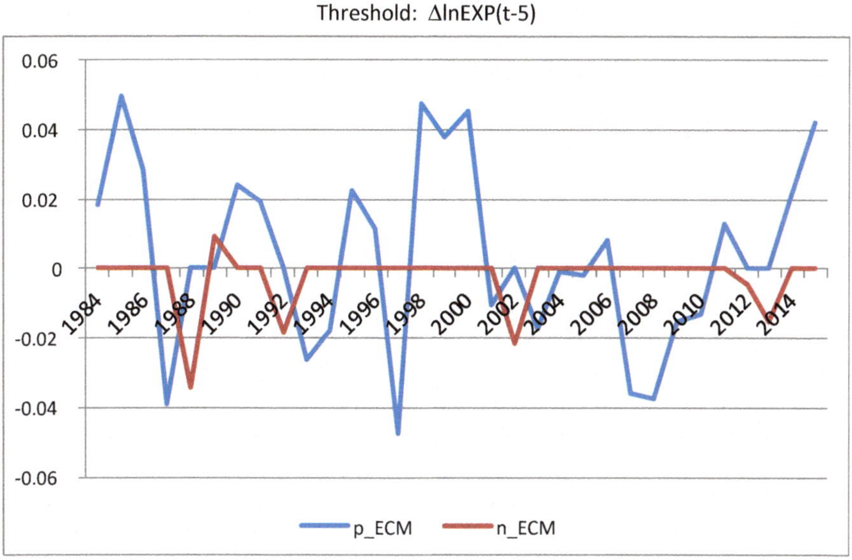

Fig. 9.9 Regimes divided by ΔlnEXP(t-5) (own computations). Symbols: p_ECM denotes regime I and n_ECM denotes regime II

two reasons: the levels are more sensitive for outliers and regime changes and a threshold model is able to detect many regimes. Thus, we report the results for logs. However, below we present the information criteria for some threshold which are most likely in the case of Turkey for the data observed in levels (Table 9.21).

One can notice that in three cases for five reported in Table 9.21 lagged loans from IMF and WB play an important role in changing the mechanism of growth in Turkey, when it is considered in levels. TFP and investment are also among the thresholds. It needs emphasizing that investment lagged by 5 years was confirmed by both the Tsay and the Hansen and Seo tests. Both tests also confirm the threshold cointegration mechanism for net export and its first difference lagged by 4 and 5 years, respectively. But the empirical models for the mentioned thresholds have higher information criteria than the five cases reported in Table 9.21.

9.4.4 Economic miracle in the Netherlands in 1980–2016

The Netherlands is a developed economy strongly related with foreign trade. The economic structure of the country is based on the principles of an open economy. It features a stable industry sector, low inflation and unemployment rate, and what is particularly important a current account surplus. The Netherlands belongs to the smallest but richest European countries. The following periods can be distinguished in the history of the Dutch economy after the Second World War:

- The period of post-war reconstruction of the economy after the German occupation in 1940–1945, as a result of which the Dutch GDP fell by about 40% (van Ark et al. 1996, p. 302). This period lasted until the early 1950s.
- The 'Golden Age' covering the 1950–1973 time period.
- 1973–1979, a period of shocks on the currency and raw material markets and a slowdown in economic growth.
- 1979–1990, it is the time of restructuring the economy.
- After 1990, a period of stable growth with the exception of slowdowns covering the years: 2002–2004 and 2008–2010.

During the post-war reconstruction, the main goals of the Dutch economic policy were to reduce inflation and the budget deficit as well as to reduce foreign debt. The Netherlands was a major beneficiary of the Marshall Plan. The aid received within the plan amounted to 4.9% of GDP and was one of the highest in Western Europe. The Industrial Organization Act, passed in 1950, created the basis for regulating the relationship between employers and employees and for establishing the Social Economic Council. In 1945, the Central Planning Bureau was also established. In turn, during the 'Golden Age' period there was a threefold increase in GDP and labour productivity and almost twofold increase in GDP *per capita*. According to van Zanden and Griffiths (1989, pp. 210–212), fast, balanced, and stable economic growth in this period was primarily a consequence of the high growth rate of the world economy, limiting trade barriers and the development of various forms of international economic integration, in particular the EEC. Since the 1960s, the growth of the country has been based on natural gas resources. The sale of natural gas generated huge revenues for the Netherlands for decades. However, it had also the unforeseen consequences because a boom of the energy sector causes underdevelopment of the others. In the economic literature, it is referred to as 'the Dutch disease' (see Corden and Neary 1982). de Haan et al. (1994) reported widely the characteristics of the post-war economic growth in the Netherlands. Thus, export was the driving force behind the Dutch economy. It was related with positive balance of payments, high level of investment expenditures, and an extensive public sector. These were standard actions for the policy of state intervention, creating a high level of effective demand. The 'Golden Age' period is also the time of major structural changes. There was a decline in the share of agriculture and industry in the GDP volume produced, with a simultaneous increase in the productivity of the factors of production employed in these sectors. As reported by Van Ark et al. (1996, p. 305), the average rate of economic growth in the Netherlands in 1947–1960 was 7.2%, while in 1960–1973 it was 4.5% with the rate of private investment at the level of 15%. The 'Golden Age' also saw intensive industrialization of the Dutch economy. This resulted from the economic policy giving tax preferences to companies in which retained earnings were shaped at a level exceeding the dividends paid. As a result, from 60% up to 80% of the investments were financed from the company's own funds (de Kam and de Kam 1988). Thanks to the system of wage negotiations conducted within the framework of the Board of Mediators and the Foundation of Labour and Social Economic Council, until the early 1960s, it was possible to control strictly the level of remuneration. The Netherlands was then a country with a relatively low level of wages. This strengthened the international competitiveness of the Dutch economy, which, in turn, influenced the balance of payments and led to increases in the number of jobs. The increase in real wages in the 1960s resulted in an increase in production costs and intensive processes of substituting work by capital. On the one hand, this significantly worsened the situation on the labour market, on the other hand, however, the expansion of traditional, labour-intensive sectors of the economy was stopped. The situation improved after discovering and commencing the exploitation of natural gas deposits. Therefore, it should be recognized that in the period of 'Golden Age' a solid foundation for further economic development was created. The economic growth of the Netherlands and the increase in productivity, when compared to other countries of Western Europe, was then relatively high with slower GDP growth *per capita*. However, while in the 1950s this increase was due to the increase in investment outlays, labour-intensive technical progress, and employment growth under the conditions of stable and relatively low wages, in the 1960s it was based on technical capital-intensive progress, increases in productivity under the conditions of rising costs of work and reducing the number of working hours. During the 'Golden Age' period, an expansion of activities for the construction of a 'welfare state' took place. The reference point for its construction was social reforms carried out in Great Britain by W. Beveridge in 1942. The implementation of the idea of the welfare state was manifested in the establishment of the right to social assistance for all citizens residing legally in the Netherlands, the introduction of a general pension for people under 65, as well as the survivor pension and statutory unemployment insurance. In turn, in the field of charity and healing, the dominant position of religious and social organizations was maintained (Kraus et al. 2008). The 'Golden Age' period and, in particular, the years 1947–1960 can be regarded as the time of the Dutch economic miracle. The economic development of the Netherlands was characterized by an increasing level of remuneration with a relatively low employment rate, strong links with the global economy, the growing scale, and share of public expenditure in GDP. Thus, the Dutch economic miracle concerns a small country whose history has made it an important element of the core structure in the world economy system, and whose economy is characterized by a high degree of openness. This economic miracle was the result of a successful implementation of the idea of state welfare policy of state intervention in the sense of Keynesian economics. A significant role was also played by institutional factors related to the organization of an effective social dialogue involving the most important social partners representing various interest groups, religion as a base for business ethics and charity system, participation in the structures of European integration, and an efficient education system, especially professional.

The construction of the welfare state caused a systematic increase in the share of public expenditure for consumption purposes from 37.7% in 1955 to 61.6% in 1990 (van Ark et al. 1996, p. 318). The period 1970–1990 was characterized by a further decrease in working time and a sharp increase in the use of temporary forms of employment. In comparison with other European countries, due to capital-intensive investments and a developed vocational education system, the Dutch economy continued to maintain high labour productivity, despite the fact that the total productivity growth slowed down. However, the developed social security system increased the number of inactive people and reduced labour supply and the previously mentioned significant increase in public spending. The social partners agreed to introduce unemployment compensation for 3 years, which dulled the incentives to look for a job. Intensification of unfavourable phenomena in the labour market and deterioration of public finances at the end of the 1980s led to changes in the economic policy consisting in limiting the growth rate of wages, reducing the budget deficit, and adjustments in the social security system aimed at reducing the proportion of professionally inactive population relative to the professionally active population.

In the time period 1990–2015, the growth rate of GDP *per capita* in the Netherlands was comparable to the economic growth rate of OECD countries (OECD 2017, pp. 257–259). However, three cases of a negative growth rate could be noted in the period of the 2009–2013 financial crisis. From 2009 onwards, hourly productivity was growing more slowly in the Netherlands than in other OECD countries. In Fig. 9.10, the GDP and GDP growth rates in the Netherlands are reported.

The limitation of regulations on the real estate market, in particular in the area of rental of flats and houses, increased labour mobility, limited the value of housing benefits paid, and intensified investments in this sector. The changes introduced in the tax system supported employment, in particular in the case of people with low incomes and favoured the maintenance of lower income inequalities, when compared to other European countries, which is in line with the idea of the welfare state. The changes implemented stabilized the Dutch economy after the period of collapse in 2008–2010.

It needs emphasizing that the Netherlands is a ‘Core’ economy and it gained its position in the 1960s and what was observed between 1980 and 2016 is a

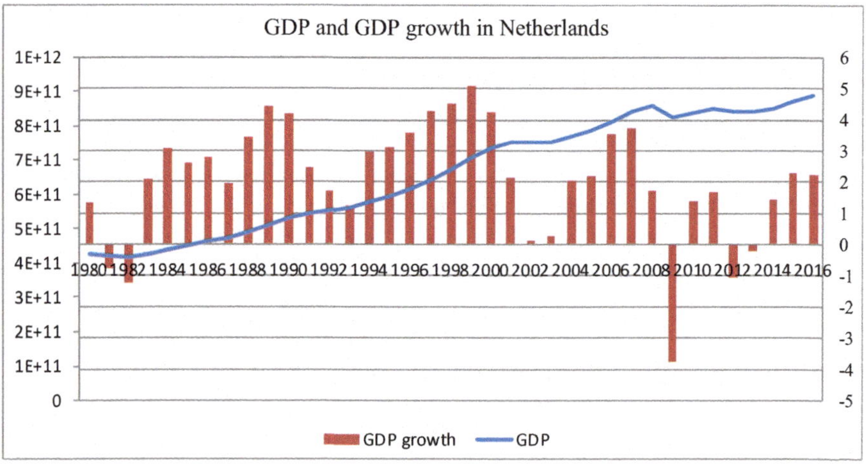

Fig. 9.10 GDP and GDP growth rate (PPP) in the Netherlands in 1980–2016 (Based on the World Bank http://databank.worldbank.org/data/)

Table 9.22 Long run equation in the case of the Netherlands GDP trend (in logs, extracted with HP filter) (own computations)

Variable name	Coefficient	Standard error	*p*-Value
Const	−1.304	0.676	0.0641
lnFDI	−0.006	0.004	0.0933
lnN_E	0.069	0.010	<0.0001
lnDEFLATOR	0.320	0.083	0.0006
lnPD	0.098	0.009	<0.0001
UNEM	−1.098	0.132	<0.0001
lnTFP	1.594	0.112	<0.0001
SR	−1.228	0.151	<0.0001
Time	0.025	0.002	<0.0001
R^2	0.999	AIC	−224.629
DW	2.285	BIC	−210.131
QLR test (*p*-value)	1.77E-122	Year of break	2001

QLR test represents Quandt test for structural breaks (Quandt 1960)

consequence of growth that moved the Dutch economy to the stable growth path. The identified mechanism of growth shows a highly developed economy case.

The econometric analysis of the Dutch economy was started with the testing for unit roots as well as structural breaks which was reported in Chap. 7. Following the results, testing for threshold type cointegration was proceeded according to the steps presented in the previous section. Tables 9.22, 9.23, 9.24, 9.25, 9.26, 9.27, and 9.28 present the results of the analysis. In Table 9.22, a long run determinant of growth can be observed. The following factors drove the Dutch economy in the long run: FDI, net export, GDP deflator, public debt, unemployment rate, total factor productivity, and short interest rate. The year 2001 indicates a structural break in the error correction mechanism as reported by the Quandt test.

In Tables 9.23 and 9.24, the results of testing for a threshold variable in three tests are presented: Enders and Siklos test, Kapetanios test, and our approach.

The results of testing for threshold cointegration allow confirming this hypothesis in cases of many thresholds. First of all, the Enders and Siklos test value was close to confirm a momentum TECM. The Kapetanios et al. test indicated the following thresholds: ECM(t-1) and ΔECM(t-1), SR(t-2) and ΔSR(t-1) and LR(t-2). Our test indicated additionally PD(t-1) and DEFLATOR(t-1) and (t-5), ΔUNEM(t-2), ΔI (t-3), and ΔLR(t-5). It did not confirm the results of the previous test in the cases of ECM(t-1) and ΔECM(t-1), SR(t-2) and LR(t-2). Thus, only ΔSR(t-1) was confirmed by two tests for TECM.

In Table 9.25, we present two best estimated TECMs for the economy of the Netherlands.

The lowest values of AIC and BIC were obtained for public debt and GDP deflator lagged by 1 year. The estimated models for these thresholds are presented in Table 9.26.

When looking at the adjustment parameters, one can easily notice that there is a substantial difference between the parameters above and below the thresholds. In the

Table 9.23 Enders and Siklos test results for HP_log_GDP in original and Kapetanios et al. versions (constant number of observations) (own computations)

Threshold variable	Threshold value	H[1]: $\rho_1 = \rho_2 = 0$ p-value	H[2]: $\rho_1 - \rho_2 = 0$ p-value	Remark
Original Enders–Siklos test				
ECM(t-1)	0	<0.0001	0.397	Linear cointegration
ΔECM(t-1)	0	<0.0001	0.129	Linear cointegration **/Threshold cointegration**
Kapetanios et al. test				
ECM(t-1)	**0.000**	**0.000**	**0.001**	**Threshold cointegration**
ΔECM(t-1)	**0.000**	**0.000**	**0.001**	**Threshold cointegration**
lnPD(t-1)	5.811	0.000	0.580	Linear cointegration
ΔlnDEFLATOR (t-1)	0.009	0.002	0.104	Partial cointegration TAR-X
ΔlnPD(t-1)	0.097	0.001	0.215	Linear cointegration
ΔSR(t-1)	**−0.002**	**0.000**	**0.010**	**Threshold cointegration**
UNEM(t-2)	1.074	0.000	0.002	Partial cointegration TAR-X
lnTFP(t-2)	4.603	0.000	0.673	Linear cointegration
SR(t-2)	**1.046**	**0.000**	**0.097**	**Threshold cointegration**
LR(t-2)	**1.064**	**0.000**	**0.039**	**Threshold cointegration**
ΔUNEM(t-2)	0.002	0.000	0.000	Partial cointegration TAR-X
ΔlnI(t-3)	0.063	0.016	0.017	Partial cointegration TAR-X
lnNI_EU(t-4)	−0.715	0.000	0.185	Linear cointegration
lnFDI(t-4)	2.967	0.000	0.000	Partial cointegration TAR-X
lnI(t-4)	4.997	0.017	0.007	Partial cointegration TAR-X
Δhp_lnGDP(t-4)	0.041	0.006	0.152	Linear cointegration
ΔlnFDI(t-4)	−0.331	0.033	0.175	Linear cointegration
ΔlnTFP(t-4)	−0.005	0.000	0.160	Linear cointegration
hp_lnGDP(t-5)	6.290	0.000	0.143	Linear cointegration
lnN_Ex(t-5)	1.610	0.029	0.009	Partial cointegration TAR-X
lnDEFLATOR (t-5)	4.342	0.000	0.005	Partial cointegration TAR-X
ΔlnNI_EU(t-5)	0.090	0.010	0.097	Partial cointegration TAR-X

(continued)

Table 9.23 (continued)

Threshold variable	Threshold value	H[1]: $\rho_1 = \rho_2 = 0$ *p*-value	H[2]: $\rho_1 - \rho_2 = 0$ *p*-value	Remark
ΔlnN_Ex(t-5)	−0.057	0.035	0.015	Partial cointegration TAR-X
ΔLR(t-5)	−0.007	0.000	0.005	Partial cointegration TAR-X

Significant thresholds in the case of threshold cointegration are in bold

Table 9.24 Our version of the Enders and Siklos test (variable number of observations) (own computations)

Threshold variable	Threshold value	H[1]: $\rho_1 = \rho_2 = 0$ *p*-value	H[2]: $\rho_1 - \rho_2 = 0$ *p*-value	Remark
ECM(t-1)	0.000	0.062	0.000	Partial cointegration TAR-X
ΔECM(t-1)	0.000	0.015	0.000	Partial cointegration TAR-X
lnPD(t-1)	**5.811**	**0.033**	**0.000**	**Threshold cointegration**
ΔlnDEFLATOR (t-1)	**0.009**	**0.000**	**0.000**	**Threshold cointegration**
ΔlnPD(t-1)	0.097	0.012	0.000	Partial cointegration TAR-X
ΔSR(t-1)	**−0.002**	**0.003**	**0.000**	**Threshold cointegration**
UNEM(t-2)	1.074	0.638		TAR-X
SR(t-2)	1.046	0.101	0.000	Partial cointegration TAR-X
LR(t-2)	1.064	0.004	0.000	Partial cointegration TAR-X
ΔUNEM(t-2)	**0.002**	**0.087**	**0.000**	**Threshold cointegration**
ΔlnI(t-3)	**0.063**	**0.001**	**0.001**	**Threshold cointegration**
hp_lnGDP(t-5)	6.290	0.132		TAR-X
lnDEFLATOR (t-5)	**4.342**	**0.000**	**0.000**	**Threshold cointegration**
ΔLR(t-5)	**−0.007**	**0.079**	**0.000**	**Threshold cointegration**

Significant thresholds in the case of threshold cointegration are in bold

Table 9.25 Best estimated TECM models according to AIC and BIC with respect to threshold value (own computations)

Threshold variable	AIC	BIC
lnPD(t-1)	−368.442	−355.354
ΔlnDEFLATOR(t-1)	−317.479	−307.369
lnDEFLATOR(t-5)	−313.707	−303.401
ΔUNEM(t-2)	−301.347	−285.545
ΔLR(t-5)	−262.722	−252.73
ΔSR(t-1)	−242.117	−227.552
ΔlnI(t-3)	−240.636	−228.557

Table 9.26 Two best TECM models for GDP in the Netherlands in 1980–2016 (own computations)

Dependent variable	Threshold variable		Value of threshold		Threshold variable		Value of threshold	
ΔHP_lnGNP	lnPD(t-1)		5.811		ΔlnDEFLATOR (t-1)		0.009	
	N1=	10	N2=	25	N1=	25	N2=	9
	BIC=		−368.442		BIC =		−317.479	
Variable	I regime	I *p*-value	II regime	II *p*-value	I regime	I *p*-value	II regime	II *p*-value
Const	0.032	0.000	−0.015	0.000	−0.008	0.000	0.030	0.000
ΔSR	1.174	0.000	−0.049	0.000			−1.616	0.000
ΔDeflator_GDP	0.684	0.000	−0.022	0.040	−0.076	0.002		
ΔFDI					−0.001	0.016		
ΔNI_UE					−0.002	0.066		
ΔI	−0.158	0.000	−0.008	0.107			−0.223	0.000
ΔDP	−0.014	0.092					0.080	0.000
ΔTFP			0.043	0.026	0.059	0.022	2.205	0.000
ΔUNEM			−0.034	0.011			−1.571	0.000
ΔN_Ex	−0.080	0.002	0.003	0.011			0.092	0.000
ECM(t-1)	−0.375	0.036	−0.060	0.002	−0.074	0.016	−2.878	0.000
Δhpt_GDP(t-1)			1.259	0.000	1.155	0.000		
ARCH LM(4)	(0.228)		(0.127)		(0.407)	ARCH LM(3)	(0.360)	
Ljung-Box max Q(1)	(0.555)		(0.976)		(0.073)		(0.996)	
Q(2)	(0.586)		(0.999)		(0.144)			
Q(3)			(0.488)		(0.276)			
Q(4)			(0.285)		(0.336)			

For ARCH LM and Ljung-Box tests, *p*-values are given in brackets

Table 9.27 The results of the Tsay test for selected thresholds (own computations)

Threshold variable	*C*(*d*)	*p*-Value	Decision
ECM(t-1)	13.951	0.175	Linear cointegration
ΔECM(t-1)	22.117	0.036	TAR-X
lnPD(t-1)	2.399	0.992	Linear cointegration
ΔlnDEFLATOR(t-1)	**35.152**	**0.000**	**Threshold cointegration**
ΔlnPD(t-1)	3.259	0.953	Linear cointegration
ΔSR(t-1)	10.232	0.249	Linear cointegration
SR(t-2)	7.705	0.808	Linear cointegration
LR(t-2)	10.065	0.261	Linear cointegration
ΔUNEM(t-2)	**16.793**	**0.079**	**Threshold cointegration**
ΔlnI(t-3)	10.274	0.329	Linear cointegration
lnDEFLATOR(t-5)	**25.288**	**0.001**	**Threshold cointegration**
ΔLR(t-5)	**15.987**	**0.003**	**Threshold cointegration**

Table 9.28 The results of the Hansen and Seo test for selected thresholds (own computations)

Threshold variable	LM	*p*-Value	Decision
ECM(t-1)	20.483	0.000	TAR-X
ΔECM(t-1)	17.359	0.000	TAR-X
lnPD(t-1)	**118.603**	**0.026**	**Threshold cointegration**
ΔlnDEFLATOR(t-1)	**160.063**	**0.000**	**Threshold cointegration**
ΔlnPD(t-1)	56.412	0.000	TAR-X
ΔSR(t-1)	**19.437**	**0.000**	**Threshold cointegration**
SR(t-2)	34.600	0.001	TAR-X
LR(t-2)	26.451	1.000	Linear cointegration
ΔUNEM(t-2)	**23.326**	**0.000**	**Threshold cointegration**
ΔlnI(t-3)	**26.839**	**0.000**	**Threshold cointegration**
lnDEFLATOR(t-5)	**5.6331**	**0.003**	**Threshold cointegration**
ΔLR(t-5)	**268.077**	**0.0001**	**Threshold cointegration**

case of lnPD(t-1), the adjustment parameter in the first regime equals −0.375 and in the second one it is equal to 0.060. This means that the division made by lagged public debt refers to the following situation: above the threshold the adjustment to the long run was faster than in the case when public debt is below the threshold value. In the case of DEFLATOR, the regime above the threshold adjusts with much slower speed than the regime below the threshold value.

Validation of the results was made on two levels. The first one is the distinction between a linear and nonlinear (threshold type) model with the Tsay test (Tsay 1998; comp. Chap. 8). The second one was made using the Hansen and Seo test (Hansen and Seo 2002: comp. Chap. 8). The tests were calculated for thresholds identified in Table 9.24.

It needs emphasizing that both tests (Tsay and Hansen and Seo) confirmed those thresholds that were identified by the procedure modified by the authors. Namely,

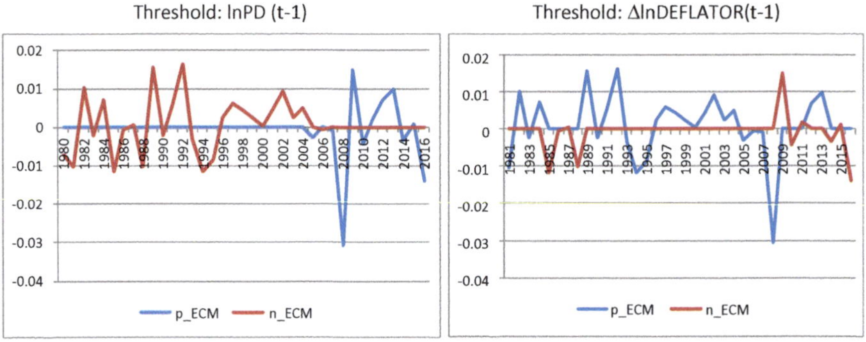

Fig. 9.11 Regimes divided by lnPD(t-1) and ΔlnDEFLATOR(t-1) (own computations). Symbols: p_ECM denotes regime I and n_ECM denotes regime II

the Tsay test identified DEFLATOR, UMEP, and LR while PD and I were additionally confirmed by the Hansen and Seo test.

Taking the above into account, we can state that public debt as well as the increase in the GDP deflator lagged by 1 year generates the mechanism of intense economic growth in the Netherlands.

Figure 9.11 presents the ECM processes in two regimes for the models presented in Table 9.26.

It can be seen that the regime of intense economic growth in the Dutch economy identified by PD(t-1) threshold variable covered the following years: 1980–2004 and 2006. The second regime covered the years 2005 and 2007–2016. In the case of GDP deflator, the results are more diversified. The entire scope of results is presented in the next section (Table 9.29).

9.5 The Economic Miracles in Ireland, Spain, Turkey, and the Netherlands: A Summary

In this section, we summarize the periods of an economic miracle detected in the four different economies, i.e. Ireland, Spain, Turkey, and the Netherlands. The Netherlands is mentioned here as the last one, since it is an economy from 'the Core', which is a kind of benchmark for such countries as Ireland and Spain. Ireland developed the new technologies sectors which place it within TFA, while Spain depends mostly on traditional sectors. On the contrary, Turkey is a developing economy and its road to the core seems to be a long one. In this chapter, we discussed the processes of growth and economic policy foundations in all of the mentioned countries.

We identified an economic miracle period, managed by the increase in the FDI in the case of Ireland which is in line with the qualitative analysis of the Irish economy provided in the original Irish literature and in Chap. 5 of this book. The Irish

Table 9.29 Periods of economic miracles identified by the TECM approach (own computations)

Endogenous variable	Threshold variable	Years of regimes	Endogenous variable	Threshold variable	Years of regimes
Ireland					
GNP_ levels	ΔHP_GNP_{t-4}	I: **1996–2009**;2014–2016	GNP_ logs	$DEFLATOR_{t-2}$	I:1981–1996
		II:1984–1995; 2010–2013			II:1997–2016
	SR_{t-5}	I:1984–1997; 1999		Δln_FDI_{t-1}	I:1982; 1985; 1987–1993; **1995–2000**; **2002–2003; 2005;2007;**2009; 2012–2015
		II:1998; 2000–2016			II:1981;1983–1984; 1986;1994; 2001; 2004;2006;2008; 2010–2011
		I:		LR_{t-3}	I:1982–1998;2013
		II:			II:1999–2012; 2014–2016
Spain					
GDP_ levels	No threshold	I:	GDP_ logs	ln_GDP_{t-5}	I:2004–2015
		II:			II:1984–2003
		I:		$DEFLATOR_{t-2}$	I:1983–1990; 1992–1995
		II:			II:1991;1996–2015
Turkey					
GDP_ levels	ΔEXP_{t-5}	I:1991;1998;2000–2002; 2004;2006–2012;2015–2016	GDP_ logs	No threshold	
		II:1985–1990;1992–1997 1999;2003;2005;2013–2014			

(continued)

Table 9.29 (continued)

Endogenous variable	Threshold variable	Years of regimes	Endogenous variable	Threshold variable	Years of regimes
The Netherlands					
GDP_ levels	SR_{t-2}	I:**1981–1995**; 2009	GDP_ logs	ln_PD_{t-1}	I:**1980–2004**;2006
		II:1996–2008;2010–2016			II:2005;2007–2016
	$DEFLATOR_{t-5}$	I: 2003–2016		$\Delta DEFLATOR_{t-1}$	I:1981–1984; 1989–2008; 2012–2013
		II:1984–2002			II:1985–1988; 2009–2011; 2014–2016
	PD_{t-1}	I: 2005; 2007–2016		$UNEM_{t-2}$	I:1982–1991; 2015
		II:1981–2004;2006			II:1981; 1992–2014;2016

The periods of regimes indicated by the best three TECM models (if applicable) with the dates of regimes. The years of miracle were in bold economy relies on democratic and market institutions that, together with the EU membership as well as development of IT sectors, give it a strong basis for stability. Ireland induced a much higher growth rate that any European economy in the same period and, after a short recovery after the 2007–2009 crisis it outdistanced them placing itself very close to the core.

In the case of Spain, the growth rates were relatively stable. The highest rate in1987 (GDP in PPP) was about 5.54%. It seems that Spain found its own endogenous path of growth with little evidence to support an economic miracle.

With regard to the Netherlands, the level of growth had been reached together with the recovery of the US and other European economies after the World War II. It was in a great magnitude accelerated by the natural gas leading to the Dutch disease. In the 1980s, the economy was mainly led by the demand side related with the flexible employment system and high salaries. However, gaining the level of Core countries, which happened in the 1960s, the growth rate was lower. In the entire analysed period, it did not exceed 5% (maximum in 1999, GDP in PPP). What has been observed is that it is the period after the miracle when a stable growth path was found.

The case of Turkey is in opposition to the market economies analysed. As the political (election) cycle dominates the economic institutions and rules, the ups and downs are much more frequent than in other economies. That is why short periods of accelerated growth are substituted by lack of money, currency crises, and the government's interventions into the economy.

In general, we focused on the logarithmic transformation of the data. Since the results obtained are diverse, we decided to analyse both outcomes of testing for threshold, i.e. levels and logs to extend the conclusions. The periods of the identified economic miracles, conditionally on the threshold variables and on the data transformation (level or logs), are summarized in Table 9.29.

It can be seen that in two of the countries the periods of economic miracles have been found. These are Ireland and the Netherlands. In the case of Spain, the GDP deflator indicates partially the period of intense economic growth. In the case of the GDP as a threshold, the division for regimes is rather related with the housing bubble which is partially responsible for the boom in the first decade of the 2000s. The viewpoint that in Spain a generally stable and linear growth took place is strongly supported by the data. The results for Turkey confirmed that the government tries to build the export-oriented economy; however, it suffers from lack of stability and follow a kind of cycle.

The applied methodology, i.e. the TECM approach supported with the Tsay test and the Hansen and Seo test, has brought us to the identification of thresholds and periods of intense economic growth in the economies under study. It can be stated that the TECM approach presented in Chap. 8 and applied in Chap. 9 contributes to applied econometric modelling of economic growth in market economies.

9.6 Conclusions

In this chapter, the economic miracles in selected economies have been a subject of analysis. The GDP and GNP series taken for analysis were expressed in real terms. As has already been mentioned, in the case of Ireland and in the case of the Netherlands, evidence supporting the intense economic growth periods between 1980 and 2016 has been found. In Ireland, it has been induced by FDI and in the Netherlands by public debt. In the case of Spain, the GDP deflator serves as a threshold variable. These show that the mechanism of growth was different even in the developed European economies. Spain got on the path of endogenous growth. The same concerns the Netherlands, however after its rapid growth in the 1960s and the 1970s it is generated by internal resources like savings. In the case of Ireland, the endogenous growth is based on multinational companies that located their direct investments there.

The case of Turkey is more complicated. Firstly, it is a developing country, strongly depending on a political cycle. Secondly, the institutions are not very solid. And thirdly, after short periods of very high rates of growth the lack of money causes different problems with finding a stable growth path in the long run.

It can be stated that relatively short length of time series analysed allowed taking into account only a two-regime case instead of three regimes. As Stigler (2010) mentioned, a three regimes approach is quite natural in economic purposes. It allows extracting the most extreme cases related with intense growth (or on the opposite side—recession) rates. Thus, the research can be repeated when new information is obtained.

One may ask whether the presented empirical findings can contribute to economic theory. The first important remark is that they are in line with contemporary economic theory. The second part of the answer is positive; however, the contribution is related rather to the interpretation of the results than to these results themselves. It needs to be emphasized that the way of testing for individual thresholds proposed in Chap. 8 and applied in this work contributes to the applied econometrics' further development.

9.7 Databases

http://www.economywatch.com/
http://www.cso.ie/en/statistics/
http://stats.oecd.org/
https://data.worldbank.org/
https://www.imf.org/en/data/
https://ec.europa.eu/eurostat/data/database/

https://www.ilo.org/global/statistics-and-databases/lang%2D%2Den/index.htm
https://www.bde.es/webbde/en/estadis/infoest/bolest17.html
https://fred.stlouisfed.org/

Acknowledgement The authors are grateful to Ali Akarca for his inspiring discussion on the initial results for Turkey.

References

Acemoglu D (2009) Introduction to modern economic growth. Princeton University Press, Princeton

Acemoglu D, Robinson JAS (2013) Why nations fail. The origins of power, prosperity and powerty. Profile Books, London

Aghion P, Durlauf SN (2005) Handbook of economic growth, vol 1B. Elsevier, North-Holland, Amsterdam

Akalin G (1995) The Turkish economic development since 1923. Achievements and failures. Turkish Public Administration Annual 1994–1995, pp 91–107

Akarca AT (2017) Economic voting under single-party and coalition governments. Evidence from the Turkish case. Economic Research Forum. Working paper no 1128, pp 1–20

Akarca AT (2019) Political determinants of government structure and economic performance in Turkey since 1950. In: Osińska M (ed) Economic miracles in the European economies. Springer, Cham

Anserson CW (1970) The political economy of modern Spain: policy making in an authoritarian regime. University of Wisconsin Press, Madison

Atiyas I (2016) Replace discretion with rules: how policy reform can boost economic performance. Econ Res Forum Policy Brief 10:1–6

Balcerowicz L, Rzońca A (2014) Puzzles of economic growth. The World Bank, Washington, DC

Barro BJ, Sala-i-Martin X (1992) Convergence. J Polit Econ 100(2):223–251

Barry F (2002) The Celtic Tiger era: delayed convergence or economic boom? ESRI Quarterly Economic Commentary. The Economic and Social Research Institute, Dublin

Barry F, Bradley J, Hannan A (2001) The single market, the structural funds and Ireland's recent economic growth. J Common Mark Stud 39(3):537–552

Bergheim S (2008) Long-run growth forecasting. Springer, Berlin

Best MH (2018) How growth really happens. The making of economic miracles through production, governance, and skills. Princeton University Press, Princeton

Billio M, Ferrara L, Guégan D, Mazzi GL (2013) Evaluation of regime switching models for real-time business cycle analysis of the Euro area. J Forecast 32(7):577–586

Boehlke J (2019) Intense economic growth in economic history and economic theory. In: Osińska M (ed) Economic miracles in the European economies. Springer, Cham

Boehlke J, Fałdziński M, Gałecki M, Osińska M (2017) Dynamics of Economic Growth in Ireland in 1980-2014. St Petersburg State Polytechnical Univ J Econ 10(2):7–20

Boehlke J, Fałdziński M, Gałecki M, Osińska M (2018) Economic growth in Ireland in 1980–2014. A threshold cointegration approach. Argum Oecon 2(41):157–188

Boratav K, Yeldan E, Köse AH (2001) Turkey, globalization and social policy, 1980-1998. In: Taylor L (ed) External Liberalization and Social Policy. Oxford University Press, Oxford and New York

Bruzda J (2007) Procesy nieliniowe i zależności długookresowe w ekonomii. Analiza kointegracji nieliniowej. Wydawnictwo UMK, Toruń

Burns AF, Mitchell WC (1946) Measuring business cycles. National Bureau of Economic Research, New York

Cable V (2009) The storm. The world economic crisis and what it means. Atlantic Books, London

Caselli F, Coleman WJ II (2006) The world technology frontier. Am Econ Rev 96(3):499–522
Cassidy M (2004) Productivity in Ireland: trends and issues. Cent Bank Ireland Quart Bull 83–106
Chan KS (1993) Consistency and limiting distribution of the least squares estimation of a threshold autoregressive model. Ann Stat 21:520–533
Corden WM, Neary JP (1982) Small open economy. Econ J 92(12):825–848
de Haan J, de Jong H, Van Ark B (1994) Characteristics of economic growth in the Netherlands during the post-war period. CEPR Discussion Papers 932, C.E.P.R. Discussion Papers
de Kam CA, de Kam F (1988) Tax reform in a Welfare State: the Case of the Netherlands, 1960–1987. C. Abraham de Kam
Dowrick S, Nguyen D (1989) OECD comparative economic growth 1950 – 85: catch-up and convergence. Am Econ Rev 79(5):1010–1030
Dungey MH, Vehbi T (2011) A SVECM model of the UK economy and the term premium. https://ssrn.com/abstract=1903533. Accessed 27 Feb 2017
Ekanayake EM (1999) Exports and economic growth in Asian developing countries: cointegration and error-correction models. J Econ Dev 24(2):43–56
Enders W, Siklos PL (2001) Cointegration and threshold adjustment. J Bus Econ Statist 19 (2):166–176
Engle RF, Granger CWJ (1987) Cointegration and error correction: representation, estimation, and testing. Econometrica 55(2):51–276
Etxezarreta M, Navarro F, Ramón Ribera R, Soldevila V (2011) Boom and (Deep) Crisis in the Spanish economy: the role of the EU in its evolution. In: Workshop on Alternative Economic Policy in Europe, Vienna, September 2011
Feridun M (2008) Currency crises in emerging markets: the case of post-liberalization Turkey. Dev Econ 46(4):386–427
Feridun M (2012) Liability dollarization, exchange market pressure and fear of floating: empirical evidence for Turkey. Appl Econ 44(8):1041–1056
Gazioglu S (2003) Capital flows to an emerging financial market in Turkey. Int Adv Econ Res 9 (3):189–195
Granger CWJ, Teräsvirta T, Anderson HM (1993) Modeling nonlinearity over the business cycle. NBER Chapters. In: Business cycles, indicators and forecasting. National Bureau of Economic Research, New York, pp 311–326
Growiec J (2012) The world technology frontier: what can we learn from the US States? Oxford Bull Econ Statist 74(6):777–807
Hagemejer J (2018) Trade and growth in the new member states. The role of global value chains. Emerg Mark Financ Trade 54(11):2630–2649
Hamilton JD (1989) A new approach to the economic analysis of non-stationary time series and the business cycle. Econometrica 57:357–384
Hansen BE, Seo B (2002) Testing for two-regime threshold cointegration in vector error-correction models. J Economet 110:293–318
Hodrick R, Prescott EC (1997) Postwar U.S. business cycles: an empirical investigation. J Money Credit Bank 29(1):1–16
Honohan P, Walsh B (2002) Catching up with the leaders: the Irish Hare. Brookings Papers on Economic Activity, Human Development Report
Kapetanios G, Shin Y, Snall A (2006) Testing for cointegration in nonlinear smooth transition error correction models. Economet Theor 22(6):279–303
Kraus K, Geisen T, Piątek K (2008) Państwo socjalne w Europie. Historia - Rozwój – Perspektywy. Toruń, WydawnictwoNaukowe UMK
Krolzig HM (1997) Markov-Switching vector autoregressions: modelling, statistical inference and application to business cycle analysis, Lecture notes in economics and mathematical systems. Springer, New York
Llopis S, Teresa M (2006) The Spanish economic miracle: a disaggregated approach to productivity growth, 1958 – 1975. J Iberian Latin Am Econ Hist 2:383–419

Malaga K (2011) The main strands and dilemmas of contemporary economic growth theory. Argumenta Oeconomica 26(1):17–24
Mankiw NG, Romer D, Weil D (1992) A contribution to the empirics of economic growth. Q J Econ 107:407–437
Myro R (2019) Determinants of economic growth in Spain: a historical viewpoint. In: Osińska M (ed) Economic miracles in the European economies. Springer, Cham
Nonneman W, Vanhoudt P (1996) A further augmentation of the Solow model and the empirics of economic growth for OECD countries. Quart J Econ 111(3):943–953
Nurhan Y (1999) Short-term capital inflows and their impact on macroeconomic structure: Turkey in the 1990s. Dev Econ 37(1):89–113
Nurhan Y, Ulengin B, Cimenoglu A (2009) An analysis of the interaction among savings, investments and growth in Turkey. Appl Econ 41(6):739–751
O'Leary E (2015) Irish economic development. Taylor & Francis, London
OECD (2017) Economic Policy Reforms 2017: going for growth. OECD Publishing, Paris
Osińska M, Kufel T, Błażejowski M, Kufel P (2018) Modeling mechanism of economic growth using threshold autoregression models. Empirical Econ. https://doi.org/10.1007/s00181-018-1560-2
Piński A (2013) Zakazane bogactwo. Editorial House Penelopa, Warsaw
Potter SM (1995) A nonlinear approach to US GNP. J Appl Econ 2:109–125
Prados de la Escosura L, Rosés J (2009) The sources of long-run growth in Spain, 1850-2000. J Econ Hist 69(4):1063–1091
Prados de la Escosura L, Sanz JC (1996) Growth and macroeconomic performance in Spain, 1933 – 1993. In: Crafts N, Toniolo G (eds) Economic growth in Europe since 1945. Cambridge University Press, Cambridge
Prados de la Escosura L, Rosés JR, Villarroya IS (2010) Stabilization and growth under dictatorship: the experience of Franco's Spain. CEPR discussion papers 7731
Proietti T (1998) Characterizing asymmetries in business cycles using smooth-transition structural times series models. Stud Nonlinear Dynam Economet 3:141–156
Quandt R (1960) Tests of the hypothesis that a linear regression system obeys two separate regimes. J Am Stat Assoc 53:873–880
Roubini N, Mihm S (2010) Crisis economics: a crash course in the future finance. The Penguin Press, London
Sala-i-Martin X (2002) 15 Years of new growth economics: what have we learnt? UPF Economics and Business Working Papers 620:9–10
Solow RM (1956) A contribution to the theory of economic growth. Q J Econ 70:65–94
Stigler M (2010) Threshold cointegration: overview and implementation. Revision 5: April 2013. https://cran.r-project.org/web/packages/tsDyn/vignettes/ThCointOverview.pdf. Accessed 20 Jun 2018
Subasat TS (2014) The political economy of Turkey's economic miracle. J Balkan Near East Stud 16(2):137–160
Swan TW (1956) Economic growth and capital accumulation. Econ Rec 32:334–361
Szczepaniak M (2015) Irlandia. Przemiany gospodarcze. CeDeWu, Warszawa
Szczepaniak M (2019) Factors of economic growth in Ireland. In: Osińska M (ed) Economic miracles in the European economies. Springer, Cham
Teräsvirta T (1994) Specification, estimation, and evaluation of smooth transition autoregressive models. J Am Stat Assoc 89(425):208–218
Teräsvirta T, Anderson HM (1992) Characterizing nonlinearities in business cycles using smooth transition autoregressive models. J Appl Econ 7(S1):19–36
Tiao GC, Tsay RS (1994) Some advances in non-linear and adaptive modelling in time-series. J Forecast 13:109–131
Timmer MP, Inklaar R, O'Mahony M, Van Ark B (2012) Economic growth in Europe. A comparative industry perspective. Cambridge University Press, Cambridge

Tisdell C (ed) (2013) Handbook of tourism economics: analysis, new applications and case studies. World Scientific, Hackensack, NJ

Tokarski T (2009) Matematyczne modele wzrostu gospodarczego. Wydawnictwo Uniwersytetu Jagiellońskiego, Kraków

Tokarski T (2011) Ekonomia matematyczna. Modele makroekonomiczne. Polskie Wydawnictwo Ekonomiczne, Warszawa

Tong H (1990) Non-linear time series: a dynamical system approach. Oxford University Press, Oxford

Tortilla G (2000) The development of modern Spain. An economic history of the nineteenth an twentieth centuries. Harvard University Press, Cambridge

Toussaint É (2011) Core vs periphery in the EU. http://www.cadtm.org. Accessed 20 Aug 2018

Tsay RS (1998) Testing and modeling multivariate threshold models. J Am Stat Assoc 93 (443):1188–1202

van Ark B, de Haan J, de Jong HJ (1996) Characteristics of economic growth in the Netherlands during the Postwar Period. In: Crafts NFR, Toniolo G (eds) Economic growth in Europe since 1945. CEPR/Cambridge University Press, Cambridge

Welfe A (ed) (2013) Analiza kointegracyjna w makromodelowaniu. Polskie Wydawnictwo Ekonomiczne, Warszawa

Yeldan E, Khakimzhanov S (2005) The political economy of reform failure and macroeconomic mis-management; Turkey, 1980–2002. In: Lunndahl M, Wyzan ML (eds) The political economy of reform failure. Routledge, London, pp 89–114

Yeldan E, Unuvar B (2015) An assessment of the Turkish economy in the AKP era. Research and policy on Turkey. Routledge, London

van Zanden JL, Griffiths RT (1989) Economische geschiedenis van Nederland in de 20e eeuw. Aula, Utrecht

Chapter 10
Economic Miracles in the Light of Imperfect Knowledge Economics

Jerzy Boehlke and Maciej Gałecki

Abstract Imperfect Knowledge Economics (IKE) is one of the latest trends in economics, which gained recognition after the outbreak of the global financial crisis in 2007. Its main assumption concerns the imperfect knowledge of market participants. No one knows fully the cause-and-effect mechanism behind the phenomenon that is in interest of the researcher. No theoretical model can fully describe reality. What is needed for this are variables derived from several models, theories, and the change of these variables over time. The structural break plays a huge role in describing and interpreting economic reality. In this context, the definition of 'an economic miracle' cannot be developed. Interpretations of an economic miracle are possible only within an individual economy. The phenomenon of the economic miracle is related to a structural break, most frequently in several factors of accelerated growth. Identification of accelerated growth factors is possible by using threshold models of error-correction or threshold cause-and-effect models without cointegration. The type of the test used (the Enders-Siklos test, modifications of the Enders-Siklos test, the Tsay test, the Hansen-Seo test) is of great importance to confirm the nonlinear nature of the model. The asymmetry between thresholds can be identified by a statistical difference of parameter evaluations with the same variables or by a variance-covariance matrix of parameter estimates or a random component.

Financial support from research project no. 2015/17/B/HS4/01000 supported by the National Science Centre in Poland is gratefully acknowledged.

J. Boehlke
Department of Economics, The Faculty of Economic Sciences and Management, Nicolaus Copernicus University, Toruń, Poland
e-mail: jurekbo@umk.pl

M. Gałecki (✉)
Department of Econometrics and Statistics, The Faculty of Economic Sciences and Management, Nicolaus Copernicus University, Toruń, Poland
e-mail: mgalecki@umk.pl

M. Osińska (ed.), *Economic Miracles in the European Economies*,
https://doi.org/10.1007/978-3-030-05606-3_10

10.1 Introduction

The chapter describes the paradigm of Imperfect Knowledge Economics. This is a new trend in economics, which has gained recognition after the outbreak of the global financial crisis in 2007. We talk about imperfect knowledge when no one has access to a model that would provide a full description of the cause-and-effect mechanism. The imperfection of knowledge causes that market participants do not perceive the world through the prism of the same model. As a result, IKE assumes that market entities, acting on the basis of various preferences, limitations, and causative factors, adopt different strategies for predicting the future as well as various consequences of their own decisions. Predictions made by individuals change the cause-and-effect mechanisms that determine the behaviour of markets at times and in ways that cannot be predicted in advance. Moreover, changes in the social context, including the evolution of institutions, values, and standards, contribute to the emergence of market instabilities, i.e. to changes of the cause-and-effect mechanisms over time.

The central issue of IKE is the theory of consistent expectations hypothesis (TCEH). According to TCEH, a set of existing economic models may at most indicate a market participant which explanatory variables may be potential causes and suggest how these variables may affect the results. The theory of consistent expectations hypothesis assumes that variables stemming from various theories or only a certain part of them may be needed to explain data obtained for a specific period. Following TCEH, a set of these variables can be modified over time. IKE lays great emphasis on structural breaks and their impact on econometric modelling and the description of reality. The purpose of this new trend is to find an alternative way of modelling macroeconomic changes as well as changes taking place on financial markets as a result of emerging structural breaks.

The objective of the chapter is to present the major assumptions of IKE, to show why this trend allows us to describe 'economic miracles', and to show the important role in econometric modelling that can be played by the theory of consistent expectations hypothesis. In addition, the chapter shows the significant role that is played by structural breaks which are not predetermined and the interpretation of results using the qualitative features of theoretical models of economic growth and changes in economic policy.

The chapter is composed of four subchapters. The first subchapter provides an overview of IKE, its genesis, main assumptions, an empirical example of modelling changes in the exchange rate in the aspect of significant structural breaks in the dollar currency market in the 1970s. The second subchapter presents the economic theoretical models underlying 'the economic miracle' in the economies discussed, and it also explains why IKE allows us to study the phenomenon of 'an economic miracle' without defining the very concept of an economic miracle. The third subchapter shows the applied econometric algorithm, tests, and econometric models. The fourth subchapter uses the qualitative premises stemming from theoretical models explaining economic growth and from the economic policy conducted by a given country in order to interpret the results obtained.

10.2 Characteristics of Imperfect Knowledge Economics

Imperfect Knowledge Economics (IKE) has become one of the newest current theories beside economics of complexity and institutional economics. IKE gained recognition after the outbreak of the global financial crisis in 2007. The main representatives of the IKE are the following: Frydman and Goldberg (2007), Frydman and Phelps (1983), Juselius (2007), Soros (1987), Johansen (1991), Johansen et al. (2000), and Thygesen and Gros (1990). This trend also includes Phelps (2003), Demsetz (1969), Froot and Stein (1991). We can also mention Pedersen (2008).

IKE are combined Stiglitz's information asymmetry (Stiglitz and Weiss 1992), Kahnemann's (Kahneman and Tversky 1979) behavioural economics and Keynes's (Keynes 1973) and Hayek's (Hayek 1945, 1978) economics in terms of decision-making. According to contemporary schools in economics, IKE refers to the New Keynesian Economics, which focused its research mainly on the search for compounds between micro- and macroeconomic theory explanation. New Keynesians focused on the importance of rigidity of nominal and real characteristics in the market functioning. They also showed that markets have not always worked fully effectively as the successors of the classical theory would like it to happen. IKE remains in opposition to the New Classical Economics and the New *Neoclassical* Synthesis, but only partly. This is because it does not agree with the economic equilibrium and growth as defined by Robert Lucas. On the other hand, it demonstrates a high concordance to the Austrian School of Economics, especially, when the role of uncertainty in the economy is analysed. Both currents divided according to the use of the language of mathematics in economics and importance of forecasts. Both streams differ in their individual approach to math language application as well as the significance of forecasts.

Imperfect Knowledge Economics developed the Kahnemann's and Tversky's prospect theory (Kahneman and Tversky 1979) by creating models based on limited rationality of individuals. The theory characterized an identification of important economic representations of change and show how they matter for a description of situation on the financial markets and what consequences entail in the economic policy. The aim of IKE is to find an alternative approach to macroeconomics and finance modelling opening economic analysis to non-routine change. Such an approach requires rethinking conventional approaches to empirical research, which have assumed away the importance of such change. For example, the fixing of the causal mechanism that underpins change leads to insuperable epistemological problems in modelling aggregate outcomes and lies at the root of contemporary models' failure to explain these outcomes in many markets. This mechanism considered in the context of market decision-making is not fully intelligible to anyone, including economists or market participants themselves. The exclusive pursuit of models that 'can be put on the computer and run' has been misguided. In this context, IKE contributes to the development of a more insightful approach to modelling market outcomes and the consequences of government policies. Hence, the imperfect knowledge of the part of market participants and economists is placed at the centre of the analysis. It does not seek the explanation of how exactly market outcomes unfold over time. IKE eschews to relate precisely a change in outcomes to a set of causal factors that has, in turn, been pre-specified by an economist. In other words, IKE assumes that the only one causal mechanism does not exist.

IKE allows constructing its models of aggregate outcomes by relating them to individual behaviour. Behaviour is represented using mathematical models but any of them is thought to be a complete one. Market participants decision exhibit regularities and are context dependent. The ways in which market participants make and alter their decisions may be formalized with qualitative conditions. These conditions only partially predetermine economic representations of change. In a world of imperfect knowledge, the aggregate outcomes that are predicted deviate systematically from their representations of market participants' forecasts of those outcomes. No one can fully pre-specify a change before it happens. Typical contemporary models are characterized by the change in the composition of the set of causal variables and in their influences on outcomes are fully pre-specified. IKE models do not imply sharp predictions of change, but they do generate qualitative implications, which is important to understand the salient features of the empirical record. The perspective of imperfect knowledge restricts the models sufficiently to enable an economist to distinguish empirically among alternative explanations of economic phenomena. The first examples of IKE models (Frydman and Goldberg extracted among others with models: Frenkel 1976, Bilson 1978, Dornbusch 1976, Frankel 1979, Hooper and Morton 1982, Meese and Rogoff 1983, 1988, Rogoff 1996) explained exchange rate dynamics, particularly their persistent and often large misalignments to PPP, as well as movements in the market premium on holding a speculative asset.

The knowledge is defined as imperfect if no one has access to a fully predetermined model that adequately represents full description the causal mechanism that underpins outcomes in all time periods, past and future. Imperfection of knowledge makes that individuals are not constrained to view the world through the prism of a common model.

As a result, IKE assumes that market participants, who act on the basis of different preferences, constraints, and causal factors, will likewise adopt different strategies in forecasting the future as well as the consequences of their decisions. Thus, it refers to rational expectations hypothesis models (REH models) and indicates that they presume that individual market participants endlessly disregard systematic information in their forecast errors. In a case of imperfect knowledge, market participants make use of diverse forecasting strategies. Treatment of these strategies in the REH model has to presume gross irrationality. IKE also supposes that insightful selection of the causal variables with fully predetermined models in order to properly describe the dependence between causal variables and the aggregate outcomes in a selected historical period. Time passes makes, that the market participants eventually alter the way that they make decisions. In the same period the social context changes in ways that cannot be fully foreseen. Disregarding these key factors of change restricts the usefulness of such models for illuminating the historical record to limited periods of time.

One of the key empirical implications of imperfect knowledge is that even if a fully predetermined model's structure adequately represents outcomes in terms of a set of causal variables during a particular period of time, it will be inadequate during other periods. When such models are used to analyse time-series data, they should always be tested for possible structural changes. The application of such test procedures should not require a researcher to fully pre-specify when structural change might occur or which causal variables might enter the structure of the post change representation.

IKE is compatible with the presumption that market participants in capitalist economies are motivated by purely self-interested concerns, but it does not necessarily require. Individual decisions depend on forecasts of future market outcomes. These outcomes are not only a result of the actions of many individuals, but they also depend on future economic policies, institutional changes, and political developments. Even if individuals are presumed to be purely self-interested, the way that they deploy resources depends as much on the social context as it does on their personal motivations. An individual himself cannot fully determine how he will form and revise his forecasts. IKE supposes that a researcher cannot ascertain completely whether an individual behaves rationally or irrationally, that is, he cannot completely evaluate whether he pursues his objectives reasonably or unreasonably.

Like contemporary models, IKE models show an individual's preferences, constraints, and forecasts of future outcomes. IKE as well imposes qualitative conditions on its representations at an initial arbitrary point in time. But it does not fully pre-specify how its representations of preferences and forecasting behaviour change between an initial point and all other points in time. It is assumed that without some regularity in economic life, no economic theory that aimed for generality would be possible.

One can consider two types of regularities on the individual level:

1. An individual's preferences or forecasting strategy may share certain qualitative features at different points in time.
2. The way that any of the causal variables affect an individual's preferences or forecasting behaviour may change over time, but these changes may share certain qualitative features.

IKE represents future outcomes as uncertain. The appropriate model relates the distribution of the outcome variables at a future time to its distribution at an initial time in a qualitative way only. Hereby, IKE's partially predetermined probabilistic representations of change are compatible with Knight (1921) and Keynes (1921, 1936; see: Keynes 1973 ed.) insight that economists cannot fully pre-specify the consequences of individual decisions or future market outcomes and their chances of occurrence. IKE model allows changing in the probability distributions of the variables which describe the outcome.

According to IKE, adding a stochastic component to a model confirms that the causal mechanism that drives individual behaviour and market outcomes is imperfect unless the probability distribution of the stochastic terms in the model and its evolution over time is fully predetermined. Otherwise, one determined how imperfect knowledge unfolds between the initial time and all other times, past and future. The distinguishing feature of the IKE models is that they do not require an economist to pre-specify either the potential set of causal variables that underpin change in outcomes or the influences of these variables in its representation. This is an important assumption because as it has been already mentioned, no researcher can specify the full set of exogenous variables and their effect.

But this is not that an economist is not required to represent these aspects of the causal mechanism. IKE considers the idea that the stock of extant economic models summarizes economists' insights concerning the causal rules that underlie market outcomes. Furthermore, these insights are shared by market participants. This idea is base of the theory of consistent expectations hypothesis (TCEH) proposed by Frydman and Phelps (1990). According to TCEH, a set of extant economic models at best indicates to a market participant, or to an economist attempting to represent its behaviour, which causal variables may be important for forecasting market outcomes, it also suggests, in a qualitative way, how these variables may influence those outcomes. TCEH supposes that the observed empirical data can result from many theories or some parts of them. Under TCEH, series of the variables can be modified in time. Good examples of such an approach are monetary models analysed by Frenkel (1976), Bilson (1978), Dornbusch (1976), Frankel (1979), Hooper and Morton (1982).

Thus, the appropriate procedure begins by deleting one explanatory variable at a time from the irrelevant variables sets, starting with the variable with the lowest t statistics. When all insignificant variables are deleted, the inverse procedure should be done. It consists in adding these variables back into the regression one at a time to check whether some of them may be significant once they are included as part of the reduced model.

The example of the exchange model considered under the IKE shows that the TCEH uses qualitative features of three monetary models to represent an individual's forecasting strategy. If the models all agree on how a particular causal variable influences the future exchange rate, then the TCEH representation constrains the sign of the weight that is attached to this variable. Otherwise, TCEH leaves this sign parameter unconstrained. By using a different individuals prediction models, TCEH allows avoiding an inconsistency between the individual and the aggregate model levels. IKE constrains the model representations only partially.

It can be seen that creative forecasting behaviour of the part of purposeful individuals alters the causal mechanism which specify market outcomes in ways and at points in time that cannot be fully pre-specified. Also, the changes in the social context, including the evolution of institutions, values, and norms are all important in engendering temporal instability in causal relationships in real-world markets.

10.3 Economic Miracles in Selected Economies in the Perspective of IKE

The cases of 'economic miracles' discussed in this book can be described, explained, and interpreted on the basis of various theoretical concepts. This applies to both the whole group of the cases discussed and to each of them separately. The reasons for such a situation are both substantive and methodological.

The case of Turkey may certainly be the subject of interest in the political theory of the socio-economic change cycle, but it is impossible to disregard the Keynesian theory of balance of payments, or more precisely, the absorption theory proposing the combination of devaluation and stabilization policy in the economic policy. The latter should reduce the absorption of the national economy, i.e. the size of global expenditures to neutralize the inflationary effects of devaluation. The assertion formulated by Keynes that the interest rate is too high for the level of investment expenditures to lead to the state of balance with full employment. This view is still present in Turkey's economic policy. The opening of the Turkish economy to foreign markets resulted in shifting the accents in the country's economic policy to a monetary equilibrium, which was to be a way to eliminate disturbances on the capital market. Certainly, in Turkey's economic policy one can notice the influence of the theory of rational expectations seeking an answer to the question of how to conduct a stabilization policy to avoid a recession. The mechanism of generating and balancing foreign debt in the case of Turkey can also be described and explained within the framework of the centre-periphery theory.

In turn, the example of the Spanish economy may be subject to explanations of traditional Keynesianism, in particular with regard to the stabilization policy issues, construction of the public sector, and infrastructure investments, but also subject to the Keynesian economic growth theory stressing the role of state intervention in controlling growth processes, in particular in building the desired sectoral structure of the economy, theoretical concepts concerning the international economic integration and North's theory of economic transformations (North 1990) created within the institutional trend, and the theory of comparative advantages. Similar to the case of Turkey, the concepts developed within the social sciences describing the relationship between the political and economic spheres, such as, for instance, Lindblom's analysis of socio-economic systems, will be useful (Lindblom 1977). He was one of the early developers and advocates of the concept of incrementalism in policy and decision-making. According to Lindblom, decision-making process is always characterized by imperfect knowledge and bounded rationality of individuals. All changes are evolutionary rather than revolutionary. The institutional approach, and in particular the theory of property rights, transaction cost theory, and the agency theory can create an important basis for describing and exploring the way the ownership structure is shaped in the Spanish economy, the scale and scope of state intervention, the role of trade unions, integration with the EU, and internationalization. When comparing the cases of Turkey and Spain, it should be noted that they differ due to their positions in the global economy system. In contrast to Turkey, in the case of Spain, Ireland, and the Netherlands, cultural differences affecting the shape and operation of the institutional order are less significant (the importance of religion, the attitude to political power, the system of social values, the shape of the dominant business model, etc.). The cases of Turkey and Spain also differ, which is quite obvious, in the so-called historical path of dependence (Arthur 1989; David 2000), which the modern evolutionary economics has developed for the basis of analysis. It defines the shape and effectiveness of the existing institutional order, opportunities and directions of change as well as individual and collective expectations. An evolutionary approach to historical changes of socio-economic systems is compatible with methodological background of IKE. It confirms that the proposed way of analysis of 'economic miracles' is quite useful and reasonable while it is mainly directed not to explain but to interpret this phenomena.

Imperfect Knowledge Economics of Frydman and Goldberg is currently an interesting methodological proposal that respects the assumptions of the methodological individualism, referring to the ideas of Hayek and Knight. IKE is a manifestation of a critical attitude towards models based on the hypothesis of rational expectations and behavioural models. The basic objection to the creators of this type of models is a non-successful attempt to build equations precisely describing market behaviour. According to Frydman and Goldberg, such an approach does not have chances of success due to the imperfection of knowledge. This knowledge relates to the knowledge possessed by economists and all participants of the market game on the behaviour of individuals and the rules governing these behaviours. Particularly, the knowledge of the latter is incomplete and not entirely validated so economists cannot succeed in creating correct models of market behaviour. It is difficult, therefore, to seek a precise explanation of economic phenomena in terms of general laws that can be described by mathematical equations. The imperfect knowledge of economists is a derivative of the imperfect knowledge of market participants. In the model building process, of course, we use all regularities found, treating them as limitations. The results obtained fall within certain areas delimited by these constraints. Acquiring this imperfect knowledge leads to determining the possible directions of change. The longer the analysis horizon, the greater the degree of knowledge uncertainty. In the mathematical description of market behaviours, the system of inequalities should be used rather than the system of equations. IKE does not provide any general rules as explanations of economic phenomena and processes. It is true that the creators of IKE do not question the existence of regularities in economic behaviours. However, they argue that these regularities are far from the concept of a rule, and their mathematical description allows only cutting off a certain group of possible results that are very unlikely so that they can be omitted in the model. These regularities are also characterized by low stability and are dependent on the social context and the moment in which they occur. Thus, IKE belongs to anti-naturalistic epistemological concepts, which means that the researcher is condemned to the necessity of constant interpretations of research results. According to Duhem-Quine's thesis, the number of possible interpretations is infinite.

An important role within IKE is played by the assumption of the irreversibility of history. This means that history (the concept of the historical dependence path mentioned in the characteristics of the case of Spain) does not define the future. It makes it difficult or even impossible to build forecasts based on rational expectations. It condemns researchers to search for the correct language of concepts and interpretation of the obtained research results. In the investigated cases of 'economic miracles', the diversity and the necessity to interpret them make it impossible to build one model of this phenomenon within one of the main paradigms in economic thought (e.g. neoclassical or Keynesian), or a model synthesizing the achievements of many paradigms.

Taking into consideration all those mentioned above methodological issues, the authors' intention was not to develop a definition of 'an economic miracle'. The cases discussed clearly show that there is no single definition of 'an economic miracle', which is consistent with the assumption of IKE that there cannot be only one cause-effect mechanism standing behind the economic miracle. Such a definition could not arise on the grounds of IKE. The presented empirical cases show that despite identifying even common factors of accelerated economic growth, each of the considered economies is characterized by different theoretical models and the resulting economic policy and institutional determinants. The same accelerated growth factor has a different impact on the Turkish economy than in the case of the economy of Ireland. Periods of 'the economic miracle' also differ within the considered economies. In this context, what matters is the qualitative interpretation of a non-linear econometric model and not the definition of 'an economic miracle'.

10.4 IKE and Econometric Models

The empirical test procedure presented in Chap. 8 of this book has been designed in such a way that a number of possible model specifications describing relationships between the observed series of variables in selected economies were allowed.

It was agreed that within the assumed threshold structure of short-term dependencies, in individual cases these variables will be revealed, which in the analysed period had the greatest impact on growth processes, which was then subjected to qualitative verification by reference to the economic history and economic policy pursued by individual countries. At the same time, it was assumed—which has been verified empirically—that long-term models reflecting the balance in the economic systems surveyed are characterized by instability. Against the background of this observation an iterative test procedure was proposed that consists in four stages.

1. Testing structural breaks at a not-predetermined moment for each variable and its increment.
2. Testing structural breaks at a non-predetermined moment for the rest of the long-term equation.
3. Estimating the values of threshold variables and for threshold variables lags.

4. Testing for threshold cointegration or non-linear dependence without cointegration.

The study did not presuppose which factors are responsible for accelerated economic growth. The choice of variables for the study was dictated by the theory of economics, the history of the economy of a given country, previous empirical research, as well as by cooperation with researchers from the countries concerned. The starting point for the identification of factors of accelerated growth was conducting tests for structural breaks at a not-predetermined moment. The tests of Andrews and Zivot (1992) and Bai-Perron (1998) were used and presented in Chap. 7. However, without taking into account each of the variables separately, the residuals of the long-term equation were tested with the Quandt test (Quandt 1960). Searching for structural changes (breaks) Frydman and Goldberg (2007) used two recursive procedures: the CUSUM test (Brown et al. 1975) and the Quandt ratio (QR) technique (Quandt 1960). Each time, regardless of the country and the nature of the variables, at the beginning, a long-term equation was assumed with all potential accelerated growth factors. For the final form of the cointegrating equation, the Quandt test was carried out, which in all studied cases indicated structural breaks in the residual processes. The identified structural breaks led to threshold cointegration testing or non-linear models without cointegration (TAR-X as it was called in Chap. 8 and 9) relative to the linear ECM model. The procedure was not limited to one test only. The Enders-Siklos test (2001), its modification (Kapetanios et al. 2006, Bruzda 2007 and authors modification presented in Chap. 8), the Tsay test (1998), and the Hansen-Seo test (2002) were used. We proposed our modification of the Enders-Siklos test, indicating the importance of asymmetry not only in a long-term adjustment but also in short-term (see: Boehlke et al. 2017 and Chap. 8). Periods of accelerated economic growth and recession cannot be described in the same way as is in the case of an identical, not dependent on the threshold variable, short-term component (increments of variables without an ECM component).

The range of the tests results from their mutual complementarity. The Enders-Siklos test concerns only threshold cointegration within the value of a cointegrating vector. This limits the identification of factors of accelerated economic growth. It becomes plausible using the modification of this test. Identification takes place based on a statistically significant difference in parameter ratings for the ECM. It does not touch the variance matrix of the covariance of a random component—hence the Tsay test. The Hansen-Seo test uses both the asymmetry of parameter estimates (not only for the ECM) and the properties of the random component. In the light of the IKE assumptions, each of the variables examined in the study was used as a potential threshold variable, and the switching value was calculated using the Chan method (Chan et al. 1985). For the ECM component, a value of zero was assumed in advance. The Enders-Siklos test was used to examine both zero values of the error correction component and the values estimated using the Chan method.

Recognition of important structural changes is a key aspect in econometric modelling in the spirit of IKE. The presence of structural breaks enforces specific econometric modelling techniques. Several solutions are possible. Application of

0-1 variables to the linear form of the econometric model, the change of the linear model parameters over time, or the use of a non-linear structure of the econometric model. In order to show what structural changes are important for identifying factors of accelerated economic growth, the authors focused on the non-linear structure of econometric models (TECM, a threshold cause-effect model without cointegration). Hence, the threshold cointegration testing procedure and estimation of the parameters of the threshold error-correction models (TECM) in the variant where only the ECM component creates regimes, but also the proposed by the authors version of the TECM model in which the increments of variables and ECM depend on the threshold variable. The scope and impact of factors that stimulate the economic boom are different from those affecting the recession. It must be emphasized that IKE looks for an alternative way of modelling macroeconomic changes as a result of emerging structural breaks.

The relationship between the research procedure and IKE is evident in the huge role of structural breaks and their identification for econometric modelling, in the non-linear nature of econometric model equations, in resigning from setting threshold variables and their values in advance, in using available alternative tests regarding the issue of threshold cointegration and in combining obtained results with qualitative considerations resulting from economic theory, economic history, and previous empirical results.

10.5 Interpretation of the Empirical Results from the IKE Perspective

The research objective of the study was to identify the factors affecting accelerated economic growth. Four different economies were selected for the empirical study, which in the last 30–40 years have experienced a period of above-average economic growth. In each of these countries, we have a different model of the economy, which resulted in accelerated growth. In Ireland, the model of the open economy and foreign direct investments were decisive, in Spain it was Keynesianism and industrialization, in Turkey the political cycle (the classic approach) and the balance of payments mechanism as well as the peripheral country development model. In the Netherlands, it was the neoclassical synthesis. However, we cannot assert that in the future the application of any of the theoretical models will lead to accelerated economic growth. The definition of 'an economic miracle' does not follow from only one theory of economics. Each case is unique and results from various institutional conditions and economic policies. Ireland, Spain, and the Netherlands joined the EU at different times and used its funds to a different extent for their socio-economic development. Turkey is not a member state of the EU and its external funding comes mainly from loans obtained from the World Bank and the International Monetary Fund. Turkey, unlike Ireland, Spain, and the Netherlands, does not benefit from the free flow of capital, people, goods, and services on the Community market and is exposed to higher currency and interest rate risks. Institutional

Table 10.1 Factors of accelerated economic growth in Spain—the combined results of the Chan, Tsay, Hansen-Seo, and Kapetanios tests and of other tests used in the research

Variable name (in logs)	Year	Variable name (in levels)	Year
SR(t-1)	1986	SR(t-1)	1986
DEFLATOR(t-4)	1987	DEFLATOR(t-4)	1987
ΔDEFLATOR(t-5)	1992	ΔPD(t-5)	1987
LR(t-5)	1996	Δhp_GDP(t-5)	1987
TFP(t-5)	1997	ΔFDI(t-3)	1988
hp_GDP(t-5)	2000	LR(t-5)	1996
ΔLR(t-5)	2001	hp_GDP(t-4)	2000
ΔN_Ex(t-5)	2002	ΔLR(t-5)	2001
PD(t-1)	2004	ΔEMP(t-5)	2008
ΔPD(t-1)	2005		
ΔFDI(t-3)	2006		
GDP(t-4)	2006		
ΔTFP(t-4)	2006		
NI_EU(t-5)	2006		
N_Ex(t-5)	2010		
EMP(t-5)	2012		

Symbols like in Chap. 7. (own computations)

conditions, the economic model applied to determine economic policy, point to various factors of accelerated economic growth in the countries discussed.

Tables 10.1, 10.2, 10.3, and 10.4 contain variables ordered chronologically for Spain, Ireland, the Netherlands, and Turkey, which played the role of the threshold variables and indicated in at least two tests (two modifications of the Enders-Siklos, Tsay, and Hansen-Seo tests) the cointegrated threshold model (TECM) or threshold model without cointegration (TAR-X). One of the confirmations of non-linearity resulted either from the Tsay test or from the Hansen-Seo test (details are presented in Chap. 9 of this book).

For threshold variables expressed as a percentage (SR_t, LR_t, U_t), no logarithms were used. The transformation was defined as follows: $x\_{it} = (x_{it}/100) + 1$, where x_{it}—is the variable after transformation. This type of transformation resulted in the indication of the same year for the value of the threshold variable.

Regardless of whether the variables were logarithmized or not, in Spain the accelerated economic growth is related to short- and long-term interest rates, price levels, public debt growth, increase in foreign direct investment, and the real GDP level (the endogenous growth theory), and the long-term interest rate increase. The year 1986, in which the short-term interest rate reached the switch value (the threshold value of the threshold variable) is the year of Spain's accession to the EU. A year later, the threshold value reaches the level of prices. Since the moment of Spain's accession to the EU, the first variables responsible for the accelerated economic growth have been the tools related to monetary policy. Myro (2019) indicates the importance of the increase in foreign direct investment, immigration, labour productivity, debt growth, the increase in trade, and Spain's accession to the

Table 10.2 Factors of accelerated economic growth in Ireland—the combined results of the Chan, Tsay, Hansen-Seo, and Kapetanios tests and of other tests used in the research

Variable name (in logs)	Year	Variable name (in levels)	Year
PD(t-3)	1984	ΔEMP(t-5)	1987
ΔTFP(t-2)	1989	SR(t-5)	1995
ΔPD(t-4)	1993	LR(t-3)	1996
DEFLATOR(t-2)	1995	I(t-5)	1999
SR(t-5)	1996	PD(t-5)	2002
LR(t-3)	1997	ΔNI_EU(t-1)	2004
ΔDEFLATOR(t-1)	2002	ΔLR(t-5)	2004
ΔFDI(t-1)	2003	DEFLATOR(t-2)	2005
ΔN_Ex(t-2)	2004	NI_EU(t-1)	2010
FDI(t-3)	2006	Δhp_GNP(t-4)	2010
Δhp_GNP(t-5)	2007	N_Ex(t-5)	2010
ΔNI_EU(t-4)	2008	TFP(t-2)	2013
NI_EU(t-5)	2008		
ΔEMP(t-5)	2008		
ΔSR(t-4)	2011		
TFP(t-2)	2014		
I(t-4)	2014		

Symbols like in Chap. 7. (own computations)

Table 10.3 Factors of accelerated economic growth in the Netherlands—the combined results of the Chan, Tsay, Hansen-Seo, and Kapetanios tests and of other tests used in the research

Variable name (in logs)	Year	Variable name (in levels)	Year
ΔDEFLATOR(t-1)	1985	LR(t-2)	1987
LR(t-2)	1987	ΔPD(t-2)	1991
ΔNI_EU(t-5)	1987	ΔI(t-5)	1997
N_Ex(t-5)	1990	DEFLATOR(t-5)	1998
ΔLR(t-5)	1992	ΔN_Ex(t-5)	2003
ΔI(t-3)	1995	SR(t-2)	2008
DEFLATOR(t-5)	1998	Δhp_GDP(t-5)	2010
ΔN_Ex(t-5)	1998	ΔLR(t-5)	2010
ΔSR(t-1)	2004	ΔUNEM(t-2)	2014
PD(t-1)	2006		
ΔPD(t-1)	2007		
SR(t-2)	2008		
ΔUNEM(t-2)	2014		

Symbols like in Chap. 7. (own computations)

Table 10.4 Factors of accelerated economic growth in Turkey—the combined results of the Chan, Tsay, Hansen-Seo, and Kapetanios tests and of other tests used in the research

Variable name (in logs)	Year	Variable name (in levels)	Year
WB_L(t-5)	1986	ΔEx(t-5)	1988
ΔEXR(t-1)	1989	LR(t-5)	1990
SR(t-4)	1989	DEFLATOR(t-4)	1992
LR(t-5)	1990	I(t-1)	1993
IMP(t-5)	1993	ΔDEFLATOR(t-4)	2001
ΔFDI(t-5)	1995	ΔN_Ex(t-5)	2002
EXP(t-4)	1997	ΔI(t-5)	2005
EXR(t-1)	2000	IMP(t-2)	2006
PD(t-1)	2001	EXR(t-3)	2008
ΔDEFLATOR(t-4)	2006	ΔIMP(t-4)	2013
ΔEXP(t-5)	2010	TFP(t-1)	2014
ΔIMP(t-5)	2011	N_Ex(t-4)	2014
ΔN_Ex(t-4)	2013		
TFP(t-1)	2014		
UNEM(t-4)	2014		

Symbols like in Chap. 7. (own computations)

euro area. All these factors are reflected in the threshold variables presented in Table 10.1.

In the case of Ireland's economy, where foreign direct investments are of great importance for accelerated economic growth, the measure responsible for economic growth is the increase in gross national product. In addition to the factors that have worked in the Spanish economy, it is worth paying attention to the inflow of European funds. Their low level during the financial crisis affected the value of the threshold variable. During the financial crisis, net exports and employment growth also reached their switching positions. The periods of accelerated economic growth is also matched by periods of lowering interest rates and increasing labour productivity as well as increasing internal investments.

In the case of the Netherlands, looking through the prism of the threshold variables, i.e. the factors of accelerated economic growth, the model of the neoclassical synthesis works. The important factors for a significant revival are the characteristic factors for both Spain and Ireland, but not all of them. The ones excluded are the lack of work productivity and foreign direct investment.

When analysing the range of factors of accelerated economic growth, the Turkish economy appears to be the most diversified of the discussed ones. The financial resources obtained from the World Bank and the International Monetary Fund are of great importance for the recovery of the economy. The first loan in the 1980s of the twentieth century becomes the value of the threshold variable. The trade exchange is of great importance for the Turkish economy, which is confirmed by the threshold variables of exports and imports. The years 2000 and 2001 were a period of crisis, at that time the exchange rate (expressed in relation to the US dollar), public debt, and

Table 10.5 Years of breaks in ECM as indicated in the Quandt test (own computations)

Country	Year (variables in levels)	Year (variables in logs)
Spain	1992	1993
Ireland	1994	2000
The Netherlands	1995	2001
Turkey N_Ex	2001	1999
Turkey EXP; IMP	1997	1986

inflation (increase of the GDP deflator) had their switching positions. Other factors responsible for accelerated economic growth are the same as in the case of the economies discussed previously.

The results of the Quandt test advocate the use of the described procedure using threshold models. In each linear cointegration equation in the residual process (ECM component), there was a structural break. For example, in Turkey the year 2001 was the year of the economic crisis and in 1999 it joined the G-20 group (Table 10.5).

10.6 Conclusions

The cases of the 'economic miracles' discussed above show that there is no single golden recipe for above-average economic growth. This conclusion is compatible with modern methodology accepting anti-naturalistic approach in scientific cognition theory. Each of the countries considered applied its economic policy, behind which there was a different model of the economy. In the case of the Netherlands, its economy can be described by the neoclassical synthesis model. Ireland represents an open economy model with a large role of foreign direct investment. Spain represents the Keynesian model of the economy and the process of industrialization. In the case of Turkey, we see a political cycle (the classic approach), the mechanism of the balance of payments, and the development model of the peripheral country. In addition to the theoretical models of the economy, infrastructural resources and external financing (the European Union, the World Bank) were of great importance in identifying the factors of the 'economic miracle'.

Identification of structural breaks in both individual variables and the process of the residual long-term economic growth equation allowed us to assign significant changes or events in the economic policies to the dates obtained. The econometric tools used confirmed the advantage of non-linear models (threshold models with or without cointegration) when describing the phenomenon of 'an economic miracle'.

References

Andrews K, Zivot E (1992) Further evidence on the great crash, the oil price shock, and the unit root hypothesis. J Bus Econ Stat 10(10):51–70
Arthur WB (1989) Competing technologies, increasing returns, and lock-in by historical events. Econ J 99(394):116–131
Bai J, Perron P (1998) Estimating and testing linear models with multiple structural changes. Econometrica 66(1):47
Bilson JFO (1978) The monetary approach to the exchange rate: some empirical evidence. IMF Staff Pap 25:48–75
Boehlke J, Fałdziński M, Gałecki M, Osińska M (2017) Dynamics of economic growth in Ireland in 1980–2014. St State Polytech Univ J Econ, Ec/2017 10(2):7–20
Brown RL, Durbin J, Evans JM (1975) Techniques for testing the constancy of regression relationships over time (with discussion). J R Stat Soc B 37:149–192
Bruzda J (2007) Procesy nieliniowe i zależności długookresowe w ekonomii. Analiza kointegracji nieliniowej. Wydawnictwo UMK, Torun
Chan KS, Petruccelli J, Woolford S, Tong H (1985) A multiple threshold AR(1) model. J Appl Probab 22(2):267–279
David P (2000) Path dependence, its critics and the quest for 'historical economics', Working Paper. Oxford: All Souls College, Oxford University
Demsetz H (1969) Information and efficiency: another viewpoint. J Law Econ 12(1):1–22
Dornbusch R (1976) Expectations and exchange rate dynamics. J Polit Econ 84:1161–1174
Enders W, Siklos PL (2001) Cointegration and threshold adjustment. J Bus Econ Stat 19 (2):166–176
Frankel JA (1979) On the mark: a theory of floating exchange rate based on real interest differentials. Am Econ Rev 69:610–622
Frenkel JA (1976) A monetary approach to the exchange rate: doctrinal aspects and empirical evidence. Scand J Econ 78:200–224
Froot KA, Stein JC (1991) Exchange rates and foreign direct investment: an imperfect capital markets approach. Q J Econ 106(4):1191–1217
Frydman R, Goldberg MD (2007) Imperfect knowledge economics: exchange rates and risk. Princeton University Press, Princeton
Frydman R, Phelps ES (1983) Individual forecasting and aggregate outcomes: 'rational expectations' examined. Cambridge University Press, New York, pp 1–30
Frydman R, Phelps ES (1990) Pluralism of Theories Problems in Post-Rational-Expectations Modeling, paper presented at the 1990 Siena Summer Workshop on Expectations and Learning
Hansen BE, Seo B (2002) Testing for two-regime threshold cointegration in vector error-correction models. J Econ 110:293–318
Hayek FA (1945) The use of knowledge in society. Am Econ Rev 35:519–530
Hayek FA (1978) The pretence of knowledge, nobel lecture, 1974, in new studies in philosophy, politics, economics and history of ideas. University of Chicago Press, Chicago, pp 23–34
Hooper P, Morton J (1982) Fluctuations in the dollar: a model of nominal and real exchange rate determination. J Int Money Financ 1:39–56
Johansen S (1991) Estimation and hypothesis testing of cointegration vectors in gaussian vector autoregressive models. Econometrica 59(6):1551–1580
Johansen S, Mosconi R, Nielsen B (2000) Cointegration analysis in the presence of structural breaks in the deterministic trend. Econ J 3:216–249
Juselius K (2007) The cointegrated VAR model: methodology and applications. Oxford University Press, London
Kahneman D, Tversky A (1979) Prospect theory: an analysis of decision under risk. Econometrica 47:263–291
Kapetanios G, Shin Y, Snall A (2006) Testing for cointegration in nonlinear smooth transition error correction models. Economet Theor 22(6):279–303
Keynes JM (1921) A treatise on probability. London: Macmillan

Keynes JM (1936) The general theory of employment, interest and money. New York: Harcourt, Brace and World
Keynes JM (1973) The collected writings of John Maynard Keynes. Macmillan for the Royal Economic Society, London and Basingstoke
Knight FH (1921) Risk, uncertainty and profit. Houghton Mifflin, Boston
Linblom C (1977) Politics and markets. The world's political–economic systems. New York: Basic Books
Meese RA, Rogoff K (1983) Empirical exchange rate models of the seventies: do they fit out of sample. J Int Econ 14:3–24
Meese RA, Rogoff K (1988) Was it real? The exchange rate–interest differential relation over the modern floating-rate period. J Financ 43:993–1048
Myro R (2019) Determinants of economic growth in Spain: a historical viewpoint. In: Osińska M (ed) Economic miracles in the European economies. Springer, Berlin
North DC (1990) Institutions institutional change, and economic performance. Cambridge University Press, Cambridge
Pedersen D (2008) Imperfect knowledge economics—a solution to the exchange rate disconnect puzzle. University of Copenhagen, Copenhagen
Phelps ES (2003) Knowledge, information and expectations in modern macroeconomics: in honor of Edmund S. Phelps. Princeton University Press, Princeton
Quandt R (1960) Tests of the hypothesis that a linear regression system obeys two separate regimes. J Am Stat Assoc 53:873–880
Rogoff K (1996) The purchasing power puzzle. J Econ Lit 34:647–668
Soros G (1987) The alchemy of finance. Wiley, New York
Stiglitz JS, Weiss A (1992) Asymmetric information in credit markets and its implications for macro-economics. Oxf Econ Pap 44(4):694–724
Thygesen N, Gros D (1990) The institutional approach to monetary union in europe. Econ J 100 (402):925–935
Tsay RS (1998) Testing and modeling multivariate threshold models. J Am Stat Assoc 93 (443):1188–1202

Printed by Printforce, the Netherlands